BY PROFESSOR WENDELL

THE TRADITIONS OF EUROPEAN LITERA-
TURE FROM HOMER TO DANTE

THE MYSTERY OF EDUCATION √

PRIVILEGED CLASSES √

THE FRANCE OF TODAY

LIBERTY, UNION, AND DEMOCRACY

THE TEMPER OF THE SEVENTEENTH CEN- √
TURY IN ENGLISH LITERATURE

A LITERARY HISTORY OF AMERICA

WILLIAM SHAKSPERE. A Study in Elizabethan
Literature

STELLIGERI AND OTHER ESSAYS CON-
CERNING AMERICA

RALEGH IN GUIANA, ROSAMOND AND A
CHRISTMAS MASK

ENGLISH COMPOSITION. Eight Lectures √
Given at the Lowell Institute

A HISTORY OF AMERICAN LITERATURE.
(With C. N. Greenough)

CHARLES SCRIBNER'S SONS

THE TRADITIONS OF
EUROPEAN LITERATURE

FROM HOMER TO DANTE

THE TRADITIONS OF
EUROPEAN LITERATURE

FROM HOMER TO DANTE

BY

BARRETT WENDELL, *1855-1921*
PROFESSOR EMERITUS OF ENGLISH IN HARVARD UNIVERSITY

NEW YORK
CHARLES SCRIBNER'S SONS
1920

NOTE

Separately to acknowledge my debts to the friends, colleagues, and assistants who have helped this book take form would at once demand undue space and perhaps now and then commit them to views other than their own. I cannot refrain, however, from expressing my gratitude to Mr. Charles Knowles Bolton, of the Boston Athenæum, for his constant and considerate kindness during the seasons when I have written there almost daily. The preparation of the Bibliographic Suggestions was originally undertaken by Dr. Frederic Schenck. After his untimely death it was taken up by Mr. Daniel Sargent. When Mr. Sargent was called to Europe, it was completed by Mr. Edward Motley Pickman, who has also made the Index. I cannot too heartily acknowledge my deep sense of what they have done for me; nor too gravely express the sorrow brought to all his friends by Frederic Schenck's death. If I felt sure that the book deserved such honour, it should be dedicated to his brave and happy memory.

B. W.

Portsmouth, New Hampshire
15 August, 1920.

CONTENTS

PAGE

INTRODUCTION 1

BOOK I

THE TRADITIONS OF GREECE

CHAPTER

I. TO 500 BEFORE CHRIST 9

I. Historical Traditions, 9. II. Homer, 16. III. The
Lost Epics and Hesiod, 28. IV. Lyric Poetry, Alcæus,
Sappho, Anacreon; Pindar, 33.

II. THE FIFTH CENTURY BEFORE CHRIST . . . 45

I. Historical Traditions, 45. II. Æschylus, 50. III.
Sophocles, 61. IV. Herodotus, 70. V. Thucydides,
78. VI. Euripides, 87. VII. Aristophanes, 97.

III. THE FOURTH CENTURY BEFORE CHRIST . . 104

I. Historical Traditions, 104. II. Xenophon, 108. III.
Plato, 114. IV. Demosthenes, 122. V. Aristotle, 128.
VI. Theophrastus; Menander, 135.

IV. FROM 300 B. C. TO THE ROMAN CONQUEST OF
GREECE (146 B. C.) 140

I. Historical Traditions, 140. II. Theocritus, 148.

V. THE GREEK TRADITION 153

BOOK II

THE TRADITIONS OF ROME

I. TO 100 BEFORE CHRIST 161

I. Historical Traditions, 161. II. Literary Traditions:
Plautus; Terence, 170.

vii

CHAPTER   PAGE

II. THE FIRST CENTURY BEFORE CHRIST . . .   179

I. Historical Traditions, 179. II. Cicero, 190. III. Cæsar, 200. IV. Lucretius, 206. V. Catullus, 213. VI. Sallust, 219. VII. Virgil, 221. VIII. Horace, 243. IX. Elegiac Poetry: Tibullus, Propertius, 256. X. Ovid, 260. XI. Livy, 270.

III. THE FIRST CENTURY OF THE CHRISTIAN ERA   278

I. Historical Traditions, 278. II. Literature under Tiberius: Velleius Paterculus; Valerius Maximus; Phædrus, 290. III. Literature under Nero: Seneca; Lucan; Petronius; Persius, 294. IV. Literature under the Flavian Emperors: Pliny the Elder; Quintilian; Silius Italicus; Valerius Flaccus; Statius, 300. V. Martial, 306. VI. The Younger Pliny, 311. VII. Tacitus, 314. VIII. Juvenal, 321.

IV. THE SECOND CENTURY OF THE CHRISTIAN ERA   330

I. Historical Traditions, 330. II. Literary Traditions: Suetonius, Apuleius, Pervigilium Veneris; Lucian, Galen 336.

V. THE ROMAN TRADITION   342

BOOK III

THE TRADITIONS OF CHRISTIANITY

I. RELIGION AND EMPIRE   351

II. THE OLD TESTAMENT   362

III. THE NEW TESTAMENT   372

IV. THE CHURCH   379

BOOK IV

THE TRADITIONS OF CHRISTENDOM

I. THE THIRD CENTURY   391

I. Historical Traditions, 391. II. Literary Traditions, 395.

CONTENTS

CHAPTER   PAGE

II. THE FOURTH CENTURY 397

I. Historical Traditions, 397. II. Ausonius; The Fathers of the Church, 404.

III. THE FIFTH CENTURY 419

I. Historical Traditions, 419. II. Literary Traditions, 424.

IV. THE SIXTH CENTURY 425

I. Historical Traditions, 425. II. Boethius, 431.

V. THE SEVENTH CENTURY 436

I. Historical Traditions, 436. II. Literary Traditions, 441.

VI. THE EIGHTH CENTURY 442

I. Historical Traditions, 442. II. Literary Traditions, 450.

VII. THE NINTH CENTURY 452

I. Historical Traditions, 452. II. Literary Traditions, 455.

VIII. THE TENTH CENTURY 457

I. Historical Traditions, 457. II. Literary Traditions, 459.

IX. THE TRADITION OF THE DARK AGES . . . 460

BOOK V

THE TRADITIONS OF THE MIDDLE AGES

I. THE ELEVENTH CENTURY 467

I. Historical Traditions, 467. II. The Song of Roland, 479.

II. THE TWELFTH CENTURY 486

I. Historical Traditions, 486. II. Literary Traditions, 497. III. Romantic Epics: "Chansons de Geste" and "Romans," 501. IV. Minor Forms of Poetry, 512. V. Latin Lyrics, 519. VI. French Lyrics, 526. VII. The Troubadours, 531.

CHAPTER   PAGE

III.   THE THIRTEENTH CENTURY **540**

I. Historical Traditions, 540. II. The Romance of the
Rose, 551. III. Reynard the Fox, 556. IV. The Golden
Legend, 558. V. The Saints: Dominic; Francis of As-
sisi; Louis; Thomas Aquinas, 564. VI Lyrics: Latin,
French, and Provença¹, 574. VII. Italian Lyrics, 580.
VIII. Dante, 586.

IV.   THE TRADITION OF THE MIDDLE AGES . .   **613**

BIBLIOGRAPHICAL SUGGESTIONS **617**

INDEX **641**

THE TRADITIONS OF EUROPEAN LITERATURE

INTRODUCTION

Though this book is intended for general readers, it originated in lectures given at Harvard
College between 1904 and 1917. Years of dealing with Harvard students had shown me not
only that Americans now know little of the literary traditions of our ancestral Europe, but also
that they are seldom aware even of the little
they know. Beginning with no more clear purpose than to help these needs, I gradually came to
see my object more definitely; it was at once to
revive knowledge which was sinking beneath the
level of consciousness, to indicate the gaps which
each man must supply for himself, and to en-
courage in all the habit of so thinking things together instead of scrutinising them apart that
each might gradually come habitually to see in
perspective whatever he might know or learn
about the traditions, historic and literary, which
have accompanied our civilisation to the point
where we are part of it.

This task is so obviously beyond the power of
any modern scholar that it mercifully limits itself. Nobody can fully have mastered even all
the languages involved, not to speak of the erudition in which centuries have enshrouded unnumbered facts concerning them and the matters

1

they set forth. All we can attempt is to take a
recognised point of view and to give account of
what thence remains visible. Our own point of
view is fixed by the accident that we are English-
speaking Americans of the Twentieth Century of
the Christian Era. The traditions of history and
literature consequently ours are evidently those
which, we need not ask why, have chanced among
ourselves to survive the times of their origin. The
test of such survival must soon become fairly
clear: it has little to do with their positive value
or their actual truth; it is whether they have so
endured that Englishmen and Americans of general culture may now hold them proper matters
of literary allusion. If so, we may rightly dwell
on them as much as may be; if not, whatever
their importance in other schemes than ours, we
may contentedly neglect them.

The moment we thus approach our subject,
one welcome condition of it appears. If only because human beings have so long been aware of
what we touch on, the matters before us would
have relative importance. So far as these matters
are literary, they prove on even slight scrutiny to
have positive importance. A pleasantly reassur-
ing fact in the history of human expression is that
the names and the works which have survived
have done so largely because, though each originally came to light in historical conditions as
distinct as those which surround us now, each
has proved, when its original surroundings have
faded, to appeal for one reason or another to
generations widely different from that which it
chanced to address in the flesh. It has thereby
proved itself more enduring than any contempo-

rary could confidently have asserted it; something in its substance, or in its form, or oftener in both, has such general human interest as to be independent of momentary limitation. Thus the classics, ancient and modern, have slowly revealed themselves as standards of perception; whoever comes to know them has a measure by which he can test or correct his impulsive judgment concerning new works of literature, or works presented to him for the first time. Even cursory glances at classics may therefore provide men with perhaps the most fundamental element of culture.

Just as the purpose of this book defined itself slowly, and consequently in the most natural way, so did the method. To treat any considerable subject intelligently, one must somehow arrange it under definite headings or—to use a convenient big word—categories. These categories may take any form; and in recent times they have often taken forms which, however agreeable to the habitual thought of their makers, turn out to be arbitrary or at least debatable; even poetry and prose, for example, are less easy to separate than you would guess until you try to draw a sharp line between them. Common sense is enough to assure us that the more nearly categories follow the habit of human thought, and thus agree with facts assumed by everybody, the more easily they can be remembered, the more firmly grasped, and the more confidently thought with. Among the few definite facts in human record are those of chronology. Though the groups of years which we call centuries are doubtless arbitrary, the centuries have two pervasive help setting forth our subject in five successive parts or books: I. The Traditions of Greece; II. The Traditions of Rome; III. The Traditions of Christianity; IV. The Traditions of Christendom; and, V. The Traditions of the Middle Ages.

BOOK I

THE TRADITIONS OF GREECE

CHAPTER I

TO 500 BEFORE CHRIST

I

HISTORICAL TRADITIONS

Though few could readily define what the word European means, when applied to a subject so broad and so vague as traditions, almost everybody can feel with something like certainty its general significance. The ruins of Egypt, for example, and the sculpture and the painting which have been found among them are not European; no more is what travellers find in India, ancient or modern; no more are the temples or the admirable fine art of China or of Japan. The Book of the Dead is as alien to Europe as are the hieroglyphics in which it is written. So are Sanskrit hymns, and Confucian precepts, and the story of the Forty-Seven Ronins. So, indeed, when we come to scrutinise familiar things, a candid mind must probably find even the moods and the expressions recorded for us in the Bible; otherwise we could hardly have that sense of illumination cast by a few days in the Near East on the scriptural stories which we half thought we wholly understood. On the other hand there are relics of long-past times which any European or American must instantly feel comparatively his own. The forms of Grecian temples and of Roman arches or amphitheatres still affect our architecture; we still make statues

9

after the manner which was first clearly defined
in Periclean Athens; we think in terms like those
idiomatic in Rome and in Greece, as distinguished
from those in which Egyptians thought or the
diverse peoples of Asia. Our religious history
has doubtless made the Old Testament vastly
more familiar to twelve or fifteen of our ancestral
centuries than we can ever again find the Odyssey.
Yet whoever will take the trouble to read, side
by side, the Book of Ruth and the story of Nau-
sicaa[1] will probably come to feel, perhaps with
surprise, that Ruth was written ages ago by some
one whose nature was far less like ours than was
the nature of the poet who ages ago set down the
story of the Phæacian girl, at play with her hand-
maids.   Though such reflections as these may not
carry us far towards the precision of definition,
they can hardly help even better serving our present purpose; for they will bring us to a point where,
without troubling ourselves about definitions, we
can clearly perceive that for us the word European
generally means something directly ancestral to
ourselves.

As soon as we come to this understanding, another fact must grow clear.   The first records of
such expression as we now call European are by
no means so general in character as that word
has become and must inevitably remain.   Rather
they are extremely local.   Centuries and centuries
ago there chanced to develop in the southeastern-
most region of Europe a civilisation and a language
not originally extensive, but clearly different from
any other which had hitherto existed.   Though
it hardly came to what we should now call fully

[1] Odyssey, VI.

developed political existence, though it was centred not in an organised state, but in many and widely various cities most of which controlled no great extent of the territory about them, and though, indeed, it flourished quite as much on the Asiatic as on the European shores of the Ægean Sea, it gradually became something which made those who possessed it think of themselves, despite their incessant mutual conflicts, as distinct from others. They were Greeks; all the rest of the world—North, South, East, and West—was barbarian, babbling in terms unintelligible to the cultivated ear. Whatever Greece may be now, there were ages between antiquity and these times of ours when Greece was living Greece no more, when the spirit and the heritage of its traditions persisted, if at all, only in regions which to ancient Greeks would have been vaguely and negligibly barbarous. The course of time, however, has proved the originally peculiar civilisation of Greece and the traditions which it came to cherish historically ancestral, like nothing else, to every phase of the development of Europe. Thither, most of all, we must look to see whence, in almost everything but the body, we ourselves came.

So looking, one historical date soon shows itself truly as important as mere tradition has made it seem to careless moods. In the year 500 before Christ, Greece already existed, and already possessed traditions, both historical and literary, which have never quite faded from European memory. At that time, the existence of Greece, and with it the future, if not the existence, of its traditions, was threatened by an Asiatic power whose civilisation was what the Greeks

called barbarous and we should call alien. If
the Persian wars of the first twenty years of the
Fifth Century before Christ had overwhelmed
Greece, as some three hundred years later Carthage
was overwhelmed by Rome, there might doubtless
have survived antique records of what Greece had
been, but these would have survived in something
other than the Europe which has ensued through
twenty-five hundred years. The whole northern
half of the Eastern Hemisphere might rather have
developed under such conditions as we now think
Asiatic. The relics of Greece, in such event, might
at best have seemed remote, fragmentary, and
broken, like those of Twelfth Century Provence
through the seven centuries which now separate
us from the Albigensian crusade. Both historically and in literature, nevertheless, something
might probably have remained. We shall see
our way most clearly through the periods which
are to follow, if we begin by asking ourselves what
that something would probably have been.

At least a little while ago, the Wonder Book of
Hawthorne and his Tanglewood Tales were familiar in American nurseries, and with them the
stories of Perseus, Andromeda and Medusa, of
Midas, of Pandora, of Hercules and some of his
labours, of Bellerophon, of Theseus and the Mino-
taur, of Cadmus, of Jason and the Golden Fleece,
and more. Thus told, in staid New England
terms, diluted from the voluptuous Latin of Ovid,
they might well have seemed as odd to a Fifth
Century Greek as we find old German pictures of
the Garden of Eden, where Adam and Eve, with
no clothes to speak of, have a stolid Nuremberg
house to sleep in. But just as, unlike the Greeks,

none of us would have the shadow of doubt as to who Adam and Eve were, so your Greek would have known, long before the Persian Wars, who the heroes were, and the worthies, and the monsters—man-bulls and winged horses—that Hawthorne has made or kept freshly familiar for us. This body of heroic legend is compactly and systematically summarised in the third chapter of the French History of Ancient Greece written as a school-book by Monsieur Charles Seignobos. Just as it stays ancestral to us, it was ancestral, and nationally ancestral, to historic Greece.

In the year 500 historic Greece was by no means confined to the region which has borne and bears its name. Its commercial energy had led to wide colonial expansion in every direction where the shipping of that period could regularly proceed. To confine ourselves to what subsequently became Europe, Sicily was virtually Greek, and Southern Italy. The city we now call Naples, for example, was already Neapolis—which is literally the Greek for Newtown, or Newton. Massillia existed—to this day called Marseilles—establishing a civilisation which was never to be wholly broken at the mouth of the Rhone. The temples of Paestum and of Girgenti still stand, ruinous and solitary, to show what the monuments were like in dozens of colonial cities once throbbing with Greek life. These colonial regions, however, bore to Greece itself some such relation as that of America, during its first four centuries, to the Europe from which its own civilisation has been so lately derived. Though they were not alien to Greece, like the antique and rigid civilisation of Egypt or of Assyria, or like the crescent empire of Persia, they were something else and newer than the central origin from which all had sprung.

Apart from its community of language and of tradition, meanwhile, Greece had not developed into what we should now call national unity. It virtually consisted of a number of distinct cities, each controlling more or less adjacent territory, each tenacious of its own political and local traditions, and all disposed to incessant and intriguing quarrel. They had certain common grounds of meeting, such as the oracular Sanctuary of Delphi, or the templed plain of Olympia where they came together for some of their athletic contests. In general, however, each thought first of itself, and next of how to down its neighbours. Among them already two or three emerged to stay more memorable in tradition than the rest. Thebes had been the legendary home of Cadmus and of Œdipus. Sparta, whence the Trojan Paris had fled with Helen, the half-divine queen of Menelaus, stayed monarchic, military, more conservative, and more compactly powerful than any of the others. Athens, the city of Ægeus and of Theseus, and the principal shrine of the goddess Athene from whom its name was traditionally derived—though for centuries Europe was apt to call her rather by her Latin name of Minerva— loomed already to the front as the chief centre of Greek intelligence and Greek expression. It is from Athens, accordingly, or at least through Athens, that the Greek traditions mostly came which have remained the common possession of subsequent Europe. The word *acropolis*, for example, is the Greek name for *citadel*—a general term for that part of any Greek city which domi-

nated the rest of it and was most securely fortified.
To us, however, it chiefly means, as it meant to
the Athenians, their own local stronghold, still
grand with the ruin of their special shrine, the
Parthenon. So, whatever the actual history of the
Greeks before the year 500, we traditionally think
of it in something like Attic terms. Outlying antiquity—Egypt and Assyria, Babylon and Nineveh,
the shadowy legends of Crete—seems not only
remote, but alien. Sparta, still loyal to the already venerable polity of Lycurgus and generally
dominant to the southward, seems vaguely threatening to the institutions ancestral to ourselves.
The pitiless code of Draco, the shrewd wisdom
of Solon, the benevolent tyranny of Pisistratus,
weakening into the self-indulgence of Hippias
and Hipparchus overthrown by the liberty-loving
outbreak of Harmodius and Aristogiton, seem
comparatively our own. So does the restlessly
intelligent succession of incessant political experiment, tending further and further from the
restraints of monarchy and of aristocracy to the
untested license of democracy.

All this, no doubt, is now far away. Even now,
however, we are dimly aware of it. We are dimly
aware, as well, of other traditions existing along
with it—of the Seven Wise Men, for example,
and some of their precepts, such as "Know thyself" and "Nothing beyond measure." What
remains more distinct among the relics of that
olden time is the literature which had already
come into its Greek existence, and which persists
to this day. Of this the chief works, already immemorially antique, were the Iliad and the
Odyssey.

II

HOMER

By the beginning of the Fifth Century, the Iliad and the Odyssey were already, as they have always remained, traditionally ascribed to Homer. Who Homer was, too, when he lived, and where, had even then become matters of dispute. We need not trouble ourselves with the controversy. Whether he ever actually existed or not, whether the two great poems which bear his name are by the same hand,[1] on what lost ballads or court poems they may perhaps have been based, and all the other myriad and unprovable conjectures about them are not really our concern. Just as the Bible has existed and exists for Christendom, so Homer existed for historic Greece—remote, antique, perennial, and familiar. His language, like that of Scripture for us, was no longer such as men used in daily life, and indeed may have been not quite such as they had ever used; nevertheless, partly by reason of its own existence, it was permanently and superbly comprehensible. Above all the rhythmic sweep of it had fixed the hexameter as the primal idiom of heroic expression for antique Europe.

Few if any modern languages can be forced into this metrical form. If we may trust those who know most of the matter, indeed, no modern ear can quite unhesitatingly imagine how the hex-

[1] The late Samuel Butler, an ingenious Englishman just now rather admired, believed the Odyssey to have been written by a youngish woman of Trapani, in Sicily, where a public place has consequently been named for him.

ameter line sounded to the Greeks. It seems to
have depended on two circumstances both no
longer familiar—the fact that a long vowel was
dwelt on perceptibly longer than a short, and the
fact that the modification of sound later indicated
by Greek accents was not a stress, such as modern
European ears are used to, but a modulation of
the voice, raised or lowered a note or so above or
below the normal pitch. The nearest approach
to the consequent effect now to be heard anywhere is probably the traditional chanting of
Sanskrit hymns in certain Buddhist ceremonies
of China, and other Asiatic regions. The hexameter line may nevertheless be somehow pronounced in the stressed and emphatic accents
demanded by modern habit; and a couplet of
Coleridge—"The Homeric Hexameter Described
and Exemplified" [1]—beautifully tells what this
poetic line has come to be for us:

Strongly it bears us along in swelling and limitless billows,
Nothing before and nothing behind but the sky and the
  ocean.

Every line of Homer can still be read in this swift,
sustained manner.

This vehicle, of course, was not peculiar to
Homer, any more than the most idiomatic poetic
line in English—the line common to blank verse,
the sonnet, the heroic couplet, and other technical
forms—is peculiar to any one English poet.
Traditionally, however, the hexameter was most
familiar, and therefore most enduringly influential, in the Iliad and the Odyssey. Nothing could

[1] He translated this, I am told, from Schiller. Whether Schiller invented
it I have not inquired.

better have suited the swift, simple, noble mood
of their sustained though excursive narrative.
In substance they detail two long episodes from the
legendary—and perhaps vaguely historic—story
of the Trojan War.   The outline of this story
was familiar to all historic Greece, and stays so
everywhere.   Paris, one of the numerous princely
sons of Priam, King of Troy,—or Ilium, as the
Greeks called it,—was asked by three goddesses
to award to one of them the prize of supreme
beauty.   After the artless manner of unsophis-
ticated nature, each offered him a bribe—one wisdom, another power, and the third the love of
women.   He chose the third.   As a result he
incurred the displeasure of Hera, or Juno, the mistress of power, and of Athene, or Minerva, the
mistress of wisdom; but under the protection of
Aphrodite, or Venus, the mistress of love, he presently eloped from Sparta to Troy with Helen, the
most beautiful of all women, and the wife of the
Spartan King, Menelaus.   Menelaus proceeded
to collect his fellow Greek princes, who resented
his treatment, and they all went to Troy, with a
view of reclaiming Helen.   The Trojans resisted
their claims; the consequent war, in which the
two offended goddesses favoured the Greek side,
lasted ten years.   In the end Troy fell; and Helen,
duly captured, went back to Sparta, where she
ended her days in peaceful conjugal respectability.

The two great poems of Homer, though they do
not tell the whole story, assume or imply it throughout.   The Iliad relates, in extreme detail, how
Achilles, on the whole the most formidable Grecian
warrior, displeased by deprival of an engaging Trojan captive, withdrew for a while from combat, to

the great disadvantage of the Greeks; and how at last, enraged by the death in battle of his dearest friend Patroclus, he resumed his arms and overcame Hector, the eldest and most eminent of the Trojan princes. All through the Iliad the war is at its height. In the Odyssey the war is ended. Troy has fallen, and the victorious Greek princes have betaken themselves home. The course of one of them, Odysseus, or Ulysses, King of Ithaca, is long and perilous. At last he is landed, alone and unrecognised, on the shores of his country, where his faithful wife, Penelope, long supposed widowed, has been beset by inconveniently importunate suitors. These he presently does to death, and resumes his sovereign and marital rights. His journeyings have led him through all manner of regions and adventures, legendary and human. Just as the scene of the Iliad is fixed, that of the Odyssey is shifting, wandering, panoramic; in the Iliad the heroic life of the Trojan conflict is in its full flush, in the Odyssey it is already an heroic memory.

Though to feel anything like the complete effect of these poems, throbbing with life in every incident they dwell on, and inexhaustible in their implication of antecedents and surroundings, one must read them through and often—though, indeed, their full glory begins to fade as soon as one forgets the surgent splendour of their hexameter rhythm—three comparatively short passages will give, even in translation, an impression of what is to be found there. The first consists of the beginning of the Iliad, to the fifty-second line, pungent with the smoke of the pyres which consume the Grecian dead, slain by pestilential shafts

from the clanging silver bow of Apollo. Here one
instantly feels the supreme simplicity and swift-
ness of this pristine poetic method, its matchless
freedom from self-consciousness, and its unsurpassed precision of imagination. Even though
Homer sometimes nods, these qualities pervade
his work from beginning to end.

The second is an episode in the Third Book of
the Iliad, beginning with the line (121) where
Iris comes to summon Helen, and ending with
the mournfully tender lines (243–4) which tell
how, unknown to her, Castor and Pollux, her
brothers, lie deep in the life-bearing earth of their
own dear country, Lacedæmon. There is a short
armistice. Priam with Trojan elders about him
looks down from the walls of his besieged city and
sees the Grecian captains, for a little while at
rest from war in what one feels to be breezy sunshine. He asks Helen who this warrior may be,
and that; she tells him, knowing them all. And
as you read you can hardly help imagining them
still alive. Among them is Odysseus, not tall but
broad-breasted, deep-voiced, and wily. No single
passage more wonderfully summarises the freshness of conception which makes one feel these
heroes as real to-day as they were when poetry
first brought them into being, centuries before
Athens was historic.

The third passage is much longer; but, as we
shall see, it has chanced to have such direct influence on subsequent literature that, even for no
other reason, it would be worth reading through.
It is the Eleventh Book of the Odyssey, which
contains only six hundred and forty lines. In
the course of his wanderings, Odysseus is cast

alone on the coast of Phæecia. There received by
King Alcinous, he tells at great length what has
happened to him since Troy fell; and the adventure he describes in the Eleventh Book is very
distinct. Freed from the enchantments of Circe,
he is bidden consult the shade of the blind prophet
Tiresias as to how he may finally make his way
back to Ithaca. To do so he sails westward,
through seas unknown to men, until he reaches
the shadowy shores beneath which the dead lurk.
He makes sacrifice, filling a trench with the
blood of sheep; and the spirits swarm up to
drink it, and thus regain for an instant some
semblance of life. He sees Tiresias, and has his
counsel. He sees, too, countless shades from times
olden even to him; and mingled with them he
sees and talks with shades of those whom he has
known in life—his mother, and Agamemnon, and
Achilles, and more. Of all the heroes who a little
while ago were alive in the Trojan sunshine, he
alone is surely living here. Most of the rest are
already shadows, memories, no longer heroic
facts but immortally heroic traditions, merging
with the older traditions of their own antiquity.
Even for its contrast with the glowing actuality
of the Iliad, this book would stay wondrous. For
us, it has another significance as well. Without it,
we should never have had the Sixth Book of
Virgil's Æneid; and without that, no small part
of Dante's Divine Comedy would hardly have
taken the form in which it lives and moves.

Familiar to Fifth Century Greece as Scriptural
story to Christian Europe, or as the Bible to
Protestant England, the Iliad and the Odyssey
might probably have persisted even though the

Persian Wars had swept Greece from existence. If so, they would have been lasting records not of what Europe and European tradition have grown to be, but of the pristine mood from which, through the centuries, Europe and its traditions have developed. Between the fall of the Roman Empire and the period which we now call the Renaissance, there were hundreds of years when the Greek language was virtually unknown in Western Europe. There has never been a generation, however, to which the name of Homer was not familiar as the first and therefore the most enduring of Grecian poets, nor yet a generation to whom countless names which first spring to life in his poems would have been altogether strange. In later Europe, no doubt, Achilles and Agamemnon, Menelaus and Helen and Paris, Priam and Hecuba, Hector and Andromache, Odysseus and Penelope and Telemachus, Polyphemus, Circe, Calypso, and the Sirens—to go no further—may often have meant, and may often mean, little enough; they can never have meant, however, or mean so little as names altogether alien to our ancestral traditions—Seti, for example, of Egypt, Vishnu or Gautama of India, Jimmu Tenno of Japan. Since the Revival of Learning made Greek once more familiar, bringing back to knowledge the source whence these traditions were poured, two features of the Iliad and the Odyssey have grown increasingly clear.

The first is chiefly of historic interest. Whoever made them, and however they are made, they fixed, long before authentic history began, the epic idiom of Europe. What we mean by epic poetry is doubtless hard to define, but not to

feel. When heroic story is told in terms themselves heroic, the task is done; all that is left for us
is to listen. So far as we are concerned now, if we
have a shade of doubt as to what we mean, it is
enough to glance once more at that passage from
the Third Book of the Iliad; as Homer told his
story there, so Europe has instinctively tended to
tell heroic story ever since. In that passage,
however, we can instantly see at least two literary
devices, Homerically normal, which would hardly
have occurred to any poet of much later times.
One appears at the very beginning, where the
goddess Iris comes, in the form of Laodice, to
summon Helen to the wall of Troy: this antique
world is at once human and superhuman. Deities
and men still mingle together—as the Lord God
walked in Eden when Adam and Eve hid there.
The second device is more formal. When Helen
comes within earshot of the old men who cluster
about Priam, there is a famous simile to describe
the cracked utterance of senility: "Like grass-
hoppers that in a wood sit on a tree and utter
their lily-like voice"—a reedy chirp is what the
words mean—"even so sat the elders of the Trojans upon the tower." Because in Homer gods
and men appear together, and similes are elaborately stated, so you will find things in Virgil,
deliberately following literary conventions instinctively established ages before; and from
Virgil these devices have been copied or adapted,
again and again, at least till the days of Camoens
and those of Milton; and Fielding burlesqued
them in Tom Jones, under King George the
Second. When anything has once been excellently
done, nobody can again attempt the like without

some fettering consciousness of the masterpiece
he would imitate or rival.   One refreshing merit of
Homer is that throughout his work you somehow
feel what appears like blissful freedom from any
inhibitory models.   Despite the conventional fixity
of his epithets, and other details which imply ante-
cedent custom, he never seems consciously hampered by academically fixed types of expression;
he rather seems eager only to make his words fit
his meaning.   Thereby he unwittingly creates a
type of expression never thenceforth to be quite
ignored.

The second feature of the Iliad and the Odyssey
which is now as clear as their historic importance
is perhaps the deepest and the surest proof of
why they are great.   Fully to feel it, you must
come to know at least a little of them in the
original Greek.   To do something like this is
not so hard as it might seem.   They have been
frequently translated;   and each translation is
of course a fresh effort to render their meaning
and their spirit clearer to the unlearned than it
has been before. The first enduring English
translation is that of Chapman, made under
Queen Elizabeth and James I;   the most nearly
popular is probably still that of Pope, made in
George the First's time;   as both of these are
rhymed, it is well to compare with them a translation in that English form, blank verse, which
English custom has now made our idiomatic
vehicle of heroic poetry—Cowper's, or Bryant's,
or Lord Derby's; and, to remind ourselves that
none of these metrical versions has any metrical
likeness to the hexameter, it is well, in addition,
to glance at a prose translation—such as those

in which Andrew Lang collaborated with Butcher and with Leaf and Myers. Take whatever passage you choose—the three on which we have already touched, or any of them, will serve. Read it in all four English versions, remembering that different as the versions may seem each stands for the same great original; and the composite effect will begin to give you a growing sense of what that original is like. Then, if you know your Greek alphabet, and have even a slight notion of hexameter rhythm, turn to the original lines; at least here and there, they will suddenly flash into the fulness of life which each separate version has attempted and variously failed to reproduce. Each time you thus recur to them, you will find in them a quality which will impress you the more the better you know them. No matter how familiar they may become, it is hardly possible to read them without a sense that they are always as new as if you had never read them before. Age cannot wither nor custom stale them.

Some such quality, no doubt, pervades all enduring literature, at least for those who love it; and most lovers of literature, having their special favourites, will now and again find it in works and men where it is not quite apparent to everybody. The more widely and certainly it is recognised anywhere, the more assured you may be that the work or the man thus appealing to humanity through the ages is great. To be so beyond dispute it must be sanctioned by the consent of the generations. Thus tested, two comparatively modern poets slowly but admirably emerge as somehow greater than the rest—the Italian Dante and the English Shakspere. In all an-

tiquity, their only incontestable fellow is Homer;
in European literature, as in the untortured region
of the Divine Comedy[1] where, pagan and unre-
deemed, antique worthies forever long for that
salvation which is hopelessly denied them, Homer
stays first of poets still. Dante never knew him
in the Greek. It is only since the Fourteenth
Century that Greek has been brought back to
European life. From the moment that it was,
there has been increasing consent that here the
tradition which Dante accepted was profoundly
right. Great though other antique poets be,
Homer—swiftly, simply, nobly primal—is greatest.

He has created, or at least brought into permanent being, many now traditional characters:
Achilles, for example, and Hector, and Penelope,
and Odysseus, to go no further. As we consider
these, and those with whom they mingle, and the
world about them all, one phase of their primality
grows increasingly clear. They are full-grown
men and women, who live amid conditions as
normal to them as conditions of our own time are
to us. The great difference between them and any
such men and women as now cluster about us lies
in the fact that, for all their years, sometimes
running into age, they have qualities, hard to define but easy to feel, which resemble those of
modern savages or modern children. Although
their dignity is incontestably heroic, it resembles
rather the dignity of babies, or of naked Islanders,
or even of the higher animals, than that of civilised later Europe. Their passions and their reasoning are European, but not those of European maturity. Not children themselves, they combine

[1] Inferno, IV.

implicitly to set forth Europe in its world infancy.
This is what Homer records.

Just how the work which traditionally bears his
name was preserved is not certain. The form in
which we now possess it is based on that sanctioned
by the critical scholars of Alexandria, two or three
centuries before Christ. By that time, it had
long been reduced to writing; but whether writing
was in literary existence when the poems were
made has been disputed. Very probably they
were for an indefinite period transmitted orally,
through professional reciters, bards, or whatever
you choose to call these antique protagonists of
publishers and libraries. All this makes less
difference than we should now be apt thoughtlessly
to suppose. Printing has for centuries made
literature and other forms of written language so
increasingly copious that we instinctively assume
them to be addressed primarily to the eye. Even
lyric poetry, of which the soul is the sound, we
rarely read aloud to ourselves. Throughout European antiquity, the case was different. In the Confessions of St. Augustine there is a casual passage
which goes to the heart of the matter. Augustine
was a highly cultivated man of the Fourth and
Fifth Centuries of the Christian Era—a professor
of rhetoric, or literature as we might now called it,
at a period when not only the great literature of
Greece but also that of Rome had long been complete. Writing about the habits of St. Ambrose
in his study at Milan, he specially notes that
"when he was reading, he drew his eyes along over
the leaves, and his heart reached into the sense,
but his voice and tongue were silent." [1] Even so

---

[1] St. Augustine: Confessions, VI, iii (ed. Loeb, 273).

late as when all pagan antiquity was virtually a
thing of the past, the notion that any page could
be read inaudibly was not instantly familiar to
an accomplished university man, concerned with
letters from his childhood.   Throughout the whole
course of antique literature in both Greece and
Rome, any written text was assumed to be of the
nature which we still recognise in a musical score;
its primary task was not to convey meaning, but
to indicate to the eye the sounds by which meaning might presently be conveyed to the ear.   A
manuscript was hardly more than a memorandum,
which should assure textual accuracy of utterance.
Some faint trace of this once universal practice
may still haunt our fancy when we read the pages
of plays, of sermons, or of public speeches.   So the
lines with which Andrew Lang closes the sonnet
prefatory to the translation in which he had his
part are hardly figurative; he is almost literal
when, touching on those who turn back to Homer
even now, he says:

> They hear like ocean on a western beach
> The surge and thunder of the Odyssey.

III

THE LOST EPICS AND HESIOD

How remote Homer already seemed to Fifth
Century Greece is curiously implied in a tradition
related by Herodotus.[1]   Not very long after the
death of Lycurgus, who is supposed to have
flourished about the Ninth Century before Christ,

[1] I, 67–8.

the Spartans were informed by an oracle that if
they wished to get the better of the Tegeans,
in Arcadia, they must remove to Sparta the bones
of Orestes, son of Agamemnon. Where his bones
lay the Spartans did not know. A Spartan who
chanced to visit Tegea was surprised to find there
a smith working in iron—a detail which, although
iron occurs in Homer, implies the legend to have
come from a time when iron was a novelty, and
bronze the usual base metal. The smith happened
garrulously to mention that he had lately un-
earthed some gigantic bones, evidently from an age
more heroic in stature than his own. The Spartan,
finding the circumstances to fit certain obscure
parts of the oracular utterance, assumed the
bones to be those of Orestes, adroitly managed
to get hold of them, and brought them to Sparta.
Whereupon the Spartans became habitually victorious over the Tegeans; so they were as sure of
their Orestean relics as ever Venetians were of
St. Mark's.

Though this story, of course, throws no manner
of light on the question of when Homer made his
poems, it clearly places in an extremely distant
past the incidents and the characters he touches
on. In the Eleventh Book of the Odyssey, for
example (l. 461), the shade of Agamemnon refers
to Orestes as still probably living; he was too
young anyway to have gone to the Trojan War.
And Homer's instinctive objectivity seems on the
whole to set forth human life in terms of his
own day—much as the maker of Chevy Chase
does when compared with the conscious antiquari-
anism of Scott. Whatever else, the Trojan War as
Homer tells of it seems contemporary, and as

Herodotus alludes to it seems already almost as ancient as it seems to us.

During this indefinitely long interval, a considerable amount of other Greek literature had come into being, still more or less known by name. Little of it, however, has been preserved; and the chief importance of that little is that it confirms the supremacy of the Iliad and the Odyssey. To begin with, such masterpieces as these would in any event imply the existence of what may be called a school about them—just as the masterpieces of Shakspere, even if no other trace of the great period of English drama were left us, would imply that he was chiefly master of his art because his art was there to be mastered. On the lesser epics than Homer's we need hardly touch; some of them are said to have concerned other episodes of the Trojan War than those with which he dealt; another, or others, which dealt with the story of Thebes, have an accidental importance because they became sources of lasting tragedies during the Fifth Century at Athens. In any special treatment of Greek literature these would need attention. Here, concerned chiefly with the literary traditions of Europe, we need only mention that minor epics once existed.

We must linger longer, however, over the didactic poet whose name the Fifth Century had already come traditionally to group with Homer's. A familiar passage in Herodotus[1] mentions Hesiod and Homer as if they had been contemporaries, four hundred years or so before the words were written. Nothing could more distinctly indicate how completely traditional, as distinguished from

[1] II, 53.

historical, both of these names had already become by the Fifth Century. We have already reminded ourselves that there is a reasonable doubt as to whether such an individual as Homer ever existed; if he did, nobody can ever be sure exactly when he flourished. The one certainty is that the poems attributed to him somehow emerged from the depth of Grecian antiquity. With Hesiod, the case is different. Though his dates may be doubtful, we can hardly doubt either that there once was such a man, or that he lived pretty obscurely in the region of Mount Helicon, or that the personal details which occasionally appear in his work are on the whole genuine. An almost inevitable inference is that, even though the Homeric poems may have taken their final form somewhere about Hesiod's time, they originated earlier. The surviving poems attributed to Hesiod, indeed, are comparatively personal, and therefore distinctly later in character. He is now conjectured to have flourished during the second half of the Eighth Century.

Compared with Homer, his work is not copious, and certainly is not entertaining. It consists of two didactic poems, called the Works and Days and the Theogony, and of a fragment concerning the Shield of Hercules. All three are in hexameter verse, and the purpose of the first two is primarily instructive. A familiar passage in the Theogony (26–28) may be taken to signify that the Muses, generally occupied in making fictions sound like truths, are equally disposed to inspire poets who prefer to express truth directly. The Theogony proceeds compactly to set forth the genealogy of the gods, and such matters.

The Works and Days, in which there is more or less personal detail concerning legal disputes between Hesiod and his brother Perses, contains considerable ethical matter, sometimes epigrammatic in proverbial conciseness, and a good deal of precise advice about methods of agriculture. Perhaps the most familiar legend contained in this poem is the story of Pandora and the caskets, which occurs near the beginning. Neither this nor the much more extensive agricultural passages are in themselves impressively memorable. What makes the latter deserve our attention for a moment is hardly more than that they happened, centuries later, to inspire the Georgics of Virgil. In Augustan Rome, as in the Athens of Herodotus, Homer and Hesiod were the two first great poetic names of traditional Greek antiquity. Virgil tried to rival Homer in the Æneid, and to rival Hesiod in the Georgics. Whatever his success, there can be no doubt that the Æneid has never obscured the Iliad or the Odyssey, but that without the Georgics, held by many lovers of Virgil his highest technical achievement, the Works and Days might very likely have been virtually forgotten. Through the Georgics, Hesiod has had an evident influence on later literature; without them he would probably have had little. As surely as epic narrative makes permanent appeal to human beings, so didactic admonition—however admirable it may be—has the fatal fault of generally boring them.

There were other traditional names in the times of Herodotus besides those of Homer and Hesiod; among them was that of Æsop, often attached to fables even still, though none of the work originally attributed to him survives. For our present purposes these lesser facts may generally be neglected. The true thing for us to remember is that if the Persians had overcome Greece in the early years of the Fifth Century there might always have remained from what was by that time immemorial Greek antiquity at least two still extant records, in hexameter verse, of what Greece might have been—the supreme epic poetry of Homer, and the far less stirring didactic poetry of Hesiod.

IV

LYRIC POETRY

To Fifth Century Greece, Homer and Hesiod were already traditional, prehistoric. They did not comprise, however, all the literature which it inherited and has transmitted to us. By the year 500 another kind of poetry, some later phases of which were then contemporary, had produced masterpieces of its own, to this day unsurpassed. The names of its chief masters remain familiar, but hardly their actual work; for its excellence was of a kind completely beyond the resources of translation, and since ancient times general readers have seldom known enough to enjoy the original Greek.

Though the name—lyric—by which we now describe this later phase of early Greek poetry is of Greek origin, and sounds Greek, it is said never to have been used in its general sense by the Greeks themselves. For them, so far as they applied it to poetry, it stayed literal, referring only to such verse as was sung to the actual accompaniment of the lyre. This very fact may well remind us of something now generally forgotten. Originally poetry was not what we now conceive it formally to be—only a modulated, rhythmic arrangement of language; even in its epic form, it was almost certainly sung or chanted, rather than merely recited, and at least often the movement of it was probably sustained by the notes of some simple accompanying musical instrument. The Greek instrument most familiar in tradition was the lyre—a small portable harp, carried by the left arm and played by the right hand. To this day the most usual symbol of music is a conventional drawing or image of what it is supposed to have looked like. Now, most probably, even the narrative material finally collected in such epic poems as the Iliad and the Odyssey first came into existence as more or less distinct episodes, regularly sung and sometimes improvised. When these first took the form which has proved permanent, they may very likely still have been sung. The fact that their narrative meaning provides interest enough to hold the attention has had a good deal to do with their subsidence into something now thought of as wholly apart from music.

All the while, however, both in days before the full splendour of the epic hexameter was developed and in later days, as well, there must probably have been, as there always is everywhere, actual song. Until pretty lately, too, if we measure time by the centuries, actual song had a quality which the extremely elaborate development of modern music has tended not only to obscure but even to suppress. At present, the music of any song first attracts the attention, and lingers longest in memory. Originally, and we may generally believe for ages, the music of any song was so comparatively elementary that attention was attracted rather by the words, and the words might well be remembered when the music was partly if not wholly forgotten. Thus the words of a song were bound to do for those who listened no small part of the office now done by music alone. In this fact lies the true secret of that phase of poetry and indeed of that quality throughout poetry to which modern custom has given the name of lyric. Definitions of this term have been numberless, various and confusing. But any one can understand, or at least can feel, what the term broadly means: when any arrangement of words in poetry excites you to such emotion as nowadays would most normally be excited by music, pure and alone, you have heard the lyric note.

There is general agreement that the great lyric period of poetry in Greece, coming later than the epic, extended from somewhere in the Seventh Century to somewhere in the Fifth, and that on the whole it was at its height in the Sixth. For two or three reasons, however, the relics of it which have survived, mostly in small fragments, though they must always be traditionally important, can never touch us anything like so closely or so certainly as the epic poetry which preceded them does, or the dramatic which followed them. In the first place, the Greek music to which they were sung has almost, if not quite, perished; scholars may conjecture what it was like, but nobody can surely know. Our Greek lyrics, indeed, are little more than the words of "Auld Lang Syne" might

be, or of the "Marseillaise," if the tunes of them
had been altogether lost. In the second place, no
one now knows quite how the Greek words were
originally pronounced and modulated; scholars
can somehow manage to read the lyric metres just
as they can read hexameter lines, in rhythmically
consistent ways. At best, however, this must
be like French after the school of Stratford-atte-
Bowe. In the third place, even such approach
to the lyric original as may thus be made must
mostly, if not utterly, disappear when one attempts translation. Try, if you like, to see what
becomes of any song of Shakspere's—such as
"Full fathom five thy father lies"[1]—when turned
into French, or German, or Italian. Something
like the literal meaning of it, which is its body,
may perhaps be left; but little vestige of the lyric
music which is the soul that gives it being. Lyric
translation must at best be parody. However
exquisite, its beauty can never quite reproduce
that which it tries to render in terms other than
those of which the final excellence is that they are
just what they are. One might as well hopefully
attempt to keep a plucked flower in dewy freshness.

Tradition, accordingly, has preserved for us
not so much the Greek lyrics themselves as certain facts about them—the names of the poets
who made them, for example, and some of the
technical forms which these poets invented or preferred. Of these technical forms the most nearly
enduring is thought to have been perhaps the
earliest. The elegiac couplet, which in form is
closely related to the hexameter line, may almost

[1] Tempest, I, ii, 396.

be used now. Coleridge at once described and exemplified it thus:[1]

In the hexameter rises the fountain's silvery column,
In the pentameter aye falling in melody back.

Later than ancient times, however, have known elegiac verse not so much in the original Greek as in its secondary form, the Latin. It happened to be the favourite measure of Ovid, who has more than once been the most widely popular of Latin poets. Two other forms of Greek lyric verse have stayed to some degree familiar—the Alcaic stanza or strophe, frequently employed by Alcæus, and the Sapphic, believed to have been invented by Sappho. Both occur again and again in the Odes of Horace, which for centuries have been known to every English schoolboy. How little either adapts itself to modern use, however, may be seen at a glance when we turn to Alcaics by so masterly a poet as Tennyson,[2] or to English Sapphics by so consummate a master of rhythm as Swinburne.[3] At least in form, these lyric utterances were made for ears perhaps finer than ours but, better or worse, other than ours have come to be.

When we turn from the form of Greek lyrics to their substance we shall find similar conditions. Beyond question, the lyric poets of Greece were

[1] Again, I believe, he translated from Schiller.

[2] *e. g.:* O Mighty mouthed inventor of harmonies,
O skilled to sing of Time or Eternity,
God-gifted organ-voice of England,
Milton, a name to resound for ages—

[3] *e. g.:* All the night sleep came not upon my eyelids,
Shed not dew, nor shook nor unclosed a feather,
Yet with lips close and with eyes of iron
Stood and beheld me.

known, admired, studied, and reverently imitated
by the lyric poets of Rome; beyond question, the
considerable body of Latin lyric verse still in existence is full of allusion to things Greek; of the
original Greek, however, amazingly little is left
us.   Compare, if you will, the admirable pages
concerning Sappho[1] in Professor Mackail's Lectures on Greek Poetry with the one hundred and
seventy fragments or mentions of her work collected and translated by Mr. Henry Thornton
Wharton, and stated to comprise every authentic
trace of her now extant.   The marvel is how from
such crumbled ruin, Mackail has managed to
rescue anything at all.

For our present purpose, accordingly, we must
be content to remember that Greek lyric poetry
excellently existed by the beginning of the Fifth
Century, that the names of some of its masters—
Alcæus, for example, Sappho, Anacreon, and
Pindar—have never faded from tradition, and that,
as the contrast of the last of these names with the
three others may well remind us, it had already
taken two pretty distinct forms.

These forms correspond with what must have
been true throughout the history of vocal music.
Song, the moment we stop to think, must evidently
proceed either from a single voice or from more
than one.   Song written for a single voice must
generally, or at least most fitly, express or pretend
to express the mood of an individual singer; song
written for more than one or for many voices,
however harmonised or not, must more fitly concern not individual emotion but collective, setting
forth not the mood of any single singer but that

[1] 92–112.

which for the while may be taken as common to the congregations or the choirs, the ogling chorus girls or the convivial roysterers, who sing it together. On the whole, the lyrics of Alcæus, of Sappho, and of Anacreon—to go no further—are written as if to express individual emotion; without exception the surviving odes of Pindar are written to express collective emotion, and collective emotion of a kind so different from any now usual that, even for no other reason, they would be hard for us to understand.

As conventionally named, they celebrate athletic victories in one or another of four great periodical contests of the Greeks—the Olympian, the Pythian, the Nemean, and the Isthmian games. Though thus remotely similar in purpose to the joyous and dancing doggerel with which American undergraduates have been accustomed to rejoice over the result of an intercollegiate football game, they are in many respects much more nearly like processional hymns of the Church. To come anywhere near sympathy with them, we must somehow try to fuse, in grave yet enthusiastic harmony, two states of feeling now habitually and discordantly separate—that of sport and that of religion or something like it. Some such fusion, though now unusual, may still exist: not very long ago a celebrated football captain, equally eminent in the Young Men's Christian Association, was said often to prepare himself for the fray by prayer; he never went so far, however, as to establish the custom of crowning his triumphs by choral services of thanksgiving; and his preliminary state of mind was generally thought exceptional. In Pindar's time something as near

it as Greek things can ever be to modern seems to
have been normal.

At least, we can be fairly sure that these odes,
like the lost odes which Pindar and others wrote
for occasions of patriotic or civic celebration,
were intended for what we may call serious performance. They were not only sung; they were
sung processionally in elaborate movements which
had many characteristics of solemn, rhythmic
dance. The nearest approach to such rendering
now extant may possibly be found in the slow ritual
perambulation of certain religious solemnities.
Yet the sombre sense of eternal reward or punishment which pervades Christian tradition gives to
our religious functions a reverent intensity completely foreign to the religious conditions of Greek
antiquity, when religion was at once more legendary and more conjectural than it became in Christian Europe. A better modern parallel for the
Odes of Pindar, indeed, may perhaps be found in
a phase of fine art never fully developed until the
Nineteenth Century—the music-drama of Richard
Wagner. Here, as all who have heard and seen
it will remember, powerful dramatic poetry—
usually serious and symbolic in purpose—is set
to peculiarly and subtly appropriate music, and
is performed with a precision of arrangement,
movement, and gesture where the slightest divergence from the canon would more or less disturb the triple artistic harmony.

This comparison has for us the advantage of
bringing to mind how much of Pindar has long
been irrevocably lost. It is not hard to imagine
that the tradition of how a music-drama of Wagner's was originally performed might in time dis-

appear, and the very fact that we have already almost forgotten the precise instruments for which John Sebastian Bach wrote, or even Mozart, should remind us that the music of Wagner, as we know it now, might well fade from human knowledge until it vanished from human memory. All the while, the poetic text of Tannhäuser, of Tristan and Isolde, or of Parsifal might survive virtually intact. If so, it would probably be recognised and admired as highly developed poetic literature; but little vestige would remain of the multiplex power exhibited by its full original rendering. With the Odes of Pindar this has actually been the case for ages. Their music is forgotten, and so is their ritual movement or dance or whatever you please to call the visible phase of their performance; all we have left are words originally meant to be sung with music and with processional movements peculiar to themselves.

If only for this reason Pindar would at best be rather a tradition nowadays than a fully living literary fact. Another reason lies in his frequent obscurity, remarked even when his work was almost new. Neither of them can quite eclipse the swift and fiery flash of his utterance, nor yet the sustained splendour of sonorous phrase for which he was held matchless. These great qualities, however, defy translation. So, as we have seen, do the purpose and the mood of the poems in which they are preserved. Accordingly the influence of Pindar on literature—an influence by no means at an end—has been of a curiously, and perhaps uniquely, accidental character. To understand it, you must glance at one or two of his

Odes in the original Greek. There is no sort of
need that you should know even the Greek alphabet. Any eye can soon, if not instantly, observe
that they are generally written in groups of three
rather long stanzas. The first, called the Strophe,
consists of lines evidently and to all appearances
arbitrarily varying in length—in an instance at
which the volume chances to open, for example,
one line contains nineteen syllables and the next
eight. The second stanza, called the Antistrophe,
is equally irregular to the eye; but when you
compare it with the strophe you will find the apparent irregularities of each precisely to correspond; irregular in themselves, they formally co-
incide with each other. The third stanza, called
the Epode, you will find as irregular as either of
the others, but not a bit like them. You may be
tempted to infer that Pindar has thrown regularity to the winds. But glance at the next group
of three stanzas: you will find the metrical structure of strophe and antistrophe to correspond
with that of those in the first group, and that of
the two epodes similarly to agree with each other.
What at first looks like almost wanton irregularity
thus proves to be elaborately regular. The cause
of the apparent irregularity, meanwhile, is probably the nature of the music and of the rhythmic
postures, or dances, for which the lines were
written.

At least in English literature, the fundamental
regularities of Pindaric structure have long been
neglected or forgotten. The apparent irregularities of it, on the other hand, have been remembered,
and have had a sort of fascination for many poets
by no means inconsiderable. Artlessly reproduc-

ing the looks of it, they have produced memorable
works of poetic art. The so-called Pindaric Odes
of Cowley, for example, were sometimes held in
the Seventeenth Century to be even more admirable poetry than the minor poems of his contemporary Milton; and Nineteenth Century imitations of them have given our literature such masterpieces as Wordsworth's Ode on the Intimations
of Immortality; as Coleridge's Dejection; and in
America as the Commemoration Ode, in which
Lowell recorded the noblest spirit of our Northern
States during the Civil War. Such free structure as you will find in all these is traditionally
called Pindaric; though its only real likeness to
Pindar is visual, and though it is bound together
by the device of rhyme, never used by the ancients, it could not have come into existence
without the grand precedent of the choral Odes
of Pindaric Greece.

The names we have touched on by no means
comprise the lyric poetry of Greece. In the conventional canon long accepted there were nine lyric
poets; and there were countless lyric poems from
other hands than theirs. For our present purpose, however, it is enough to remember that by
the beginning of the Fifth Century Greece already
possessed not only epic poetry and didactic but
lyric, too, and that though the influence of this
has been chiefly secondary it has been permanent.
For one modern who can in the least appreciate
the extant lyrics of Greece, there are hundreds
and thousands who can still, if they choose, make
something out of the extant lyrics of Rome, and
these were deliberately based on Grecian models.
Even if the Persians had prevailed in the Fifth

Century, therefore, at least some trace of the Greek lyric might probably have remained.

One fact about it we have not remarked, a fact equally true of Hesiod and of Homer. When and where the Homeric poems were made, nobody can ever be quite sure, but everybody agrees that they were not originally made at Athens. Hesiod was almost certainly of a stock which had emigrated from Asia Minor to Bœotia and lived in the regions dominated by Thebes. Though the lyric poets were apt to wander over the Grecian world, and at one time some of them did their best work in Sparta, they were generally from the eastern shores of the Ægean Sea: Sappho came from Lesbos, and so did Alcæus, if we may believe the stories of them; Anacreon was of Teos in Asia Minor. Pindar, a true Greek, was of Bœotia like Hesiod before him; so late as the time of Alexander the Great, his house was preserved at Thebes as a sort of literary shrine. And so on. Whatever else, early Athens was not yet what Fifth Century Athens was to be—the virtual centre of Greek expression, in all its phases.

CHAPTER II

THE FIFTH CENTURY BEFORE CHRIST

I

HISTORICAL TRADITIONS

If our purpose were to study and to summarise the facts of history, we should have to dwell on the Fifth Century long. Our immediate concern, however, we can hardly too often remind ourselves, is only with traditions which have so lingered in literature as to become part of the habitual thought of Europe. Tendencies, events, truths of great importance may often not thus have survived; if so we may neglect them. Things in themselves less weighty, or even legendary, may sometimes be more noteworthy for us. Our true business, when considering any century, is only to ask ourselves what traditions were in existence when it ended which did not exist when it began. In the case of the Fifth Century—the supreme period of "the glory that was Greece"[1]—tradition chances to be fairly harmonious with history.

When the century began, the principal historical fact from the Greek point of view was the recent and rapid growth of the Asiatic power of Persia. Under Cyrus Persia had conquered Lydia and brought to ruin the once dazzling fortune of the Lydian king, Crœsus. Incidentally, we may well

[1] Poe: To Helen.

45

remind ourselves that legendary anecdote, preserved in literature, has made Crœsus traditional
both as a type of wealth and prosperity—a fact
which has some sort of historical sanction—and
as a contemporary of the Athenian Solon, which is
at best doubtful. The conquest of Lydia had
brought under Persian domination virtually all
the Greek regions of Asia Minor, thus concen-
trating the national life of the Greeks, so far as
this may ever be thought of as politically united,
in Greece itself and its colonies to the westward,
such as Southern Italy and Sicily. Under Cambyses the Persians had invaded and conquered
Phœnicia and Egypt. Under the first Darius,
who was on the Persian throne in the year 500,
it had already made incursions into European
regions to the north of Greece. Such expansion of
an Asiatic power clearly threatened the existence
of Greece, and with it that of subsequent Europe.
Had it prevailed, the civilisation of the whole
European world might probably have taken on a
character such as we now think of as Oriental.
Broadly speaking, something like what happened
when the Turks possessed themselves of the regions
where European traditions originated might have
happened to begin with.

Instead, our historical traditions are on the
whole true in remembering the Fifth Century as
comprising three periods which together not only
directed the future traditions of Europe, but to a
considerable degree controlled their course. The
first is that when the Greeks, forced by circumstances into something like political union, held
back and defeated the Persian invaders, thereby
securing a European independence of Asia; the

second is that when the civilisation of Athens was at its highest and most powerful, to such degree that the Athenians dreamed of what we should now call imperial domination throughout the regions where Greek civilisation prevailed; the third is that when the internal dissensions of Greece, culminating in the Peloponnesian War, fatally broke Greek union, or perhaps rather proved the Greeks so incapable of long-united action that they must ultimately submit to some imperial control other than their own.

Broadly speaking, the historical traditions of the first of these periods are based on events which happened during the second ten years of the Fifth Century. It was in the year 490 that the seemingly overwhelming forces of Darius, already on Attic soil and with strong naval support, were defeated by the Greeks, under the Athenian general Miltiades, on the Plain of Marathon, little more than twenty miles from Athens across country. This defeat resulted in the withdrawal of the Persian invaders for a period of some ten years. In 480, they returned under Xerxes, the son of Darius, after preparations as elaborate as those of Spain to overwhelm the England of Queen Elizabeth, or those of Germany to destroy France in 1914. At the narrow pass of Thermopylæ, the Persian tens of thousands were held in check by the Spartan king, Leonidas, with only three hundred men; all but one of these devoted defenders of Greece fell on the spot, and the sole survivor, deeming life in such circumstances a disgrace, had the happiness to fall a year later in victorious battle. Sweeping on, the Persians occupied and virtually destroyed the city of Athens. The

Athenian fleet, however, remained intact. Under
the command of Themistocles, it decoyed the far
more numerous Persian navy into the narrow
strait of Salamis, and there, almost within sight
of Athens, so crushingly defeated the invading
enemy that they withdrew in consternation. A
year or so later the Greek victory at Platæa, in
Bœotia, completed the liberation of Greece, and
of Europe, from the danger of Asiatic dominion.

The fleeting period of Athenian ascendency
ensued. In historic fact, and in detail, it is at
once dissentious and confusing. For one thing,
Themistocles, the victor of Salamis, was compelled
to fly from his country, and ended his days as an
unpatriotically confidential guest of the Persians.
What has survived in tradition, however, is clear,
inspiring, and on the whole true. The increasingly democratic and turbulent government of
Athens was for years under the virtual control
of its most eminent citizen, Pericles, whose name
is now generally given to the age he dominated.
Athens was fortified as never before; and at the
same time was enriched with works of fine art
such as never had existed previously and have
never been surpassed. What we possess of them
now are only fragments or ruins. Every art
flourished. As we have already reminded ourselves, to be sure, little trace of Greek music survives; and with painting, unless we count as
painting the exquisitely drawn figures on vases
and other pottery, the case is the same. But the
remains of the Parthenon, to go no further, are
still so nearly preserved as to demonstrate the
wondrous approach to perfection of Grecian architecture; given a structural and artistic purpose,

none before and none afterwards was ever so nearly attained. Sculpture, too, was at its height —freed from the cramping limitations of archaic convention and not yet trembling into the restlessness or subsiding into the literalness which too anxiously copy the changes of human movement and the details of facial expression. The Elgin Marbles, stripped from the Parthenon but kept safer in the British Museum than they could have been anywhere else, are so instinct with life that when you think of them you hardly remember them actually to be little more than vestiges of what they were when they were made. With them, as with the temple they adorned for twenty centuries, tradition associates the name of Phidias. With the name of Pericles tradition remembers that of his mistress Aspasia. And while all these names were those of living humanity, there came into existence, as we shall see, at least two considerable phases of European literary art—the drama and history.

These phases of Greek expression persisted through the third, and disintegrating, period of Fifth Century Greece. On the details of this period, so far as they concern considerations so general as ours, we shall touch when before long we consider the work of its contemporary historian Thucydides. Here we need only remind ourselves that in the year 431 the incessant dissensions of the Greeks broke into war between Athens and Sparta, each with their adherents. Two years later Pericles died. Various constitutional and political confusions at Athens ensued. With one or two intervals of truce, the war lasted for twenty-five years. The military power of Athens was finally broken by the defeat of an imprudent expedition against enemies in Sicily, particularly at Syracuse. And when the Fifth Century ended, the greatness of Athenian empire was already a memory.

II
ÆSCHYLUS

If the Persians had prevailed in 490, the surviving literature of Greece would have consisted, as we have seen, only of epic, didactic, and lyric poetry. Its last developed form would have been the choral ode of which the greatest and for modern times the only surviving master was Pindar. Pindar's work, to be sure, was mostly done after the year 500, when he was probably little more than twenty years old; he is said to have died after the middle of the Fifth Century. In general, however, he only carried to its highest excellence a kind of poetry which had existed before him.

A new kind of poetry to which we now come, nowhere near its full development when the Fifth Century began and virtually complete when it ended, is not only the highest literary achievement of this noble period of antique fine art, but makes such inherent human appeal that, though it has taken various forms, it has never ceased to exist. In our Twentieth Century of the Christian Era, indeed, the most widely vital phase of literary expression throughout the European world is probably the drama. It is rarely poetic nowadays; it is often and generally vulgar; but it is so pervasively alive that if a great poet should anywhere arise, he might well find it at this moment his best means of commanding human attention.

This very fact is apt to bewilder untrained readers who turn to the primal drama of Fifth Century Greece. At that period the theatre was not, as it is now, principally a place of amusement; it had, indeed, a character for which we can hardly find a better name than religious. Though its actual origins are known only by allusions or references, there seems little reason to doubt that they were closely associated with festival ceremonies in honour of the god Dionysus—later much confused in tradition with the Roman Bacchus. Among other things, he was the presiding deity of the vineyard season, and of the process of generation as well. In both aspects he lent himself to celebrations not only of a seriously symbolic nature, but also of a gayety often extremely ribald. The serious phase of his worship seems immemorially to have taken the form of choral odes, touching with more or less elaboration on this or that of his exploits. They were generally in what is called dithyrambic verse, which appears to have had all the apparent irregularity of Pindar's and none of the regularity involved in his balance of strophe and antistrophe, epode with epode. The ribald phase meanwhile seems immemorially to have permitted, at least in speech and gesture, reckless license. From the serious phase, Greek tragedy is thought to have developed; and from the ribald, Greek comedy. This divergence of origin is very likely one chief reason why, even to this day, critics have so often been disposed to discuss tragedy and comedy as distinct and separate kinds of literature.

Though no error could be greater than to suppose the Odes of Pindar to be themselves the
origin of Greek tragedy, they may accordingly help
us to understand how this later form of literature
originated. Pindar carries the traditional choral
ode of his own antiquity to its highest and final
literary form. From the same origin, another line
of development led to the other kind of expression,
which first survives in the tragedies of his contemporary Æschylus, said to have been only two or
three years the younger and to have died ten or
fifteen years before him. The dithyrambic odes
which celebrated episodes in the career of Dionysus
frequently concerned his various relations with
human beings. The moment the monotony of
their unmixed choruses was varied by the inter-
polation of what we might now call a solo by one
of the company, generally supposed to have been
the leader, the performance would evidently take
on a freshly animated aspect. To introduce a
second speaker, originally perhaps the tragic poet
himself, who should converse with the soloist,
would evidently enhance this animation. The
step to impersonation on the part of the new
speaker is obvious. Thus tragedy is thought to
have come into existence; and by the Fifth
Century it had so far developed as not only to
have traditional names of its own, such as that of
Thespis—actors have been called "Thespians"
ever since,—but also to concern itself with pretty
much any accepted divine or heroic story, whether
directly connected with Dionysus or not. So far
as Greek tragedies have survived, indeed, they do
not extremely emphasise him.

Æschylus, an Athenian some twenty-five years

old in 500, is said to have begun his work as a
tragic poet at about that time, to have fought both
at Marathon and at Salamis, to have brought his
art to a point previously unapproached and in
some respects never surpassed, and to have maintained his full power until his death, which occurred
in Sicily a little before the middle of the Century.
In all he is thought to have written at least ninety
dramas; mentions or fragments of more than
seventy exist; but in complete form we possess
only seven—selected in antiquity as masterpieces,
and used then and thereafter for classical texts,
much as modern schools or colleges might use a
few selected plays of Shakspere.

The plays of Shakspere, as everybody knows,
were written for something similar to modern performances in regular playhouses; and if successful
were occasionally and perhaps often repeated.
The tragedies of Æschylus, on the other hand,
were written for something more like ritual presentation on single occasions of solemn festivity;
they appear, generally, to have been offered in
competition with other poets for a poetic prize,
such as was annually awarded at Athens; and the
conditions of their performance in the vast open-
air theatres of the Greeks were wholly different
from anything to which modern times have been
accustomed. For one thing, by the Fifth Century,
tragic actors wore megaphonic masks, and height-
ened their stature with high-soled boots or buskins.
These devices, which survive even now, like the
lyre, in the guise of conventional theatrical symbols or ornaments, imply that the chief feature of
ancient dramatic art was not action but elocution.
Facial expression, indeed, was out of the question.

The condition of a Greek performance which is
strangest to us, however, and therefore the most
perplexing as we read a Greek drama now, is the
constant presence and the frequent dominance of
the chorus. We can come nearest to understanding such dramatic works, perhaps, if we consider
them as a phase of expression in which the character and the action now assumed to be the basis of
the drama have not yet completely emerged from
the choral ode of earlier times, and must therefore have had, to enhance their inherent power,
the full freshness of æsthetic novelty.

Another phase of their novelty is almost as
foreign to us nowadays. At least for two or three
hundred years, a new play has often if not generally concerned a new subject. A considerable
part of its preliminary interest has consequently
lain in the fact that the audience does not know
exactly what is going to happen. In the Greek
theatre, on the other hand, the subjects of tragedy
were always familiar; the interest of the audience
was excited not so much by what happened as
by the manner in which what must of course happen was presented. Of the seven surviving tragedies of Æschylus, for example, one—unique in
dealing with an historical subject—concerns the
defeat of the Persians, and incidentally contains a
wonderful description of the battle of Salamis,
where the poet had personally taken part; two—
Prometheus Bound and the Suppliants—concern
prehistoric legends; one—the Seven against
Thebes—concerns the Theban story of Laius,
Œdipus, and their descendants, which was then
almost as familiar, in now lost epic form, as the
Trojan story of Homer has remained; and a con-

secutive group of three—Agamemnon, the Libation Pourers (Choephori), and the Eumenides—relate, in magnificent succession, one tremendous episode of the Trojan story itself—that fatal misery of the house of Atreus on part of which, as we have already seen, the shade of Agamemnon touches in the Eleventh Book of the Odyssey. The central figure of the three is Orestes, doomed by ancestral crime to matricidal expiation, itself freshly criminal. Every one of these seven stories was perfectly well known to all who came to see and hear how Æschylus would set them forth; and the same was probably true of all his many tragedies now long lost.

In view of all this, it is amazing that within a few years an open-air performance of the Agamemnon, with conjecturally restored music and choral movement, proved absorbingly impressive to American audiences, hardly any of whom knew a word of Greek, or had much notion of the story. Perplexed though they may have been, they could not help feeling the colossal power of this primal dramatic poetry; and whoever was among them must always feel, when turning to the printed text, that at best the text alone, unacted and undeclaimed, is only a libretto. Even thus, however, and even in translation, it remains grandly poetic. The time you may give to Mrs. Browning's version of Prometheus Bound, or to Robert Browning's version of the Agamemnon—which, if possible, should be compared with the freer but clearer version by Edward Fitzgerald—will nowise be wasted. All three of these versions are memorable English poems; and they all render in English something of the spirit which keeps

alive to this day the first fully developed tragic
poetry of Europe.

The essence of tragedy is to be found in an
eternal conflict which nothing can ever long disguise. Human beings come into this world amid
environments utterly beyond their control; no
man can choose his parentage, or his country, or
his century, or his station. If by chance men
grow to maturity, such conditions as these must
always to no small degree control them—both
physically and morally; certain deeds may be in
their power, more must always stay hopelessly
beyond it, and even what they can do must inevitably be conditioned if only by their sense of
principle, or duty. However virtuous, they cannot escape the past. Neither can they avoid the
future. If there be such a thing as the present,
it can never be more than a ceaselessly shifting
point of division between these unfathomable
depths. And in the depths of the future only
one fact looms certain: human life must swiftly
end, generation after generation, in human death.
Yet on what men do while their fleeting earthly
existence remains conscious must depend the irrevocable heritage to be borne by their posterity;
just as nothing can modify what has been, so
nothing can modify what shall have been when
men have done it. For a little while they feel
as if they were free to do what they will; so, perhaps, if we grant that they are creatures of their
past, they may be; even if they be, their freedom
can last no longer than they cast their shadows in
the sunshine. At best, life is a struggle, during
the little while when each man lives, between his
individual being and the implacable environments

of the past which is behind him and the future
which must soon bring his earthly existence to a
close. Fate you may call these surroundings of
us all, or whatever else you will. Nothing can
avert them, or even long obscure them. In the
ceaseless conflict between each man and the
uncontrollable force which must always surround
him the essence of tragedy lies.

If we may trust those who know Æschylus best,
no poet in all European record has ever more
deeply felt, or more stupendously set forth, this
ultimate tragic truth. What is more, you need
go no further than the English versions of his
work on which we have already touched, to make
sure that he is essentially aware of both its terms—
of environment and of individual consciousness.
Pretty clearly, however, and perhaps partly because he is the first great master of that species
of poetry which he brought into enduring European
literature, he may well perplex modern readers by
the intensity with which he dwells on the fact of
environment, as distinguished from the fact of
individual existence. Though he thus gains in
grandeur, he inevitably makes less intimate and
instant appeal to human sympathy. In his Agamemnon, for example, whether you have the fortune to have seen it acted or like most of us must
confine yourself to its printed pages, you can
hardly help so deeply feeling the sweep of fate
that you half forget the men and the women,
Agamemnon himself and Ægisthus, Clytemnestra
and Cassandra, whom this fate sweeps on towards
their doom. At best, you remember how the sacrifice of Iphigenia, years before, had stirred her
mother Clytemnestra to depths which could not

dream of stillness until with adultery and murder she had wrought expiatory vengeance on the husband and father who had done the deed; and you feel, in turn, how nothing less than the expiatory vengeance of Orestes, years later, which plunges him, as the murderer of his mother, into new and deeper crime, can atone for the doing to death of his father Agamemnon. What manner of man Agamemnon felt himself to be you care little in comparison, or what manner of woman Clytemnestra. Partly, no doubt, this is by reason of the constant dominance, throughout the drama, of the chorus; partly, however, and to no small degree, it comes from the mood of the poet who tells the story. Others have told more wondrously what the subtleties of human nature are; he tells best of all what the environment must forever be wherein for its little while human nature has struggled and must struggle until humanity shall come to an end.

As we have already reminded ourselves, the tragedy of Agamemnon, though itself complete, does not stand solitary in the work of Æschylus. It is the first of a group of three distinct but consecutive tragedies, originally made for consecutive performance, and together setting forth a story too extensive to be comprised in any single one. Though no other group of three plays happens to survive from Fifth Century Greece, such groups, at least when the Century began, were the usual form in which tragic poetry was written. They are commonly called Trilogies. Among the extant works of Æschylus, to go no further, the Seven against Thebes is known to have been the third drama of a trilogy in which it was preceded

by one concerning Laius and another concerning
Œdipus; the Prometheus Bound was the first or
the second drama of a trilogy, too, where it was
followed by a drama called Prometheus Unbound—
though whether the third of the series, which was
named Prometheus the Fire Bearer, began or ended
it has been more or less disputed. Originally, we
are told, such tragic trilogies were regularly followed by a fourth drama, of distinctly different
character, where the chorus was composed of
Satyrs, and the subject, whether connected with
the trilogy or not, was treated in a spirit of broad
and ribald burlesque. The only extant example
of such comic afterpiece, however, chances to be
a dreary drama of Euripides called the Cyclops;
it concerns the adventure of Odysseus with Polyphemus, it is animated—if at all—only by the
buffoonery of conventional drunkenness, and those
who know it in Greek generally pronounce it as
empty in the original as it is when translated.[1]
We therefore have no means of knowing what
an Æschylean tetralogy—as the full group was
called, of three tragic dramas followed by a comic
—may originally have been like. Without the
trilogy of which Orestes is the central figure, we
should be equally in the dark concerning the three
tragic dramas, taken by themselves.

Of this remaining trilogy, the first part—the
Agamemnon—is the most interesting, perhaps the
most powerful, and certainly the only one which
has been translated into anything like English

---

[1] It is fair to add that Shelley translated the Cyclops and that many of
his devotees agree with him that the play is delightfully funny. Somehow,
though, you must worship Shelley very religiously if you would share his
notions of fun.

poetry; it is consequently more positively memorable than either of the dramas which follow it. For our present purpose, however, the second play of the series—the Choephori, or the Libation Pourers, as the title is usually translated—is in one respect more interesting to novices who desire any definite impression of Æschylus. The most nearly satisfactory English translation is probably that of Doctor Plumptre—pedestrian and uninspired, but nevertheless literate. Similar in general treatment to the Agamemnon, it deals with the story of Orestes and his sister Electra—the children of Agamemnon and Clytemnestra. Electra has remained at Argos, with her mother, who has married Ægisthus; but Electra has never for an instant forgotten her pious duty to the memory of her murdered father. Orestes has long disappeared; no one knows whether he is alive or dead. At length, he secretly returns, pays due filial honour to the tomb of Agamemnon, makes himself known to Electra, and with her aid avenges their father by taking the lives both of their mother and of her husband, who had been first the adulterous paramour of Clytemnestra and later accomplice in Clytemnestra's crime. Whereupon, the Furies swarm about Orestes, avenging his mother, and driving him into renewed and maddened exile. Give yourself up to the story, and you can hardly fail somehow to feel the imaginative power with which Æschylus has told it; yet you can hardly fail, either, to feel that his whole way of telling it is almost an obstacle to any modern mind. We are used now to dramas where the incidents and the characters are presented as if they were visibly and audibly before

us; compared with any such method, that of
Æschylus seems almost ritual—more nearly like
the solemn recital of some Scriptural story in an
elaborate religious ceremony. To get the full
effect you must probably read, and ponder on, the
whole short drama; the Greek has in all only one
thousand and seventy-four lines. If you lack
time or patience for such reading, you may find
something of the effect in the portion between the
first speech of Electra[1] and her full acknowledg-
ment that Orestes may be close at hand;[2] her
exchange of speeches with the chorus, for example,
resembles a responsive chant, like that of the
Anglican Psalter.

The reason why this drama may interest us
more than the others in the trilogy is accidental.
A drama on the same subject by Sophocles happens to have been preserved; and so has one by
Euripides. This opportunity for observing how
the three great tragic dramatists of the Fifth Century dealt, each characteristically, with the same
story is unique. What in each case is something
less than the best work of its author, therefore
becomes, for our present purpose, his most certainly distinct.

III

SOPHOCLES

The surviving work of Sophocles, the second
great tragic poet of the Fifth Century, includes,
like that of Æschylus, only seven dramas, selected
and preserved for educational purposes, and

---

[1] Line 83; Plumptre, line 86.   [2] Line 210; Plumptre, line 203.

supplemented by fragments of others, often very short, which have happened to be quoted by later authors of classic antiquity. The subjects of his seven extant dramas resemble those of the extant dramas of his great predecessor. One, the Maidens of Trachis, concerns prehistoric legend— the story of Heracles, or Hercules as Roman and later times have often called him, unwittingly done to death by his wife Dejanira with the poisoned robe of the slaughtered centaur Nessus. Three, and on the whole the most memorable, concern— though not as a formal trilogy—the Theban story: Œdipus the King, Œdipus at Colonus, and Antigone. The remaining three—Philoctetes, Ajax, and Electra—concern separate episodes in the story of Troy. All these subjects, and all those of his numerous dramas which have not been preserved, were perfectly familiar, like the subjects treated by Æschylus, to the audiences for whom he wrote. What appealed to their interest was not the story of any of these tragic poems; it was the manner in which this story was presented by the poet.

Though the life of Sophocles overlapped that of Æschylus for some forty years, and though for twelve or fifteen of these years they were artistic rivals, the younger tragic poet really belonged to a later generation. At the time of the battle of Marathon, where Æschylus fought, Sophocles was no more than five years old; on the occasion of the battle of Salamis, where again Æschylus fought, Sophocles—who was somewhere about fifteen years old and is said to have been remarkably handsome—was called upon, if we may trust tradition, only to take part in a choral ode, cele-

brating the Grecian victory. It was eleven or
twelve years later, in 468, that he is first reported
to have won the prize for tragic poetry. The
power thus attested he retained, seemingly un-
diminished, throughout his long life. He is said
to have lived to the age of ninety, dying only a·
year or two before the fall of Athens at the close
of the Peloponnesian War. His full maturity accordingly came when Athens was at the very
height of Periclean power; and, though he saw this
power bent, he did not survive till the moment
when it was broken. By chance, perhaps the
most impressive portrait-statue of all European
antiquity makes his aspect now almost as familiar
as his name. It is not of his time, nor even itself
an original work of art; it is thought to be a marble copy of a bronze statue set up at Athens some
fifty or sixty years after he died. Taken only as
it stands now, however, in the Lateran Museum at
Rome, it seems incomparable. He looks, as somebody has said, like one who has risen in response
to the applause which is his due; and throughout twenty-five centuries this applause has never
ceased.

Yet any modern reader who should approach
his work by itself, particularly in translation—
and no English translation of it has such literary
merit as has been attained in translations from
Æschylus and from Euripides—may well find it
perplexing, at least to begin with. It was made
for presentation under the same conditions which
surrounded the tragedies of Æschylus; as in them,
a considerable, even though clearly a smaller,
part of its utterance is assigned to the chorus, and
its formal methods are widely different from any

to which we are now used. We have utterly lost
both the music and the rhythmic motions which
were originally part of it. Taken by themselves,
therefore, we may well find the texts of Sophocles
perplexing, archaically strange. The moment we
compare them with the work of Æschylus, however, they take on another aspect. To discuss
whether this aspect is higher or lower, better or
worse, would be fruitless, and perhaps imperti-
nent. There can be no doubt of two things—
Sophocles is clearly different from Æschylus, and
at least a considerable part of the difference is
due to the fact that he treats his subjects with
something far more like human sympathy. This
difference is analogous to that between the earlier
sculpture of Greece and the Phidian sculpture
of Periclean Athens; something like it may be
observed in the development of widely different
phases of European art—such as Italian painting,
or the English drama under Queen Elizabeth and
King James the First. If one may generalise,
when a great school of expression dealing with any
kind of human affairs has gathered new creative
energy, it begins by breaking the bonds of outworn convention and proceeds to closer and closer
imitation of actuality, until the sense of actuality
—or perhaps a sense of the new conventions which
have incidentally come into being—freshly limits
and finally smothers its imaginative impulse.
There is hardly anywhere a clearer instance of
what this generalisation means, at least in its
earlier phase, than you may find when you consider the work of Sophocles not alone but in its
relation to that of the poet, a generation older, who
had virtually created the tragic poetry of Europe.

The real, permanent relation between Æschylus and Sophocles is implied in what, even now, is generally said or written about them by those who know and love them best. You may have read much concerning Æschylus without finding your attention particularly directed to the personages in his dramas; what his admirers dwell on is rather his dramas as they stand complete—setting forth with unsurpassed grandeur of both conception and diction how the sweep of irrevocable fate whirls to doom the conscious beings who for a little while raise their heads above the surface of the relentless stream of life. The moment you turn to what is said or written about Sophocles, you will grow aware of a difference: at least before long, your attention will be called, even though you hardly know quite how, to the grandly generalised yet human beings to whom his imagination has given individual life. In the sense in which men discuss a character of Shakspere's, there is hardly such a thing as a character among the personages of Æschylus; but you will find the Antigone of Sophocles, for example, or his Œdipus, almost as distinct and as inexhaustible to those who love his work as Hamlet is or Lady Macbeth to those who love their Shakspere. Something similar is implied in the effect of his dramas when performed before modern audiences. As we have already reminded ourselves, a performance of the Agamemnon of Æschylus, in open American air, with restored music and choral procession, was deeply and absorbingly impressive. Even those who felt its splendour most profoundly, however, can hardly imagine how this tragic thing could be pent within the walls and the roof of such a theatre

as we are now used to. The Œdipus of Sophocles,
on the other hand, literally translated into both
English and French, has occasionally been acted,
with tremendous effect, on our regular stage. Those
who saw Mounet-Sully play the part, with all the
modernities of lights and scenery about him, had
little sense of strangeness in the drama; what they
felt was rather its power and his as he embodied
an antique but human character. The tragedy
of Sophocles, in short, proved capable of translation not only into a living language but even into
the theatrical terms of the present day. Though,
like the text of Æschylus, the text of Sophocles is
only a libretto, such as that of a Wagner music
drama might be if both the music and the original
methods of acting were completely lost, the text of
Sophocles, alone and unsupported, proves to this
day not only enduringly poetic, but also dramatically practicable.

The most memorable characters in the extant
work of Sophocles are Œdipus and Antigone; his
most powerful dramas are certainly those which
bear their names. By comparing either of these
with the Prometheus Bound or with the Agamemnon of Æschylus, you may most impressively
come to feel the characteristics of each great
tragic poet when at his best. As we have already
reminded ourselves, however, the accident that
the Electra of Sophocles deals with the subject
with which Æschylus deals in the Choephori, or
Libation Pourers, makes a comparison between
these somewhat secondary tragedies more definite
and therefore perhaps more suitable for our immediate purpose.[1] Fully to feel the difference,

[1] *Cf.* p. 61.

you should read both of them through—no great
task, for the Electra of Sophocles has only 1510
lines, which added to the 1074 lines of the Choephori make no more than 2584 lines in all. A
mere comparison of the opening scenes, however,
will go far to define the contrast. In both plays,
Orestes presently appears, secretly returning to
pay filial honours to the tomb of his father, Agamemnon; in both he is accompanied by his friend
Pylades, who speaks in neither. In the Choephori, however, Orestes proceeds at once to perform his ceremonial duty, almost as a priest might
do reverence before an altar; his conduct is not
human but ritual. In the Electra of Sophocles,
on the other hand, there comes in with him a nameless attendant—called a pedagogue in the Greek
—whose prologue-like opening speech states tó
him and incidentally to the audience where they
are and what is the general situation; and his
own answer to this speech, before the voice of
Electra is heard behind the scene, sets forth what
in every sense of the term we may call a plot;
here, in short, there is nothing ritual at all.

A similar contrast you will find by comparing the
passages in the two plays concerning the way in
which the return of Orestes comes to the knowledge of Electra. We have already touched on
the ritual treatment of this matter by Æschylus;
in the Choephori, Electra goes straight to her
father's tomb, and there discovers the tress of
hair which Orestes has ceremonially deposited
upon it. In the Electra of Sophocles, on the other
hand,[1] her sister, Chrysothemis, comes joyously
in, with the tress of hair which she has found on

[1] Lines 871–933; Plumptre, lines 871–932.

the tomb and believes to have been cut from the head of Orestes, and Electra for a long time cannot be persuaded that it is his. An even sharper contrast may be found by comparing the passages about the death of Clytemnestra: in Æschylus,[1] after what amounts to a solemn responsive duet, she is led off to slaughter; in Sophocles,[2] having been induced to suppose Orestes dead, she is behind the scene, contentedly preparing for his formal funeral, and you hear her cries of despair when he reveals himself and strikes her down. Electra, in this case, who at that period of the action has long disappeared from the Choephori, stays in the centre of the theatre, listening to the sounds of horror, and so rejoiced that the murder of her father is avenged as for the while to forget how this vengeance could have been achieved only by the murder of her mother. These comparisons, as we ponder on them, may well make us feel almost as if the tragedy of Sophocles were conceived and set forth in modern terms.

To correct such impression, we need only return to this tragedy by itself. The moment we forget Æschylus, Sophocles must appear to us almost as remote as the older poet. Though in Sophocles the chorus is decidedly less prominent than in Æschylus, the chorus even in Sophocles might well impress any uninitiated reader of these days as the most conspicuous and perplexing feature of his dramatic method. Accepting this, too, a modern reader might well feel his sense and his presentation of the sweep of fate—of the environment which must always and forever relent-

---

[1] Lines 902–929; Plumptre, lines 890–917.
[2] Lines 1398–1421; Plumptre, lines 1398–1421.

lessly surround humanity—to be the dominant
note of his work; and his sense of the other factor
in tragedy, of the humanity which fate besets
during our little while of anxious life, to be at
best rudimentary. The truth is, however, that
beyond any other tragic poet in the literature of
Europe Sophocles was profoundly and equally
aware of both terms in that tremendous conflict
between humanity and its environment wherein
the essence of tragedy lies; and therefore that the
distinguishing feature of his poetic genius may be
found in the balance with which he keeps himself
from laying undue stress on either term of the
conflict.

Some such balance those who know him best
discern even in the detail of his poetry. Above
and beyond all else, he has the serene poise of
mastery. Thus, more than the elder tragic poet
whose work began earlier than his, and more than
the younger tragic poet who was the contemporary
of his later days, he seems in the end to embody
the most deeply characteristic spirit of his time.
His long life began only a few years after the Fifth
Century began, and ended only a few years before
it ended. His maturity came literally in the full
Age of Pericles at the very time when the Parthenon was built, and when Phidias made sculpture
at once ideal and real. The words Periclean,
Phidian, and Sophoclean mean, in different ways,
the same thing; and there is no fourth to match
them.

Though, as we have seen, Sophocles wrote on
almost to the end of the Century, his quality as a
tragic poet was fully developed by the year 450.
Æschylus was then dead. Even if the Fifth Cen-

tury had no other claim to place in the traditions
of European literature, the first half of the Century
would therefore be enduringly memorable for
having added to the traditions of epic, didactic,
and lyric poetry which it inherited a fourth tradition which it created. During these fifty years
Æschylus brought tragic poetry into lasting existence; and Sophocles brought it well within the
range of human sympathy.

IV

HERODOTUS

At just about the time when tragic poetry had
thus developed its most beautiful balance, another kind of literature, widely different in both
form and purpose, first took permanent shape.
Its purpose was not to celebrate legend or to express imaginative emotion but intelligently to record facts—to tell as truthfully as might be how
the Greek world where the writers lived had originated and was behaving. Its form was accordingly free from the shackles of metre, and far
more nearly resembled the language used in daily
life; we have long called this form prose. Neither
purpose nor form was a novelty; both had existed
perhaps immemorially. Until this period, however, neither had so highly developed as to produce a literary masterpiece; or, if by chance either
had, no such masterpiece has been preserved.
The work of the first two surviving Greek historians, on the other hand, has qualities which
have hardly been surpassed. For narrative skill
and sustained interest Herodotus remains endur-

ingly excellent; for thoughtful and animated statement of contemporary fact, no writer has excelled
Thucydides; and together they give us a marvellous impression of how the Fifth Century began
and how it ended.

Both of them were contemporary with a considerable part of the career of Sophocles, and both
might have seen or known Euripides, too, the
third and last great writer of Greek tragedy.
Thucydides was also contemporary with much of
the career of Aristophanes, our only surviving
writer of Greek comedy. For reasons of chronology, therefore, as well as for the more obvious
reason that on general principles a given kind of
literature may conveniently be treated all at once,
it may now seem volatile to distract attention
from the later course of Fifth Century drama to
that of history as written in the Fifth Century.
Two considerations, however, justify this interruption: quite to understand the change in the
drama, we shall be the better for reminding ourselves afresh of the historical circumstances which
surrounded it; and any reader who has cared to
turn, as he reads, to the texts we have touched on,
may well have found his task by this time something of a strain. Poetry is not only harder to
read than prose, but lends itself much less readily
to translation. Just here, prose gives us what
Herodotus often and deliberately gave those whom
he addressed—a welcome chance to take breath.

In so doing, though, we must freshly remember
one feature which all antique prose had in common with antique poetry, and which modern prose
and even modern poetry has considerably if not
altogether lost. Nowadays we read print with

little sense that the words before us were originally
symbols representing vocal sounds.   At least until
the time of St. Augustine, on the other hand, as
we have already remarked,[1] few thought of a
written page as anything else than a memorandum
from which somebody might read aloud.   The
moment, consequently, that you compare any
translation of Greek prose with the original text,
you must begin to feel how much of the original
has been lost.   In the original, it is hard to prevent the voice from laying stress on the word
which has most meaning; in almost any modern
version, it is almost as hard not to throw your
emphasis on words more or less insignificant.
Ancient words were always addressed to the ear;
modern words are generally addressed to the eye.
Granting this, however, there can be no doubt
that the substance of voiceless prose is far less
hard to grasp than that of voiceless verse; for
the primary purpose of prose is not to stir or to
edify but to inform.

Herodotus has so long been called the father of
history that we are apt to forget his perhaps
deeper claim to respect: so far as surviving European literature goes, he is also the father of
prose, almost as distinctly as Homer is the father
of poetry.   Though both had predecessors, both
so eclipsed their predecessors as to make them,
from our point of view, virtually invisible.   In an
auroral past, however, antique to Greece itself,
Homer stays primally and almost legendarily im-
personal; Herodotus, in the full light of a recorded century, is distinctly individual.   A gentleman of Halicarnassus, in Asia Minor, he was born

[1] *Cf.* p. 27.

about half-way between the battles of Marathon
and of Salamis. His birthplace, though Greek
by origin and tradition, was under Persian dominion; his general situation may therefore be likened
to that of a good French Alsatian born between
1870 and 1914. His natural sympathy was with
one side of a great conflict; his youthful surroundings went far to make him familiar with the manners and customs of the other. He had the best
of Greek education; among the writers we have
touched on he quotes Homer, Hesiod, Alcæus,
Sappho, Pindar, and Æschylus—and he quotes
many more now known only by name, or from
fragments. When he was about twenty years old,
political troubles at Halicarnassus, which resulted
in the execution of at least one of his kinsmen,
appear to have driven him from his native city,
never to return there. The details of his wanderings
and of his travels are not clearly determined; it
is certain, however, that he was for a while resident at Athens, when the power of Pericles was
flourishing, that at one time or another he journeyed not only over the whole Greek world but
into outlying regions like Scythia and Egypt, that
the merit of his historical work was fully recognised, and that because the constitution of Athens
forbade him as foreign-born to attain full rights
of citizenship there he became a citizen of Thurii,
an Athenian colony in Southern Italy, where he
died at somewhere about the age of sixty.

His general sympathies, at least as his work reveals them, were nevertheless enthusiastically
Athenian. The opening paragraph of his History,
virtually a compact preface, states his purpose to
set forth the great and marvellous deeds of both

Greeks and Barbarians,—a term by which he really means the Persians and the peoples who came under Persian dominion,—and the causes which brought them to war. Another way of putting this would be to say that in the full light of Fifth Century Athens he set himself the task of telling how the Greece of which Athens was the momentary leader had grown into its independent national consciousness.

Evidently, this Greece was surrounded by regions which it called barbarous; evidently, too, both Greece and its Barbary had emerged from an antiquity already as immemorial as any antiquity is now. Something of these circumstances, as they concerned both space and time, had been recorded by earlier geographers or chroniclers; and so had the principal facts of Grecian topography and story. This material, however, of which Herodotus apparently made full use, had never attained the dignity of enduring literature. He supplemented it by wide travel and extensive personal inquiry. He deliberately put it into a form which he meant to be permanent; and, for want of satisfactory prose models, he carefully imitated the methods of Homer, to the point of breaking by frequent episode what might otherwise have been the tedium of narrative too long sustained. There was never more conscientious artist than this Father of History and of Prose, devoted to the celebration of how Greece came to her victory over Persia, and fortunate enough to do his work before time had swiftly shown how short the life of politically independent Greece was to be.

As his history has come down to us, it is divided into nine books, each conveniently named for one of the Muses. Professor Bury[1] points out that this division, though made by Alexandrian editors under the Ptolemies, really indicates the structure of the work, and also that the whole work might have been further grouped in three triads, each consisting of three Books. There are reasons to think that the last three Books, which deal with the reign of Xerxes, and the final defeat of the Persians—bringing into literature the names of Thermopylæ, Salamis, and Platæa,—were written first; and that the other six—the first three concerning the reigns of Cyrus and of Cambyses, and the second three concerning that of Darius and culminating with the Greek victory at Marathon, were added as a colossal and magnificent introduction. However this may be, the nine Books, as we have them, are composed together with remarkable artistic skill, leading us excursively but surely from legendary antiquity, and often through remote regions, to that climax of Greek warfare when, as we can now see, what for the while appeared only the defeat of Persians finally assured the existence of the spirit and the civilisation which, in contrast with the Asiatic, has now for twenty-five centuries been European. The story they tell is that of the manner in which our whole Western world was born.

Herodotus is by no means a philosophic historian. All he surely does is to collect facts as well as he can, and to set them forth in fluent and pleasant narrative style. He is more nearly critical, however, than you might at first think. An amusing example of his method and his limitation occurs in his account of Egypt. Cambyses, the

---

[1] The Ancient Greek Historians (Harvard Lectures), 1909, p. 38,

successor of Cyrus on the Persian throne, added
this already immemorially antique dominion to
those of the Persian crown. Egypt accordingly
coming within the range of Herodotus, he devoted
the whole Second Book of his History to an account,
descriptive and historical, of this perennially fascinating region; and until modern ingenuity de-
ciphered hieroglyphic inscriptions and otherwise
discovered the actual facts of Egyptian history
through tens of centuries, Egyptian tradition as
known to Europeans was mostly based on Herodotus. Many of his names, indeed, still familiarly
persist—Cheops, for example, Mycerinus, and
Rhampsinit; it is not very long since his name of
Sesostris was generally replaced by the true one
of Rameses; and so on. He was not content to
learn his Egypt from record or report, or such
works as the geography of Hecatæus, now no longer
in existence, which he is thought to have availed
himself of in a manner such as modern prejudice
would hold plagiaristic. He travelled to Egypt,
he saw all he could there, and he made every inquiry in his power. Among other things, of course,
he visited the pyramids, already, though not yet
ruinous, more than three thousand years old; and
he gives a probably correct account of how they
were built. Naturally, however, he was unable
to read hieroglyphic inscriptions; so he unsus-
piciously accepted, and set down, the statement
of his local guide—an evident pleasantry, most
likely provoked by vexatious questioning—that
the inscription on the pyramid of Cheops, which
was probably the "cartouched" name of that half-
legendary monarch, recorded how much had been
spent for the radishes, leeks, and onions consumed

by the workmen who had built this artificial moun-
tain;[1] and he proceeds to conjecture how much
more must have been spent for tools, clothing,
and solidly nutritious food. It is fair to add that
he was not often caught so napping; the quiet
good sense of his comment on the preposterous
story is far more characteristic. His implication,
too, that these luckless labourers had no wages
seems to be true.

Even though he cannot be accepted as a final
authority on history, accordingly, he may be confidently regarded as an honest story-teller, who
not only tells us most of what we know about such
memorable facts as Marathon, Thermopylæ, and
Salamis, and such memorable personages as Darius
and Xerxes, Miltiades, Leonidas, and Themistocles,
but also, in his matchless episodic digressions, collects an incomparable treasury of legend, tradition,
and anecdote. He can never cease to be interesting; and there are few clearer contrasts between
the mood of Europe and that of Asia than you will
find by comparing his narrative with that in the
Books of Genesis and Exodus. His Egypt, for
example, though resembling that of Joseph, and
of Moses, and of their Pharaohs, is in many aspects much more like ours.

The substance of his work lends itself far more
readily to translation than can ever be the case
with poetry, or with prose whose purpose is more
or less poetic. In Rawlinson's English version—
on the whole our best—he stays thoroughly readable. Almost the only device which has become
quite strange nowadays is one which may be due
partly to his study of Homer as a narrative model,

[1] II, 125.

and partly to the fact that his work was written to be read aloud. Instead of telling what eminent men thought and purposed, he deliberately puts declamatory speeches into their mouths, more or less like those uttered by Homeric heroes; a casual example may be found in what Miltiades says to Callimachus shortly before the battle of Marathon.[1] This convention was followed by most of the ancient historians, Greek or Latin; and a trace of it survives even in the imaginary eloquence attributed to John Adams by Daniel Webster when called on, in 1826, to eulogise the lately dead second President of the United States. These formal declamations, however, leave undisturbed the narrative and anecdote which surround them. So long as men like good stories well told, they will not tire of Herodotus.

Not long after the middle of the Fifth Century, accordingly, Greek literature already had both poetry—epic, didactic, lyric, and dramatic—and admirable narrative prose. To this point, also, the course of Greek literature, like that of plastic art in Greece, had shown little symptom of decline. Each new phase of it had created an unprecedented type which has endured.

V

THUCYDIDES

By the middle of the Fifth Century Thucydides, the second of the great Greek historians, was certainly alive, and may have been some twenty years old. If so, he was only twelve or fifteen

[1] VI, 109.

years younger than Herodotus; in any event, he was no younger than an eldest son of his predecessor might have been, and was old enough to have remembered the effect produced at Athens by the history of Herodotus when it was a novelty. Although his own work is therefore almost contemporary with this, it nevertheless impresses one almost as if produced in a different epoch.

To some extent, the difference may be due to circumstance. Thucydides, a man of the highest rank in Thrace, where he possessed considerable property, was also closely related to eminent families at Athens, was an Athenian citizen, at one time during the Peloponnesian War held an important military command, and by reason of defeat was condemned to long banishment, which he seems mostly to have passed on his Thracian estates. He was thus both a full contemporary of the historical period he has recorded, and to some extent a participant in its action; while Herodotus was neither. As a matter of literary tradition, however, the difference probably goes deeper. For one thing, the history of Herodotus, held by some to have been written for public reading, has evident histrionic qualities; that of Thucydides, though doubtless intended to be read aloud, can hardly have been written with any view to public performance, which would indeed have been somewhat beneath his dignity. Again, the history of Herodotus, setting forth the great deeds which freed Greece and Europe from the danger of Asiatic dominion, ends at a time when he was less than ten years old; that of Thucydides, recording the progress of a civil war ultimately fatal to Greek independence, begins at a time when he

can hardly have been less than twenty-five and
perhaps may have been forty. Between the end
of Herodotus and the beginning of Thucydides
there is accordingly a historical gap of just about
half a century; and this half century included
almost all of the Age of Pericles—a period of which
there is no important historian. Herodotus writes
its magnificent prologue, Thucydides its fatal
epilogue; neither tells its story. Yet each wrote
in the full maturity of middle life. The contrast
between the periods each dealt with would in any
case have gone far to make their work different.
Whoever celebrates an heroic past can never be
quite like one who notes down the occurrences of a
disintegrating and baffling present.

Almost as a matter of course, therefore, both the
method and the proportions of the history of
Thucydides contrast strongly with those we have
glanced at in the history of Herodotus. Two-
thirds of the older historian's work consists of his
colossal and almost epic introduction to the still
almost epic three books in which he finally records the already well-past defeat of the forces of
Xerxes. If we may trust the opening paragraph
of Thucydides, he perceived when the Peloponnesian War broke out, in the year 431, that this
was to be the most critical incident in the history
of Greek independence, and accordingly determined to record whatever happened as soon as
possible after it had occurred. The first of his
eight Books he devotes to a summary introduction; the other seven record the annual progress
of the war until the twenty-first of its twenty-
seven years. His work, never finished, breaks off
abruptly. His temper throughout may be called

philosophical; that is, he states his facts not so much for their own sake as for the reason that when duly recorded they will give the future data to think with. Except in his numerous speeches, however, which Professor Bury believes frequently to express his personal opinions,[1] he seldom philosophises directly; at least apparently he preserves the character of a dispassionate observer, content that conclusions be drawn, when the time comes, by others. Very likely, as some recent critics think, he was deliberately partisan, stating this fact or that in such manner as would induce readers to take his view of it, and occasionally suppressing matters inconveniently favourable to other opinions than his. However this may be, he manages throughout to appear unbiassed. Fair or not, he has hardly been surpassed in what looks like judicial fairness. He professes, probably with truth, to have collected and sifted his material scrupulously. He writes more like a judge, summing up evidence, than like an advocate emphasising facts to support his side of the case; so his prose, as he tells what men were, and what they did and what happened to them, has a literary quality almost Shaksperean. He often seems an almost final model for those who would provide others with a firm and solid basis for historical generalisation.

The moment you try thus to use him, however, you will grow aware of his limitations. History as we now conceive it, at least when we want to philosophise, is perhaps the most intricately complicated subject with which would-be philosophers can possibly deal. Superficially a matter of delib-

[1] *Op. cit.*, chap. IV.

erate politics, strategy, and tactics, more or less
conditioned by chance, it has other phases—economic, social, cultural, whatever else—so fundamental that wise men may well come to think it
really a manifestation of natural force, hardly if at
all more manageable by men than geology is or astronomy. To generalise about it at all, if we
come anywhere near this opinion, we need immeasurably more data than have yet been collected, and very likely more than ever can be.
And all that Thucydides gives us, despite his unsurpassed power of statement, is an account of
how individuals behaved in attempting to control political or military affairs when at any moment accident might interfere with their best-laid
plans. You may read him through and through
with no perception that the half-century of Greek
history which came between the close of Herodotus, in 479, and the beginning of his own work,
in 431, had any economic or social aspect, or that
the Age of Pericles had produced a single work of
art or of literature. He tells you of politics, of
soldiering, of such freaks of chance as the plague
at Athens, and of public characters so far as their
conduct was public. Here he virtually stops.

This very limitation, on the other hand, con-
centrates his astonishing intensity—a quality the
more remarkable when we remember that, so far
as record goes, he had no model for just the kind
of history which he attempted. His omissions,
indeed, are probably deliberate. The task he had
set himself was not to write a general account of
his times, but rather to make the most careful
study he could of a war actually in progress when
he wrote. Whatever had no direct or apparent

bearing on this was therefore not within his scope; whatever concerned it, he set forth as firmly as he could. Though he lacks the charm of Herodotus, accordingly, his unsurpassed force and his apparent truthfulness make Herodotus in comparison seem pleasantly old-fashioned. Though Thucydides be the harder to read, he rewards every effort which he demands. To appreciate him, as to appreciate any great master, you must read him through. Characteristic passages, however, will give an impression of his qualities. His account of the last days and his summary of the character of Themistocles,[1] for example, shows how he can deal with matters already past—such as Herodotus dealt with throughout. His almost dramatic funeral oration,[2] put into the mouth of Pericles eulogising the first Athenians who fell in the war, at once implies the character and the bland idealism of Pericles and illustrates how Thucydides developed the already conventional use of speeches in what he meant to be authentic history; the method is something like that of Shakspere, when with frankly dramatic purpose he wrote the funeral speeches of Brutus and of Antony over the body of Julius Cæsar. The passage describing the plague at Athens[3] reveals at least two phases of Thucydidean mastery: coming directly after the funeral oration of Pericles, it so contrasts with this as both ironically and dramatically to emphasise how slightly idealism can foresee the chances of reality, and how relentless these chances must be; taken by itself it is one of the

---

[1] I, 135–138. The most readable English translation is Jowett's; but any will do.

[2] II, 35–46.   [3] II, 47–52.

three tremendous accounts of pestilence in European literature—the other two are Boccaccio's introduction to the Decameron and Defoe's description of the Plague at London. Finally, if you will take the time to read the Sixth and Seventh Books, which deal with the fatal expedition to Sicily, you will not waste a moment; should this task prove, as it probably may, too arduous, you will find the grim end of the story[1] incomparable for precision, clearness, and sheer narrative power. It has often been held the greatest masterpiece of military history ever achieved.

Whatever else, when with memories of Herodotus hovering in the background you ponder on the effect of Thucydides, you can hardly help feeling how he once for all sets forth, for enduring tradition, the fate of the glory that was Greece. When Sophocles was born this was dawning as if it might blaze forever; before Sophocles died, it was forever clouded. The memory of it stays so gleaming that we are apt to forget its fragility; it was at its best for less than a single long human lifetime. Somehow, too, Thucydides implicitly tells us why. His Greece, no doubt, is not primal; its intelligence is not only fully mature but often seems unsurpassed. In one aspect, however, this intelligence remains primitive or at least youthful, hardly ever imagining any more than children imagine, or than the restless spirit of reform imagines which throughout the ages persists childish, that intelligence cannot control events and remake the Golden Age unresisted and unfailing. Such a quality needs, for anything like endurance, the saving grace, which Greece lacked, of instinctive

[1] VII, 70–87.

common sense, recognising among other unwelcome facts that the most nearly sure means of historic and social growth must be sought in compromise. Nothing else can long avert conquest or anarchy; any government of men can persist only so long as the men in power stay strong enough to impose their will on those who disagree; there is more hope for peoples who consent humbly to submit themselves to the unintelligent but colossally sensible government of law—usually right in decisions, however blundering in the reasons given for them. The very excellence of Greek intelligence during the Fifth Century, despite the admirable self-control of its expression, was therefore a fatal cause of anarchic political weakness. Here, on the whole, were men who still fancied each for himself that he could have his own way.

When we compare this impression with that produced by the men who live in Herodotus, and then recall that produced by the Homeric heroes, we shall find the three tending,—at least in comparison with any impression produced by later Europe,—despite their evident differences, to group themselves together. The characters of Thucydides, and those of Herodotus too, are no longer like those of Homer, full-grown men at once European and yet somehow temperamentally in a state variously resembling that of modern infancy;[1] at the same time, for all their maturity of unbalanced intelligence, they have not yet grown to what modern minds would instantly recognise as complete maturity of character. Their racial inexperience keeps them still youthful, if only in their blindness to such limitations of human independence

[1] *Cf.* p. 26.

as wise experience has long been compelled sadly
to recognise. Achilles, for example, Miltiades,
and Alcibiades, when we compare them as a group
even with Romans, and still more when we compare them with Europeans of modern times,
merge together, grown men yet still juvenile; and
their composite embodies not only Greece but the
swift and beautiful childhood of Europe.

All three of the masters who have given us each
his own part of this triple composite, deal with
what has traditionally been accepted as history;
and none of them, so far as we know, had precise
models for the aspect in which he presented it.
Surely, though, Homer set forth in matchless
hexameters the splendid legends of heroic antiquity,
Herodotus in always fluent and limpid prose heroically celebrated a national past still within the
bounds of human memory, and Thucydides, struggling with a language not yet quite tamed to the
severity of his purpose, philosophically recognised
and did all he could to help explain the troublous
perplexity of contemporary circumstance. Taken
alone, the history of Thucydides is a masterpiece
of classic grandeur; compared with Herodotus,
it seems by very reason of its intense concentration to have lost something of that serene exten-
siveness of view which marks Herodotus, the father
of prose, as belonging to the Age of Pericles,
Phidias, and Sophocles. When we compare both
of them together with Homer, we can hardly help
feeling more deeply still that the course of Greek
expression is tending toward the limitation of
imaginative freedom by an inexorable sense of
fact. In Thucydides the development of history
in Greece,—with which we have interrupted our

glance at the development of dramatic poetry, the other great form of literature developed there during the Fifth Century,—has clearly taken a shape still original but no longer surgingly crescent.

It was amidst such things as he records, and to a great extent while he was recording them, that the work of Euripides was at its highest, and that the work of Aristophanes began. When we turn now to them, completing our glance at dramatic poetry, we shall find their relation to Æschylus and Sophocles variously analogous to the relation we have already tried to define between the work of Thucydides and that of Herodotus. For all their imaginative power, they too are comparatively hampered by increasingly insistent perception of fact.

VI

EURIPIDES

Though Euripides, traditionally said to have been born at Salamis on the very day of the battle which saved Greece, can hardly have been much more than fifteen years younger than Sophocles, the contrast between them is much greater than that between Sophocles and Æschylus, who were far less nearly of an age. Euripides, even in his own day, was recognised as an innovator, welcome to those who liked a new phase of art, and by no means so to those who preferred the maintenance of artistic tradition. As a tragic poet, to be sure, he was throughout compelled to observe certain of the conditions imposed on tragedy by the circumstances of its development: his subjects had

to be heroic and considerably religious in character,
the unavoidable chorus forbade his methods to
approach what we should now consider anything
like direct portrayal of life, and the use of masks
and stilted buskins prevented freedom of expression or of action. Compared with any such
dramas as make instant appeal nowadays, his
must therefore seem almost ritually formal, and
dependent for stage effect rather on elocution than
on representation either of human beings or of
human conduct. Compared with those of his
great predecessors, however, they take on another
aspect, almost modern. He is said to have died
in the year 406, a few months before Sophocles—
both happily spared knowledge of the final collapse of Athenian power, two years later. For a
full half century they had been rivals—one magnificently sustaining the old tradition of tragedy,
the other and the more popular sturdily asserting
a new.

A fortunate chance enables us to see pretty distinctly what this new tradition was, in comparison
with that sanctioned by custom. Among the surviving dramas of Euripides is one concerning
Electra, a subject also dealt with, as we have
already seen,[1] by both Æschylus and Sophocles.
When compared with the Choephori, or Libation
Pourers, of Æschylus, the Electra of Sophocles
seems, as we reminded ourselves, like things we
are used to. Compared with the Electra of Euripides, however, it appears uncompromisingly
antique. The Electra of Euripides, accordingly,
though not the most powerful of his nineteen surviving works, becomes for our purposes the most

[1] *Cf.* pp. 60, 67.

distinctly characteristic.[1] What is more, as it contains only 1,359 lines, all three of the dramas now before us are comprised in 3,943 lines, about as many as are in Hamlet; so to read through all three is no great task. Euripides opens his in a manner substantially and doubly new to us. A peasant —called in Greek "Autourgos," or a man who does his own work—enters, and devotes a soliloquy of fifty-three lines to a precise statement of the situation with which the action begins. Though evidently a minor character in the drama, he thus makes his first appearance as the speaker of what amounts to a formal prologue, much as the Richard III of Shakspere does in the chronicle-history which bears that sovereign's name. Some such prologue generally occurs, until the device begins to seem mechanical, throughout the extant tragedies of Euripides. The substance of the Peasant's prologue is even more characteristic than this newly conventional use of it. The general situation is the same as that with which the dramas of Æschylus and of Sophocles open: Agamemnon has been murdered by Clytemnestra, who has married her paramour Ægisthus; Orestes has disappeared; and Electra remains pretty desperate in Argos. Both Æschylus and Sophocles, however, represent her as still of acknowledged princely rank. Euripides, on the other hand, sets forth how, by way of avoiding trouble concerning succession to the throne, Ægisthus and Clytemnestra have compelled her to marry the Peasant,

[1] Gilbert Murray's translation is the most literate. All his translations of Euripides are noteworthy English poems. On the whole, too, they appear quite as like the original as the careful but rather more diffuse versions of A. S. Way, which are printed with the Greek text in the Loeb Classical Library.

an incidentally loyal creature who states that he
has secretly refrained from asserting his marital
rights; and when, after the prologue ends, she
makes her appearance, she enters with a water-
jar, doing something like menial work. In comparison with the classical dignity of her other
presentations, accordingly, the situation is either
astonishingly more human or, if you prefer, senti-
mentalised to a degree which may conveniently
be described by the sadly abused word romantic.
Anyhow it appears much more nearly real; and
indeed when new may well have appeared almost
altogether so.

A similar contrast appears when you compare
the two treatments of how Electra recognises
Orestes.[1] We have already compared the presentation of this incident by Sophocles with that by
Æschylus.[2] In Euripides, an old man enters—
comparatively an almost comic character—who
has been a servant of Agamemnon, and deeply
resents the social degradation of Electra. He
tells her how he has just found on her father's
tomb the new-cut lock of hair which figures in
both of the other versions. Orestes, still unrecognised, enters while they are discussing this,
to which Electra attaches no importance; and the
old man presently recognises Orestes, mostly by
reason of a scar on his brow—a traditional dramatic trick until the absent strawberry mark on
the left arm which brings about fraternal reunion
of Box and Cox. Here, in comparison with either

---

[1] Lines 487–584. In Gilbert Murray's admirable version the lines are
not numbered; the passage begins on p. 30, of the single-volume edition,
and ends on p. 37.
[2] *Cf.* p. 67.

of the other treatments, is at once something like what we should now think dramatic action and a rather meretricious theatrical device. You will find a similar contrast in the passages describing the murder of Clytemnestra,[1] set forth by Euripides at considerable length;[2] he makes Electra lure her mother into the Peasant's hut, where Orestes is awaiting them to wreak his atoning vengeance in Electra's presence. Nowhere near so grandly classic as the heroine of Æschylus and of Sophocles, the Electra of Euripides is much more like a human being.

Here we come to what seems the fundamental fact in the dramas of Euripides. Tragic though they stay, and in many ways limited or controlled by the conditions and the traditions of the Greek theatre, they strongly emphasise the human factor in tragedy, comparatively neglected by Æschylus,[3] and brought by Sophocles into no more prominence than is needed to balance it with the other factor of tragic conflict[4]—fate, environment, whatever you will.[5] Whether this nearer approach to human sympathy makes Euripides greater or less than his predecessors has been often and fruitlessly disputed. There can hardly be a doubt that his comparative popularity, from his own time onward, is due to the appeal he thus makes to human nature, the one fact which poets, readers, and spectators must always and inevitably have in common. Here, at least, generation after generation have found something addressed to themselves, something which they can understand instinctively and without deliberate imaginative

[1] *Cf.* p. 68.   [2] Lines 998–1157; Murray, pages 64–73.
[3] *Cf.* p. 57.   [4] *Cf.* p. 69.   [5] *Cf.* p. 56.

effort. It has been summarised in a quatrain of
Mrs. Browning, not itself remarkable yet somehow
haunting the memory.[1] In the previous stanza
she has four commonplace lines about "Æschylus,
the thunderous," and four still more commonplace
about "Sophocles, the royal." Then come those
which linger:

> Our Euripides, the human,
> 　With his droppings of warm tears,
> And his touches of things common,
> 　Till they rose to touch the spheres.

To return to the Electra of Euripides, you will
find that it ends with a stage device for which
there is no precedent in the dramas of Sophocles or
of Æschylus. At the end of the Choephori, to be
sure, the Furies reveal themselves to Orestes, beginning the merited tortures with which the third
drama of the Trilogy is concerned.[2] In the Electra of Sophocles, there is no divine interposition.
In the Electra of Euripides, on the other hand,
the demigods Castor and Pollux—on earth brothers
of Clytemnestra and Helen—suddenly appear in
the air; and Castor, who speaks for both, brings
the troubles of Electra to an end by arranging
her marriage with Pylades, the bosom-friend of
Orestes, and only afterwards pronounces the con-
science-smitten doom of Orestes himself.[3] It seems
probable that these god-like apparitions were represented by actors mechanically lifted off their
feet. At all events, such interventions frequently
occur in the dramas of Euripides, where divine
visitants are apt to solve the complications of the

---

[1] Wine of Cyprus, XII. 　　[2] Lines 1046–1074; Plumptre, 1038–1064.
[3] Lines 1233–1359; Murray, pp. 78–83.

plot; and the device has given rise to the term *Deus ex machina*[1] (the God in the machine) commonly used from Roman times to describe any personage introduced from nowhere to unravel narrative or dramatic intricacies which have got inconveniently snarled. Whatever their dignity, these interjected deities have little other artistic purpose than to save poets and writers the trouble of inventing solutions more logical. And, though their function may thus partake of the godlike quality of mercy, they are hardly impressive enough to excite any deeply religious or even earnest emotion. At least comparatively, these gods of Euripides are pretty thinly theatrical. They are not such deities as any one could ever quite have believed in. Here is one simple reason why those who disapproved of Euripides found him, among other objections, irreligious.

A less obvious practice of his points the same way. Though, as a matter of necessity, he retains the chorus, he uses it at once more freely, more separately, and perhaps more negligently than Sophocles; and, as we have seen, it looms larger still in Æschylus. The dramas of Æschylus, indeed, represent a phase of tragic poetry not quite fully emerged from its origin in choral odes.[2] Those of Euripides represent a phase where the choral ode is subsiding into the background, and tending towards something little more essential than lyric interludes, analogous to the music played between the acts of modern plays in Amer-

[1] The term, usually supposed to be originally Latin, is said first to occur, and only allusively, in the Hermotimus of Lucian (86), a Greek dialogue of the Second Century A. D.

[2] *Cf.* p. 54.

ican theatres. It is tending, as well, towards
philosophic comment on lines of thought which
the action may have started. To enter into the
philosophic opinions of Euripides would lead us
now too far afield; but chapters and books have
been written about them, and doubtless more will
be. Whoever thus independently preaches must
be prepared to have his orthodoxy scrutinised.

Of one thing, meanwhile, there can be no doubt.
Compared with either of his predecessors Euripides
was popular, and has remained so. The familiar
lines of Milton's sonnet, "When the Assault was
Intended to the City," remind us how, at least in
tradition,

> Sad Electra's poet had the power
> To save the Athenian walls from ruin bare.

There was a similar tradition that Athenian cap-
tives in the quarries of Syracuse owed privileges,
and perhaps their lives, to the chance that they
could recite Euripidean lines. Again, only seven
dramas of Æschylus have been preserved, and
only seven of Sophocles. Of Euripides, on the
other hand, who is said to have written more
than ninety, we still possess nineteen: and his
influence on the drama in later languages than
Greek has been preponderant—on Seneca in Latin,
for example, on the Samson Agonistes of Milton,
on Racine in French, on Alfieri in Italian.

Milton, as we have just seen, thought of him as
the author of Electra, and the preface to Gilbert
Murray's translation of this drama pronounces its
heroine the most profoundly studied of all those
left us by Fifth Century Greece. By themselves,
however, certain other works of Euripides are per-

haps more positively memorable. The surgent
splendour of the Bacchæ makes many hold it his
masterpiece; the tenderness and pathos of the
Alcestis combine with its happy ending in appeal
to general modern feeling; the Medea has a sav-
age intensity befitting the half-barbarous and
half-divine origin of its passionate, wronged, and
merciless heroine; the Hippolytus, with its para-
doxical contrast between the accursed lust of
Phædra and the fantastic purity of her husband's
son, is perhaps melodramatic—whatever that
abused term may mean—but none the less absorbing. The character of the Nurse there, too, though
not the detail of her speeches, reminds one of that
masterpiece of dramatic realism, the Nurse in
Shakspere's Romeo and Juliet; and Racine's
Phèdre, which is based on the Hippolytus, more
nearly holds the stage than any other tragedy of
Seventeenth Century France. Considering his inevitable limitations of subject, scope, and method,
at the same time, Euripides very adroitly avoids
monotony. Throughout his dramas, nevertheless,
you will find the characteristics we have perhaps
tediously dwelt on when we compared his version
of the story of Electra with those of Æschylus and
of Sophocles. Greater or lesser than his great
predecessors, he is less grand and far more nearly
human. Compared with them, he takes a long
step towards reality, bringing heroic personages
down towards the level of this earth where we
live and move and have our being.

They are no longer like Periclean, Phidian,
Sophoclean ideals; in their veins runs something
like the blood of life. Thus, not altogether fantastically, we may group them with the virtually

contemporary historical personages and incidents of Thucydides, as compared with those of Herodotus, a little earlier in fact and measurelessly so in spirit. Though the surge of Greek invention which we have admired from Homer's time onwards persist throughout this later period of the Fifth Century, it is at last near the period where, if not yet ebbing, you begin to feel that it cannot rise much higher.

Of other tragic poets who flourished in these years only the names are left us. We need hardly regret the loss of their works, nor even much lament the loss of far more work by Æschylus, Sophocles, and Euripides than survives; for the fragments of it preserved by grammarians and critics are at best no better than the tragedies we still possess. These, thirty-three in all, are enough to define both the nature and the course of this great phase of European literature, unknown when the Fifth Century began and complete, in its primal form, when the Century ended. Had these hundred years added nothing else to literary tradition, they would stay memorable for their tragic poetry. As we have seen, besides, they also added to European literature the great tradition of historical prose. Thus doubly memorable, they would still have— even if neither of these monuments had been preserved—another claim to lasting memory. For towards the end of them there came into permanent existence another form of literature, in its kind unsurpassed.

VII

ARISTOPHANES

As we reminded ourselves when we first touched on dramatic poetry,[1] this phase of literature originated in choral odes or something like them made for the festivals of the god Dionysus; and the worship of this deity had two distinct phases. One, of solemn character, developed into tragedy, the other, concerned with obvious aspects of his conduct as the god of generation, was ribald to a degree which would now seem inconceivably remote from any European ideas of religion—and indeed would make the wildest grotesques of mediæval sculpture appear, in comparison, devoutly austere. This developed into comedy, which appears to have existed and flourished throughout the growth of tragedy. The very extravagance of its license may perhaps be one reason why it was later in taking permanent form; so far as words and conduct went, it seems to have been bridled only by the limits of invention imposed by nature on those who made it; within the limits of conventional dramatic conditions, they were permitted, not only every imaginable violation of general decorum and decency, but also the wildest range of personal abuse and of what Americans would nowadays call topical allusion. So long as their audience laughed, their work was well done; and few human emotions are at once more genuine and more transitory than such as excite laughter. For centuries the rude

[1] *Cf.* p. 51.

but persistent bases of it have now been condemned as obscene—a word which literally means
that they should be kept out of sight; and
the personal or topical bases of it fade out of sight
by themselves as, year by year, the men, the
politics, and the manners concerned are swiftly
forgotten. So old fun is apt either to make men
pruriently snicker and whisper, or else to be lifeless as corked champagne. Fun must sparkle,
and the very essence of effervescence lies in momentary freshness. To laugh healthily, you must
laugh loud.

It is perhaps more surprising, therefore, that
Greek comedy survives at all than that the eleven
examples of it still in existence are all by one man,
and that his literary career began with the last
quarter of the Fifth Century. Of the life of Aristophanes little is known. He was Athenian; he
was probably born after 450; his first appearance
as a comic poet, though precocious, seems to have
occurred well after the Peloponnesian War broke
out; and he lived for some fifteen or twenty years
after the Century ended. His extant comedies
imply that his sympathies were conservative or
even reactionary, at a period when the state of
things he cared for was swiftly bound nowhere;
the Symposium, or Banquet, of Plato, represents
him in good company. That is about the whole
story.

His work is at once hard to understand and
harder to translate. To appreciate anything like
its full meaning you must know every traceable detail of the political and social conditions
momentarily existing when each comedy was
written; you must guess what others, now beyond

recovery, may perhaps have been; and you must admit insoluble the problems occasionally presented by personal or topical allusions. When you try to render into another language what despite these difficulties you have discovered, you will find any modern language to fail. It could hardly manage the fundamental need of expressing serious purpose in terms of unbridled license and broad burlesque, reduced to a metrical form of exquisitely varied exactitude. When it strives to combine with this the need of animating the lines with incessant, unexpected fun, both witty and humorous, and of sweetening the whole with passages, mostly choral, unsurpassed for lyric beauty, the task becomes superhuman; and yet until the task is accomplished in a style of seemingly spontaneous, idiomatic ease, you can hardly even approach Aristophanic effect. There is no need to say that nobody has done so. The double wonder is that Aristophanes remains so fascinating to all who care for him in the Greek as to keep them incessantly attempting the impossible with a courage which he would have been the first to laugh at, and that after all they have managed to give English readers even a shadowy notion of what he was.

Fortunately for us here and now, the Comedy of Aristophanes which most instantly concerns the traditions of literature has been translated into English better than any other. Gilbert Murray's version of the Frogs is licentious, to be sure, only in its dainty avoidance of Aristophanic license; and its lyric beauties never reach the point of haunting charm. On the other hand, it is clear, swift, idiomatic, easy to read, and so faithful to the fun of the original that when read aloud it will often excite spontaneous laughter. The subject of the Frogs is the state of dramatic literature in the year 405. The death of Euripides the year before, shortly followed by that of Sophocles, had left the tragic poetry of the Greeks, as we can now see, virtually complete. There were plenty of tragic poets, and there were to be a great many more, but none to vie through the ages with the three great Fifth Century masters. This truth instantly impresses the divinely prescient god Dionysus, who bereft on earth of tragic artificers able duly to celebrate his festivals, feels impelled to bring back one of them from the shades. He appears in broadly comic conventional character, disguised as Heracles,—one of whose feats was the recovery of Alcestis from the dead,—and very much and reasonably afraid of the discomforts and misadventures he may have to undergo; among other things this Aristophanic deity is the most abject imaginable coward. Charon compels him to earn his passage across the Styx by taking a very inexpert hand at the oars; on the way he is scared and chaffed by a ghostly chorus of Stygian frogs, to whom the name of the comedy is due. All of which, despite Gilbert Murray's skill, may perhaps seem a little dull in Twentieth Century English. When we fairly get to the Shades, however, things wake up. For a good many years, it seems, there had been no question that in this mildly dismal eternity Æschylus was entitled to all the honours due the greatest of tragic poets; when Euripides followed beyond the grave, he proceeded to claim these dignities for himself. Æschylus violently disputes the claim, and the last half of the Frogs[1] is devoted to their quarrel. They appeal to Pluto, abusing each other with incessant quotations or parodies of their own verses. After much fluctuation, Pluto decides in favour of Æschylus, who takes the occasion to pronounce Sophocles, and not Euripides, second to himself. The comedy ends with his start back to Athens—which implies that, whatever happens to Euripides, the tragedies of Æschylus are not going to be shelved. There could be no broader burlesque; and certain passages—particularly that where Æschylus caps line after line of Euripidean prologue with two ridiculous words which fit both sense and metre,[2] yet state that Ægyptus, Dionysus, Cadmus, Pelops, and other divine or heroic beings have lost the Greek equivalent for their cakes of soap—are durably laughable. Incidentally, this buoyant popular criticism of almost contemporary poetry keeps the tragic poets astonishingly alive. It is not in the least judicial; it does not even pretend to be fair; but it contagiously expresses the mood which, from those days to ours, has resented the vulgarising of fine art, and has been impulsively disposed to regard changes as probably for the worse. The most wonderful thing about it is that, if you will let it recall you to the poets it concerns, you will find yourself appreciating and enjoying them decidedly more than when you read them first.

Most of our Aristophanic comedies concern matters either political or social, and therefore cannot be understood without considerable study of the conditions amid which they were written;

---

[1] Lines 755–1533; Murray (1908), pp. 58–108.
[2] Lines 1198–1248; Murray, pp. 88–91.

all have animation, to be sure, and passages so generalised both as fun and as poetry that you can hardly fail to find plenty of reason why they are excellent; most, however, need a good deal of annotation, except for the initiated, and sometimes even for them. With one, however, this is less the case, if indeed it be comparatively the case at all. The Clouds, originally produced some twenty years before the Frogs, ridicules the influence of new-fangled philosophy on good old beliefs and manners, much as crusty Victorian churchmen did their best now and again, over their port, to laugh down evolution or the higher criticism; and the central figure of the comedy is a fantastic caricature of Socrates, who is traditionally said rather to have enjoyed this exhibition of himself on the popular stage. Beyond question, the Socrates of the Clouds, though his mask probably resembled the grotesque features of the real man and his costume the odd untidiness for which the real man was noted, has little more than a name in common with the character whom Benjamin Franklin thought worthy to place in the self-admonishing maxim "Imitate Jesus and Socrates." Dr. Henry Jackson's matchless article on him in the Encyclopædia Britannica[1] tells the true story incomparably for such purposes as ours. For more than one reason, nevertheless, the Socrates of the Clouds is worth our attention; no other account of this remarkable man is anywhere near so early, none other indeed is fully contemporary, and no other so clearly reminds us that Fifth Century Athens was the city where that life was lived which will live forever in the faithful

[1] Ninth edition; reprinted, with little change, in the Eleventh.

reminiscences of Xenophon and the idealised dialogues of Plato. These works themselves belong not to the Fifth Century but to the Fourth. The man they concern, however, passed all his years but the very last in the Fifth. To think of the Fifth without remembering that he was there would be almost as incomplete as to think of it without remembering Pericles or Phidias. Were any easily accessible English version of the Clouds half so readable as Gilbert Murray's translation of the Frogs, we should dwell on this comedy longer; for next to the Frogs it is the most important contribution of Aristophanes to the traditions of European literature.

Aristophanes, as we have seen, lived and wrote for some years after the Fifth Century ended. On the whole, however, his true place is in the last quarter of it. When his work began, the Century had already added to its inheritance of epic, didactic, and lyric poetry its own contributions of tragic poetry and of history; to these Aristophanes added the primal enduring example of comic poetry. No other hundred years of Europe has been quite so splendidly creative, even in literature alone. Though essentially European, however, that literature still remained, and complacently supposed itself nationally Greek and locally Athenian. Athens held everything else provincial or barbarous.

CHAPTER III

THE FOURTH CENTURY BEFORE CHRIST

I

HISTORICAL TRADITIONS

Again we come to a Century where, if our purpose were historical, Greece might detain and perplex us long. Concerned, however, only with facts which the Fourth Century brought into such traditional existence that they have remained matters of general literary allusion, we can summarise them pretty simply.

When the Fourth Century began, we have already seen, the imperial power of Athens was broken. Athens remained, however, an important centre of trade and of culture. The Age of Pericles, which has never faded from tradition, was still well within the limits of human memory. There were times, for nearly fifty years, when something like imperial recovery may have seemed more than possible. On the whole, however, the most significant circumstance in completely Greek perspective, seems the most nearly familiar name in military tradition from the first half of the Century. Just who Epaminondas was and what he did is perhaps generally forgotten; so indeed may also be the names of his living victory at Leuctra, and of what he believed his dying victory at Mantinea; but hardly, if he is remembered at all, the

fact that he was not of Athens but of Thebes.
There had been a while when Spartan power
looked dominant; Theban power suppressed that;
and Theban power virtually ended when Epaminondas fell.   For our purposes it is enough to remember that almost to the middle of the Century
the history of Greece proper is in a state of kaleido-
scopic confusion.

To the northward of Greece, meanwhile, the
power of Macedon was rapidly assuming a form
more portentous than any previously known in
Europe.   This region, from the Athenian point
of view, was semi-barbarous; but its culture and
its fashion were Greek, much as those of Prussia
were French under Frederick the Great.   Its government was a monarchy, increasing in organisation and in strength; its best-remembered military
device, the phalanx, was more formidable than
anything previously known.   In 359, a youth
named Philip became king.   For twenty years
his authority increased, while that of the dis-
cordant Grecian states diminished.   In 338 his
victory at Chæronea made him military master
of Greece; the next year he was formally acknowledged as commander-in-chief of the Greeks; and
what might have ensued if he had not been assassinated in 336, when only forty-seven years old,
nobody knows.

It could not have been more wondrous than what
came to pass.   The next thirteen years comprise
the imperial career of Alexander, who succeeded
to his father's throne at the age of twenty, and
whose death at thirty-three prevented the consoli-
dation of an empire European in origin, unprecedented in extent, and professedly Greek in cul-

ture. He began by reducing Greece itself to sub-
jection, incidentally destroying Thebes but sparing the house of Pindar. Then he swept over Asia
Minor, and down through Syria; and Egypt sub-
mitted to him, and he founded at the mouth of
the Nile the great seaport, Alexandria, which still
bears his name. Then he turned his attention to
Persia itself, where he completely overthrew the
power of Darius III, and took possession of Babylon, of Susa, of Persepolis, and of Ecbatana.
Then he pressed eastward even to India, where
troubles with his troops prevented him from push-
ing on to the Ganges. Forced temporarily to
withdraw, he went down the Indus, and so westward across burning deserts. He got as far as
Babylon, where he died of a sudden fever in the
year 323. There had never before been so triumphant a short life as his; and there has been none
since. His military genius was of the highest.
Wherever he went he founded cities on Greek
principles, and introduced Greek forms of art.
His name survives to this day in India—transmuted into Sikanda, or some such form; you can
long trace Greek influence in Indian sculpture.
And so on. No wonder his head was turned; in
Egypt he is said to have declared himself the son
not of Philip but of Zeus; in the Orient he assumed something like the character of its native
sovereigns, requiring his courtiers and generals to
prostrate themselves at his feet. There were
times when he drank hard; in an outburst of fury,
towards the end of a feast, he killed with his own
hand his loyal friend Clitus; the excesses described in Dryden's Alexander's Feast are not
far from literal truth. Yet if need were he could

bear without complaint the hardships of a common soldier. Though he did not live to accomplish what he had begun, his Century stays traditionally his, and the tradition of him has never been forgotten or even much dimmed. To this day, for example, the most classic form of French verse is called Alexandrine because it is based on that in which a French poem purporting to describe the exploits of Alexander was written in the Twelfth Century, some sixteen hundred years after Alexander was dead and gone.

From the confusion with which the Fourth Century began, accordingly, there emerges in the mid-century this tremendously distinct fact of Macedonian empire, when Europe, reversing the earlier Persian story, possessed herself of the Levant, of Egypt, and of southwestern Asia. And though no longer purely Greek, the Europe which did so cherished and spread the cultural traditions of Greece.

On the death of Alexander, however, something like the old confusion ensued. Greece itself relapsed into internal quarrels and warfares. The Hellenised Orient was disputed among the generals of Alexander, several of whom established separate independent monarchies. In actual history all this is important. In tradition it has mostly faded. The single clearly surviving fact is what happened in Egypt. Here, one of the generals, Ptolemy by name, founded with its capital at Alexandria a Grecian dynasty destined to hold the throne until its last sovereign descendant, Cleopatra, took her life rather than surrender herself to be exhibited in triumph by the Roman conqueror who was soon to be Augustus Cæsar.

Yet, somehow, Athens held her course as the direct heir of Periclean culture.   In sculpture the Fourth Century gave us the work of Praxiteles; and when you compare the Hermes of Olympia with the Elgin marbles, and feel the difference, you will be at pains to choose which you would keep if you must lose one.   In literature, too, though the great period of Greek poetry was complete, the Century produced new masterpieces of prose.

II

XENOPHON

Though probably the least important Fourth Century writer on whom we shall touch, and indeed less so than any other Greek within our present scope, Xenophon is among the most widely familiar.   His admitted lack of that indefinable quality called genius has combined with a not very strongly founded opinion that his prose is unusually good to make him at once comparatively easy to read, and suitable for those who are trying to learn the Greek language.   So his work has been much used in schoolbooks, even to this day.   The circumstance, with its dismal consequences of grammatical analysis, deprives him, to be sure, of anything like popularity—which he once and deservedly enjoyed; at the same time, it almost cruelly saves him from oblivion, at once giving him an eminence rather above his merit, and fixing in schoolboy minds the notion that all the trouble they are put to when trying to penetrate the mysteries of elementary Greek will lead them only

into vistas of tolerably animated polite commonplace.

He was by birth an Athenian gentleman, at a
time not unlike our own, when persons of his condition, who once enjoyed perhaps more consideration than they deserve, are condemned by democratic enthusiasm to be rather impotent objects
of popular distrust. In the year 400 he appears
to have been somewhere between twenty-five and
thirty years old, and had already had his two
most noteworthy experiences: friendship with
Socrates, and a considerable part in the celebrated
retreat of ten thousand Greek mercenaries from
what promised to be annihilating defeat in Persia.
The confusion of Athenian politics led to his exile.
For some years he lived a life of literary leisure
under the more congenial and aristocratic dominion of Sparta. He is thought to have died before
the middle of the Century.

His writings are rather more copious than we
generally remember. The most carefully studied,
the Cyropædia, pretends to be an idealised life
of the great Persian, Cyrus, and introduces a good
deal of matter concerning education; it was
early included in the Loeb Classical Library. He
wrote, too, a number of treatises or pamphlets
about constitutional matters, about horsemanship
both military and civil, about hunting, and about
other things. For our purposes, none of these is
remarkable. Other works of his, however, touch
on three distinct matters, all worth our attention.
The first is his Hellenica, an actual history.
Xenophon took up the history of Greece at the
point where Thucydides left it, and carried on the
turbulent story until the death of Epaminondas.

His later sympathies were Spartan; he had nothing like the power of Thucydides, nor yet the advantage of creating what amounted to a new form of historical expression. So this history bears to the book which it attempts to continue a relation like that of Smollett's chapters on the history of England to the more impressive work of Hume. It has a certain value, partly for want of an immediate rival; but it is manifestly inferior. Had Xenophon done no more than this and his lesser works, he would hardly have risen above our present horizon.

His most familiar work, on the other hand, commonly supposed by schoolboys to be all he wrote, has two claims to our attention: it clearly records with considerable spirit a distinct episode in military history, and the general character of this episode so contrasts with the historical matters treated by Herodotus and by Thucydides as to make it strongly typical of the last two or three years of the Fifth Century. Herodotus almost epically celebrates the national victories with which that Century began; Thucydides superbly collects the story of the virtually civil wars in which the fruits of those victories were lost; Xenophon circumstantially tells what happened to a large body of Greek mercenaries, shortly after the Peloponnesian War came to an end. At just about this time Artaxerxes II succeeded to the throne of Persia; after the good old Oriental fashion his brother Cyrus attempted to supplant him, and accordingly hired a considerable force of Greek soldiers, no longer needed for hostilities among the Greeks. In the expedition Xenophon took part. The name, Anabasis, by which his

account of it is commonly called, properly applies
only to the first of his eight Books; for it means
something like "advance," and seven of the Books
are devoted to what happened to the Greeks after
Cyrus had been defeated and killed at Cunaxa, not
very far from Babylon. They made their way
across hostile country to the Black Sea. Xenophon's narrative of how they did so, and incidentally of the part he played in the retreat,—
as he always writes of himself not in the first person but in the third, he can commend himself un-
blushingly,—is said by the few who have been
allowed to read it without stopping for grammatical
excursions to be clear and interesting. Certainly
we possess no earlier record of a distinct military
operation so detailed, so apparently precise, and
so nearly animated. When we stop to think, however, there can be no doubt that he rather overemphasises what was at best a technically creditable tactical episode, important mostly to the few
thousand Greeks who thereby managed to escape
annihilation, and that these, at the moment, were
only soldiers of fortune, prepared to fight for the
highest bidder. Remember the mood of Herodotus, and Marathon, and Thermopylæ, and Salamis;
compare with these the mood of an autobiographer
whose great achievement is that he kept his skin,
and the skins of others, intact; and you will
ironically feel the difference between the beginning and the end of the great Fifth Century.

The remaining work of Xenophon, though less
generally known, is on the whole his most memorable. As a youth he had come under the influence
of Socrates, whom he appears to have known well.
Socrates at the age of seventy was condemned to

death by a majority vote of a fantastically democratic popular court, on the grounds of irreligion
and of corrupting the young; refusing more than
one means to avoid his penalty, he drank the
poisonous draught commanded by Athenian law,
and slept in peace. The account of his end by
Plato,[1] accepted as historical, is among the noblest passages of world-literature. Xenophon,
who loved and respected his memory, defended it
in a long, somewhat rambling series of recollections, now generally known by its Latin name,
Memorabilia. They come half-way between the
extravagant caricatures of Aristophanes, and the
idealised dialogues of Plato, and thus, when compared with either of them, have an appearance
of literal fidelity. Though this may be delusive,
—for one thing, Socrates is frequently presented
as speaking, and of course nobody could remember his exact words after an interval of years,—it
may be at least traditionally accepted; and it
makes the Memorabilia substantially interesting
beyond almost anything else on which we have
touched. Even in Dakyns's clear and fluent English version, to be sure, you will hardly have
patience to read them through. Open them at
random, though, as you might open a volume of
recent memoirs or letters, and you will have an
instant sense that what your eye lights on is not
only true but living. The oftener you do so, the
oftener you will be disposed to do so again. In
the end you will feel them to justify the loving
summary of the character of Socrates with which
they end.[2] Their definite and simple task is accomplished. Thus, in the perspective of European

[1] Phædo, 114–118.   [2] IV, viii, ii.

literature Xenophon takes his place as the first
enduring writer of anecdotic biography.

At least two of his minor works give other
glimpses of Socrates. The Economist, a longish
treatise on the Science of the Household, takes the
form of a dialogue between Socrates and one Cri-
tobulus; and the Symposium, or Banquet, introduces Socrates in a convivial company whose conduct and speech are occasionally such as unpleas-
antly to recall Macaulay's[1] celebrated comparison
of the morals of Plato with those of Sir George
Etherege. Negligible in themselves, at least for
students so cursory as we are now, these dialogues
have the interest of showing what Xenophon
could do when measured with Plato. For the
method of both and the substance of one—the
Symposium—are to be found in celebrated works
of that justly celebrated philosopher. The comparison is perhaps unkind to Xenophon. Without
it his portrait-sketches of Socrates might appear
stronger than they do now. With it, one feels
him, for all his loyalty and for all the fidelity of
his purpose, fatally free from insight. He implies what Socrates looked like and how he behaved; he tells you what kind of things Socrates
said, and how these affected the great variety of
Athenians to whom, through fifty years or more,
Socrates incessantly said them; but somehow
Xenophon keeps hopelessly outside of the character
he is attempting to portray. He does enough to
make Socrates both real and memorable, but hardly enough to make Socrates immortal. Doubtless,
the Socrates of Plato is variously idealised; very
probably the Socrates and the Athens of Xeno-

[1] Early in his essay on the Comic Dramatists of the Restoration.

phon—incidentally full of such social amenity as
one instinctively feels must have existed at a
period which produced the fine art of Fifth Century
Greece—are very like facts. These facts, too,
would be priceless if we had nothing else to balance
the extravagances of Aristophanes. As they stand,
however, they sink into little more than record of
how the last quarter of the Fifth Century was remembered by a cultivated Athenian gentleman,
condemned by circumstance to a life of literary
leisure during much of the first half of the Fourth.

Had this been the chief literature of the Fourth
Century, accordingly, we should have had from
that period only evidence of how the great phase
of literature brought into permanent being by
Herodotus, and brought nearer earth by Thucydides, was politely declining. Happily for everybody, this very period has given us literature as
priceless as any from the great Century it followed.

III

PLATO

Philosophy, which literally means love of wisdom, is as old as humanity. You can hardly
imagine men without desire for knowledge, without
aspiration toward truth. Such desire and aspiration they have always expressed, sometimes in the
crude form of aphorisms and proverbs, sometimes
in recurrently futile effort to think into order the
dazzling confusion of perception. By the Fifth
Century, both phases of expression were immemorial in Greece; and if our concern were with
philosophy we might already have mentioned

them, touching on such names as Thales, who is said to have flourished in the Seventh Century, and Pythagoras, whose traditionally more familiar name is usually placed in the Sixth. When Athens was at her height in the Fifth, there seems to have been considerable philosophical activity, along with the fine art and the literature on which we have dwelt. This, indeed, is what the Clouds of Aristophanes satirises and attacks. The old order was changing and with it the old faiths; compared with the gods of Æschylus, those of Euripides are feebly divine. In such conditions, as in our own times, you will generally find anywhere numerous more or less honest purveyors of new truth, beautifully systematic at first sight, but apt soon to prove filmy and flimsy.

When the Fourth Century began, this kind of thing, even though permanently traceable, had not yet developed into lasting literature. From Homer down, no doubt, there was much detached aphorism scattered through Greek poetry and Greek tradition; this, however, was either incidental to the poems—epic, lyric, or dramatic—where it occurred, or else took the form of separate and fragmentary sayings, such as "Know thyself." By the Fifth Century, too, there were philosophic poets, of whom the most eminent was probably the Sicilian Empedocles. One reason why their hexametric statements of doctrine do not quite rise to the level of world-literature may very likely be that, so far as they have been preserved, they survive only in few and broken fragments. A more substantial reason why Fifth Century philosophy produced no literary masterpiece is pretty clear that, as a matter of principle, Soc-

rates, by far the most important Athenian thinker
of that period, never wrote a line. Neither did he
ever have anything like a school, or centre of systematic teaching; the fact that Aristophanes represents him as the head of a regular establishment
for instruction was itself, when the Clouds appeared, an incisive thrust of satire, implying that
Socrates was really what he had all his life professed himself and persistently tried not to be.
There can be no doubt that his eccentric and often
vexatious habit, throughout his career, was to
mingle with men in public places, to pretend to seek
the wisdom they believed themselves to possess, to
ply them with ingenious questions until they were
driven into mazes of contradiction, and then to proceed to speculate about the rays of truth which
might begin dimly to illuminate the darkness of
an ignorance which he professed himself to share
with them. He was often stimulating, generally
salutary, and seldom negligible; his purpose,
though now and again disguised by irony and
humour, was honest and high; his conduct, granting the accepted morals of his time, was blameless
to the point of saintliness; but he was frequently
irritating, and hardly ever conclusive. All this
clearly appears in the Memorabilia of Xenophon,
one of the younger men whom he most deeply influenced; but nothing, as we have already seen,
can make Xenophon of more than secondary literary importance. So the Socrates of world-
literature is hardly more Xenophon's than he is
that of Aristophanes; he is the Socrates set forth
in the Dialogues of Plato.

Like Xenophon, Plato was a gentleman of
Athens, who could remember the last fifteen or

twenty years of the Fifth Century and who wrote
during the first half of the Fourth. Like Xenophon,
he was deeply influenced by Socrates. Unlike
Xenophon, he took as little part as possible in
public affairs, and he was himself a man of the
highest intellectual and literary power. Even if he
had written nothing, indeed, Plato might still be
traditionally remembered as one who never ceased
to think forward with the impulse given him by
Socrates, and whose comparatively systematic
teaching has made the name of the place where he
habitually taught—the Academy, which seems to
have been a kind of public park, very near Athens
—a general European name for institutions of
learning or of instruction. And even if he had
never taught, his writings would stay memorable,
not only for the portrait-sketches of Socrates on
which they seem originally to have been based,
nor yet only for the uncodified philosophic system
or tendency which they increasingly developed, but
also for the artistic skill and beauty of their literary form.

It was perhaps the lifelong colloquial habit of
Socrates which first led Plato to set forth the
character and the doctrines of his master in dialogues; thus, whatever else, he could best represent that unique, inspired, grotesque figure, incessantly mingling and talking with all sorts and
conditions of men. Besides this particular advantage, the form of dialogue has two or three
general conveniences: it is animated, it allows
considerable variety, and above all it never quite
commits a writer to the opinions thereby put
into the mouths of other human beings. Yet, as
these speakers, however distinctly characterised,

are really his own creatures, he can use them when
he likes as vehicles for himself, with a freedom
both artistic and intellectual hardly to be enjoyed
otherwise.   Given the form, it has never been
better used than by Plato, who first established
it in the enduring literature of Europe.   Quite
apart from what he has to say, the manner in
which he says it is admirable.

To go no further, the first page or so of the Republic gives a glimpse of daily Athenian life almost
as lastingly fresh as are the heroic incidents of
the Iliad ;   the beginning and the end of the
Symposium, or Banquet, take one into the heart of
antique, and to us exotic, conviviality; and the
two dialogues concerning the last days of Socrates,
the Crito and the Phædo, are masterpieces of narrative told through the speeches of clearly individualised characters.   Throughout, indeed, the Dialogues of Plato exhale the atmosphere of social
Athens and the politeness which kept its most
vagrant excesses within the limits of classic decorum.   Not long ago a reader who accidentally
opened Jowett's translation, with no knowledge
of Greek, no disposition to philosophic speculation, and a general impression that time-honoured masterpieces are tiresome, was surprised to
find how, if you skip the passages which bore
you, the Dialogues can still impress you, carelessly turning the pages, as not only interesting
but often amusing, like animated and witty con-
versational books of one's own time.   Thus to
dwell on the mere surface of works inexhaustible
for depth may perhaps appear inadvertent.   By
itself, however, that surface has had permanent
effect on European literary tradition.   Though

no later writer of dialogues has surpassed, and indeed none has quite equalled, the primal animation of Plato, you will find his method and the semblance of his devices imitated through the centuries, much as the drama of Rome, of France, and of Italy has imitated the methods and devices of Euripides. Except for Plato's dialogues, Romans might never have used the form; and, confining ourselves to English, we might be at pains otherwise to see why Dryden should have chosen it when discussing dramatic criticism, Addison when writing about medals, or Mr. Alexander H. Stephens when, a few years after the American Civil War, he wrote two large volumes justifying the constitutional principles of the Southern Confederacy. Masterpieces of any art are tyrants that die hard.

Though the order in which Plato's Dialogues were written can never be certainly known, one fact about them seems generally admitted. He began by an effort to set forth, for all future time, the character and the general teachings of Socrates, who without such record might soon fade into little more than a name. As his work proceeded he tended increasingly to think for himself, and to use the characters in the dialogues as vehicles for speculative opinions of his own. At last his Socrates became pretty shadowy; and the longest of the dialogues, the Laws, — which is generally thought his latest, — drops Socrates altogether, consisting of a political discussion between an Athenian, a Cretan, and a Lacedæmonian. Even here, however, Plato never expresses himself directly; throughout, he sets forth what he has to say after the Socratic manner.

Men meet, and fall to talking about whatever subject he chooses them to deal with; they question one another politely and adroitly; incidentally they express a considerable variety of more or less tenable opinion. Their desire is by inquiry to ascertain or at least to approach truth. They never arrive, however, at anything much more conclusive than the discovery of probabilities for which the writer escapes complete responsibility by always putting his arguments into the mouth of somebody else.

Such a method you might well expect to lead nowhere. Beyond question, however, no European philosopher has had more enduring influence than Plato. This has fluctuated. At times it has blazed; at other times it has only feebly glowed; but it has never been more than eclipsed, and unless men change beyond recognition it never will be. To enter into the details of any philosophic system is clearly beyond our present scope. Very broadly, however, we may do well to remind ourselves of the character or tendency of Plato's. So long as this world lasts, life will stay baffling, confusing, and often to all appearances desperate; nothing can ever quite clear from it the clouds of error, of ugliness, of sin, vice, and wickedness. Yet these are so far from comprising the universe, that in thoughtful moments, as you gaze on them until your eyes begin to see deeper, they grow to seem like the vapoury clouds of earth dimming the full reality of sunlight. Beyond falsehood, ugliness, and evil glow the radiant, quenchless facts of truth, of beauty, and of good. Seek these, and even though you never attain mastery of their infinitudes you shall forever find in their exhaustless depths more and more illuminating light. Reality, as we call it, is transitory, delusive, phantasmal. Beyond it, about it, above it stays the serene eternity of immutable ideals. Even a glimpse of ideals may help assuage the troubles, alleviate the miseries, correct the blunders of daily life, as we pass from cradle to grave. Nothing but recognition of ideals, and, if so may be, knowledge of what they may reveal to such understandings as ours, can ever help us towards the calm security of wisdom. He does best who throughout our passing years most tirelessly seeks.

There are men and there are generations to whom moods like this appeal beyond all others. Whether they know it or not, such men and such generations are the secular disciples of Plato. Even still, when we carelessly try to name ideals beyond reality—such as love grown to exceed the transitory delusions of the flesh—we are apt, with no thought of Fourth Century Athens a few years before Philip's victory at Chæronea, to call them Platonic.

Had this been all that the Fourth Century contributed to the literary tradition of Europe, the period would accordingly be memorable for bringing into our enduring literature the fact of philosophy and the form of the dialogue. These, as we have seen, belong to the first half of the Century. The next quarter of it added two more primal names to the literature of Greece. These are Demosthenes and Aristotle.

IV

DEMOSTHENES

Demosthenes and Aristotle were of about the same age, and are said to have died within a few months of each other. In 375 both were boys; by 350 both were past thirty; and neither survived for more than a year the death of Alexander. Chronology therefore gives no help towards deciding which to dwell on first. For at least two reasons, however, it seems best that we choose Demosthenes: he was a native citizen of Athens, so deeply concerned with civic and public matters that his career implies the history of his time; and his work established in lasting literature a distinct form of expression. The career of Aristotle, on the other hand, who was of Stagira on the seacoast near Macedonia, and first came to Athens as a student, is comparatively independent of history, and his work, although second to none in positive importance, is not so primal. Without him European literature would have possessed at least one phase of philosophy, in the works of Plato; while, until Demosthenes revealed himself as the supreme master of Grecian oratory, oratory had hardly taken its independent literary place. There is a third reason, too, for permitting him to interrupt our glances at Fourth Century philosophy; nothing else could more prudently remind us how, throughout such considerations as ours, we are compelled by the conditions of language to treat consecutively matters which were really contemporary. Had we touched on Aristotle first, we might have been at more pains to remember that philosophy had not completed its Fourth Century development before oratory, the other characteristic form of great Fourth Century expression, began.

Demosthenes, there is hardly need to say, no more invented oratory than Plato invented philosophy, Herodotus history, or Homer poetry. Like them he only carried a form of thought and expression so far beyond the point where he found it as not only to make its origin comparatively negligible, but also permanently to influence its future course. Masterpieces, though apt to survive alone, seldom if ever come into being so; the very existence of a masterpiece implies the previous existence of an often traceable tradition, or school, thereby so crowned that posterity tends to forget the foundations on which great works must always rest. Without a cloud of dramatists encompassing him round, for example, we could never have had Shakspere; yet, though some hundreds of their plays exist, the growth of Baconian heresy already proves how nearly the dust of no more than three English centuries has buried them. When such oblivion may overtake literature made in our own language, and itself its own excuse for being, we need wonder little that the Greek origins of oratory seem important only to students of Greek history.

This form of expression is distinctly different from all we have previously considered. Broadly speaking, the office of poetry is at once to stir and to please, occasionally conveying information; that of history is to inform, meanwhile exciting attention and incidentally giving pleasure; that of philosophy is to explain perplexities and pleasantly to stimulate thought. Whatever else, all the literature we have as yet glanced at, from Homer to Plato, may be regarded as having fulfilled its purpose when those who read or hear it are duly informed, stirred, and pleased. At least to this extent, a finished work is the chief end contemplated by poets, historians, or philosophers; so far as any of these desire to influence those whom they address, their prime purpose is to influence only opinion or mood, or at most to induce sympathy. The object of oratory, on the other hand, is by no means accomplished when an oration is written or delivered, nor yet when hearers or readers completely and sympathetically understand. Generally speaking, unless an oration makes men behave otherwise than they might have behaved if let alone, it is only a display of rhetorical fireworks. It is not an end in itself, it is rather a secondary matter—an instrument or weapon useful for attaining such ends as are sought by practising lawyers and practical politicians.

The course of Athenian history, at least from the period of the Persian Wars, had tended to give increasing importance to eloquent speeches. Decisions of grave consequence, both political and legal, were apt to be made by a majority vote; the court which condemned Socrates, for example, consisted of some five hundred citizens, a large minority of whom voted in his favour. Such conditions, in days when nothing like what we should now call public prints existed, made oratory almost uniquely efficient. A man who, for better or worse, could persuade an assembly to act as he happened to desire was a man to be counted with. When his momentary purpose was accomplished, however, his means of accomplishing it became an outworn tool—at best a matter of record, on which later tools could be modelled when required. By the time of Demosthenes, two, requisites of such tools were clearly understood: an excellent speech must apparently appeal to reason, the more soundly the better; it must also, and more subtly, appeal to emotion or prejudice. The difficulties here involved are obvious: your orator must be master of his craft to the point of craftiness, yet he must often if not generally appear artless, spontaneous, sincere, and fervid. At his worst he is an adroit trickster; at his best, he has to control genuine impulse with histrionic skill. Throughout he is compelled to devote himself with all his art and with all his heart to questions which begin to be matters of the past as soon as his work is done.

In view of all this, the wonder is not that Greek oratory has chiefly historical or legal interest, but rather that any Greek orator should ever have emerged, as Demosthenes unquestionably has emerged, into the full eminence of world-literature. The historical circumstances of his time, the known facts of his life, and the substance of his extant works are admirably summarised in the short monograph about him by S. H. Butcher. He was the orphan son of a well-to-do Athenian man of business. Despite physical disadvantages which have given rise to anecdotic tradition,—such as the tale of how he cured thickness of utterance by practising speech with his mouth full of pebbles, —he was compelled at twenty or so to bring suit against a dishonest guardian, and to plead his cause in person. For the legal career thus accidentally begun he proved to have unusual gifts. From time to time he wrote a good many speeches for other litigants whom Athenian practice required to speak for themselves. He early took interest in public matters, particularly when they concerned foreign policy. He was passionately patriotic, enthusiastically cherishing ancestral Athenian tradition. He was an assiduous student of Thucydides. He was among the first to perceive the danger of Macedonian aggression. So long as there was any hope, he opposed Philip with such intensity that the word Philippic, originally the name given three or four of his orations, has ever since been a general term for political denunciation. After Chæronea he did his best to preserve what was left of Athens. He lived through the reign of Alexander. In the confusion which followed Alexander's death, he was forced to seek sanctuary in a temple not very far away. Pursued thither, already under sentence of death, he took his life, heroically disdaining unmerited indignity. And before long his name and his statue were held venerable in the city he had tried to save.

Of the surviving speeches attributed to him, twenty-five remained unquestioned when Butcher's monograph was published. Eleven of these are political, like modern speeches in Parliament or in Congress; the rest are forensic—seven concerned with public or political affairs, and seven with private law-suits. To appreciate or even quite to understand work so partisan and occasional needs more knowledge of history and of detail than most of us can ever possess. Translation, too, must generally throttle the life of oratory almost as fatally as it disenchants the magic of lyric poetry; the soul of both lurks quivering in the meshes of their original sound and rhythm; cut or even disturb a single strand, and something escapes. Yet through more than two thousand years Demosthenes, at least in tradition, has held his own. Even when he was alive, he was generally recognised as the greatest master of the art he professed and practised; whether he succeeded or failed at any given moment, he did what he tried to do better than it had been done before, and on the whole as well as it could imaginably be done.

Although his policy failed, accordingly, for he fought against the stars, he has none the less been admired by posterity, recurrently studying and imitating him as the primal model of what oratory ought to be. He stands to all Europe, Butcher clearly points out, in some such relation as that of Edmund Burke to the parliamentary eloquence of England. Both were consummate masters of language; both counted with human nature; both were faithful students of history; both sincerely believed in the constitutional traditions of their national inheritance; both raised occasional eloquence to the height of enduring political thought excellently expressed; both have thus won secure place not only in history but in literature. Yet each, to do his work, was perforce a man of his own time; and the time even of Burke is dead and gone. How much of either must be counted as humanly temporal, how much may be accepted as humanly eternal, nobody can quite tell. The one sure thing is that the methods of Burke long survived the parliamentary conditions where they originated, and that the methods of Demosthenes, originating in the democratic conditions of Fourth Century Athens, have more or less directly affected European oratory ever since. To go no further, Cicero was aware of them, and Burke was aware of them and of Cicero as well, and Daniel Webster, aware of both Cicero and Demosthenes, was aware of Burke into the bargain. Orators do things still—assert principle, for example, appeal to prejudice, denounce opponents —not only because these things must be done anyhow but also, and perhaps considerably, because these were the methods fixed in tradition by the master who finally brought oratory into literature, while Philip and Alexander were conquering the liberties of Greece.

V

ARISTOTLE

It was just before Demosthenes made his first public appearance, pleading for himself against his dishonest guardian, that Aristotle first came to Athens.[1] Born of a respectable family at Stagira, a sea-coast town close to the borders of Macedon, he is said, as traditionally descended from Æsculapius, the god of medicine, to have been compelled in boyhood to supplement his regular education by such anatomical studies as were then practicable. His father appears to have had friendly personal relations with the Macedonian court,

[1] The facts here are mostly taken from the popular monograph on Aristotle by Sir Alexander Grant (1877).

before the time of Philip. At about the age when men now begin university work, Aristotle was sent to complete his education at Athens. There he became a pupil of Plato; and there he remained for some twenty years. In the course of this sojourn he was recognised as the ablest man who had ever sat at Plato's feet; so, although he had gradually diverged from Plato's doctrine, being given to strongly independent thought, he probably aspired to the mastership of Plato's school when Plato died—much as a distinguished university man might now aspire to succeed an elderly college president whom he personally respected but whose teachings he believed old-fashioned. When a more orthodox successor to Plato was chosen, Aristotle left Athens, and is said presently to have been selected by Philip as the private tutor of Alexander. In Alexander's time he returned to Athens, with a comfortable endowment from the Macedonian crown. The name of the school he thereupon established— Lyceum—has become almost as familiar in tradition as that of Plato's Academy. He lectured, with unsurpassed effect, until the death of Alexander. The subsequent confusions at Athens drove him, as they drove Demosthenes, from the city. Just how he died is not known; very likely he succumbed to the organic disorders often brought on by a habit of life mentally active and physically indolent.

He had written copiously. So far as is known, his earlier work, some of which survives, often took the Platonic form of dialogue, but was apt to be controversially opposed to various phases of Platonic doctrine; it is thought to have been published,—that is, frequently copied and thus placed at the disposal of whoever wished to buy it. His later work, on the other hand, which comprised the whole body of his mature teaching, is often thought to have been kept only in private copies, used as notes for his incessant lectures, sometimes complete enough to be read unchanged, sometimes more like memoranda to guide impromptu discourse. These came near getting lost; at last, however, some two hundred years after his death, they were brought to Rome, duly edited, and finally published there. Meanwhile his reputation had not only survived but strengthened; it has never faded out of sight.

His works, as we now possess them, are probably a considerable part of those published at Rome during the First Century before Christ. In two ways they sharply differ from anything we have hitherto dwelt on: they imply a temper so intent on thought, rather than on expression, as to prefer verbal precision to literary grace; and, more profoundly, they attempt to reduce the chaos of experience to semblance of order not by speculative inquiry or occasional aphorism, but by dogmatic system based on critically scrutinised fact. They are not precisely what we should now call scientific; in the Fourth Century before the Christian Era, true science, for want of data, was possible only in its most highly generalised and purest form of mathematics, and even then was elementary. On the other hand, they bring into world-literature and permanently establish there the kind of thought, recurrent through the centuries and now for a while dominant, from which science—that is, knowledge finally to be verified by observation or experiment—must sooner or later result. Dante wrote better than he knew when he called Aristotle "Maestro di color chi sanno." [1]

The contrast between his method and that of Plato may be seen at a glance. Both, for example, wrote about government, Plato in his Republic and his Laws, Aristotle in his Politics; both touched on oligarchy and democracy. Here is a bit from Plato's Republic, where Socrates is talking with one Adeimantus.[2]

Socrates speaks first:

Can we any longer doubt, then, that the miser and money-maker answers to the oligarchical state?

There can be no doubt.

Next comes democracy; and how does the change from oligarchy into democracy arise? Is it not in this wise? The good at which such a state aims is to become as rich as possible, a desire which is insatiable.

What then?

The rulers being aware that their power rests upon their wealth, refuse to curtail by law the extravagance of the spendthrift youth because they gain by their ruin.

To be sure.

There can be no doubt that the love of wealth and the spirit of moderation cannot exist together in citizens of the same state to any considerable extent; one or the other will be disregarded.

That is tolerably clear:

and so on, for many pages.

Compare with this the manner in which Aristotle sets forth a similar opinion;[3] he may be imagined a lecturer stating his own views:

---

[1] "Master of them that know," Inferno, IV, 131.
[2] VIII, 555: Jowett III, p. 261.   [3] Politics, tr. Jowett, III, 7.

The true forms of government are those in which the one,
the few, or the many govern with a view to the common
interest; but governments which rule with a view to the
private interest, whether of the one, or of the few, or of the
many, are perversions. . . .   Of forms of government which
regard the common interests[1] we call that in which one rules
kingship or royalty; that in which more than one, but not
many, rule aristocracy (the rule of the best).   But when
the citizens at large administer the state for the common
interest, the government is called by the generic name—a
constitution. . . .

Of the above-mentioned forms, the perversions are as
follows: of royalty, tyranny; of aristocracy, oligarchy; of
constitutional government, democracy.   For tyranny is a
kind of monarchy which has in view the interest of the
monarch only; oligarchy has in view the interest of the
wealthy; democracy, of the needy; none of them the
common good of all.

Even so slight an example shows Plato suavely
conjectural and Aristotle dogmatically authoritative.   If you wish to dispute Plato, he may
take refuge behind the shadow of Socrates; when
you face Aristotle, you must tackle the Master
himself.

The Master you must tackle, too, cherished no
less a purpose than to reduce all knowledge, physical and metaphysical, to final system.   In so doing
he came into sharp contradiction of the master at
whose feet he had begun his philosophic study.[2]
Plato held that ideas are more real than facts.
Somewhere, for instance, there is an immutable
Idea of Man, of which the countless individuals
whom we perceive as men are only various, transitory, incomplete, and delusive manifestations.

---

[1] I permit myself, to make this passage clearer, a slight rearrangement
of Jowett's words.

[2] See Sir Alexander Grant, Aristotle, 8–10.

Aristotle, on the other hand, held—with what would seem a good deal more like common sense —that an abstract idea of Man can be derived only from generalisation based on observation of individual men, and that apart from them it can have no real existence whatever. We are straying already into thickets of philosophy where realists and nominalists have quarrelled, and may again quarrel long, quite aside from our own path. Our proper concern is nowise with philosophy, but only with the moods of the two philosophers who successively yet together brought philosophy into the tradition of European literature; and just here we must not wander far from Aristotle.

He did not achieve his purpose, of course; nobody can possibly know everything, and, even if anybody could, human life is not long enough to allow the lucky creature completely to state universal truth. Aristotle's copious work was nowhere near finished; a considerable part of it, furthermore, has very likely disappeared, ages ago. Two pieces of it, however, which happen to survive, at once concern such pursuits as ours, and historically indicate both how his mind worked and how it has influenced posterity. He wrote treatises on Rhetoric and on Poetry; in each case he examined the practice of the Greeks and based thereon a statement of generalised principles as to what had actually been done; in each case, his manner, and to all appearances his temper, was vigorously authoritative; in each case his generalisations have again and again been accepted as finally indicating not what Greeks had done by his time, but rather what everybody ought everywhere and always to do. His rational conclusions

from observation have thus often been held omniscient and irresponsible commands.

The posthumous history of his works has had
much to do with this distortion. As we shall remind ourselves later, there were six or eight centuries between the fall of the Roman Empire and
the development of what we have complacently
thought modern civilisation when little knowledge
of Greek survived in Western Europe. During
much of this period, Aristotle was only a name;
when at last he became once more a teacher, such
versions of him as first appeared among our fore-
fathers were probably Latin translations from the
Arabic translations of his writings which were
studied, largely under the influence of Averroes,
in the universities of Moorish Spain. At that time
the general temper of European learning tended to
accept authoritative teaching as final. The doctrine of the Church, for example, was generally
assumed to be true; and the business of doctors
was accordingly, once for all, to enlighten ignorance. This temper accepted Aristotle as the highest of merely human authorities; as the man who
without divine inspiration came nearest to understanding what nothing short of divine inspiration
could ultimately explain. Thus the father of our
scientific spirit was for generations held infallibly
above investigation; orthodoxy always distrusts
experiment. In such guise he appeared to Dante,
who set forth in final poetry the doctrine of
Thomas Aquinas.

As for us, hastily summarising, we must be content to record that, somewhat as Euripides brought
tragic poetry nearer earth than Sophocles, and as
Thucydides brought history down from the half-

epic heights where Herodotus lingered, so Aris- totle brought philosophy out of the poetically speculative condition where Plato had made it part of literature, and into its first enduring semblance of systematic order. By themselves, Euripides, Thucydides, and Aristotle are magnificently Greek, classical, primal; compared with their great pred- ecessors, they mark long steps from the past that had been towards the future that, for better or worse, was to be; they no longer quite aspire; their task is rather to master and to subjugate. At least, and perhaps most profoundly, their mood is less youthful than the moods they inherited; and of the three, Aristotle, who lived not in the Fifth Century but in the Fourth, is most mature.

VI

THEOPHRASTUS; MENANDER

So far as important surviving literature goes, no other names of the Fourth Century are compara- ble with the four at which we have glanced. For historical reasons, however, we can hardly neglect two more, those of Theophrastus and of Menander. Both men flourished at Athens during the second half of the Century; both lived into the next; both left rather popular writings; and both had con- siderable influence on the literature of subsequent times.

Of the two, Theophrastus was about a genera- tion the older. Without entering into any details of his life, we may remind ourselves that he studied under Aristotle, that he is said to have succeeded the Master as head of the Lyceum—or Peripatetic

—School, and that he wrote philosophical and scientific works meritorious in themselves, but of
no lasting importance as literature.   What makes
him of literary consequence is that tradition attributes to him a short collection of character-
sketches, now numbering thirty.   They are colloquial, rather epigrammatic, and to all appearances
based on life; taken together they give one some
such notion of every-day Athens as you may get
of George II's London from the engravings of
Hogarth.   A casual example of what the Characters, as they are called, brought into literary
being may be found in the first sentence describing "The Stupid Man":

> The stupid man is one who, after doing a sum and set-
> ting down the total, will ask the person sitting next him
> "What does it come to?"

And so on, for about a page of print.   Incidentally, the Greek work here translated by Sir Richard Jebb as *stupidity* is *anæsthesia*, whose modern
meaning is an excellent instance of how the centuries affect language; the fact that you know
what a word means now is no reason why you
should suppose yourself to understand what it
used to mean.   Again we stray.   Taken by themselves, the Characters of Theophrastus would
hardly deserve attention in a consideration so
cursory as ours.   They chanced, however, in far
later times, to stimulate imitations among the
English and the French.   Without them, to go
no further, we should hardly have had the *Carac-
tères* of La Bruyère or the numerous "Character-
Writings" of Seventeenth Century England.   Without these we should hardly have had, in their

present form, the sketches of character in the
essays of Addison and of Steele. Without these
sketches—Sir Roger de Coverley, for example—we
should hardly have had the novels of Richardson
and of Fielding; and without them the whole
popular literature of the Nineteenth Century might
have taken another turn. So Theophrastus has
his place in the ancestry of prose fiction.

There is a tradition that Menander, some thirty
years younger than Theophrastus, was more or
less associated with him, perhaps as a pupil. The
work of Menander, however, was nowise philosophic. At the end of the Fourth Century, he was
among the most popular writers of comedy; and
his light plays, surviving those of his contemporaries, became the standard examples of what
Greek comedy had grown to be a century after
Aristophanes. None of them now exists. Almost
to the end of the Nineteenth Century, indeed, Menander was directly known only in occasional fragments quoted by later writers: of these the most
familiar to English-speaking tradition is "Evil
communications corrupt good manners," [1] imbedded in the Fifteenth Chapter of the First Epistle
to the Corinthians. He was also known to be
the original model from which certain Latin
comedies of Plautus and of Terence had been
translated, adapted, or imitated. From these extant works, even if no other evidence had existed,
it would have been clear that Menander's comic
method was completely different from that of
Aristophanes, and distinctly subsequent. Instead
of broadly satirising, with extreme license, the men
and the incidents of the moment, Menander, with

[1] I Cor., 15, 33.

deft fluency, conventionally sketched, in plots now long since grown trite, typical phases of private life. His characters meanwhile appeared to have had some such generalised quality as marks the avowedly generalised Characters of Theophrastus. So much was to be gathered from his Latin imitators and from a good deal of critical and allusive mention. The relation of Latin comedy to that of Seventeenth Century France is a matter of common knowledge. Without Plautus and Terence, Molière could never have been just what he was and is. Molière, furthermore, improved on his models, being a decidedly more gifted poet than either of them. A probable conclusion appeared to follow, and was long accepted. The loss of Menander was supposed irreparably to deprive us of early comedy as much better than Molière's as his is better than the Latin.

Since 1895, we have had consolation for this grief. Somewhere in Egypt fragments of Menander have been discovered, by no means complete but consecutive enough to give a notion of his dramatic method, and of how he presented character. These are generally agreed to be disappointing. Apart from a certain swift and gay ease, they are on the whole inferior to any equal amount taken from his comparatively laborious Latin imitators. It seems at least possible that Plautus and Terence are about as much better than he was as Molière is better than they. If so, his true value proves, like that of Theophrastus, rather historical than positive. He made something which, whatever his reputation, we moderns might serenely have neglected if it had not later developed into a form more important than it ever attained in his hands. Traditionally, none the less, he stays among the great.

Neither he nor Theophrastus, however, looks very large beside even the polite merit of Xenophon, far less beside the greatness of Plato and Aristotle and Demosthenes. We have touched on the two later men only to complete our glance at what the Fourth Century contributed to the literary tradition of Europe. That Century had inherited not only the traditions of epic and of lyric poetry inherited by the Fifth, but also the dramatic poetry and the history brought by the Fifth Century—the century of Pericles—into final existence. To this inheritance the Fourth Century—the century of Philip and of Alexander—added two other forms of primal prose—philosophy and oratory; to this it also added two lesser phases of literature destined to ripen into the fiction and the comedy of modern Europe. So the Century ended. In the year 300, enduring European literature still stayed altogether and only Greek.

CHAPTER IV

FROM 300 B. C. TO THE ROMAN CONQUEST OF GREECE (146 B. C.)

I

HISTORICAL TRADITIONS

The Third Century before Christ was the last when Greece can be considered anywise independent; about the middle of the Second Century, in the year 146, the power of Rome, which had already mastered the Greek colonies in southern Italy and in Sicily, finally took possession of Greece itself. Thenceforth, until the collapse of the Western Empire, more than six hundred years later, Greece remained politically a part of the united Roman dominions. And from the beginning of the Third Century, indeed, the historical traditions familiar to subsequent literature belong not so much to Greece, the primal fact of European antiquity, as to Rome, the secondary.

This interposition of Rome, to which we must soon come, was more instantly evident in the middle of the Nineteenth Century than we may find it now, in the first quarter of the Twentieth. Until 1875, at least in America, we still called many Greek things by Latin names; one thought of Zeus, for example, as the Greek equivalent of Jupiter. And though the Olympic Hermes of Praxiteles was dug up a little too late for anybody to describe him as Mercury, we might still be perplexed by an offhand mention of the Venus of Milo under the name of Aphrodite. That wondrous Grecian statue, by the way, is now thought to have been made as late as the Third Century, if not later; certain details, particularly of the drapery, deny it a place in the Fifth Century or even in the Fourth. There can be no question, however, that it reminds one rather of the great periods which were past when it was modelled than of what generally marked that to which it is now assigned.[1] Greek sculpture stayed Greek, but not Athenian. Phidias and Praxiteles too were dead and gone. The art they had grandly practised was tending towards such literal precision as that of the Dying Gladiator, such writhing restlessness as that of the Laocoön group, or such graceful sentimentality as that of the Belvedere Apollo or of the Hunting Diana—whom nobody calls Artemis—in the Louvre.

Of late years, the period of Greek history between the time of Alexander and the Roman Conquest has usually been described by the word Hellenistic. What was going to be Europe was no longer only or quite Greek; yet Greek influence, though not of the first political or military importance, was bringing regions formerly barbarian within the range of Hellenic civilisation. It extended westward, and saturated the traditions of Rome, over which we must soon linger long. It extended eastward, to various places beyond the scope of observation so cursory as ours. More memorably for us at this moment, it extended southward, where until the days of

[1] See Ernest Arthur Gardner: A Handbook of Greek Sculpture: 1911.

Augustus Cæsar it dominated the diuturnal humanity of Egypt as Persians and Shepherd kings had dominated it centuries before, as Romans and Mahometans were to dominate it centuries later, as the British Empire has now benevolently dominated it for thirty or forty years. How large this Hellenistic Egypt looms in tradition we can see by comparing the names of two generals, both eminent under Alexander, and both founders of independent dynasties; one is Seleucus, the other Ptolemy. Just who either was and what he did only students of historical detail remember. Hardly anybody, for some two thousand years, besides, could have felt sure without reference to authorities whether Seleucus and his successors began their independent career in Mesopotamia. Even to this day, meanwhile, almost everybody could have told you that the Ptolemies flourished in Egypt, and fixed their capital at Alexandria. Historically, indeed, this Egyptian Hellenistic tradition is the most familiar of all. Just as we may summarise the Fifth Century as that of Pericles, and the Fourth as that of Philip and of Alexander, so we may summarise the Third as the first century of the Ptolemies.

At this time, too, Greek literature, so far as it persisted, tended to become less important in Greece than in Egypt. Athens, no doubt, remained, as indeed it remained throughout antiquity, a traditional centre of culture. In the year 300, Theophrastus had not yet finished his career there as a lecturer and a writer, nor Menander his as an enduring master of comedy; and the Academic school founded by Plato still flourished. Apart from these maintainers of already somewhat waning traditions, however, only two Athenian names of the Third Century or of the Second seem certainly within the range of our cursory consideration. Two facts about both are significant: both belong to the first half of the Third Century, and the importance of both has nothing to do with history but concerns only philosophy. One name is that of a philosopher—Epicurus; the other is that of a school of philosophy—the Stoics. Its founder was Zeno of Citium; conceivably to avoid confusion with an earlier philosopher, Zeno of Elea, his teaching has generally been remembered as proceeding not from him but from the place—the Stoa—where he taught. What he taught is another question. Like the doctrines of Epicurus, that of the Stoics would lead us into philosophic mazes. Two or three facts about their existence are all we can touch on now. In the first place, these two new and divergent systems of philosophic teaching tended, like many new-fangled notions throughout history, to supplant the orthodoxies—here the older schools of philosophy, Platonic and Aristotelian, Academy and Lyceum—whose founders were dead. In the second place, they were at odds with each other; very generally speaking, the opinions of Epicurus tended toward extreme emphasis on the material aspect of the universe, and those of the Stoics toward extreme emphasis on the spiritual. Naturally enough, each school was disposed to misrepresent the other, the Stoics declaring the Epicureans prone to wallow in sensual delight, and the Epicureans retorting that the Stoics were foolish dreamers. How far from conclusive either charge was we may perceive when we touch on the

Epicurean poem of Lucretius written when the
Roman Republic was at its last gasp, and on the
Meditations of the Stoic emperor, Marcus Aurelius,
written when the Roman Empire began to totter
down its fatal decline.　In the third place, nevertheless, a distorted echo of those antique disputes
lingers to this day.　Without remembering why,
we think of epicures as men content with fleshly
joys, and of stoics as men austerely ready without
the consolations of revealed religion to bear either
those ills we have or fly to others that we know
not of.　The words *epicure* and *stoic* will stay
part of our language as long as the language lasts,
transmuting yet preserving the chief if not the
only persistent tradition established for posterity
by Third Century Athens.

　Though no tradition quite so familiar survives
from Ptomelaic Alexandria, the general influence
of Alexandria from the beginning of the Third Century to the time when European tradition became
rather Roman than Greek, was for our purposes
paramount.　In the year 300 Alexandria was both
a new city, founded within the memory of men
not beyond middle age, and the seat of a new
dynasty eager to secure itself on a throne commanding the most considerable commerce in the
contemporary world.　One means of doing so was
to make the new capital brilliant.　Brilliancy is a
matter both of fashion and of intellect; if either
shine anywhere, people flock to it from elsewhere.
What happened at Alexandria under the Ptolemies
was not unlike what happened at Paris under
Napoleon, and at Berlin between 1870 and 1914.
A powerful new sovereignty tried to make the seat
of its government at once gay and learned.　Only

the learned phase of Third Century Egypt, and indeed of Egypt through several centuries then to come, has traditionally survived; and only one feature of that has stayed traditionally familiar. Even to the present day, however, people generally though vaguely remember that among the treasures of Alexandria there was once an unprecedented library.

This library was originally, and long remained, a conspicuous feature of what was generally known as the Museum, or abode of the Muses. Though the word *Museum* had probably been used earlier, its wide familiarity and its general diffusion throughout modern Europe is probably due to the fame attained by the Museum of Ptolemaic Alexandria. This was not the kind of institution which its name would now usually imply; it was rather such as we should now call a university. By the time when it was established, Greek literature had passed through the stages at which we have glanced, from antique Homer to contemporary Menander. It had not yet, however, been systematically studied; for one thing, texts were in a state of confusion inevitable when they could be reproduced only by repeated process of often careless manuscript copying; incidentally, too, a good deal of spurious work had got mixed up with the genuine. One prime task of Alexandrian scholars was to separate the genuine texts of Greek literature from the spurious, and having done so to restore them, as nearly as possible, to their original form.

The methods and the limitations developed by these prototypes of the learning at present prevalent about us are excellently summarised in F.

W. Hall's Companion to Classical Texts.[1] For our
purposes, it is enough to note that the Greek
Classics, as we now possess them, remain substantially as they were fixed by the studious criticism of Alexandria; the Books into which they
were divided, for example, are generally of Alexandrian origin, and the accents and breathings
which have bothered schoolboys for two thousand
years are said to be Alexandrian inventions.
Compare this kind of thing with Athenian traditions of the same period—Epicureans and Stoics,
let us say, with whoever settled the standard text
of Herodotus or of Pindar—and you will feel the
most important difference between Hellenic and
Hellenistic temper: Greece remained on the whole
intelligent, while barbarous regions appropriating
Greek inheritance could not make themselves
much better, or worse if you prefer, than erudite.
The most enduringly familiar name from this
period of scholarly industry is typical; among
other things, an eminent Alexandrian professor,
named Euclid, produced in the Third Century before Christ an elementary treatise on geometry
which was not altogether supplanted as a text-
book when English and American boys went to
school in the Nineteenth Century of the Christian
Era. A good cursory impression of his surroundings and of their tendency and history may be
derived from a glance at the Encyclopædia Britannica article on the "Alexandrian School."

This encyclopædic summary gives hardly due
emphasis to a name deservedly conspicuous
throughout Roman times, but eclipsed later partly
because the works of its bearer have perished, and

[1] Pp. 32-39 (Oxford: 1913).

partly because admirable Latin imitations of them
have survived. Callimachus, the first remembered
librarian of Alexandria, was not only a man of
great energy and learning, but so industrious a
writer that he is said to have produced some eight
hundred books. Among these were specially admired elegies and epigrams, without which we
could hardly have had, in their actual form, the
elegiac poetry of Rome, or the poems of Catullus,
or the epigrams of Martial. The services of
Callimachus to the course of both learning and
literature were accordingly great. As we have
seen, however, only a few broken fragments of his
writings have been rescued from the wreck of
antiquity.

Another work finally accomplished at Alexandria
has been more fortunate. Among the people who
flocked to Ptolemaic Egypt were many Jews who
had mostly forgotten their ancestral language and
habitually thought in Greek. Chiefly for their
benefit, a translation of Hebrew Scripture into
Greek was undertaken in the Second Century.
The name this traditionally bears—the Septuagint
—is derived from a legend that it was accomplished by seventy-two learned men in seventy-
two days. Really, as it now survives, it seems
to have been the work of several hundred years.
Substantially, whatever its history, it still exists,
and throws much light on the state of Old Testament texts when the Ptolemies ruled the dominions
of the Pharaohs.

Ptolemaic, accordingly, we may on the whole
call the Greek traditions so far as they here concern us, both of the Third Century and of the half-
century which ensued before Greece was finally

conquered. How completely we are warranted in doing so will be evident when we compare the familiarity of this name with the oblivion which has overtaken two others. The last stand of Greece, in the year 146, was made at Corinth, which the Romans presently captured, sacked, and destroyed. The Greek general who tried to defend it proves to have been called Diæus, the Roman general who defeated him was called Mummius; to ascertain what either was called, however, you must turn not to world tradition but to your most conveniently accessible book of reference.[1]

II

THEOCRITUS

What Alexandrian life was like when Alexandrian learning was founded happens to be compactly recorded for us in a little sketch which has been called the most graphic of all Greek antiquity—the Fifteenth Idyl of Theocritus. Matthew Arnold's translation of this, in his essay on Pagan and Mediæval Religious Sentiment,[2] is at once the best English version and the easiest to find. It tells how two prettily frivolous Alexandrian women met and gossiped on their way to a festival of Adonis, and thus puts in admirable setting the graceful hymn they there heard sung;

[1] In my case here this happened to be Shuckburgh's Greece to A. D. 14. Seignobos does not mention the needless names.

[2] Essays in Criticism, I, VI. The whole essay is worth reading, for such purpose as ours; it contains also a translation of St. Francis of Assisi's Canticle of the Sun.

the whole thing is compressed into 159 hexameter
lines, more than half of which are trippingly colloquial. Though feathery in lightness it implies
the atmosphere where for their little while these
butterflies hovered in Ptolemaic sunshine; the
hymn meanwhile, pretty as themselves and not
much more significant, tells us what sort of attrac-
tion lured them out of doors. You think of Tan-
agra figurines, perhaps, or of the curled portraits
painted, with demure eyes, on the wooden slabs
which replaced amid their new-fashioned mummy-
wrappings the archaic and conventional masks of
immemorial Egypt. There is a glittering court
above such beings, and a surging mass of many-
coloured bazaar-like creatures about and beneath
them; and dashing Greek soldiers keep things in
semblance of order. It is all bright, gay, fleeting,
transitory, ominous. To have known such life,
you feel, would surely have been a momentary
pleasure, just as it would have been to enjoy, when
he was the last new maker of poetic novelty, the
dainty art of Theocritus.

He was by no means the only poet of his time,
nor perhaps the most apparently important. We
have already glanced at the poetic excursions of
the librarian Callimachus. There were plenty of
others who knew by heart the poetry of ancestral
Greece, from Homer down, and who exquisitely
imitated both its lyric beauties and sometimes its
epic animation. What is more, they were not
altogether ephemeral. Much as modern Europe
came to understand the primal glory of Grecian
fine art only when men began to perceive how far
this outshines the secondary expression of Rome,
so the Romans themselves delighted in Alexan-

drian poetry before they fully recognised the transcendent beauty of those elder Greeks whom the Alexandrians venerated as the Masters. In the Æneid, for example, as every one can see, Virgil beautifully imitated a parodied Homer; but those who have read the Argonautica of the Alexandrian Apollonius Rhodius assure us that without this now obscured poet's account of how Jason dealt with Medea we should never have had quite as it lives for all time the tenderly pathetic story of Æneas and Dido. Before Virgil imitated Homer in the Æneid and Hesiod in the Georgics, too, he had already imitated Theocritus in the Bucolics, or Eclogues. This accident has doubtless had a good deal to do with the persistence of Theocritus as an influence on the poetry of later Europe; most probably, however, he might to some degree have survived without it. For he happened to introduce into lasting literature a form of poetry—the Pastoral—which, despite its evident artificiality, has proved to appeal recurrently and genuinely, at least to the whims of taste and in all likelihood to some less unstable phase of human emotion.

Not much is known about Theocritus. It seems probable, however, that he was early familiar with the countryside of Sicily, where even to this day you may sometimes hear among the hills the sweet, shrill notes of wooden pipes played by shepherds as they watch their feeding flocks. The sound is haunting, at once human and almost as straight from the heart of nature as the song of a bird; at a distance, the shepherd looks like a creature not of humdrum life but of poetic fancy. Get near enough, inspect him carefully enough, and you will no doubt find him dirty, rude, cunning, and foolish; but a glimpse of him is like a peep into a world more primally innocent than this coarse, naughty world of ours. So far as Theocritus has lastingly influenced literature, he did so by translating this pretty aspect of Sicilian hillsides into graceful, trifling, mostly hexametric poems, where the shepherds and shepherdesses, though suggested by nature, are no longer what rustics must really be everywhere, but are presented as rustics appear to sentimental passing strangers. The name given his sketches befits them. An Idyl has been thought of these two thousand years as a fantastically artificial variety of poetry; but the literal meaning of the Greek word is almost exactly what a *Glimpse* means in English. You catch sight of something that sets your fancy playing; you look at it no more, but let your fancy play; which was very pleasant to Ptolemaic courtiers and fashionable folks of Alexandria. This was the public to which, amid the decadent Hellenism of the Third Century, Theocritus appealed as the best new maker of verses.

Somehow, his appeal has never quite died. The names of his idyllic personages linger always familiar—Daphnis, for example, Thyrsis, Tityrus, Amaryllis, Corydon, and Lycidas. Virgil, as we have already observed, acceptably imitated him for the revived fashion of Augustan Rome; and Virgil was imitated far and wide twelve or fifteen centuries later. And Spenser's first work was the Shepherd's Calendar, which tried to bring pastoral conventions a little nearer the nature from which they had been wandering ever since Theocritus first led them astray. When we remember,

though, that Spenser's own lament for the death
of Sir Philip Sidney disguises Sir Philip as a shepherd called Astrophel, we shall remind ourselves
at once how deep and how vagrant the influence
of the pastoral has proved.   It has given English
literature our two noblest mortuary poems, the
Lycidas of Milton and the Adonais of Shelley.   It
has shown itself, on the other hand, in such graceful trifles as the Pastor Fido of Guarini, the Aminta
of Tasso, and the Sad Shepherd of Ben Jonson.
Without it, we might hardly have had in their
actual form the ballets of Italian opera, nor the
Dresden china figures which made gay with flowery
colour the light boudoir of the Eighteenth Century.   Without it, Marie Antoinette might hardly
have played the milkmaid in her toy village at
Trianon, nor English-speaking children have told
you all about Little Bo-Peep.

And this recurrently fascinating prettiness was
the last thing established among the literary traditions of Europe by the antique, unique originality
of primal Greece.

CHAPTER V

THE GREEK TRADITION

There could be no greater mistake than to suppose that we have glanced at all the literature of Greece. Any systematic account of the matter, even though extending no further than the point where we have now arrived, would call instant attention to many names and tendencies of the full classical period, from the time of Homer to that of Theocritus, on which we have not touched. Furthermore, there is one fact about Greek literature which, though commonly forgotten, gives it unique interest quite apart from its merits. So far as the relations of literature with living language are concerned, this first of European literatures has never quite stopped. From the remote antiquity when Greek epics were reduced to writing until the present day every century has produced something normally expressed in Greek, by men who thought and spoke the Greek of their times. The Greek language, of course, has altered a good deal in the course of its three thousand years; you would hardly expect a modern Athenian instantly to grasp a sentence written, or still more spoken, after the manner of Periclean Athens. For all this, classical Greek, throughout recorded history, has stayed more or less intelligible to the Greeks, somewhat as Chaucer is to Twentieth Century Englishmen or Americans; and any of us who fails after a few minutes to make out what on the whole a page of Chaucer has to say ought to consult not the dictionary but the doctor.

At the same time, there is good reason, in such a scheme as ours, for considering as distinct the period over which we have now lingered as long as we can. So far as there was any European literature from the time of Homer to that of Theocritus, this literature was wholly and only Greek. Its allusions, for example—religious, historical, or literary—were either directly or implicitly Greek; if they touched on foreign things,— Egyptian, for example, Colchian, Macedonian,— they regarded them as more or less barbarous. Anybody was assumed to know who Theseus was, or Zeus, or Solon; nobody would have had the slightest idea of who Romulus was, or Jupiter, or Numa Pompilius; and the names of Moses or Jehovah or David would have meant no more to Socrates or Epicurus than those of Aztec or Peruvian heroes or gods or statesmen would have meant to big-spectacled students of Confucius and Mencius before the Chinese Empire crumbled into a make-believe republic. The sovereigns of Memphis, no doubt, and the deities, the Nile and the Euphrates, too, and Scythia and the misty shores of encircling Ocean, were not altogether unknown; but they, and names like them, were familiar only as things other than Greek, foreign, barbarian, different, remote, alien as the colossal torpor of the defaced Pyramids is to the quenchless life of the ruined Parthenon. Until the time of Theocritus nothing but Greece exhaled the spirit destined to animate immemorial Europe.

After that time came a change. A few names of those who have later written in Greek and of the things they have written about may serve to remind us of its nature and its course. In the

Second Century before Christ, the Greek Polybius
wrote about the already portentous history of
Rome until the end of the Punic Wars; in the First
Century before Christ, it is thought, appeared the
first of the collections of Greek lyrics—at the time
both old and new—on which centuries later the
Anthology—the Greek word for nosegay—was
based; in the First Century of the Christian Era,
Josephus wrote in Greek about the Jews; at the
same time the Greek writings now collected in the
New Testament were at least coming into existence; when the Second Century of our Era began,
Plutarch was probably at his best, whose perennially popular Lives—as we shall soon remind ourselves again—concern Roman traditions quite as
much as those of the Greek language in which he
thought and wrote; it was during this Second
Century that Marcus Aurelius made in Greek the
Stoic memoranda which often seem the noblest
spiritual record of Roman paganism; it was in
Greek that the Byzantine Fathers, Chrysostom
and more, set down their Christian doctrine; and
throughout the history of the Eastern Church
Greek has liturgically lived on, much as Latin lives
in the Western.   Until the fall of Constantinople,
less than fifty years before the discovery of America, Greek remained the literary language of that
region, where its course had stayed uninterrupted
since literature began there.   Even under the
Turkish domination of the Sixteenth and the Seventeenth Centuries there are traces of Greek ballads
and the like; and by the Eighteenth Century that
modern phase of Greek was already growing up
which is now said to bring forth more newspapers
in proportion to the calculable number of their

readers than any other contemporary tongue. Glance back at this record, and you will see that of all the things we have touched on only the Anthology is purely Greek. Everything else treats in later than classical Greek terms of matters which the elder Greeks would have held barbarian.

We need hardly remind ourselves, the while, that among living tongues few are much less known to foreigners than modern Greek. To men who habitually think in English, or French, or German, or Italian, or Spanish, for example, it presents itself much as a negligible dialect of barbarians might have presented itself to Periclean Athenians. This obvious fact implies the actual history of classical Greek. From the Second Century before Christ to the Third Century of the Christian Era the Greek literature on which we have touched was as familiar among educated Romans as Latin literature is to Catholic churchmen, or as French has been to cosmopolitan Europeans from the time of Louis the Fourteenth. Even then, however, your every-day Roman was apt to find the Greek language beyond his range, as bluff and un- lettered Casca does in the second scene of Shak- spere's Julius Cæsar.[1]   Cassius, plying him with questions as to what has just happened when Cæsar refused the crown, asks:

> Did Cicero say anything?
> *Casca :*   Aye, he spoke Greek.
> *Cassius :* To what effect?
> *Casca :*   Nay, an I tell you that, I'll ne'er look you i' the
>   face again; but those that understood him
>   smiled at one another and shook their heads;
>   but for mine own part, it was Greek to me.

[1] I, II, 277-283 (Cambridge edition).

From the time of Marcus Aurelius, it began to become Greek to everybody this side the Eastern Empire. By the Sixth Century it was almost unknown throughout Western Europe; so it remained for hundreds of years; in the Fourteenth Century, a scholar so alert as Petrarch is said never to have come across anybody who could teach him to read the original text of Homer. Though Greek traditions and even Greek works grandly survived, they long survived only as they had been transmitted or translated by men who thought and wrote in Latin. It was thus that Dante knew them; and thus we must henceforth try to think of them at least until we come to the period, a century or more after Dante's, when the dead grammarians of the Renaissance finally restored to our ancestral possessions the literal records of Greek antiquity.

From then till now—that is, for more than five hundred years—they have been so constantly and so admirably studied that very likely they can now be better understood and appreciated than ever before. To-day we can hardly consider them for any reason without turning to them, as we have turned here, directly, forgetting while we do so that in this aspect they are not so much the traditions of the centuries which were to ensue on them as the facts on which those traditions were based. Thus viewed, they reveal a few general characteristics which we may do well to summarise.

In the first place, ancient Greeks, who first displayed the type of mind which was destined to become European, and who happened to possess a language of unsurpassed beauty and flexibility, were little if at all hampered when they attempted the miracle of expression by the notion or the certainty that any previous and foreign people had already done what they were trying to do. Their problem, at least when we compare them with subsequent Europeans, was therefore simply to grasp the ideas they wished to set forth and to discover the words and the artistic forms most nearly suitable for their purpose. In the second place, their unsurpassed and in some respects disproportionate intelligence was artistically controlled by an instinctive distaste for unrestrained emotional excess. Though not remarkable for practical common sense, they had an artistic sense of the highest order. In the third place, this quality combined with the unique simplicity of their artistic problems to make their productions at once enduringly fresh and evidently excellent. Thus, though they had little if any conscious purpose of hampering the future, their accomplished works could not help seeming to be models of how such things ought to be done, and therefore affecting not only the subsequent expression of Greece but also that of all the Europe to which Greek influence has ever extended. So, finally, they brought into enduring existence the primal types of epic poetry, of lyric poetry, of dramatic poetry, of historical prose, of philosophical prose, of oratory, and of pastoral poetry which were destined to modify the thought and the utterance of all subsequent Europe.

For ages, however, subsequent Europe was generally to know these things not as they originally were, but only as they seemed when peered at through the veil of the interposed traditions of Rome.

BOOK II

THE TRADITIONS OF ROME

CHAPTER I

TO 100 BEFORE CHRIST

I

HISTORICAL TRADITIONS

A little while ago we touched on the fact that in the year 100 of the Christian Era Plutarch was probably at his best. His name is very familiar; ever since his Lives were translated into French and a little later into English, between three and four hundred years ago, they have been the most popular and therefore the most nearly original source from which our notions of antique worthies have been derived. So, although mention of him at this point violates our general purpose of considering the traditions of literature century by century, it is none the less just here that he is most worth our attention. For no one else so clearly marks the manner in which later times have generally fused the Greek traditions at which we have glanced with the Roman to which we now turn.

What little we know about him[1] is mostly derived from his own works. He was born at Chæronea, in Bœotia, during the reign of the Emperor Claudius, some four hundred years after the victory of Philip there had ended the liberty of Greece. He was educated at Athens, then still unruined and the traditional seat of philosophic culture. He

[1] Compactly summarised in Bernadotte Perrin's Introduction to the Lives: Loeb Classical Library, 1914.

represented Chæronea as deputy to the Roman
governor of Greece. He travelled widely. He
must have passed many years at Rome, where
both political duties and his personal accomplishments made him intimate with the best society of
his time. He lectured, mostly on moral philosophy. He ultimately went home to Chæronea
and there passed his later years, widely recognised
as a philosopher and a man of letters. He probably lived into the reign of Hadrian, when the
prospect of the Roman Empire looked bright.
He was a loyal Roman citizen, or if you prefer a
loyal subject of the Cæsars. Yet, although he
could read Latin, he never confidently mastered
any other language than his native Greek. Quotations from the Greek classics abound in his
works; he makes hardly any from the Roman.
There are none, it is said, from Virgil; there is a
little dispute as to whether one may be from
Horace or not. Even so late as the Second Century of the Christian Era, it appears, a lettered
Greek might still hold barbarous any literature
except his own.

When we come to other than literary traditions,
however, this had long ceased to be the case. If
Greece remained the principal source of intelligence, learning, philosophy, and culture, Rome had
already been for some three centuries the centre
of law, of government, of authority. By Plutarch's time the whole antique world was almost
equally familiar with the historical traditions of
both; and whoever pondered on how life should
be conducted could not neglect either. This problem was what most occupied him. His philosophic works, usually called Morals, and about

as long as the Lives, generally concern questions
of how people ought to think and to behave. His
fondness for this kind of speculation permeates the
Lives themselves. Fifty of them survive, all but
four in pairs—one Greek and one Roman; and
most of the pairs are followed by formal moral
comparisons. The series conventionally begins, for
example, by parallel lives of Theseus and Romulus,
with a comparison of these legendary founders of
originally diverse national traditions; and, to go
no further, there are parallel lives of Demosthenes and Cicero duly compared, and of Alexander
and Cæsar where the comparison has been lost.
Throughout, antique worthies are treated rather
biographically than historically; they are characterised, with abundance of anecdote; and for all
the narrative power which has kept the work
popular, they are chiefly regarded as instances of
conduct which has at once exemplified and influenced national ideals, finally merging in the common human ideal of what we now call European
antiquity. How much they have to do with our
own traditions, a single and typical fact must
serve to remind us: they are the basis, in our own
literature, of the Coriolanus, the Julius Cæsar, and
the Antony and Cleopatra of Shakspere. What
is more to our purpose at this moment, the making
of them, somewhere about the year 100 of the
Christian Era, proves how by that time even a
Greek man of letters who had never found need
thoroughly to learn the Latin language recognised
that the heroic and historic traditions of what was
growing to be Europe already included not only
the primal traditions of Greece but also and
equally the secondary traditions of imperial Rome.

His Roman Empire was really, as it supposed
itself, the third phase of consecutive Roman history and government. There had been a time,
already remotely antique, when the government
of Rome, then only local, was royal. A revolution, probably in the Sixth Century before Christ,
had expelled royalty—of which the name was
thenceforth detestable to Rome, much as it now
happens to be among the citizens of the United
States. The ensuing Republic—this word is the
literal Latin for Commonwealth—had shown two
divergent tendencies: amid the social disputes
which for centuries had kept Rome recurrently
turbulent, aristocratic privileges had gradually
diminished; and through these same centuries,
the military and administrative force of Rome had
gradually extended until, in the First Century
before Christ, a paradox was clear—an unstable
central government was virtually bound to keep
in stable order the whole civilised world. During
that Century a new series of revolutions turned
the central power into a military autocracy, to
persist for about five hundred years. What we
are apt to forget is that the title of its sovereigns,
now held superior to any borne by kings, was
originally unpretentious; the Latin word *Imperator*
—or *Emperor*, as we call it in English—meant
nothing more nor less than *General*, and *Cæsar*
was a family name. Thus the imperial title—
Empereur—of the Napoleons, like the imperial title
—*Kaiser*—of German monarchs implicitly em-
balmed during our Nineteenth Century the secular
abomination of royalty traditional to republican
Rome.

What the actual history of this long development had been, no one knew when Plutarch wrote; it is more or less disputed even among our most learned contemporaries. Two facts about it, however, were already certain by the year 100 before Christ. A considerably legendary account of things which had occurred earlier than what our present chronology calls the Third Century before Christ was generally known, and conventionally accepted, by the Romans; and what had ensued during the Third Century and the Second was considerably a matter of historical record. These traditions, utterly strange to the classic traditions of Greece, were as familiar to Plutarch as those of his own Greek ancestry. More than any one else, except Livy, he has kept them so for us.

They begin with the legend of the wolf-suckled twins Romulus and Remus, shadowily demi-divine and said to descend through Æneas from the royal race of Troy. The founding of Rome was traditionally placed about the middle of the Eighth Century. The Seventh Century and most of the Sixth comprised the period of the seven Roman kings, from Romulus to Tarquinius Superbus. Their sovereignty came to an end through an aristocratic revolution excited by the reckless conduct of Sextus, the son of Tarquin. He violated the Roman chastity of the beautiful matron Lucretia. She sent for her husband Collatinus and their kinsman Brutus; she told her poignant story, and took her life in their presence. They roused the people, expelled the king, and established the republican sovereignty of annually elected consuls—at first patrician or noble. When Porsena, of Clusium, tried to restore the Tarquins, the bravery of Horatius, who held the bridge unsupported, saved Rome, as every schoolboy knows who has read, or has had to read, the Lays of Macaulay.

So we come to the Fifth Century—in Greece the Century of the Persian defeats, of Pericles and of the Peloponnesian War. Compared with historic facts like these, the traditions of their contemporary Rome are surprisingly nebulous; yet among them you begin to discern enduring solidities. This was the Century of the legendary Appius Claudius and his hapless victim Virginia, again revived by the Lays of Macaulay; of the first Tribunes of the People, and crescent encroachment of plebeians on the hereditary privileges of patricians; of the no too historic worthies Coriolanus and Cincinnatus; of the codified Law of the Twelve Tables; of the first Dictator and of the first Censor.

The contrast between the Greek traditions of the following Century—the Fourth, the Century of Philip and Alexander—and those then gathering about Rome is different but hardly less marked. This was the period when Gaulish raiders besieged Rome itself, when the bearded Senate was slaughtered as it sat silently defiant, and when only cackling geese saved the Capitol; and it was the Century when Samnite enemies subjugated a Roman army, compelling them to pass under the yoke at the Caudine Forks; but it was the Century, as well, when Roman power began its final advance in Italy. By the year 300 Rome was no longer only a local sovereignty; the Republic was fatally tending towards Empire.

The Third Century—in Greek, or Hellenistic, tradition the Century when the Ptolemies began

their royal course—brought Rome at last into the
full light of history and left her, after perilously
fluctuating fortunes, already virtually imperial. It
began with Italian conquests, over Samnites, and
Gauls, and Etruscans, and the Greek civilisation
of Southern Italy. Then soon came the first of
the Punic Wars which were ultimately to settle
the naval mastery of the Mediterranean, and thus
of the whole antique world. When this war began, Carthage, originally a Phœnician colony established in the region now called Tunis, was the
most important of maritime powers. It already
had firm foothold in Greek regions of Sicily. Here
it found itself face to face with Rome. The First
Punic War lasted between twenty and twenty-five
years. In the course of them, Regulus, who had
defeated the Carthaginian fleet, landed in Africa
and besieged Carthage itself; the tale of how, defeated in turn, made prisoner and despatched to
Rome with terms of peace, he advised that no
peace be made and, impelled by honour, went
back alone to his Carthaginian doom, by and by
took its place in Roman legend.[1] Before 240
Roman victories had brought the Carthaginian general Hamilcar to terms, and all Sicily was yielded
to the Republic. Then followed some twenty years
of nominal peace, during which the Romans seized
the Carthaginian island of Sardinia and the
Carthaginians established themselves iñ not yet
Roman Spain; the name of Cartagena records
them there to this day. The Second Punic War,
which virtually occupied the last twenty years of

[1] *Cf.* Horace, Od. III, V; and Kipling's tale—Regulus—which tells how
bravely this has been expounded in English schools. Collected Works,
XXVI, 279.

the Century, began with what to anything else
than Rome would have seemed annihilating defeat.
Starting from Spain, the Carthaginian general
Hannibal crossed the Pyrenees, dashed across
Southern France, passed over the Alps amid frost
and snow, descended into Northern Italy, swept
the Romans from his way there, destroyed the
flower of their army in Central Italy at the Trasi-
mene Lake, followed this victory—despite the tactical delays of the dictator Fabius—by one more
overwhelming still at Cannæ just below the spur
on the boot of Southern Italy, and betook himself
to comfortable winter quarters at Capua; and all
this in two years.   But Capua, as the saying goes,
corrupted Hannibal.   Thereafter the Romans began to retrieve themselves.   Four years later
Marcellus took Syracuse, for all the legendary
engineering skill of Archimedes; the next year,
the Romans recaptured Capua.   In five years
more they had driven the Carthaginians from
Spain, where Scipio—later to be Africanus—won
his first fame.   He soon proceeded to attack Africa.
Hannibal, recalled home to defend Carthage, he
crushingly defeated.   And the year before the
Century ended, Carthage was compelled to accept
peace on Roman terms.

The Second Century thus found Rome victorious.   During the first half of it, the principal
Roman advances were to the eastward in regions
which two hundred years before had been among
those earliest brought under the Macedonian
power of Philip and of Alexander.   Just about the
middle of the Century, the Third Punic War began, which lasted only three years.   Carthage,
though subdued, still existed, and as long as it

existed stayed at least a possible menace. The
tradition of Cato, again and again urging upon the
Senate that Carthage must be blotted out,[1] implies the story. This time, the city was almost
literally razed, under the orders of the younger
Scipio Africanus,[2] son of the Æmilius Paulus who
conquered Macedon and grandson of the Æmilius
Paulus who fell at Cannæ, but by adoption grandson of Scipio Africanus the elder. In the same
year when Carthage thus vanished, the victory of
Mummius at Corinth finally reduced Greece to
the dominion of Rome. Fifteen years later,
Scipio had virtually achieved the Roman conquest of Spain, thereafter, until centuries later
Barbarian invasions destroyed the Empire, a Roman province. What was meanwhile happening
at Rome is implied in the story of the Gracchi,
grandsons of the first Scipio Africanus, and the
"jewels" of their mother Cornelia. Radically disposed, as has often been the case throughout history with generous youth of quality, each in turn
attempted economic and social reforms, unwelcome
to the class they sprung from; and each was consequently murdered. For all this turbulence in
Rome, Roman conquests continued. They reduced
to Roman sway the region beyond the Alps which
still bears the popular name of Provence. And as
the Century ended there surged forward the dominant figure of Caius Marius. Born a man of the

---

[1] He is said to have closed speech after speech with the words "Censeo
Carthaginem esse delendam"; the common English version of this is "Car-
thago delenda est." Provokingly enough, I have not lighted on the original authority for either.

[2] For an account of how Carthage fell, see Appian, VIII, 113–136. This
passage, thought to have been condensed from Polybius, may be found in
the Loeb edition of Appian, I, 601 *seq*.

people and always illiterate, he displayed extraordinary political and military ability. He subdued the African king Jugurtha, whose heroic struggle against Rome led only to the deadly chill of the Mamertine prison. Beyond the Alps Marius met and separately annihilated the Northern hordes of the Teutons and of the Cimbri; and when the Century ended, he was for the sixth time Consul. In that year, 100 before Christ, Julius Cæsar was born; and Cicero was six years old.

II

LITERARY TRADITIONS

PLAUTUS; TERENCE

The names of Cicero and of Cæsar loom so large in the perspective of European tradition, and each is in its kind so ultimate, that we are apt to forget a noteworthy fact about them. Except for Plautus and Terence, on whom we shall presently touch, they were earlier than any other Latin writers now extant except in fragments. By their time, nevertheless, the colossal and growing strength of Rome had been deeply affected by the finer civilisation of primal Greece. This is so far the case, indeed, that we possess hardly any monuments of earlier and purely Roman days. There are a few old walls, and cellars like the so-called Mamertine Prison, mostly uncovered by recent excavations; there are a few arched structures, such as the Cloaca Maxima, the great sewer which still drains the Forum; there are some cores of concrete, the usual method of Roman building from beginning to end. That is about all—sturdy, durable, unlovely. The triumphal arches, the aqueducts, the amphitheatres which ruinously fill one's fancy when one hears the name of Rome, belong not to the Republic but to the Empire. Everybody knows, to be sure, the austere stone coffins of the ancestral Scipios. A few portrait busts, too, survive from times little if at all later than those we have touched on. They are magnificently, uncompromisingly literal and living, incomparably stronger than the softened and Hellenised sculpture which put them out of fashion; but for all their calm dignity they lack the charm of grace. They are not rude, though; and neither was the society to which Cicero and Cæsar were bred.

So far as this society possessed a national literature it was only about a hundred years old. The most eminent of its poets was Ennius, who appears to have combined a considerable strain of Greek blood from Southern Italy with intensely Roman patriotic feeling. He fought in the Second Punic War, came to Rome about the beginning of the Second Century, and was held in high personal esteem by Scipio Africanus. He wrote copiously and variously—among other things, comedies, tragedies, satires, and a very long epic poem, called Annals, celebrating the traditions of Rome. Until the Æneid replaced it, this was held the Roman national epic. It had much to do with fixing the originally Greek hexameter as the poetic idiom of heroic Latin verse as well.[1] Only fragments of it survive, however,—some six hundred lines in all and few consecutive. Worse ruin still has overtaken

---

[1] Somewhat as Marlowe's "mighty line" established blank verse in England.

the other works of Ennius. For our purposes, he is little more than a name. One thing about him nevertheless seems clear; this chief classic of the First Century Romans owed much of his eminence to the fact that he had variously adapted the originally barbarous Latin language to what everybody acknowledged to be the finer poetic forms of the Greek. Whoever knows English poetry from the time of Henry VIII through the reign of Elizabeth will recall numberless instances of a similar process in our own literature. Throughout the life of Ennius this tendency to soften the asperities of native Roman culture was vigorously opposed by Cato, who seems to have been more impressed by the political instability, the enervating luxury, and the flexible morality of the Greeks than by their consummate intelligence or their exquisite æsthetic sense. Though the name of Cato stays traditionally great, however, little of his work remains, except in fragments. Historian, orator, and Roman, he has left us hardly more than the notions we associate with the word *censorious* when we think of his official title Censor. As a satirist, Ennius was already superseded, during the Second Century, by the more characteristically Latin Lucilius, himself now extant only in fragmentary lines, mostly quoted for linguistic purposes by later grammarians. Though the still remembered name of the tragic actor Roscius, who flourished about 100 before Christ, reminds us that Roman tragedy was once important, not a single example of the tragedy of Ennius exists, nor indeed of any Roman tragic poetry until we come to Seneca, at his best under the Emperor Nero. Of the comedies of Ennius, too, we have nothing but the names; they were never held his happiest efforts. His contemporary Plautus, however, survives; and so does the younger comic poet Terence who was born not long before Plautus died. Of all the Latin literature produced earlier than Cicero's time, the only works at once important and complete are now twenty comedies by the one and six by the other.

As we have already reminded ourselves,[1] these Latin comedies were adapted or translated from those of Menander and other writers, now lost, whose light touch animated the last form taken by dramatic poetry among the Greeks. The survival of Plautus and Terence at once testifies to their popularity, preserves—except for Aristophanes—all that we certainly know of antique comedy, and has greatly influenced the standard comedies of Italy and France. What is more, there can be no doubt that throughout the centuries, even to this day, men who have studied or familiarly read them have agreed in finding them amusing. For at least two reasons, however, they are no longer so to those who casually glance at modern translations of them: so far as they anywhere pretend to describe human experience, they deal with a state of society both foreign and past even when they were alive at Rome; and they have been so widely and so long imitated during the last five hundred years that nothing could now prevent their fun from seeming rather conventionally stale. That this is by no means the whole story, however, any reader of Shakspere can remind himself by turning to the Comedy of Errors. This is a free adaptation of a comedy by Plautus,

[1] *Cf.* p. 137.

called Menæchmi—Menæchmus is his name for
the brothers whom Shakspere names Antipholus.
Shakspere's other twins, the two Dromios, do not
occur in the Latin play; and furthermore he considerably modifies the laxity of personal morality
which Plautus assumes as normal. In more than
one aspect, however, the Comedy of Errors may
give us a better notion of what Plautus did than
we might obtain by puzzling or nodding over
direct translations from his Latin. Without him
this gay, nonsensical confusion could no more have
existed than his own plays could have existed without the Greek models on which he based them; and
if we may trust the scholars who know him best,
he not only allowed himself to modify his Greek
plots as he chose but also set forth under Greek
names various phases of contemporary Roman
character and conduct. Just such free treatment
marks the work of Shakspere, and for that matter
of all the English dramatists in Shakspere's time;
wherever their scenes are set, or at whatever period,
the language and the behaviour of their characters,
typical or individual, resembles what was current
in the England which knew or remembered Queen
Elizabeth.

Plautus appears to have been, like Shakspere
eighteen hundred years later, a man of obscure
origin who had considerable experience of life and
of the theatre before he produced his craftsmanlike
and fluent plays. He wrote, it is thought, for between thirty and forty years, of which twenty or
so were in the Third Century. Conceivably, therefore, he might have known old men who could remember Menander, still alive and at work less
than a hundred years before him. Terence be-

longed to a younger generation, and can hardly
have known Italy till after Plautus was dead.
He is said to have been born in Africa, and originally to have been a slave. His talent and attractive qualities early improved his condition; he
was precocious and died at thirty or so—born well
after the Second Punic War, dead well before the
Third. The six comedies he has left us, less exuberant than those of Plautus and more highly
polished, are supposed to be more like the Greek
works on which the art of both was modelled;
substantially, indeed, they may be rather translations than adaptations. Even so, they flow as
freely and as gracefully as if they were original.
The most familiar line from them is at once a case
in point and a typical example of how the meaning of familiar quotations is apt to change. At
the beginning of the Heautontimoroumenos, or
Self-Tormentor,—the retaining of the untrans-
lated Greek title goes far to show that the play
was probably presented as a mere translation,—an
elderly man, pestered while at work by questions
from a meddlesome neighbour, testily asks whether
the tormentor has so much time to spare that he
can attend to matters which are none of his business. The ensuing pun is hard to translate; it
may roughly be indicated as "I am a man; so
any man's business is mine." At all events, it is
a mere play on words; but the words in question
happen to be capable of serious meaning. "Homo
sum," they run, "humani nil a me alienum puto"; [1]

---

[1] The original pun is double, on *homo* and *alienus*, even treble if we include *nil* :

Men.   Chremes, tantumne ab re tuast oti tibi
        Aliena ut cures ea quæ *nil* ad te attinent?
Chrem. *Homo* sum: *humani nil* a me *alienum* puto.—
                        Heautontimoroumenos I, 75-77. (Loeb.)

taken by themselves they may be rendered "I am a man; no human lot can seem quite strange to me." And so, through centuries on centuries, this verbal pleasantry has been regarded by posterity as a noble philanthropic maxim, straight from the heart of still uncorrupted republican Rome.

If our concern were with dramatic history, we might dwell on these prototypes of later comedy long, defining them, and clearly distinguishing between them. Here it is enough to remember what is true of both. The highly conventional plots of both are taken directly from the later comedies of the Greeks. The scenes of both are generally laid in Greece—even Plautus is said to use the word *barbarous* when mentioning Rome. The names of the characters in both are apt to be Greek. All this may well remind us of the relation to Italy similarly evident in so many of Shakspere's plays. Shakspere, however, early began to individualise his characters. Nothing like such individualisation occurs in either Plautus or Terence; their characters, even when compared with those of Aristophanes, and still more with those of the tragic poets of the Fifth Century, turn out to be nothing but broadly indicated types, such as Elizabethans would have called humorous. Perhaps the nearest things to them in English may be found by turning to the earlier, and no longer very animated, comedies of Ben Jonson. In theatrical matters there must always be an element of make-believe; in surviving European drama, this element is hardly anywhere more obvious than you will find it when you ponder on

Plautus and Terence not only separately but together.

Thus taken together, they are doubtless robust, fluent, and—like Shakspere and his contemporaries —nationally idiomatic. Thus taken together, the while, they clearly mark another phase of European literature than the primal Greek, with which we have hitherto been concerned. The Greek, from Homer to Theocritus, betrays no evidence that the men who made it were ever hampered by consciousness of foreign models, superior to anything their own country had made. These earliest survivors of Latin literature, neither of whom was born until well after Theocritus—the latest Greek on whom we have touched—was dead, imply from beginning to end an ingenuous belief that if literature is to be made in their still hardly tamed language, it must be made according to standards already fixed by that elder civilisation which first brought into being the intellectual idiom of subsequent Europe. In this sense, even if they were so in no other, they were characteristically Roman. Just as the literature of Greece is fundamentally primal, so that of Rome, for all its classic dignity and all its sententious gravity and all its large urbanity, is fundamentally secondary. What is more, Plautus and Terence, earliest of enduring Latin writers, imitate not the greatest works of the literature they hold supreme but only one of its later and least profoundly memorable phases. Something similar we shall find recurring throughout European literature. Again and again, the decadence of an extinct art has lured men back to understanding of its masterpieces.

These two first survivors of the literature of
Rome, in short, may best be regarded as variously
typical rather than as positively excellent.   Their
work, and nothing else, remains to remind us of
what Roman literature was like in the year 100
before Christ.

CHAPTER II
THE FIRST CENTURY BEFORE CHRIST

I

HISTORICAL TRADITIONS

At least historically, the First Century before Christ comprises more names and facts unforgotten by posterity than any other throughout European tradition. It was the Century of Marius and Sylla, of Mithridates, of Spartacus, of Catiline, of Pompey and of Julius Cæsar, of the conquest of Gaul, of the crossing of the Rubicon and of the battle of Pharsalia, of Brutus and Cassius, of the battle of Philippi, of Antony and Cleopatra, of the battle of Actium, and of the final concentration of Roman power under the imperial sway of Cæsar Augustus. These very names almost tell their tale; after two thousand years they are as familiar as ever.

The general outline of the story which hovers about them, too, is not only traditionally but historically true. This was at once the Century when expansion of Roman dominion showed itself most indomitable, and that when the ancient forms of republican government proved hopelessly inadequate longer to control the colossal power of Rome. Both tendencies appear wherever we happen to glance at the first half of the Century. At home as well as abroad, there were incessant wars and rumours of wars. Though these have been so recorded, and of late years so studied that historians can discuss them in detail, the tradition of them, which is our immediate concern, stays confused in the distance. As we think of the confusion, however, certain facts grow more or less clear. There was a Social War, in which the peoples of Italy demanded Roman citizenship; they were ultimately defeated, and thereupon the citizenship was paradoxically given them. Thus, throughout later Roman history, citizenship came to imply not residence at Rome but political rights in the Roman Empire: it was enjoyed, the pious will remember, by the Apostle Paul, who had never been near Rome till he came there with his appeal to Cæsar. On the Social War there presently followed, at about the same time, the first war against the threatening Asiatic power of Mithridates and the first Civil War, at Rome itself, between Marius and Sylla; very broadly speaking this internal conflict was between the new and comparatively democratic tendencies embodied in Marius, and the old traditions of the aristocratic Republic embodied in Sylla. At home and abroad, the fortunes of war fluctuated. There was a time when Marius found himself a fugitive, almost literally alone, and saved himself only by asking a Cimbric soldier sent to despatch him if the fellow dared kill Caius Marius; there was another, a little later, when, forbidden to land in Africa, he bade the officer sent to prevent him go tell the governor that Marius was to be seen sitting on the ruins of Carthage. Yet, not much later, while Sylla was fighting Mithridates, Marius came back to Rome, and died there dominant. In two or three years, Sylla, victorious in Asia, was at Rome once more, and wreaked his vengeance as he pleased, with slaughter and pillage in the very Roman streets. He soon died, in his turn. This, very generally, was the story of Rome during the first quarter of the Century, when Cicero and Cæsar were boys, and grew to be young men.

The next quarter of the Century brought them both into the full light of history, and Pompey, too, who was just about of an age with Cicero. War with Mithridates broke out again; and at the same time the revolt headed by the gladiator Spartacus threatened parts of Italy itself. In both cases, the power of Rome, for all the political and social disease at its heart, proved indomitable. Pompey came forward, upset the policies established for a while by Sylla, cleared the Italian seas of pirates, and at last finally subdued Mithridates. In the same year, Cicero, then Consul, exposed and suppressed the conspiracy of Catiline, and fancied for a little while that he had saved the Republic. But Cæsar, suspected of having to do with the conspiracy, was coming towards what the traditions of the future were long to declare his own. With Pompey and Crassus he formed the first Triumvirate; preserving semblance of the ancestral forms of the Republic, they virtually seized the sovereignty, in the year 60. The following ten years comprise the whole story of Cæsar's conquests in Gaul; while these were in progress, Crassus was defeated and killed in Asia. By the year 50, Pompey was master of Rome, but Cæsar of all the North and of his Gallic war veterans; the rivals were face to face, and Cicero, with no other choice than that between them, seems—like conservative men so placed throughout history—to have been

concerned mostly with speculations as to which
of them the devil would presently take as hind-
most.

Traditionally, the third quarter of the Century
is clearest of all.   In the year 49, Cæsar crossed the
Rubicon, a little stream which divided the region
of Northern Italy legally under his command from
the territory legally under the command of Pompey.   The die was cast, he is reputed to have said.
A year later, he proved himself the winner.   At
Pharsalia, in Thessaly, Pompey was overwhelm-
ingly defeated; and seeking asylum in Egypt, with
Cæsar close at his heels, he was treacherously
murdered in his boat.   The following months
Cæsar passed in Alexandria, the first imperial
Roman lover of Cleopatra.[1]   He gradually made
her sole queen, last of the Ptolemies; then swiftly
followed his victorious campaigns in Pontus,—
whence he wrote "Veni, vidi, vici," [2]—in Africa,
and later in Spain.   By that time he was absolute
sovereign of Rome, where Cleopatra had followed
him, his acknowledged mistress, with their child
Cæsarion; but, preserving the forms of the Republic, he bore only such titles as *imperator*, or
general, as *pontifex maximus*, or chief priest, as
consul, and as *dictator*—an office finally conferred
on him for life.   The style of royalty stayed immemorially detestable to Roman tradition.

At this point the story becomes more familiar
still to all who know English literature; for the
Julius Cæsar and the Antony and Cleopatra of

[1] See the impish but not therefore negligible Cæsar and Cleopatra of
Mr. Bernard Shaw.

[2] Originally, it is said, written to the Senate, these words were finally
inscribed on a banner borne in the triumphal procession which celebrated
his Pontic victory.   They mean, "I came, I saw, I conquered."

Shakspere have translated the prose of Plutarch
into changeless English poetry. Accurate or not,
they are surprisingly faithful to their authority,
which records what happened between the year
44, when Cæsar was assassinated, and the year
30, when Cleopatra took her life. The throbbing
distinctness of individual character which makes
them so memorable is of course due to Shakspere;
but the course of the story where these characters
live and move is straight from Plutarch. Cæsar,
dominant at Rome and throughout the Roman
dominions, was imposing peace on the world, by
that time turbulent throughout living memory.
In modern terms we may roughly generalise his
policy as the declaration of practicable law enforced by an army whose chief function was to
regulate all civilisation and thus make the world
safe. This policy involved at least a modification, if not the complete abolition, of many liberties enjoyed by citizens, and particularly by men
of rank, under the time-honoured constitution of
the Republic. The wars and rumours of wars
which had convulsed the Republic ever since anybody could remember had made conspiracy and
rebellion matters of habit. A consequent conspiracy, led by conservative Roman gentlemen,
lured Cæsar to the Senate house, and there stabbed
him to death, at the foot of Pompey's statue.
Thereupon anarchy for a while broke loose again;
and among others Cicero was murdered. Very
soon, two distinct parties defined themselves: that
under Brutus and Cassius, which endeavoured to
sustain some semblance of the old republican
principles; and that under the new Triumvirate
—Cæsar's nephew Octavian, his brilliant adherent

Mark Antony, and a rather shadowy person named Lepidus—which was determined finally to assert the dominant policy of Cæsar. About two years after Cæsar fell, these forces met at Philippi in southeastern Macedonia. Brutus and Cassius were utterly defeated. The words with which the Brutus of Shakspere salutes the self-slain bodies of Cassius and of their faithful officer Titinius imply the story of Europe for centuries to come:

> O, Julius Cæsar, thou art mighty yet!
> Thy spirit walks abroad, and turns our swords
> In our own proper entrails.[1]

Julius Cæsar is perhaps the clearest of Shakspere's plays; certainly it is among the easiest to read. Antony and Cleopatra, at first confusing, demands but abundantly rewards closer attention. With astonishing fidelity to Plutarch, it tells how the unity of the triumvirate failed, to master its trinal diversities; and how Antony, betaking himself to Egypt, was there ensnared by the wiles of Cleopatra. Whatever she may have been in life, Shakspere has made her an incarnation of damning harlotry:

> Age cannot wither her, nor custom stale
> Her infinite variety.[2]

After fluctuating efforts to break her spells, Antony finds himself face to face with Octavian, already called Cæsar, in a final struggle for world-empire. Lepidus has meanwhile faded out of sight; though he flits across the stage once or twice more, he is virtually disposed of in the mar-

[1] Julius Cæsar, V, iii, 94–96.   [2] Antony and Cleopatra, II, ii, 240–241.

vellous scene[1] where all three triumvirs get perilously drunk on Sextus Pompey's galley, and he is
presently bundled helpless over the side into
safety.   There is a naval battle off Actium, on
the southerly part of the coast of Epirus; in the
midst of it, Cleopatra, who has insisted on seeing
the fray, gets frightened, and bids her ship take
flight. Antony infatuated instantly follows her,
and thus

> For lazy glances flung away the world.

Back in Alexandria, and there besieged by victorious Cæsar, he falls on his sword and dies in
the arms of Cleopatra,

> A Roman by a Roman
> Valiantly vanquished.[2]

Thereafter, rather than be displayed in the triumphal train of Cæsar, she applies the asp, a
deadly serpent, to her breast:

> Come, thou mortal wretch,
> With thy sharp teeth this knot intrinsicate
> Of life at once untie. Poor venomous fool,
> Be angry, and despatch. O, could'st thou speak,
> That I might hear thee call great Cæsar ass
> Unpolicied. . . .
> *(To her attendant)*
> Peace, peace;
> Dost thou not see my baby at my breast
> That sucks the nurse asleep?[3]

[1] Antony and Cleopatra, II, vii. This should be compared with the
original passage in Sir Thomas North's translation of Plutarch's Life of
Antony—the version used by Shakspere.

[2] Antony and Cleopatra, IV, xv, 57–58. *Cf.* Plutarch's account of his
death.

[3] Antony and Cleopatra, V, ii, 306–313.

And when Cæsar, coming too late, finds her dead, he speaks her epitaph for the centuries:

> She looks like sleep,
> As she would catch another Antony
> In her strong toil of grace.[1]

With her the kingdom of the Ptolemies ended. Egypt was fully Roman. The second Cæsar was lord of all.

At that time he was only about thirty-two years old. He lived to the age of seventy-seven, dying in the year 14 of the Christian Era. For more than forty years, which included the whole last quarter of the First Century before Christ, he was more absolutely sovereign than any European had been before, and his power has never since been surpassed. Whether he was great, or cool, or only fortunate is not now our concern. Like his uncle, Julius Cæsar, he preserved the forms of the immemorial Republic. His banners bore the legend S. P. Q. R.[2]—the Senate and the People of Rome. His title was only *Imperator*, which had always been borne by Roman generals. *Cæsar* was his family name. *Augustus*, the name by which he is traditionally remembered, was originally an innocent honorific, meaning something like our own word, *august* or *reverend*. And *Princeps*, or *prince*, need have conveyed to sensitive ears nothing much more troublous than Americans of 1799 might have detected in its English equivalent *first*, when Lee eulogised Washington as "First in war, first in peace, and first in the hearts of his

---

[1] Antony and Cleopatra, V, ii, 349-351.
[2] Wickedly parodied, years ago, by some precursor of American Trusts, who declared the initials to stand for "Small Profits. Quick Returns."

countrymen." He pretended to exercise his authority as the formal successor of republican magistrates—proconsuls, for example, tribunes and censors; in fact, however, he came thus to embody the state. Among other things he was *Pontifex Maximus*, or chief priest of the Roman religion. The history of this title is a curious instance of how time and circumstance modify not only the meaning of words, but all the associations which gather about them. Literally, *pontifex* signifies *bridge-builder;* the fact that in primitive antiquity the safety of Rome required special and constant attention to any bridge across the Tiber seems to have put such structures under the particular guardianship of the local gods and their priests. Long before the time of Cæsar, nobody remembered that the pontifical office had ever had anything to do with bridges; but the title survived as that of the chief ministers of the Roman gods. It has never quite lapsed. It is borne to this day by the Pope, still believed by millions on millions to be successor of St. Peter as Christian Bishop of Rome and apostolic head of the Catholic Church. In its religious phase, indeed, the antique Empire of the Cæsars structurally survives even now.

The theory of our ancestral Church implies that of finally imperial Rome. After generations of anarchic bloodshed, there came into existence a new ideal of empire. This is nowhere more excellently celebrated than by the great poem written to assert it when Augustus was all-powerful, the Æneid of Virgil:

Behold, at last, that man, for this is he,
So oft unto thy listening ears foretold,

Augustus Cæsar, kindred unto Jove.
He brings a golden age; he shall restore
Old Saturn's sceptre to our Latin land
And o'er remotest Garamant and Ind
His sway extend; the fair dominion
Outruns th' horizon planets, yea, beyond
The sun's bright path, where Atlas' shoulder bears
Yon dome of heaven set thick with burning stars.
Against his coming the far Caspian shores
Break forth in oracles; the Mæotian land
Trembles, and all the seven-fold mouths of Nile.[1]

Till that time, imperial power had meant only
armed conquests—Assyrian, Babylonian, Egyptian, Persian, Macedonic. Now at last there appears a sense of duty, animating the gross body of
power. The mission of Rome was to bring to
troubled mankind the solace of *Pax Romana*—of
world-wide Roman peace, strong in the majesty of
the law. Three lines of that superb prophecy of
Anchises summarise for all time the hope of this
newly golden Augustan age:

Tu regere imperio populos, Romane, memento;
Hae tibi erunt artes: pacisque imponere morem,
Parcere subjectis, et debellare superbos.[2]

(Remember, Roman, thine imperial charge;
These be thy arts: enforce the rule of peace,
Sparing the conquered, beating rebels down.)

By what means Augustus attempted to make
real this ideal purpose, we need not inquire. Traditionally the forty years of his reign are a period

[1] Æneid, VI, 791–800; translated by T. C. Williams (Boston, 1908).
[2] Æneid, VI, 851–853: Williams translates this passage thus:
But thou, O Roman, learn with sovereign sway
To rule the nations. Thy great art shall be
To keep the world in lasting peace, to spare
The humbled foe, and crush to earth the proud.

of emergence from the storms of anarchy into the calm sunlight of world-order. Two familiar likenesses of him embody the spirit of his age. The first is the youthful bust, softened from the literal austerity of elder Roman sculpture, but still strong in its gracious rendering of beauty and promise; its features were parodied again and again by imperial portraits of the great Napoleon, whose face probably had some manner of resemblance to them. The other likeness is the statue which shows Augustus imperial—idealised, no doubt, as the bare head and feet would imply, and the symbolic devices on his fretted cuirass, but mature, calm, majestic, just, and sovereign; first of those destined to reincarnate the mighty spirit of Julius Cæsar, he walks abroad, on his way to the posthumous honours of divinity.

When the First Century before Christ closed, this was his aspect, after some thirty years of imperial sovereignty. The first half of the Century had been a whirl of anarchy and bloodshed; the last quarter of it, uniting the world under the beneficent sway of Augustus Cæsar, had promised a diuturnal future to the peace of Rome. And by the beginning of our Christian era, Latin literature, hardly in lasting existence when the Century began, had produced its most memorable masters. To the first half of the Century Cicero belongs, and Cæsar, and Lucretius, and Catullus; to the full serenity of Augustan promise belong Virgil, and Horace, and Ovid, and Livy. To these eight, and to a few of their lesser contemporaries, we may now turn.

II

CICERO

Among the most interesting books about Rome is Monsieur Gaston Boissier's Ciceron et Ses Amis.[1] Based on the letters of Cicero, it at once gives a remarkably animated account of him and of his times, and shows why he is now the most fully recorded and clearly defined personage of all classical antiquity. This is not because of the circumstances which made him historically conspicuous, nor yet because of the copious orations and philosophic works which have always been recognised as the chief classical model of Latin prose. It is due to the fact that more than nine hundred letters actually written by him, or to him, still exist. For centuries between his time and ours, no doubt, they were virtually lost and forgotten. Now that they have been restored to us again, for something like five hundred years, they often seem the most precious part of his work. Their general characteristics are admirably summarised in Boissier's introductory chapter; no other such collection of any period so variously and so clearly preserves at once the personality of a great public man and the atmosphere as well as the detail of the circumstances about him.

At the time when the first of these extant letters was written Cicero was about thirty-eight years old.[2] Sprung from a respectable family of

[1] An English translation of this, by A. D. Jones, was published in 1897.
[2] The original texts, arranged chronologically and abundantly annotated, may be found in the volumes edited by Tyrrell and Purser (third edition, Dublin: 1904).

country gentry, he had received both at home and abroad the highest education of his time; he was equally familiar with the traditions of Greece and of Rome; he had gone to the bar; being blest with extraordinary diligence and wit he had there distinguished himself; and he had early taken active part in politics. His career had thus been of a kind happily usual throughout the modern history both of England and of America. By nature and by training he was attached to the state of things amid which he had been born and bred. Whoever has his way to make likes to be sure of his bearings; whoever must stake his future cherishes respect for the rules of the game. To such a man no environment could have been much more disconcerting than that where Cicero found himself. The anarchic disturbances of civil war had made everything uncertain. At Rome neither life nor property was safe; and the old Roman aristocrats, who looked with patronising contempt on "new men," such as he was, had often become at once luxuriously corrupt in private life and cynically unprincipled in political conduct. A well-born demagogue is a very dangerous animal. The conspicuous talent of Cicero had nevertheless brought him forward, both as a lawyer and as a public man; he had already made a considerable fortune; and if his work had stopped then a number of his forensic speeches and his denunciation of Verres would already have established his reputation as the most accomplished orator who ever spoke Latin.

In this aspect he is traditionally best known now. It is a commonplace that his methods have at various times been studied and imitated by public

speakers of widely different subsequent periods—
never more admiringly than in England and
America from the middle of the Eighteenth Century to the middle of the Nineteenth. It is rather
less generally understood that these methods of
his had in common with those of his imitators the
profoundly characteristic feature of being deliberately based on excellent foreign models. He was,
and he remains, the greatest Roman master of the
subtle art most enduringly mastered among the
Greeks by Demosthenes; but just as surely as
Demosthenes considered only the general principles
of his art and its best models in his native language, so Cicero never wrote a line of oratorical
Latin without a consciousness, intensified by life-
long study and culture, of his effort to rival in
what had lately been a barbarous tongue the lof-
tiest achievements of primal Greece. An often
forgotten result followed, and has never quite lost
influence. Cicero, conventionally accepted as the
most admirable master of Latin prose, really wrote
not the current Latin which everybody used for
daily purposes of thought or speech, but rather a
consciously literary dialect which attempted to reproduce effects fully attainable only by the more
subtle refinements of the Greek language. Such
work, whatever its merit, cannot escape evident artificiality; yet, accepted as itself a faultless model,
it has been held up for hopeless imitation by European schoolboys almost to this day. This is as if
some mongrel race, two thousand years hence, were
assiduously to be taught English by courageous
attempts to parody heavily Latinised examples
of our style, like the blank verse of Paradise Lost or
the balanced periods of Doctor Johnson. The clas-

sic literature of Rome never had, like the primal
Greek, the full and free grace of instinctive idiom.
It had, however, a studied polish much higher than
any fabricated by its imitators; and for such polish
there never will be a better name than Ciceronian.

The most widely familiar examples of Cicero's
oratory are probably his speeches against Catiline,
immemorially studied at English and American
schools. In the body of his extant work, these
come rather early. Only eleven of his letters, all
addressed to Atticus, have been preserved from
years before his consulship; and his correspondence
does not begin again until his consulship was over.
The traditional story of his political triumph, indeed, is principally based on orations which he
made at the time. What is to be said for the other
side must be gathered largely from inference; for
one constant, and constantly imitated, feature of
his oratory was fierce denunciation of opponents.
Before accepting Cicero's views of Catiline, one
may prudently ponder on the methods of Ser-
geant Buzfuz, a pretty sound Ciceronian, in the
case of Bardell *v.* Pickwick. These views, however, have long been sanctioned by tradition;
and may very probably have been sincere on the
part of the great magistrate who set them forth.
Elected to the consulship, he found the structure
of the State threatened by a new conspiracy, led
by Roman gentlemen of better origin than he. His
adroitness and eloquence suppressed it without
bloodshed at the capital; to Romans who remembered the atrocities of Sylla, this may well have
seemed a return to the golden age of the legendary
Republic. And Cicero, one of whose foibles was
the self-conscious self-esteem of a self-made man,

and who had been officially proclaimed *Pater Patriæ*, or Father of his Country, could ingenuously write of himself—though laughed at for the writing—such an alliterative hexameter as

> Cedant arma togæ, concedat laurea laudi.[1]
> (Let arms yield to the gown, the laurel-crown[2]
> To public commendation.)

His time, however, was out of joint. Five years later he was in exile, his house and effects at Rome confiscated and looted. For the rest of his life there is no other contemporary authority comparable with his correspondence, which now becomes copious. Read it as you will, there can be no doubt that the crashing course of history was beyond human control, and that his life-long hope to see preserved or restored the antique constitution of the Republic was futile. His exile, to be sure, lasted less than two years. Through the greater part of Cæsar's campaigns in Gaul, through the struggles between Cæsar and Pompey, as well as at the time when Cæsar was murdered, Cicero was mostly at Rome, with fluctuating fortunes and influence, and sometimes with what looked like fluctuating principles. Meanwhile he produced the greater part of his collected works, orations both legal and political, and the political or philosophical treatises which consoled or occupied his generally enforced periods of comparative leisure. After the death of Cæsar, he did his utmost to resist the resistless power of Cæsar's imperial tendency: his orations against Antony, conventionally called Philippics by reason of their essential

---

[1] De Officiis, I, 22.
[2] A Roman military victor was crowned with laurel.

likeness to the fiery but futile speeches in which three hundred years earlier Demosthenes had denounced Macedonian aggression on the liberties of Greece, at once defined his position and sealed his doom. He was among the first to be proscribed by the second Triumvirate—Antony, Octavian, and Lepidus. Starting to escape, if he could, from a country estate where he had taken refuge, he was put to death in his private conveyance by pursuing soldiers of the Triumvirs. His head and his hands were hacked off; they were brought to Antony as proof that this opponent need no longer be reckoned with; and it is said that before the relics were exposed in the Forum, the wife of Antony—just then the "shrill-tongued Fulvia"[1] of Shakspere's Cleopatra—displayed her matronly Roman charity by piercing the dried and silenced tongue of Cicero with one of her hairpins.

True or not, that ferocious anecdote defines the Rome where the first consummate literary expressions of what we now call culture were produced. This quality of culture, evident throughout Cicero's letters, as well as in every line of his more studied literary works, makes him generically different from any Greek; at least in this aspect, indeed, he seems almost modern. His letters are those of an accomplished gentleman, in the finer sense of the word; they show his complete urbanity of social habit—among other things he was reported the best diner-out of his times, and his witticisms were repeated far and wide; they also show his politely alert familiarity with intelligent thought, with fine art and with literature, Greek and Latin; they could have proceeded only from

[1] Antony and Cleopatra, I, i, 32.

a man who knew how to enjoy the cream of life.
Here if ever in the whole course of literature you
find yourself in thoroughly good company; and
thoroughly good company implies highly trained
minds and manners. His orations, whether legal
or political, could have been produced by nothing
less than assiduous and life-long study, under the
most skilful teachers, of an extraordinarily adroit
and subtle art. Whether, under any circumstances, oratory has quite so much practical value
as we are apt to assume is beside the point; Cicero
could do at will whatever can be done with it.
Here again we find him in a position possible only
when the refinements of a highly developed civilisation are for a while matters of course. And his
numerous philosophic and political treatises more
than imply the same kind of surroundings. Speaking generally, they seem to have been produced,
with remarkable speed and ease, by an almost
overactive mind which found relief and recreation
in what to most of us would be hard intellectual
work. He hardly pretends to be an original
thinker, and indeed may nowadays be conventionally credited with less original thought than he
really displays. He had read, however, almost
everything that was worth reading; he knew what
he thought about whatever he had read. And,
often modelling his form on the tradition established by Plato's dialogues, he was apt to put into
the heads of Romans—Cato, for example, Scipio,
or Lælius, as well as contemporaries of his own—
thoughts and speculations which had caught his
fancy while reading or talking about the philosophy
and the literature of the Greeks. Once more, such
expression implies not only a very highly culti-

vated condition of society, but also that phase of
culture, recurrent throughout subsequent Europe,
which eagerly recognises the standards made lasting by a finer though foreign civilisation of the
past. All this sounds as if his times were like
ours; yet, in those very times, Fulvia—a great
lady of his own race—could be believed to have
dealt with his relics as the French mob dealt with
those of the Princess de Lamballe in the first out-
bursts of their Revolutionary madness. He was
pre-eminently such a man as we might find delightfully cultivated now; and he lived and died
when persons of quality might behave like German soldiers in Belgian villages or Bolsheviki in
Russia.

A little poem by Catullus,[1] of which the deliberately equivocal grace has thus far eluded all attempts to translate it, pleasantly implies the relation of Cicero to his contemporary men of letters.
Addressing him by name, and calling him most accomplished or most eloquent of the offspring of
Romulus, it thanks him as the best of patrons or
advocates for some present or civility, or service,
in the name of the worst or most unworthy of
poets. Generally rendered literally as if it concerned Cicero's professional skill, and sometimes
thought ironic, it may just as well be taken as an
ingeniously pretty play on words; if we may trust
the dictionaries, the Latin *patronus*, which doubtless means counsel as related to client, applies
equally to the relation of a generous patron to
any kind of artist, and Cicero was at once a lover
of letters and rich enough to express literary approval by substantial gifts. So, the word *diser-*

[1] XLIX: Disertissime Romuli nepotum, etc.

tissime may signify as you please either most skilful in the choice of words or most delicately appreciative in the criticism of anything.

Cicero was really both. It was probably only when the works had survived the man, and become the permanent masterpiece of Latin prose, that the marvel of his literary achievement overshadowed, through the centuries, the other aspects of his astonishing career. He had found his language still somewhat rude; he had made it, whatever his conscious artificialities, exquisitely polished; to its native robustness he had added something as near as ever might be to the lovely subtleties of Greek flexibility. Thus he had produced something different from anything previously in existence, and something which could be admired, reverenced, and imitated wherever men could read and could try to write in Latin—as men did throughout the Middle Ages, and as orthodox Churchmen, to go no further, still do. So, thinking of him as incomparable, we seldom remember that he was bravely trying all his life to do in Latin what had already been done in another language, and that his models in this other language were not the oldest. His oratory has been reiterantly celebrated, through generation after generation, until we are apt to forget that the form of literature which he thus established in Rome, as the earliest of its great literary achievements, was late to develop in Greece. This by itself, and still more when we think of it together with the comedy of Plautus and Terence domesticating at Rome a late phase of Greek poetry, would imply the nature of that Latin literature which in European tradition followed on the primal Greek. Cicero has uninterruptedly

persisted as an acknowledged literary master; it
has been only in comparatively recent times that
we have come to perceive how, despite his ultimate
skill, his historical place in world-literature cannot
help being secondary.

For ages meanwhile he was probably regarded
not chiefly as an orator, legal or political, but as a
philosopher. Dante[1] groups him, in the "philosophic family" clustered about Aristotle, with the
shadowy Greek sages Orpheus and Linus, and with
Seneca "the moralist." His philosophic works,
secondary not only in style but in substance, were
more congenial to the mediæval mind than his
comparatively mundane letters, which almost got
lost. Even if we had lost them, however, and his
orations too, his philosophic works would preserve
the wonder of his Latinity. They would reveal, as
well, the breadth of his culture, the activity of his
mind, the selective power of his intelligence, and
the fundamental earnestness of his character. The
revival of his letters, indeed, is reported somewhat
to have shocked his admirers, not quite prepared
to find him so human. To the letters we must
turn for the man, and the oftener we do so the
more willingly we shall do so again. Tradition, of
which the letters preserve the historic basis, has
made and kept him a great moral philosopher, a
great advocate, and the greatest classical model of
Latin prose.

[1] Inferno, IV, 141.

III

CÆSAR

The parallel Lives of Plutarch sometimes appear oddly or at best artificially mated. In grouping Cicero with Demosthenes, however, he was simply and clearly right. Both were orators unprecedented and unsurpassed in the languages which they moulded to suit themselves; both were alike professional advocates and public men; both were at times what we should now call prime ministers; both tried to defend the ancestral constitutions of their countries from irresistible change; both failed; both met with violent deaths amid the crash of the systems they had hoped to save; and the forces which destroyed both had lately been incarnate in imperial conquerors. With equally simple good sense, Plutarch grouped together the lives of these conquerors, Alexander and Cæsar. The one carried Greek, or Hellenistic empire to a point which for a little while seemed fated to dominate the civilised world; the other brought into final being that Roman Empire whose principles are not yet altogether extinct. We have needed centuries clearly to discern the contrast between the two. So far as we can now perceive, the fleeting empire of Alexander was animated by no deeper ideal than that of overwhelming military force; whatever the purposes of Cæsar himself, the diuturnity of his empire came ultimately to animate it with the ideals of divine sanction and earthly peace.

These ideals, variously persistent through the generations, have made the Cæsar of tradition and of legend grandly unlike anybody who could ever have existed in the flesh. The accident that his empire was mostly Western and controlled Europe has doubtless helped his legend. Amid English ruins you will still find tower after tower traditionally bearing his name; to find the name of Alexander likewise remembered, you must voyage as far as Egypt or India. It was no such trifle as this, however, which once made the German Emperor, William II, reverently salute in the excavated Forum the spot where they declare the body of Cæsar to have been burnt. It was honest, even though men may now generally hold it pitifully mistaken, belief that the great Roman whose visible presence vanished here in smoke and flame was the first apostle of the true duty of sovereignty—to enforce by arms the rule of peace. *Pax Romana* had long endured; *Pax Germanica* should soon rise, the German sovereign planned, newly to embody the spirit of it.

The well-known facts of Cæsar's life have been repeatedly studied. We have no such record of him, however, as reveals the real Cicero in the copious correspondence on which we lately touched; nor indeed much contemporary record beyond his own military reports. He was of the highest social rank, traditionally descended from Iulus the son of Æneas, and thus both from the royal race of Troy and from the goddess Venus. He was also a man of the highest fashion, with all the accomplishments and, if we may believe scandal, with all the private vices which make fashion abhorrent to the uncouth or the godly. He had the gift of fascination, particularly for women; though most of his portraits look rather grim, the profiles re-

veal traces of that aristocratic beauty so evident
in the later members of his family from Augustus
to Nero; and nobody anywhere ever more carelessly contracted and disregarded personal debts.
As a politician he was adroitly unscrupulous; as
a military man he was a genius of the highest
order; and to find another such combination of
military capacity with administrative, Europe had
to wait for Napoleon. Above all, he had the
faculty of perceiving at critical moments just what
could be done, and of doing it with lightning de-
cision and more than lightning exactitude. Here
lies the problem concerning him which can never
be decided. There is an excellent case for declaring him to have mastered the secrets of a confusion
little less than chaotic for every other human
being of his time, and thus deliberately to have
reduced anarchy to order. The case on the other
side is about as good; he may equally well have
been no more than the shrewdest of opportunists,
fortunate enough when only seizing occasion fully
to avail himself of that tide in the affairs of men
which taken at the flood leads on to fortune.

At this point, intentionally or not, such of his
writings as have survived do him good service.
Like Frederick the Great, he dabbled in letters, and
was at his worst as a poet. His verses, however,
and various other pieces of his work have long since
vanished. His military reports are preserved:
seven Books on the Gallic Wars and three on the
Civil Wars which ensued. The merit of these
is emphasised by the chance that supplementary
matter by other hands is generally published with
them; there is an eighth Book on the wars in Gaul,
and there are separate Books about his wars at

Alexandria, in Africa, and in Spain. As literature these appendices are negligible; as literature the authentic work of Cæsar is masterly. With unparalleled simplicity and compactness, with hardly a trace of emotion or partisan feeling, he sets forth what happened, or if you prefer what he chose that people should believe to have happened. His effects are implicitly strengthened by the fact that like Xenophon he writes of himself not in the first person but in the third, as if somebody else were giving a thoroughly competent account of his campaigns. He seldom stirs you, so that his incidental story of how a daring soldier, leaping overboard with the standard, rallied hesitant troops to the invasion of Britain[1] comes with all the force of surprise. From beginning to end, though, he impresses you as a writer who knows exactly what he means to say about a commander who always knew exactly what he meant to do. To this extent, the whole range of literature contains nothing more saturated with the temper of mastery than the Commentaries of Cæsar.

More than probably this effect is deliberate. Though pretending to be only matters of succinct record, these reports were almost unquestionably intended at once to justify him in the opinion of his partisans and if so might be to convince doubters that his course had been right. To do this, he must evidently represent himself as calmly dominant over self, and men and affairs. He does so with such assurance and such confident dignity that you never hesitate to take him at his word. You can hardly help accepting his facts as true; you cannot resist the impression that the

[1] Bell. Gall., IV, 25.

man who states them has something like the colossal impersonality of greatness; you may well find yourself wondering whether the tales of his dissolute youth and his unscrupulous maturity are anything more than echoes of malicious gossip, of partisan denunciation, or of ribald songs chanted by his half-drunken soldiers. Whatever their deliberate purpose, these writings appear unaffectedly genuine. If they really are so, the man who wrote them seems far more likely to have moulded chaos to his will than only to have taken shrewd advantage of whatever happened to occur.

Though no earlier document exactly resembling the Commentaries now exists, it is thought that, like any other masterpiece, they were not unprecedented. The generals of Alexander are known to have written compact professional reports of their own campaigns. If we still had these, the works of Cæsar might more than probably prove to be as faithfully modelled on Greek originals as those of Cicero are, or the comedies of Plautus and of Terence. Here again chance has favoured him. As they stand, his Commentaries appear to us almost as primal as the hexameters of Homer seem. And certainly the temper of them—firm, judicial, masterful, solidly dominant —is magnificently Roman. Hardly any other known works can be found more nearly to justify a secular legend or tradition of which they calmly record the origin.

How various this tradition has been, three aspects of it in European literature may serve to remind us. So far as the person of Cæsar goes, to be sure, Dante gives to him only a line: [1]

[1] Inf., IV, 123.

Cesare armato, con gli occhi grifagni,
(Cæsar in armor, with his falcon eyes,)

appears among those pre-Christian worthies who are doomed eternally hopeless to live in longing. One meaning of Cæsar none the less pervades the Divine Comedy: first of human beings he embodied the supreme ideal of earthly empire, and in the lowest depth of hell his assassins Brutus and Cassius, traitors to God's anointed, suffer the worst tortures of all but one; only Judas Iscariot, traitor to God Incarnate, has sinned more deeply than they. In Shakspere's Julius Cæsar, on the other hand, they live heroic, mistaken if you will and futile in their attempt to turn the course of history, but nevertheless impelled to the deed which involved their fate by hatred of the tyranny already fatal to the wisdom and the dignity of the tyrant. And when the Emperor Napoleon III tried to set forth his ideals of government,—honestly cherished, if we may believe those who knew him best,—he presented Cæsar as the foremost Saviour of Society in all history. Which Cæsar was, or what, nobody can ever be sure. The facts fit all three versions of him, and more. If our concern were with facts, he would remain vastly impenetrable. Yet he would remain, even as a fact, perhaps the greatest of all European humanity. As a tradition he is incontestably so. No man before him and none since rises quite so dominant as he, humanly fallible as you will, but in his sovereignty the supreme traditional incarnation of the ideal of divinely sanctioned Empire.

IV

LUCRETIUS

Cicero and Cæsar, in their several ways the first masterly makers of enduring Latin prose, were not primarily men of letters. The literary eminence of Cæsar, indeed, is almost accidental; and that of Cicero, except for his philosophic treatises, —now generally esteemed less memorable than his orations or his letters,—might perhaps be regarded as incidental to his finally hapless public career. Fairly to estimate even him, we can never neglect the catastrophic history of his times, often best known from the records he made in the whirling days when no one could be sure whither things were bound.   By chance, there have happened to survive from these very times the first enduring Latin poets—Lucretius and Catullus.   Tradition has often forgotten just when they lived.   Classical literature has so long and so generally been studied as a matter of grammar, prosody, and the like, that, unless a classical author happened to figure in history as well as in letters, very competent students of the classics often neglect his historical position.   In this instance the neglect is regrettable; for different as Lucretius and Catullus are they imply together the feelings of artistic, sensitive, passionate natures surrounded by historical catastrophes of which they must be poignantly aware, yet which they can nowise influence or control.

They died within a year or two of each other, while Cæsar's Gallic Wars were at their height, and well before his crossing of the Rubicon.

Though Lucretius was probably some ten years or more the elder, neither could remember an Italy unshaken by civil wars, and both were grown men when Cicero was Consul and Catiline conspired. Ten years later, both were dead. In both, as we shall soon remind ourselves, you feel the full influence of the culture which had come to Rome from the primal civilisation of Greece. Both were none the less Roman. As we have already seen,[1] Catullus addressed Cicero as "Disertissime Romuli nepotum," which may roughly be rendered: "Finest of all the sons of Romulus"; and the opening invocation of the poem of Lucretius begins with the words

Æneadum genetrix, hominum divumque voluptas,
Alma Venus, . . .
(Mother of all who from Æneas spring,
Of men and gods the joy, dear Venus, . . .)[2]

Fourth or Fifth Century Greeks, to be sure, would have known that Æneas was a Trojan prince, but not that Romans claimed descent from him; and to Greeks the names of Romulus and of Venus would have been as unmeaning as those of Adam and Eve would have been to Cicero, or as those of Jimmu and of Daigo are now to Europeans unskilled in Japanese mythology. To both Lucretius and Catullus, however, as their allusions indicate, the native traditions of Rome were no less familiar than the exotic traditions of Greece.

In both of these poets, furthermore, you feel a

[1] *Cf.* p. 197.
[2] C. F. Johnson (1872) translates these words:
   Mother of Romans! joy of men and gods,
   Benignant Venus . . .

note of personal passion unlike anything which we have hitherto met. Here at last is something comparatively modern. Like many men of our own days, they were at once self-conscious, part of a highly complicated and swiftly altering civilisation, so placed that although they could poignantly perceive and feel they were powerless to act, and not only stirred to the depths but bewildered. Both, as Romans of the First Century before Christ, were Roman in sentiment yet veneered with a surface of alien polish. Here their likeness ends. Like so many men of letters nowadays, each felt the same conditions in his own peculiar way. No two men in all literature are much more different from each other.

Little is positively known about either. Somewhere near the year 400 of the Christian Era, to be sure, St. Jerome noted a tradition about Lucretius which has faintly persisted—perhaps because it is agreeable to orthodox Christian opinions of pagan philosophy. According to this legend, renewed in literature by Tennyson's admirable monologue Lucretius, the poet's wife, displeased by his addiction to philosophic speculation, secretly gave him a love-potion which had the unhappy effect of unseating his reason and ended in suicide. Tennyson makes him revolt from slavery to the flesh:

What Roman would be dragged in triumph thus?
Not I; not he, who bears one name with her[1]
Whose death-blow struck the dateless doom of kings
When, brooking not the Tarquin in her veins,
She made her blood in sight of Collatine
And all his peers, flushing the guiltless air,

[1] Lucretia. *Cf.* p. 165.

Spring from the maiden fountain in her heart.
And from it sprang the Commonwealth,[1] which breaks
As I am breaking now.

Without some hovering consciousness of the
breaking Republic, the mood of Lucretius may be
hard to understand; but the moment you grow
aware of the conditions of Rome throughout his
lifetime it seems the only mood rationally imaginable. The conditions of our own times, at the
beginning of the Twentieth Century, too, are very
like those of his. "Even though no single line or
passage of his," I have written elsewhere,[2] "may
quite stir the torpor of our modern habit, his whole
work may well make us tremblingly wonder
whether, after all, his be not the final word. We
need not vex ourselves with scholarly search for
whence he derived the substance of his Epicurean
philosophy; we cannot now linger over the relentless details of his philosophic system, nor yet
dwell on the reasons why, at sundry times between his and ours, he has been neglected or forgotten. What no one who reads him can help
recognising is the still vibrant passion of his mood,
and that quality of it for which I can find no
better name than despair. We men are conscious
beings, in a world of consciousness where we vainly
fancy that, at least for the fleeting while of our
conscious lives, things may somehow come under
our control. Hence comes our vain aspiration,
our vain effort, our hopelessly foredoomed futility
and disenchantment. There is but one course
which can console the wise; it is humbly to recog-

[1] The Latin word *Respublica* (Republic) literally means Commonwealth.
[2] The Ideals of Empire : Harvard Graduates Magazine, June, 1917,
p. 463.

nise that consciousness can truly be no more than passive. In a universe of conscienceless force, resistlessly pursuing its course from none can tell whence to none can tell whither, the acts of men and of nations are only manifestations thereof, as irresponsibly ungovernable as earthquakes or tempests. So, indeed, are the gods themselves, differing from us only in the deathless duration of a consciousness which permits them, like us, to see what only delusion can make either us or them fancy for an instant capable of deflection. Doubtless there are epochs when, for a while, things may seem to be subsiding from chaos into order; there are lifetimes, too, so far from troubled that lucky folks may sometimes pass from cradle to grave happy in the delusion of security. Such days as those when Lucretius lived, however, can afford no such anodynes. Blind force, his reason assured him, had made the gods and the world, fathomless antiquity, the vanished empires of the forgotten past, Homeric Greece and Troy, Persia and the Grecian victories, Rome itself—then at once dominantly imperial and mortally stricken. Men can observe, marvel, even momentarily enjoy if they admit that all the power conceivably theirs lies in the wondrous chance that they possess the power of contemplation. They may not even murmur such words as 'Thy will be done'; for will itself is a delusion. The only fact is force, material, irresistible, unchangeable, everlasting."

The mood here indicated pervades the poem De Rerum Natura (On the Nature of Things), which is both the only extant work of Lucretius, and the only surviving example of the once copious philosophical poetry of antiquity. As we have already reminded ourselves,[1] this form of literature existed among the Greeks; but of its Greek phase only traditions remain and perhaps a few scattered and fragmentary lines. Accepting, if we may believe those who know your philosophy, the atomic theories of the Greek Democritus and the moral principles of the Greek Epicurus, the Roman Lucretius, modelling his didactic hexameters on those of the Sicilian Empedocles, endeavoured to explain the universe in terms which should make tolerable the world-crash of his unhappy and bewildering environment. Far too intricate for detail here, his system is not hard to grasp and in general conception is curiously modern. All life, he holds, all existence comes from mere clash of atoms in void. There is no such thing as immortality. Religion, as men conceive and practise it, is a debasing superstition; he tells, for example, the story of how Agamemnon sacrificed Iphigenia in Aulis, and ends the episode with the line

> Tantum religio potest suadere malorum.[2]
> (Such sins and crimes religion can evoke.)

There are gods, no doubt; but the gods, like the men and the worlds, are powerlessly sentient and contemplative creatures of force and fate, itself blind, invisible, unconscious, inexorable. The tremendous grandeur of irresistible law has never-

---

[1] *Cf.* p. 115.

[2] I, 101. C. F. Johnson translates this line:

> Such and so great are superstition's crimes.

Monroe's literal prose version is "So great the evils to which religion could prompt." Compare these two learned renderings with my untutored one, and you cannot help understanding the original. This is the best way for the unlettered to approach classical texts—by harnessing a team of ponies.

theless a consoling splendour. Submit; grant that effort can avail nothing, that struggle is useless, and presently you shall find in wondering submission to the wonders of eternity a vast surcease of the pain inherent in contradiction and rebellion. In understanding lies the secret of salvation.

Despairing if you will, the fervour with which Lucretius writes—a fervour excellently imitated in the poem about him by Tennyson—grows contagious. He has one priceless poetic gift: he can command sympathy. His power of observation, too, is amazingly sensitive; and his power of intensely emotional statement is all his own. He makes quiveringly alive what from any one else might well have dried into a process of pitilessly sincere reasoning. On general principles, a philosophic poem is at best respectably dull. The poem of Lucretius, if you will read it without pausing to scrutinise or to criticise, may now and again prove absorbing. In itself, this is an artistic miracle.

He left it unfinished. It ends abruptly, in the midst of a long passage based on the terrible description of the Plague at Athens in the Second Book of Thucydides.[1] Cicero, they say, had something to do with preparing the swift, rough, palpitating hexameters for publication. If so, he had the tact to leave them individual and not to polish them into a grace which, whatever its merit, could never have been Lucretian. For something other than grace, and greater, was needful to set forth what the breaking of the Commonwealth meant to a great spirit who greatly cherished the great traditions of ancestral Rome.

[1] *Cf.* p. 83.

V

CATULLUS

In spite of its passion and its power, such philosophic poetry as that of Lucretius could never have been popular. To enter into sympathy with it demands harder thinking than every-day people enjoy. With Catullus, the other great poet who survives from the last days of the Roman Republic, the case is different. His passion seems genuine, his artistic sense is exquisite, and both are devoted, at least in his best work, to the deliberate setting forth of what appear to be his own personal emotions. This self-revelation, this implicit autobiography, is at once permanently human in its appeal and consonant with the literary mood of Europe during the past two or three centuries. Compared with any one on whom we have as yet touched, he therefore seems much more like the men we have known and lived with.

Though those who care for his work thus come to know him, as it were, with a feeling of intimacy, they know little about him. He seems to have belonged to a respectable family at Verona, or somewhere near there; and so to have been a Roman citizen of the kind whose political rights were granted only after the Social War. As a class these newly acknowledged citizens were probably more proud of their dignity and more instinctively patriotic than the habitual inhabitants of Rome; they were also probably disposed to idealise, as the secular home of Roman traditions, the mother city of the Republic. Catullus is thought to have come to Rome, with good intro-

ductions, at the age of twenty or so, and to have
been at first dazzled and later disenchanted by the
brilliant and corrupt society he found there.   He
appears never to have studied in Greece or Egypt,
but at one time to have travelled rather extensively
in Greek regions, thus resembling a modern youth
of good condition who has replaced university
training by observing foreign civilisation for himself.   At thirty or so, he retired for a while to his
pleasant native regions, where he is said to have
died prematurely.

His extant work consists of one hundred and
sixteen lyric poems, widely different in length and
in character, and arranged in no evident order.
The first of them, however, dedicating the little
book to his fellow countryman Cornelius Nepos, a
man of letters whose social graces appear to have
exceeded his artistic gifts—at least so far as his
writings are preserved—indicates that this confusion may have been chosen by Catullus himself.
Throughout he imitates or adapts, with a fresh
felicity of his own, the lyric forms of the Greeks,
implying a knowledge not only of the primal Greek
lyric poetry but also of the fastidious and prettily
overwrought parodies of it which were fashionable in Ptolemaic Alexandria; some of his work is
known to have been modelled on what were then
held the masterpieces of Callimachus.   For two
reasons he thus became exceptionally important
in the tradition of European literature: with
strong individuality, he made excellently Latin a
number of literary forms hitherto excellent only
in the original Greek; and the accident that the
Greek language was long forgotten throughout
Western Europe, while knowledge of Latin has
always persisted there, has kept him throughout

the centuries not only a name but a fact. Secondary, like all Romans, in his relation to the Greeks, he has been in his relation to posterity almost primal; for no earlier Latin writer of lyric poetry came anywhere near him, and in some respects no later lyric poet in any European language has ever surpassed him.

His influence, for example, is evident at various times in the poems which now and again have survived from among those perennially made for weddings. His two or three elaborate works of this kind, probably if not certainly modelled on Greek originals, have a grace and a charm which has recurrently appealed to later writers with similar tasks before them; and beyond any of his admirers and imitators he has managed to suffuse them with what seems genuine as distinguished from conventional feeling. He can be approached but hardly surpassed. And something like this is true of much else among the various things that he wrote. One might thus study him long. In the end, however, approach him as you will, the poems most clearly characteristic of him, as well as most certain and most unfailing in their appeal, are those which record what seems to be the story of his personal affections.

Scattered through the present order or disorder of his collected works, these, which number something like a fifth of the whole though nowhere near a fifth of his lines, may be so arranged as to tell a fairly consecutive story. They concern a mistress whom he conventionally calls Lesbia. She is thought really to have been Clodia, a woman denounced in one of Cicero's orations as equally conspicuous for rank, for accomplishments, for unscrupulousness, and for profligacy; this lady was a sister of the Clodius whose escapades with certain celebrants of female mysteries led to the divorce of Cæsar, and to the traditional saying that Cæsar's wife must be above suspicion. So far as one can make out, Catullus, coming to Rome young, enthusiastic, and disposed to idealise everything Roman, was completely fascinated by this Clodia or Lesbia; and when she smiled on him, beyond his wildest hopes, fancied that their love was mutual. Nothing could long disguise from him the fact that he was only one of numberless admirers to whom now and again, when so disposed, she carelessly accorded her capricious and frequent favours. To follow and to reconstruct the story in detail is beyond our scope now. Some notion of it may be derived from the three poems concerning her which are now most nearly familiar. The first two—the second and third in his collected works—concern Lesbia's pet sparrow: one tells how prettily she plays with the bird, the other laments the grief brought her by the bird's untimely death; and if literature contains a daintier poem than either, it is yet to be discovered. The third poem is only a single elegiac couplet, made when he had come to understand what manner of woman Lesbia was; in his collected works it is the eighty-fifth:

Odi et amo. Quare id faciam fortasse requiris.
    Nescio, sed fieri sentio et excrucior.
(I hate and I love. Why I do such a thing perhaps you
    may wonder.
    I know not, but that I do I feel and in torture writhe.)[1]

---

[1] Theodore Martin (1861) translates this couplet thus:
    I hate and love—wherefore I cannot tell,
    But by my tortures know the fact too well.

No translation can begin to convey the searing scorch of that burning Latin simplicity. *Excrucior* literally refers to the agonies of crucifixion, not yet sanctified by the history of Christianity. Conflicting and intermingling love and detestation, over which the victim has no manner of power, are like the nails that fasten hands and feet to the cross. And the lightness of the ten words which come between the first three and the last makes the climax the more tremendous.

He can be horribly obscene, no doubt; but to remember this any healthy mind must recall the ugly passages which sink from memory beside those where he sets forth his tenderness, his sensitiveness, and his suffering. And in one of his most unspeakable depths he bids us call to mind that if a poet himself be chaste there is no need that his lines be. Whatever you think of this morality, it has been more or less practised throughout the history of literature. Catullus very likely echoed it from some Greek, perhaps known to the curious, just as, when Herrick wrote at the end of his Hesperides, under King Charles I,

Jocund his muse was, but his life was chaste,

he almost translated Catullus. And anyhow the conventions of classical antiquity permitted a range of utterance by no means agreeable to the still somewhat Victorian prejudice of those who read English. Decency, after all, is a question of manners or fashion; an innocent dancing-school waltz would have shocked the most cynical Roman who ever surfeited himself at an orgy. Emotion, on the other hand, is coeval with humanity; that

of Catullus appears to be genuine. Whether it
actually is or not may of course be disputed. Again
and again, throughout literature, you will find
poems which may be taken either as passionate
statements of tremendous love-affairs or as ingenious pieces of half-dramatic imagination. You can
never make quite sure which is which; only, some
make you believe in them and others do not. From
the time of Rousseau to the present day confession
has been in much literary favour; a good deal of
Byron's popularity depended on it, for example,
and, to go no further, so does the appeal made by
Mrs. Browning's Love Sonnets from the Portuguese. This is one reason why the reckless self-
revelation of Catullus—the first enduring example
of such a mood in European literature, for surviving Greek lyrics of the kind are either fragmentary or artificial,—seems now so strangely
modern. Whatever he really was, he must always
appear to be poignantly individual.

In a very different way, the passion of Lucretius
is equally poignant. Not self-revealing, it is almost
as self-conscious. These poets were contemporary,
and contemporary with Cicero and Cæsar. If it
is possible to generalise the mood excited in sensitive spirits by the crash of the Republic, and the
spectre of world-chaos—terribly like what has
happened about ourselves since 1914—we may
perhaps call it an intensely personal sense of that
eternal conflict between man and his environment
which was so grandly and so objectively set forth
in general terms by the tragic poets of Fifth Century Greece.[1]

[1] *Cf.* p. 56.

Cicero and Cæsar, Lucretius and Catullus are the four great names of Roman literary tradition between the beginning of the First Century before Christ and the final establishment of the Roman Empire. There were other writers during the last half-century of the Republic; but in general we may consider them either as virtually negligible, like Cornelius Nepos, or as substantially lost, like Terentius Varro, whose Menippean Satires exist hardly more than in name. The only secondary Latin author of this period whom we cannot quite neglect here is Sallust. His two surviving monographs—one about Catiline, the other about Jugurtha—are at once the first examples we possess of serious historical writing in Latin, and implicitly indicate the persistence through those crashing years of characters neither so dominantly active as Cicero or Cæsar nor so passionately sensitive as their contemporary poets.

The personal history of Sallust, so far as it is known, is creditable only to his practical intelligence. A man of obscure origin and unprincipled ability, he managed, by taking the democratic side and denouncing the vices of the decadent aristocrats, to bring himself ultimately into a position where he could comfortably and safely emulate and surpass them. He had the tact, or the luck, to attach himself to the fortunes of Cæsar. Favoured by Cæsar, he so enriched himself with the spoils of African provinces that the splendour of his Roman villa—the Gardens of Sallust—has never been quite forgotten by legend; and here, while Antony and Octavian, not yet Augustus, were plotting and struggling for mastery of the world, he passed his later years in magnificent and luxurious literary leisure.

The most considerable fruits of this were five Books of Histories, believed to have been concerned with what happened throughout the Roman dominions during the years which ensued on the death of Sylla. Of these only fragments remain. His monographs on the conspiracy of Catiline, however, and on the African wars with Jugurtha some fifty years earlier, are preserved intact. In manner and in temper they are curiously unlike what we know of the self-seeking and self-made millionaire who wrote them. It is generally agreed that he modelled his literary methods on those of Thucydides. First among the Romans, accordingly, he wrote history as if it were not so much a mere record of fact as a sound basis for reflection and reasoning. Himself a partisan, he more than probably gave a partisan turn to his work, intending rather that his readers should think with him than that they should think rightly. Like Thucydides, however, he had the art—or perhaps better he learned from Thucydides the art—of seeming to write dispassionately. In consequence, when you read his clear though never quite great narrative, you find yourself quietly disposed to believe what he says, and never either excited or repelled by the intensity of his partisan feeling. He can deal with actualities as if he stood grandly aloof from them— which is perhaps the most subtle method of leading the doubtful unwittingly to agree with you. So his Catiline and his Jugurtha, who lived and plotted and fought and died, have been throughout the centuries the Catiline and the Jugurtha of European tradition.

To complete our impression of the period of Cicero and of Cæsar, this glance at their more prudent and fortunate contemporary has appeared worth while. To linger over him, however, after he has duly reminded us that supple skins can be kept intact even amid world-chaos, would be unduly to emphasise a matter not of the first importance in such a scheme as ours. And matters of the first importance are close at hand. For, if the commonly accepted dates be true, Virgil had begun to write some years before Sallust comfortably died.

VII

VIRGIL

Though Virgil was only thirty years younger than Cæsar, he belongs not only to another generation but to another world. Born when the fate of Rome seemed still in the balance, he had the fortune to pass his mature years amid the full security of Augustan promise. Ardently sympathising with the new and more serene spirit of this time, he expressed it first and best. During life he was recognised not only as the most excellent exponent of its ideals but as the longed-for master who had finally achieved the miracle of making the poetry of Rome rival, if not surpass, that of Greece. From his own day to ours the tradition thus begun has never lapsed. Though it has greatly varied and fluctuated, it has always been familiar. Meanings he could never have dreamt of have been read into his lines; he has been enveloped in clouds of superstition; he has been dissected by generation after generation of often ignorant grammarians and schoolmasters; during the Eighteenth and Nineteenth Centuries his right to eminence has been disputed, particularly by the stupid erudition of German scholars; but there has never been a time when his works themselves have not been known to every human being who has seriously studied the literature of Europe. Thus, if only thus, he would be unique.

The history of this unique diuturnity has been admirably, if somewhat dryly, summarised in Comparetti's Virgil in the Middle Ages, which traces it not only as it persisted throughout what has pretended to be literature and scholarship, but also as it took the form of fantastic popular legend, transforming the most eminent of Augustan poets into the most potent of antique enchanters. Fairly trustworthy historic facts go far to account for both phases of tradition.

Virgil, son of a well-to-do farmer somewhere near Mantua, was born there in the year 70, a time when the still recently conferred rights of Roman citizenship must generally have inspired something like enthusiastic Roman patriotism. He grew up in this pleasant Italian country, itself a part of the provinces assigned by the first Triumvirate to Julius Cæsar; and as he approached maturity Cæsar was his virtual and beneficent sovereign. He was sent to school for a while at Milan, and later studied under the best teachers at Rome. Never robust, and said to have been shy and amiably awkward, he seems to have returned to his native region, and there to have devoted himself to literary work. What must have appeared a great misfortune, when he was approaching the age of thirty, proved to be the making of him. During the subsident confusion which ensued on the battle of Philippi, the lands of his family were seized, for distribution among the disbanded soldiers of the second Triumvirate. To secure restitution, if he could, he went back to Rome. There his literary power was recognised. He became a friend of Octavian, soon to be Augustus Cæsar; a friend, as well, of Mæcenas, the most generous patron of Augustan letters; of Horace, too, a little later, and of whoever else came to distinction in the culture of the finally growing Empire. There can be little question either that he was personally lovable or that amid general social license his character was remarkable for simplicity and purity. The rest of his life passed prosperously, partly at Rome and more amid the wondrous landscapes about Naples. He lived through the first ten years or so of Augustan empire. Dying in the year 19, at the age of fifty-one, he escaped even premonition of its decline. He knew and he loved all Italy, from the Alps to the Sicilian sea. He saw it growing to be the centre of earthly peace, established and sustained by the newly conscious imperial power of Rome. And his three great works crescently and sincerely celebrate its limitless promise.

One aspect of all three works deserves our attention before we turn to them separately. Though by Virgil's time the dominion of Rome vastly exceeded anything in the earlier history of Europe, the culture of Rome remained, as indeed it always remained, to a considerable degree exotic. In literature the primal achievements of Greece, already matters of an auroral and early clouded past, appeared—as they are—unsurpassed and unsurpassable. So the conscious effort of the Romans had been to produce, in their own language, something which might vie with them. Well before this effort began, the Greek classics were no longer living and contemporary things; but rather the reverend subjects of industrious but pedantic Alexandrian scholarship. Two phases of our own ancestral literature are here similar. The effort of Elizabethan Englishmen to rival the literatures of continental Europe and that of Americans after the Revolution to rival the literature of England were impelled by motives very like that which impelled Romans to rival the literature of Greece. In all three cases, the patriotic fervour of the effort led to expressions distinctly different—and in the case of Elizabethan England magnificently and independently different—from anything earlier; but neither literature in America, nor the literature of the Elizabethans, nor the literature of Rome could ever have existed without earlier and alien models and standards. In the Second Century before Christ, as we have already seen, Latin writers had brought comedy to a point fairly to be held excellent; but so far as extant works go they had achieved no such success in other fields. During the first sixty years of the First Century, however, the work of Cicero had produced masterpieces of oratorical, philosophic, and epistolary Latin prose; that of Lucretius had produced a Latin masterpiece of philosophic poetry; that of Catullus had produced beautiful Latin lyrics; and that of Cæsar and of Sallust had brought historical Latin prose at least to the point of dignity. There remained, the more evidently, three conspicuous phases of Greek literature still unapproached in Latin. These were the latest, and at Alexandria probably the most widely acceptable at the time,—the Idyls of Theocritus,—and the two earliest—the didactic hexameters of Hesiod and the epic hexameters of Homer. It was Virgil's happy lot to establish something like all three in the lasting literature of Rome.

The first of his three great works, the Bucolics or Eclogues, consists of ten short poems in hexameter verse, comprising altogether less than 850 lines. They appear to have been begun at the time when he had returned from Rome to his native province, and to have been finished, revised, and published after what seemed misfortune had brought him to Rome again. If we may trust those who know their classics best, hardly anything could be more seemingly imitative than most of these pastoral verses. Though not sustained or literal translations they are such excellent parodies of Theocritus as could have been made only by one saturated both with the text and with the spirit of the fashionable poet most admired by Ptolemaic Alexandria. They generally profess to deal with shepherds or the like—simple country folk—who give utterance to exquisitely polished verse. Their first apparent difference from their models is that they seem even more deliberately artificial. Theocritus had really known the countryside of Sicily; and some vestiges of its human life here and there underlie the prettily fantastic graces with which he set it forth to please the

courtiers of the Ptolemies. Though Virgil really
knew the countryside of Italy, you would never
imagine this from his beribboned shepherds, modelled only on the already make-believe creatures
of Theocritan fancy. It is not always easy, indeed, quite to understand why such conspicuous
make-believes should both have appealed to the
taste of their own time and have had recurrent
and often profound influence on European literatures at later periods.

That they have done so, however, there can be
no question; and perhaps the most obvious phase
of their influence was originally almost if not quite
a novelty. The country-folk of Theocritus were
elaborately and prettily conventionalised, no
doubt, but that was about all. The country-folk of
Virgil now and again symbolise or refer to real people and events of his time; and these come nearer
the "old Algrind" of Spenser—an evident anagram
for Archbishop Grindal—or his lament for Sir
Philip Sidney under the guise of Astrophel, or his
presentation of himself as Colin Clout and of Sir
Walter Raleigh as the Shepherd of the Ocean, than
they come to much of anything in the original
Greek. Here Virgil showed something like originality; at least he turned pastoral poetry into a
channel which it was to cut long and deep, among
other ways through the Lycidas of Milton to the
Adonais of Shelley.

Another difference which distinguishes them from
their originals in Theocritus is consentingly recognised by almost all who have studied them carefully; though the Virgilian shepherds are utterly unlike any imaginable peasants, the places where they
live and sing are not only real but really Italian.

The backgrounds of Theocritus have no such definite character as you will feel when from the wide-branching beech-tree of Virgil's first line onward, you discover his fantastic personages to merge in settings conceivable only by one who had always known and loved the landscapes even still perhaps the most gracious in Europe. And in his day, these were Roman, and Rome was on the verge of acknowledged empire. Thus Rome was the more ready to recognise and to welcome Virgil's merit. For more than two centuries before his time, there had been brave attempts to make Latin hexameters which should rival those of Greece; and these had resulted in countless noble lines and in many noble poems. Until the gentle and exquisite grace of his verses appeared, however, there was little which could be held final. Here, at last, was a studied but superbly mastered beauty of expression hitherto unapproached in Latin and never surpassed. It could not have the fresh vigour of the primal Greek; but it could give a kind of delight not quite to be found in any primality. Fifteen centuries later something like it was again to illuminate Italy, when the aspirations of primitive painting culminated in the conscious and serene mastery of Raphael.

Among the Eclogues is one to which the course of history gave accidental but great traditional importance. The Fourth of the ten, containing only sixty-three lines, and commonly called by the name of Pollio, a friend and patron of Virgil in Northern Italy and Consul in the year 40, is not a pastoral dialogue but a celebration of the hope for the whole future world to be expected from a man-child not yet born. Whom it may actually have concerned can never be decided— some think this to be a child of Pollio, some a child of Octavian, some Octavian himself duly conventionalised as the coming incarnation of Empire. The coincidence of its date with the birth of Christ, however,—in the perspective of a few centuries forty years are not long,—combined with the obscure yet radiant glory of its prophetic promise, and with some of the terms by which this was set forth, to make centuries of early Christianity accept it as an unconsciously inspired Christian prophecy. The lines

> Jam redit et Virgo, redeunt Saturnia regna;
> Jam nova progenies cælo demittitur alto,[1]

for example, doubtless refer either to the return to earth of the inviolate goddess Justice, or conceivably to the Zodiacal sign under which the coming child was expected to make his appearance; but to many moods of historical Christianity they appeared almost literally to foretell the maiden motherhood of Mary. Thus the first published work of Virgil gave him not only classical eminence but a place, with the Sibyls, in the traditions of Christian Europe.

The Bucolics are commonly attributed to the years 41 to 39, during which Virgil passed the age of thirty. He is thought to have been just about forty years old when his next important work, the Georgics, was finished. As it contains, in its four books, less than 2,200 lines, his methods of poetic composition were evidently deliberate. The

---

[1] Lines 6-7:   Once more the Virgin comes and Saturn's reign;
Behold a heaven-born offspring earthward hies.
(Tr. T. C. Williams: Boston: 1915.)

origin of this poem appears to have been to some
degree political or social. Roughly speaking, the
ten years or so when it was coming into existence
began with the battle of Philippi, which finally
defeated the murderers of Julius Cæsar, and ended
with the battle of Actium, which finally established
the power of Augustus. After something like a
century of civil wars, vexing all Italy with recurrent devastation and confusion, there was both
need and longing for peace and order; and no
single feature of such prospect was more desirable
than renewed interest in peaceful agriculture, the
necessary basis of all social prosperity anywhere
throughout history. With this in view, Mæcenas
is said to have suggested to Virgil the subject
which should at once direct attention to this public need and enrich Latin literature with a work
such as might rival or replace the Works and
Days of the Greek Hesiod. By a pleasant chance,
our most nearly life-like contemporary account of
Virgil, and of his daily surroundings, belongs to
just about this period. The Fifth Satire of the
First Book of Horace, thought to be closely modelled on a similar work of Lucilius about a century
older, describes with much detail, and pleasant
lightness of touch, a journey made by Mæcenas,
in company with Virgil, Horace, and other friends,
from Rome to Brundusium, now Brindisi, probably at a time when the disputes between Octavian
and Antony demanded the presence there of the
distinguished man who was not only the chief
patron of Roman letters, but also the most trusted
political adviser of Augustus. And somehow the
trivial line[1]

Lusum it Mæcenas, dormitum ego Virgiliusque,

[1] Horace, Sat. I, v, 48.

which says only that at the end of a tiresome stage
of the journey Mæcenas refreshed himself by something like a game of tennis, while Virgil and Horace
preferred a nap, tells more of them, and of their
mutual relations, than volumes of comment.   Virgil is said to have introduced Horace to Mæcenas,
who was evidently a good friend as well as a patron to both.   In circumstances like these the
Georgics were slowly and conscientiously written.

They could not have been written without
Hesiod as an antique and reverend model.   They
could not have been written, either, without full
knowledge both of the learning and of the conscious literary graces of Hellenistic Alexandria.
More deeply still, however, they could not have
been written except by one who had always and
familiarly known the daily life of Italian country-
folk—the skies above them, their hills and fields,
their crops and their vines and their olives, their
flocks and herds, their horses and their cattle, and
the bees on which all antiquity depended for what
it knew of sweetness.   For all the studied polish
of the lines, too, these poems could not have been
written without sincere belief both in the rustic
enthusiasm which pervades them and in the beneficent promise of what was soon to be Augustan
Empire.   The famous passage beginning "O for-
tunatos nimium"[1] rings true, as it celebrates the
happy lot of husbandmen:

> Oh, more than blest, if their true bliss they know,
> Are tillers of the land! whose sustenance
> From civil faction far, the righteous earth
> Ungrudgingly bestows

[1] Georgics, II, 458 *seq.*

are the words with which Theodore Williams[1] renders the first three lines of it. They sound conventional, no doubt, but as you come to know them, they prove genuine. So does the closing passage of the whole work,[2] which Williams translates as follows:

> Thus have I made my songs of well-kept farms,
> Of flocks withal and trees, while Cæsar's power
> Was launching the vast thunder of his war
> Over the deep Euphrates, publishing
> By conquest his supreme and just decrees
> Unto the grateful nations, taking so
> His pathway to the gods.[3] The selfsame days
> I, Virgil, passed in sweet Parthenope[4]
> Busied and blest in unrenowned repose,
> I that erewhile, when youthful blood was bold
> Played with the shepherd's muse and made my song
> Of Tityrus beneath the beech-tree's shade.

The manner in which the last line of the Georgics,

> Tityre, te patulæ cecini sub tegmine fagi,[5]

echoes the first line of the Bucolics,

> Tityre, tu patulae recubans sub tegmine fagi,[6]

deliberately and rightly brings the two works together. Throughout the Bucolics, as we have seen, the backgrounds are apt to be the real landscapes of Italy; but the figures who flit before them are Theocritan and sometimes symbolic

---

[1] Boston, 1915, p. 64.   [2] Georgics, IV, 558–565: Williams, p. 121.
[3] A somewhat excessive allusion to the progress of Octavian, after the battle of Actium, through Eastern provinces formerly subject to Antony.
[4] Naples.
[5] Literally, "Tityrus, thee I sang beneath the wide-spreading beech."
[6] Literally, "Tityrus, thou who liest beneath the wide-spreading beech."

conventions or fantasies.   In the Georgics all this
is strengthened into something like larger truth.
The country-folk are real farmers or herdsmen,
never individualised, but skilled in their daily and
yearly tasks almost as they may be seen to this
day.   The growth in strength, however, is a true
growth, and not a change of spirit.   To both
works, alike and together, might still be prefixed
the three lines which Addison chose in 1701 as
the text from which to preach his fulsome Letter
from Italy:

> Salve magna parens frugum, Saturnia tellus,
> Magna virûm! tibi res antiquæ laudis et artis
> Aggredior, sanctos ausus recludere fontes.[1]

And when both works were complete, Italy as
well as Augustan promise was finally safe in lasting literature.   Addison's protest seems sincere
that, if he had the power,

> Unnumbered beauties in my verse should shine,
> And Virgil's Italy should yield to mine![2]

Virgil's Italy, indeed, was as present to Addison
as Byron's was to Nineteenth Century travellers.
It is quite imaginable, too, that the Bucolics and
the Georgics may have stirred Romans tired of
civil wars, much as Childe Harold stirred Englishmen ready to waken from the pre-revolutionary
torpidities of the Eighteenth Century.   But times
change and we human beings with them.   In a

---

[1] Georgics II, 173–175.   Williams (p. 53) renders the passage thus:

> Hail, O Saturn's land,
> Mother of all good fruits and harvests fair,
> Mother of men!   I for thy noble sake
> Attempt these old and famous themes and dare
> Unseal an age-long venerated spring
> (And uplift Hesiod's song o'er Roman towers.)

[2] Letter from Italy, 53–54.

single century Childe Harold has quickly passed
from its original warmth of true popular appeal to
the chilly recesses of literary history; and in the
course of twenty centuries such artificial conventions as those of pastoral poetry and such primal
devices as would set forth didactic purpose in poetic
terms have mostly meant little to human beings, as
distinguished from scholars, fantastics, or pedants.
We can study them, we can admire them as much
as we choose; but without considerable effort of
historical imagination we cannot sympathetically
understand how anybody could ever have enthusiastically enjoyed them. So, if Virgil's work had
stopped here, he would have remained a beautifully sincere celebrant of Italy and of the imperial
policies of Julius and Augustus Cæsar; he would
have proved himself, too, the faultless master of
Latin style who could at last make the studied
grace of Latin hexameters rival by reason of its
very differences the vigour and splendour of the
primal Greek. Thus his place in European literature would have been secure; but it could never
have been thought comparable with that of Homer,
or of the tragic poets of Fifth Century Athens.
Eminence like theirs belongs only to the few who
can tell, epically or dramatically, what seems to
"that willing suspension of disbelief for the moment which constitutes poetic faith,"[1] a genuine
human story. How true this is anybody can remind himself by merely thinking of Virgil now.
Everybody knows, in a general way, that he wrote
the Bucolics and the Georgics; but everybody
remembers first that he wrote the Æneid.

If we may trust the accepted story, this last of
his works has survived against his expressed will.

---

[1] This definition occurs somewhere in Coleridge; I forget just where.

When he had finished the Georgics, he is said soon to have begun the more ambitious poem avowedly intended not only to supplant the older Latin epics, of which the most important was the now long-lost Annals of Ennius, but also to set forth the spirit of Roman nationality, at last become Augustan Empire, in terms comparable with the primal and unrivalled epics of Homer. To this task he gave his last ten years or so. His rather sudden death, at the age of fifty-one, left it incomplete; though he had both planned and written it from beginning to end, he had not harmonised all its details, and he was dissatisfied, as indeed he might probably always have remained, with what his fastidious taste held many crudities of detail. He therefore left instructions that the work should be destroyed. These were disregarded; in spite of them it was posthumously published; and from the time of its appearance it has stayed what it is and will permanently be— the European masterpiece of deliberate as distinguished from spontaneous poetry.

Not only for its own sake but because through nearly two thousand years it has been more or less intimately known to every subsequent writer whose work survives in the literature of Europe, the Æneid should be read by all who care for our literary traditions.[1] This is no formidable task, for it contains in all less than 10,000 lines, against the more than 15,000 of the Iliad, and the more than 12,000 of the Odyssey. Thus considerably shorter than either of its original models, it obviously challenges comparison with

[1] To my mind, the blank-verse translation by T. C. Williams (Boston, 1908) more nearly approaches Virgilian effect than any other as yet made in English.

both. The first six of its twelve Books relate the adventures of Æneas on his wide-wandering voyage from sacked Troy to the shores of Italy, where Roman Empire was destined to spring from his descendants; these Books, sometimes in detail, resemble the Odyssey—Æneas, to take a single and obvious example, gives a long account of his past adventures to Dido just as Odysseus gives one to Alcinous. The last six Books of the Æneid, which tell how, once arrived in Italy, Æneas is compelled to establish his foothold there by force of arms, similarly resemble the Iliad with its surging battles and divine comminglings in the fray. The moment you begin to compare the Æneid with its originals, however, certain clear differences will instantly appear.

For one thing, as we reminded ourselves when we touched on Homer, the Iliad and the Odyssey, independent of each other, relate only episodes in the long story of the Trojan War; while the Æneid, conceived and composed as a whole, completely tells the traditional story of how fugitives from conquered Troy came to where in the fulness of time their descendants were to become the final conquerors of Greece. For another, the grand impersonality of Homer makes his noble, swift, simple lines seem like a contemporary account of the matters they set forth; and the very first words of the Æneid—

Arma virumque cano, Trojæ qui primus ab oris
Italiam, fato profugus, Lavinaque venit
Litora[1]—

[1] Arms and the man I sing, who first made way,
Predestined exile, from the Trojan shore
To Italy, the blest Lavinian strand.
—Tr. Williams.

distinctly assume, with their frank use of the first person singular, the point of view of Augustan Rome, where the poet is to tell of a legendary past, seen throughout from a remote, hard-won, and magnificent present. Homer writes heroically; Virgil writes of heroes and of heroic deeds, conscious of what had sprung from them throughout intervening ages. Again, the most salient feature of Homeric style is a grand simplicity, conscious —if conscious at all—only of how words should express meaning; and the style of Virgil is not only deliberately ingenious but full of such elaborate and imitative refinements as could have been devised only by a poet profoundly learned and admiringly familiar with the whole range of Greek expression from the original epics to the graces and affectations of Alexandrian fashion. Thus, though Virgil went far to fix poetic idiom from his time to ours, he can hardly have seemed to his contemporaries more nearly idiomatic in Latin than Milton seems to men who think in vernacular English. For all their obvious differences, indeed, the most nearly analogous poem to the Æneid in European literature is probably the Paradise Lost.

Both tell anew, and each in its way finally, stories which had long been immemorially familiar. Both imply in their writers the most extensive culture of their times. Both are intended to celebrate causes in which the writers passionately believed. In this aspect, the most obvious difference between them lies in the fact that when Milton dictated his lines the cause of the Puritans was politically lost, and that when Virgil made his lines the cause of Roman Empire stayed radiant with promise. The legendary founding of the eternal

city was believed to have occurred more than
seven hundred years before; some five centuries
had already passed since the Republic had supplanted the still traditionally detested system of
Roman royalty; fluctuating but never desperate
in fortune, the power of republican Rome had
gradually come to dominate the then civilised
world, and in the same year, already a century
past, had conquered what was left both of Greece
and of Carthage; at last, the spirit of Cæsar and
of Augustus had breathed a new soul into what
had sometimes appeared the dying body of the
Commonwealth. The closing of the Temple of
Janus, after the settlement of the East, had sym-
bolically proclaimed world-wide peace.[1] All this
was in the patriotic mind of Virgil when he set
himself the happy task of proclaiming for all time
what through centuries was to remain the acknowledged ideal of Empire.

How he probably came to choose his precise
subject, and how the legendary story of Æneas
had taken form through the centuries, has been
admirably summarised in Professor Nettleship's
compact monograph on Virgil.[2] By Virgil's time
Roman tradition had long held that the origin of
Rome could be traced to the Trojan hero whose
posterity had been destined to overcome the descendants of the victorious Greeks. And the
course of history might be held to justify this final
conquest. Nothing could ever deprive Greece of
her primality, no doubt; nothing need ever ob-

[1] *Cf.* Æneid, I, 289; VIII, 714.
[2] Classical Writers, ed. J. R. Green, 1880. The preface is dated August,
1879. The chief fault to find with this little book is that it spells Virgil
with an *e*—which is doubtless as correct classically as it is traditionally
abominable.

scure her literature, her art, her philosophy, her
scholarship, the permanent sources and frequent
inspirations of the culture both of Rome and of
what, mostly through Rome, was to be all subsequent Europe. If the higher life of Rome thus
owed so much to Greece, however, this was by no
means all. For generation after generation Greece
had been declining from her Fifth Century culmina-
tion; her decline had bred in her luxury and corruption, physical and moral; these had influenced
Rome for the worse, as surely as the nobler phases
of Greece had influenced Rome for the better; to
counteract them there was need to revive the antique manliness peculiar to Rome herself. Roman
virtue had made and sustained the Republic; it
had ripened into the serene ideal of peaceful Empire; and it had sprung not from momentarily
dominant Greece but from the chief heroic enemy
of Greece—Troy, still living in the spirit. A later
story had already intermingled with the legend of
Æneas that of the Carthaginian Dido, thus giving
antique basis to the pitiless history of the Punic
Wars. Broadly speaking, Virgil no more invented
the substance of his Æneid than he created his
frequent borrowed lines or phrases, his antiquarian
and other learning, his Roman patriotism or the
metrical structure of his hexameter lines. His peculiar task was to fuse these and more in a work
which his pervasive spirit was to make his own—
much as, sixteen hundred years later, Shakspere
brought into world-literature story after story
ready for the purpose.

Like Shakspere, however, and all other masters,
Virgil was strongly individual. To define his individuality, not so sympathetic during the past

century as it has generally proved, is hopelessly
beyond our power now. To feel it one need only
read him, even in translation; and if one have not
time or patience for all twelve Books of the Æneid
one may perhaps feel it most instantly in the First
and the Fourth of them, which mingle Homeric
memories, the humanity of Euripides, the somewhat sentimental refinement of Alexandrian epics
and profoundly Roman feeling in the tragic story
of Dido. For more than one reason, however, the
Sixth Book of the Æneid is more suitable to our
present purpose. Compactly complete and mov-
ing toward a superb climax of Augustan ideal, it
instantly suggests comparison with its obvious
model, the Eleventh Book of the Odyssey; and,
as we have already reminded ourselves, it stands
in European literature midway between that first
panoramic vision of the dead and the Divine
Comedy of Dante.

At this point, indeed, it is well worth while in
any event, to read the Eleventh Book of the Odyssey again; there are only 640 lines. Turning back
to it now, you will probably feel more deeply
than before its matchless freshness, the noble simplicity of its swift and unconscious conception and
expression, the measureless antiquity of Greek
tradition which it assumes, but above all its own
comparative antiquity. Living though they seem
by themselves, these west-bound voyagers on
windy and trackless seas belong to another and
an indefinitely earlier world than we have had in
mind ever since we first touched on the literature,
Greek or Latin, of historic times. When, beyond
the stream of Ocean they come to the dim shores
where the shadows of the dead can emerge, the

sacrifices they make resemble those of savages.
There is something almost swinish in the thirst
with which the phantoms crowd to drink the fresh
blood whence they may regain fleeting semblance
of the life they have lost, and in the terror which
forbids them draughts until they are unthreatened
by the sword. All this, no doubt, we may forget when we feel their renewed humanity, as when
unburied Elpenor tells his hapless story,[1] or as when
the mother of Odysseus appears and has to wait[2] until Tiresias has uttered his purely personal prophecy,[3] or as when she is suffered at last to reveal her
maternal tenderness[4] even though the filial arms
which try to clasp her meet through her visible but
unbodied form, or as when Agamemnon contrasts
his tragic fate—not yet avenged by Orestes—with
the happier conjugal fortune of Odysseus,[5] or as
when the spirit of Ajax stands angrily apart disdaining even in death to have speech with one by
whom in life he had been defeated.[6] We can
hardly help feeling the primitiveness of it all,
however, when we remember the confusion of the
shadowy dead,—classified only as women and men
in a semblance of being even less ordered than
theirs had been when they breathed in sunlight,—
and when we find Odysseus at last shrinking from
them, for fear that Persephone should send forth
the Gorgon whose gaze, turning him to stone,
might keep him too hers there forever.[7] And the
fair wind which wafts him back towards the living
comes like fresh air.[8]

Compared with this, the Sixth Book of the

---

[1] Od. XI, 51–83.   [2] Ibid., 84–89.   [3] Ibid., 90–151.
[4] Ibid., 152–224.   [5] Ibid., 385–467.   [6] Ibid., 541–564.
[7] Ibid., 630–635.   [8] Ibid., 640.

Æneid, a masterpiece of deliberate composition in some 900 lines, may seem according to your mood either vastly more mature or provokingly sophisticated. Its mysteries, unlike those of Homer, are not elementary and fearful but ritual and symbolic; they resemble the celebration of the Mass rather than the slaughter of victims. Like Odysseus, Æneas must make pilgrimage to reach his unearthly goal and hear the prophecy of his future; but his pilgrimage is not with companions to the edge of life, where he may summon the dead from the depths, it is with a single Sibyllic guide to the depths themselves, thrown open to him by the magic of the Golden Bough. These depths of Acheron have an order of their own, too, where the dead pass towards the Stygian ferry of Charon,

> As numberless the throng as leaves that fall
> When autumn's early frost is on the grove;
> Or like vast flocks of birds by winter's chill
> Sent flying o'er wide seas to lands of flowers;[1]

where beyond the burning flood of Phlegethon the wicked writhe in eternal torture; and where the good are happy in the Elysian Fields. So those with whom Æneas holds converse he finds each in something like his eternal place: Palinurus,[2] for example, whose tale is evidently told to rival that of Elpenor in the Odyssey; Deiphobus,[3] who similarly challenges comparison with the Odyssean Agamemnon; self-slain Dido,[4] passionately disdainful of her betrayer, as Ajax was of Odysseus; and old Anchises,[5] who combines the tenderness of Anticleia, mother of Odysseus, with the pro-

---

[1] Æn., VI, 309–312; tr. Williams.   [2] Ibid., 338–383.
[3] Ibid., 494–546.   [4] Ibid., 450–476.   [5] Ibid., 679–901.

phetic foresight of Tiresias, but speaks prophecy
not so much of what shall happen to Æneas himself as of the Roman Empire and world order destined to spring from his seed. This prophecy is
rightly not in the midst of the narrative, where
Tiresias utters his prophecy to Odysseus, but is
made its magnificent climax. And the passage of
Æneas up from the Shades is not a terror-stricken
flight; it is rather a clear-eyed awakening from a
gravely exultant visionary dream.

In this Book, as everywhere in the Æneid,
those who can read the Latin, even though stum-
blingly, may find immortally beautiful passages.
On one we have touched already—the lines in the
prophecy of Anchises which foretell the imperial
ideal to be cherished by Rome.[1] Another may be
found in the passage where Dido turns forever to
the unfailing love of her dead husband Sichæus.[2]
Lovelier still are the words which at once predict
and lament the fate of young Marcellus, who had
he lived would have been the heir and the successor
of Augustus.[3] The tradition is probably true that
when these were read to the bereaved mother of
the princely boy, she swooned in ecstasy. No
translation, of course, can begin to convey the
final beauty of lines like these. None but scholars,
perhaps, can rightly pretend even truly to feel it.
But one thing is sure; they can dreamily haunt
through the discords of a prosaic lifetime a man
who first knew them as a stupid and reluctant
schoolboy.

[1] *Ibid.*, 851–853; *cf.* p. 188, *supra.*
[2] *Ibid.*, 472–474. It may not be quite fantastic to discern here implicit
commendation of the laws by which Augustus endeavoured to revive the
forgotten sanctity of marriage.
[3] *Ibid.*, 867–886.

Thus they and their maker have haunted through twenty unbroken centuries the poetic consciousness of Europe. We may well have seemed to linger over Virgil too long, and nowise to have revealed him. For our purpose, however, we have lingered rightly. No other poet so summarised what Europe had been until the days of promise when he lived. No other so confidently proclaimed the high hope which he was never to know unfulfilled by the future. No other has ever been so persistently studied, so blindly reverenced, so fantastically misunderstood, so incessantly unforgotten. No other has been transmuted by popular legend into the most potent of wonder-working enchanters. And no other could have given rise to the rhyming lines in which a Thirteenth Century poet, quoted by Comparetti,[1] tells how St. Paul, on his journey to Rome and lingering at Naples,

Ad Maronis mausoleum
Ductus fudit super eum
Piæ rorem lacrimæ:
"Quem te," inquit, "reddidissem!
Si te vivum invenissem,
Poetarum maxime!"[2]

VIII

HORACE

The trait of Virgil which most clearly accounts for his enduring eminence is that he not only expressed the ideals of his time but also summarised

---

[1] I have mislaid the precise reference.

[2] Anybody can read the sound of these words, which mean—Led to the tomb of Virgil, he shed over him a dew of loving tears: "What I could have made thee!" he said, "if I could have found thee alive, greatest of poets!"

its past beyond any other antique poet. For such encyclopædic range, indeed, his only rival or fellow in European literature is Dante, thirteen hundred years later. In the perspective of the centuries grandeur looks solitary; yet as a matter of human experience it has hardly ever come into existence except at times of great general activity. One of its essential features, too, involves something like a limitation; its very largeness prevents it from quite implying the moods of everyday life. These have never been expressed better than by the friend and contemporary of Virgil who stands second only to him in the tradition of Augustan letters.

The life of Horace resembled that of Virgil. The son of a wise but uneducated father, who had made a modest way in his country world, the boy, born in Apulia five years after Virgil was born in Northern Italy, was given the best education of his time. He studied at Rome, and later at Athens. At the battle of Philippi, he was an officer in the army of Brutus and Cassius; but no harm came of this. His very obscurity kept him safe; and it was not in his temper to be a passionate partisan. He came quietly to Rome, where he occupied himself with poetry. He became a friend of Virgil, who is said to have introduced him to Mæcenas. The friendship and patronage of Mæcenas made his unpretentious fortune. His later years were passed at Rome and at a farm which Mæcenas gave him in the Sabine hills, not far from Tivoli. In his own range of poetry, he was recognised and has remained unsurpassed; and the very nature of this work from beginning to end implies his excellent social quali-

ties. To go no further, the Fifth Satire of his
First Book, a work on which we have already
touched,[1] describes beyond compare his friendly
relations with Mæcenas and with Virgil, as they
were tested by a rather tedious journey from
Rome to Brundusium; and the Ninth Epistle of
his First Book, commending one Septimius to the
princely youth who was later to be the Emperor
Tiberius, has been held to comprise in its thirteen
hexameter lines the most nearly faultless letter of
introduction ever written. He was favoured with
the friendship and patronage of Augustus. After
Virgil's death, whom he survived for nine years,
he was distinctly the most eminent of living
Roman poets. And when he died, almost in the
middle of the forty years through which Augustus
was sovereign, he had incomparably expressed
the temper of that newly civilised life on which
the still high hope of Roman Empire and Roman
peace was based.

His fame at the time is no wonder. The survival of it, however, and its renewal whenever
subsequent history has allowed the growth of
social graces, may fairly be held astonishing.
Hardly anything is more volatile, more transitory,
more mutable than fashion. What it chases one
day it laughs at the next. Yet, though in widely
various guises it has over and over again smiled
with Horace, it has never laughed at him.
Whether in life or in letters a friendly sense of
his charm has proved itself through the centuries perhaps the most certain proof of polite
culture. Those who cannot respond to him are
not men of the world. The temper of this recur-

[1] *Cf.* p. 229.

rent phase of humanity he has generalised beyond
any other poet. There is something significant
in the genuineness of his appeal to the great gentlemen of England in the Eighteenth Century.
Time was, and not so very long ago, when a speech
in Parliament was hardly complete without some
savour of his lines.

Among his characteristics none is more distinct than a self-consciousness which almost anybody else might have found dangerous if not
fatal. He writes of himself and from himself
again and again, yet he never loses urbane reti-
cence: always confident, he is never confidential.
As you grow to know him, accordingly, you come
to feel the pleasure of an intimacy sure not to
burden you with secrets. There is no detail of
open life, at Rome or at his Sabine farm, too
trivial for mention if it chance to fit his purpose;
there is no pleasure or petty vexation, of memory
or of passing circumstance, on which he hesitates
to touch if it suits his mood. His mood, however,
keeps him and thus keeps us all secure from the
troubles of obtrusion. To go no further, Catullus before him and Rousseau in times almost
modern will serve to remind us of what this means;
so will the self-pitying laments of Ovid's exile.
There is a shamelessness of the soul, prevalent
nowadays, more subtly obscene for its very semblance of decency than any of the body. From
this Horace was beautifully free.

His work may clearly be divided, both formally
and substantially, into two groups. The first,
with which it probably began and certainly ended,
consists of his early Satires and his late Epistles,
written throughout in hexameter lines. The sec-

ond, which broadly speaking was written after
the Satires and before the Epistles, consists of the
Epodes and the Odes, widely various in character
and in metre, which among other things made
permanent in Latin literature and thus in the
continuous literature of Europe the most enduring lyric measures of the Greeks. That their
charm has survived the use to which they have
been put as models for the Latin verse-making
of generation after generation of English schoolboys may fairly be counted among the miracles
of literary history. But there was something in
Horace, as no one knew better than he, which
nothing can quite kill.

Of this, particularly as it appears in the Odes,
tradition has now so long been aware that one is
almost startled to find him mentioned by Dante
only as a satirist. When Virgil and Dante are
met by the sovereign poet Homer[1] in the placid
shades where the great of antiquity live hopeless
yet longing, he is close followed by Ovid, Lucan,
and "Orazio satiro." [2] On reflection, however,
it is not strange that at various times the Satires
have seemed better than the Odes, just as the Odes
seem better to-day. The substance of satire is
easier to understand than that of any poem whose
merit lies greatly or even partly in lyric beauty;
the temper of satire, ridiculing foibles and denouncing abuses, subtly appeals to that complacent love of self-righteousness which lurks in
most of us; and the moral pretension of satire,
even though not always genuine, is apt at once
to make an unresisting reader forget for a while
that he is little better than one of the wicked,

[1] Inferno, IV, 79–102.　　　[2] Ibid., 89: "Horace the Satirist."

and to pacify the frequent discomfort of consciences doubtful whether they may rightly enjoy entertainment without edification. The form of Latin satire, too, presents to anybody who has studied Virgil far less difficulty than any lyric measure. It is regularly written in hexameter lines, comprehensible when you have caught the rhythm of the Æneid, and at the same time fascinating by reason of the great difference of their effect from that of epic poetry. Any one who knows the classic poetry of France may observe a similar variety in the Alexandrine couplets, or quatrains if you prefer, which equally suit the passion of Racine and the irony of Molière. Any one who will turn to Dryden or to Pope may observe the same kind of range in the English heroic couplet. For satirical purpose, the hexameter line was never used more skilfully and happily than by Horace. Lucilius, his chief predecessor in this form of literature, wrote hastily and carelessly; Juvenal, the chief Latin satirist of a later time, wrote with truculent intensity; Horace wrote with exquisitely polished urbane ease. This, indeed, is not wholly a matter of form. Lucilius before him and Juvenal after him—like satirists in other tongues than Latin from the days of Juvenal to our own—were often abusive. Compared with almost any other writer of satire, Horace is not; he is said, indeed, to have called these poems not Satires but "Sermones," which means *Talks* or, if you like a big word, *Colloquies.* To understand why, you must perhaps read all eighteen of them;[1] if you lack time or patience for

---

[1] The most fluent English translation is Sir Theodore Martin's. One could wish, however, that he had managed to combine his urbane ease with a regular use of the heroic couplet. His various metres produce a less firm effect than that of Horace's invariable though flexible hexameters.

this, you will go far on the way, and be amused while doing so, by reading only three: the Fifth of the First Book, which recounts the journey to Brundusium; the Ninth of the First Book, which describes an encounter with a bore in the Forum; and the Fifth of the Second Book, which professes to continue the interview between Odysseus, or Ulysses, and the shade of the blind prophet Tiresias in the Eleventh Book of the Odyssey. Here Ulysses is troubled about financial matters, and is gravely advised to supply his needs by one or another of the less admirable means, such as inducing a rich old man to name you in a will, believed to have been habitually resorted to by agreeable but penniless Augustans.

Had Horace written no more than the Satires, he would accordingly have been memorable. Historically, indeed, they sometimes appear the most interesting part of his work; for they give many quietly amusing glimpses of Augustan life, much as the Tatler and the Spectator, so often prefaced with gracefully translated lines from Horace, keep alive the London of Queen Anne. Like the English essayists, too, he indulges in a good deal of urbanely conventional moralising—never fervid enough to disturb you. By themselves, however, the Satires could hardly have made him the Horace of tradition. At least nowadays, and for a good while past, he has been as conspicuously the author of the Odes as Virgil has always been of the Æneid. The name *Odes*, by the way, is not that by which they were called in Latin; their original title is *Carmina*, or *Songs*. This term, which instantly avoids any confusion of them with the Pindaric and choral odes of Greece, most conveniently describes or defines them.

Whether they were actually sung or not, to begin with, their purpose, like that of the songs of Burns or of the Irish melodies of Moore, is essentially lyric.

They are lyrics, at the same time, with at least two other than purely lyric features: they were studiously intended finally to domesticate in Latin, as they did, the loveliest poetic measures of the Greeks; and throughout them you will find compactly sententious phrases, not Greek but Latin in impulse, which express once for all— beyond any power of translation—the things they mean.   To take three or four random, hackneyed examples, nothing but the words themselves can ever say just what is compressed into phrases like

Integer vitæ scelerisque purus,[1]
(Flawless of life and pure of guile),

or

Eheu fugaces, . . .
Labuntur anni,[2]
(Alas, . . . the fleeting years flow past
unmarked),

or

Odi profanum volgus et arceo[3]
(I hate and spurn the unholy crowd),

or

Dulce est desipere in loco.[4]
(It's pleasant to be careless when we may.)

---

[1] I, XXII, 1.   I cannot resist the temptation to place beside these words, and the quotations which follow, the prose into which the conscientious editor of the Loeb Classics edition of the Odes (1914) has thought proper to render them.   Here he writes: "He who is upright in his way of life and unstained by guilt."

[2] II, XIV, 1, 2: "Alas . . . the years glide swiftly by" (Loeb).

[3] III, I, 1: "I hate the uninitiate crowd and keep them far away" (Loeb).

[4] IV, XII, 28: "'Tis sweet at the fitting time to cast serious thoughts aside" (Loeb).

It is probably this exquisite finality of expression, rather than the almost faultless grace of his lyric measures, which keeps the Odes of Horace perennial. The very first of those four phrases, however, will serve to remind us how little tradition understands him. Taken by themselves, the words "Integer vitæ scelerisque purus" appear to summarise with grand simplicity an almost holy ideal of human character; thus they are quoted now, and thus gravely chanted. In the Odes, they are the pleasantly ironic opening of what has properly been called a decorous comic song. Substantially, this goes on to say with demure grandiloquence that while this excellently sincere poet strolled in the woods, composing a song about a pretty young person named Lalage, a wolf who caught sight of him turned tail and ran away; and the last two lines of the Ode—

> Dulce ridentem Lalagen amabo,
> Dulce loquentem[1]—
> (Sweetly laughing, sweetly talking Lalage
> I'll love)—

are about as far as can be from anything serious. Not that Horace was never in earnest; but you have to watch carefully if you would make sure whether he is or not.

To do so, you must know him well; and there is hardly a poet in European literature more willing and ready to be pleasantly known. Beyond almost any other he keeps familiar ease secure from the imprudent dangers of undue familiarity. As you grow to know him, too, you will feel that

[1] I, XXII, 23-24: "I will love my sweetly laughing, sweetly prattling Lalage" (Loeb).

throughout his literary life he slowly and gently matured. His earlier Satires and the book of Epodes[1] which preceded the Odes appear, in the perspective of his complete work, comparatively coarse; at least you can detect there some vestige of his obscure origin, and feel what he meant when, years later, he wrote of himself as "ex humili potens"[2] (From humble state exalted). He was a man of his Augustan time, too. He lived from the years when since long before living memory Rome had been convulsed by civil wars into the tranquil dawn of Roman peace; and he welcomed both the authority and the reforms of the strengthening Empire, reviving the traditions of the Roman past, social and religious, encouraging the gracious influence of the Greeks peerless for their intelligence and their fine art, and stimulating the pursuit of truth by philosophy. To understand his Odes you must keep all this in mind. You may understand them best, indeed, when you look back at them after reading his latest and ripest works, the Epistles.

Of these there are two Books. The first contains twenty letters, widely various in length and topic; the second contains only two, both rather long, and both concerned with general principles of literature; with this second group they sometimes place the separate letter commonly called De Arte Poetica (On the Art of Poetry). All of these poems, like the considerably earlier Satires, are in hexameter verse; all use this verse with a studied yet colloquial ease of idiom, perhaps most nearly paralleled in English by the Imita-

[1] This word seems to mean something like *couplets* or *echoes*.
[2] Od., III, XXX, 12: "Risen high from low estate" (Loeb).

tions of Horace where Pope most clearly disclosed his own lack of urbanity. If it were not for the snarling animosity of our most eminent Queen Anne poet, his composite Epistle to Dr. Arbuthnot, otherwise called the Prologue to the Satires, might now and again seem almost Horatian. Nothing can seem anywhere near completely Horatian, however, at least when we come to the mature Horace of the Epistles, unless the sensitively urbane lines, at once colloquial, sententious, and final, set forth what you instinctively feel to be sincere philosophic purpose—an honest effort to perceive and to say something as near truth as human conditions will allow. The details of any philosophical system, like those of any state of religion, at which now and again we may have to glance, are evidently beyond our present scope. So to expound the views of Horace in other words than his own, or to trace them to their clear or conjectural sources, is happily no business of ours now. Two facts, indeed, concerning the Epistles as they complete his work are perhaps enough to touch on here.

In the first place, when at last you think of his writings from beginning to end, you can hardly help believing that he really held such purpose as he set forth in the Epistle to Mæcenas which stands first in his First Book. Three Books of the Odes had certainly been published, and with unsurpassed success, when he wrote the lines[1]

[1] Ep. I, I, 7-12:

> Est mihi purgatam crebro qui personet aurem:
> "Solve senescentem mature sanus equum, ne
> Peccet ad extremum ridendus et ilia ducat."
> Nunc itaque et versus et cetera ludicra pono,
> Quid verum atque decens, curo et rogo et omnis in hoc sum;
> Condo et compono quæ mox depromere possim.

Go where I will, unceasingly I hear
A voice that whispers in my well-rinsed ear:
"Cast the old horse in time, before he fall
Dead lame, and halt, the gibe and jeer of all."
So verses now and all such toys I quit,
Work night and day to find the true and fit,
The lore of sages cull where'er I may,
And hive it up for use some future day.

(Sir Theodore Martin.)

Those who know him best assure us that from the first Satires and the Epodes through the Odes to the last of the Epistles they can feel, for all his urbanity, his tact and his occasional courtliness, something like a constant growth of polite earnestness both philosophic and, like that of all sincere philosophy, religious. Antique religion variously differed from what our ancestral generations of Christianity have made the word religion mean for centuries—and never more obviously than when the growth of Roman Empire had mingled the perhaps thin deities of early Rome with the vagrant gods of decadent Greece and with the more mysterious divinities of the East or of the unchanging ages of Egypt. But Rome could never have been Rome without the spirit which was destined to animate the Catholic Church. Horace was no prophet, as some have thought Virgil; he was no dissembled preacher of the gospel, as some have thought Seneca, two or three generations later; but like all good men he grew more serious with the years, and like all good fellows he grew so gently.

In the second place, when you want to know what he means, you must be on your guard against conventional distortions of his meaning. The

first example of this danger which comes to mind
will serve as well as a dozen to indicate it. The
Sixth Epistle of the First Book—a poem discussing the general question of how to make life most
nearly tolerable—begins with the lines:

> Nil admirari prope res est una, Numici,
> Solaque quæ possit facere et servare beatum.
>
> (Not to be wonderstruck, Numicius, is almost the one and
> only thing which can make and keep a man happy.)

This translation of the first two words into four
is clumsy enough, if you please. The first comment on them which comes to hand states them
to signify "the *ataraxia* of the Epicureans," a
rendering certainly more learned and probably
more exact. But the hobbling English is enough
to remind us that the words "nil admirari," literally meaning "to admire nothing," and commonly
quoted as if *admire* meant *approve*, are by no means
intended to recommend fault-finding. What they
really signify Sir Theodore Martin takes four
lines to suggest:

> The best, indeed the only means I know
> To make men happy and to keep them so
> Is this, Numicius: never to admire
> With too great fervour or too great desire.

The Latin word *admirari* implies rather surprise
and wonder than approbation; at least in America,
the English word *admire* has come to imply enthusiastic if uncritical delight in the object of
admiration. So, believing themselves disciples of
Horace, Americans too greatly desirous of turning up their noses are now and again apt to dis-

play the too great fervour expressly condemned by the two words they conventionally misunderstand.

We have lingered over Horace perhaps too long; but he is of the few with whom one can hardly help lingering. His own lines about himself, in the Ode which closes his Third Book,[1] prophetically summarise his history through the centuries.

> Exegi monumentum ære perennius,

they begin (I have made a record to outlast bronze);

> Non omnis moriar,

he writes five lines lower (Not all of me shall die). And the reason is that first of all, from humble state exalted, he has brought the songs of Greece into the verse of Italy.[2] He was right. For hundreds of years between his time and ours, Greek was little known in Western Europe. There has never been a time, though, when Grecian melody, in Horatian guise, has not gladdened all Europeans who would listen. Even still, most of us who come to know it at all know it first through him.

IX

ELEGIAC POETRY

TIBULLUS, PROPERTIUS

If our object were seriously to study Latin literature, we should now have to consider with care a kind of poetry, contemporary with the full powers of both Virgil and Horace, at which, con-

[1] III, XXX.   [2] Lines 9–14.

cerned only with the traditions of European literature, we need no more than glance. Among the
standard forms of Greek verse had immemorially
been the elegiac couplet, at once described and
exemplified in English by Coleridge's lines[1]:

In the hexameter rises the fountain's silvery column,
In the pentameter aye falling in melody back.

The grace and ease of this couplet, preserving the
grandeur of the hexameter yet recurrently soften-
ing its effect, had led to considerable development
of it, often for the expression of amatory senti-
ments, among the polished though not unduly
fervent poets of Alexandria, of whom Callimachus
is now perhaps the most nearly remembered. Catullus, to go no further, had already used it in
permanent Latin. Though such lines as his "Odi
et amo," [2] however, are tremendously intense,
their most ardent admirer can hardly hold them
mellifluous. To attain anything like the Augustan
polish of Virgilian hexameters, or of Horatian
Alcaics and Sapphics, the Latin Elegiac Couplet
needed development from the state where Augustan literature found it.

This development was duly given it by three
poets, one of whom died some years before Virgil,
one in the same year with Virgil, and the third
only three years later, when Horace had some eight
years more before him. Of the first, Gallus, only
fragments have survived. Of the two others,
Tibullus and Propertius, we have quite enough to
give us a clear impression not only of how they
wrote but of what they were like. Both, accord-

[1] See p. 37.   [2] See p. 216.

ingly, are worth reading and worth knowing.
However well you come to know them, nevertheless, you can hardly fail to find them comparatively
secondary, in genuine passion to Catullus, in
range and power to both Virgil and Horace, and
in traditional importance to the copious popularity of Ovid, whose work was presently to eclipse
theirs.

They are doubtless distinct. Tibullus, a few
years the elder, has a sweetness of expression, and
sometimes of sentiment, which has won affection
from those who know his verses well; these have
been sympathetically translated into English by
Theodore Williams,[1] on whose versions of Virgil
we touched a little while ago. Propertius, who
seems to have come to Rome from Assisi, thus
first and faintly brought into literary tradition,
has more power, but less amiable quality, and is
generally the object rather of admiration than of
spontaneous liking. For our purposes, however,
we may here think of them not separately but together. In the year 25, when Augustan empire
was at last apparently secure, both were writing,
and neither was thirty years old. Ten years later
both were dead. The work of both is wholly in
elegiac verse, which both use for various purposes,
Tibullus with more tenderness and more sensitive
understanding of nature and friendship, Propertius with more fervour, more feeling for Roman
grandeur, and more attention to mythology. Both,
meanwhile, are most instantly remembered, at
least traditionally, for the kind of sentiment which,
each individually, they set forth in common.
Both had, or as poets pretended to have, rather

[1] Boston, 1905.

stormy experiences in the matter of love. Neither was a miracle of constancy. Tibullus writes, at different times, of two mistresses, whom he calls Delia and Nemesis; Propertius, though he admits occasional vagrancy, reciprocated by his mistress, celebrates only the lady whom he calls Cynthia. In both cases, the love poems are not very systematically arranged, and the surviving texts, particularly of Propertius, are technically as well as otherwise corrupt; Roman love affairs at their best were not chivalrously romantic. Granting this, you may still extract from the poems of each what may very likely be, as is generally assumed, a true story of Augustan love, where the lovers and their mistresses are both human and individual. So, unless your mood be prying, you need not trouble yourself with the question of whether the stories are duly conventionalised records of amatory fact or only finished specimens of amatory poetical conventions. Should this question possess you, there can be little doubt that these elegiac lovers and mistresses appear comparatively unreal, or at best shallow, when you compare them with Catullus and Lesbia; but that they similarly appear haplessly human when you place beside them the pretty lyrics in which Horace touches on his pleasures with Lalage[1] or Neæra.[2]

Some such perplexity, you may presently remember, besets the love-poetry which came into literature twelve or fifteen hundred years later—the Sonnets of Italy and, to go no further, of Elizabethan England. Petrarch, Sidney, Spenser,

---

[1] *E. g.*, Odes I, XXII.

[2] *E. g.*, Odes III, XIV. The last stanza of this ode is particularly Horatian. The poem begins by celebrating the victorious return of Augustus from Spain. In honour of this event, the poet presently directs his

and Shakspere will occur to anybody; and perhaps also the fact that, though very likely make-believe, Laura, and Stella, and the nameless Dark Lady all seem genuine, while the seemingly cooler and more conventional sonnets of Spenser are almost demonstrably true. The one indisputable truth about all four is that Sonnet-sequences brought into literary tradition an exquisitely artificial kind of love-poetry which somehow seems at heart natural. Something very like this was brought into the lasting tradition of Latin literature by the elegiac contemporaries of Virgil and of Horace.

X

OVID

Tibullus and Propertius were probably old enough to remember the death of Julius Cæsar; Horace and Virgil were certainly old enough to remember the chaotic last days of the Republic. So the four Augustan poets on whom we have touched could personally feel the sense of relief and hope which the strengthening Empire brought

servant to go invite Neæra to sup, and incidentally to dress her hair prettily. But if she is "not at home," the invitation need not be pressed. Then comes the end:

> Lenit albescens animos capillus
> Litium et rixæ cupidos protervæ;
> Non ego hoc ferrem, calidus juventa,
>   Consule Planco.

(Grizzling hair cools tempers eager once for quarrels and strife; I would not have borne this, hot with youth, when Plancus was consul.)

Taken by themselves, the first two lines are as gravely final as the opening line of "Integer vitæ." Taken by themselves, with their slightly melancholy rhythm, the words "Consule Planco" delicately express the sense of bright, vanished times one can remember. Yet really it is all a pleasantry.

to the Roman world. With Ovid, their only important successor in surviving Augustan poetry, the case was different. Born after the murder of Cæsar, and in the year when Cicero met his end, he could know only by tradition what had preceded the sovereignty of Augustus. As he wrote of himself, when old and exiled,[1] he had seen Virgil, and he had heard Horace read, but Tibullus had died too early to be his friend, so of all his predecessors he had personal relations only with Propertius—who had succeeded Tibullus as Tibullus had succeeded Gallus in the elegiac poetry where Ovid claimed for himself the fourth place. This claim has proved just. Without him Latin Elegiacs might be a matter only of literary history. From the times when his lines were written they have never been quite neglected; and though his longest work, the Metamorphoses, is in fluent and easy hexameters, all the rest we possess are in elegiac form.

He was a country gentleman, of comfortable means though not of high rank. After what would amount to a university education, supplemented by travel, he established himself at Rome when between twenty and twenty-five years old, not long before Virgil died. He had an appetite and an aptitude not only for letters but for fashion. Through more than twenty-five years, he thoroughly enjoyed a state of society the more agreeable because active interference in public affairs had become so nearly dangerous that prudent men and women of the better sort felt unusually free to pursue pleasure. In this pursuit Ovid eagerly joined, contributing to it not only a wel-

[1] Tristia, IV, X, 45-54.

come presence but an inexhaustible stream of poetry which at once gratified and expressed the fashionable temper of the times. After Horace died, he had no conspicuous rival as a poet. If he had died himself at fifty, his career—though by no means exemplary—would have been among the most cloudlessly happy imaginable. His last years might seem pathetically different, if he had not so incessantly and monotonously insisted on his troubles. With little warning, he was ordered, probably because he knew too much about the misconduct of Julia, the profligate granddaughter of Augustus, into exile at Tomi, on the Black Sea, not far from the mouth of the Danube. There he lingered on, in climatic and social discomfort and barbarian surroundings, until the fourth year of the Emperor Tiberius. And thence he sent back to Rome, year after year, the complaining elegiac letters, reiterantly begging for pardon, which are collected in his Tristia—or Sorrows—and in his Epistles from the Pontus.[1]

This dismal conclusion of his always copious work is at once very different from the beginning of it and yet a direct result of his first poems. There is little question that these were substantially what we now possess only in a second and revised version, under the title of Amores, or Loves. Formally following the elegiac tradition then lately established by Tibullus and Propertius, they set forth with unprecedented ease and fluency the story of his relations with a married lady whom

---

[1] There was a region called Pontus on the Black Sea; but this, well eastward on the North coast of Asia Minor, was nowhere near Ovid's place of exile. So the words *ex Ponto*, in the current title of his Epistles, mean not *from Pontus* but *from the Sea*.

he calls Corinna. Who she was nobody knows, nor even whether she may not have been mostly or wholly a creature of erotic fancy. The sure thing is that even in Augustan Rome these poems were so shamelessly audacious and at the same time so admirably turned as to make a success not only of skill but of scandal. If you wish an impression of their polite indecencies, you may get it from the comparatively rude Elizabethan translation of them attributed to Christopher Marlowe.

Somewhere between the last original version of the Amores and the revised form in which they survive, he appears to have produced at least many of the imaginary letters known as the Heroides. These purport to be more or less reproachful communications, made for despatch by something equivalent to the Roman post-office, from deserted heroines of legendary antiquity to their variously vagrant lovers. The first is from Penelope to Ulysses, there is one from Briseis to Achilles, another from Phædra to Hippolytus, another from Ariadne to Theseus, another to Jason from Medea; and so on. Perhaps the most nearly interesting now is that from Dido to Æneas, evidently made to challenge comparison with the Fourth Book of the Æneid. Nothing could be more fantastically and sentimentally artificial than such pretty nonsense, and compared with the Amores it lacks the spice of effrontery. Beyond question, however, it was not only welcome when it was written but was written well enough to be enjoyed at far later and different times; without it, to go no further, Michael Drayton would never have swelled the flood of minor Elizabethan poetry with his England's

Heroical Epistles, and without these our own minor romantic traditions might very likely have lost the names of Surrey and Geraldine. On the whole, however, this rather milder sort of thing can hardly have gratified literary appetites whetted by the Amores for still sharper savours. So Ovid, always ready to please with tongue or pen, presently brought forth what has been called the most immoral, though not the most demoralising, poem ever written by a man of genius. This is his Art of Love, which begins

> Si quis in hoc artem populo non novit amandi,
> Hoc legat et lecto carmine doctus amet.
> (If any one here in Rome has not learned the art of loving,
> Let him read this and, taught by the song he has read, make love.)

His ensuing instructions, which fill three elegiac books averaging more than seven hundred lines apiece, abundantly justify his promise. This time even Augustan fashion was aghast; and one technical reason for Ovid's exile, many years later, was pretended to be the corrupting influence of his Art of Love on general behaviour and morals.

If he had died at forty he would have left us only these variously erotic elegiac poems. His reputation would have been fashionable, frivolous, very scandalous, and not much more conspicuous than that of Propertius or Tibullus. The work on which his great traditional importance is based was produced, or at least made public, not in the last years of the First Century before Christ but in the first years of the Christian Era. This fact is worth remembering: at the date conventionally assigned to the birth of Christ, Ovid was the only considerable poet in the full flush of his power. It seems probable that he found his reputation, when well on in middle age, inconveniently juvenile; and that one reason why he devoted himself to work more apparently serious and more dignified in form was a desire to throw into shadow the prolonged indiscretions of his literary youth. Whatever his motives, there can be no doubt that almost as clearly as Virgil is traditionally remembered as the author of the Æneid, and Horace as the author of the Odes, Ovid is traditionally remembered as the author of the Metamorphoses.

All the rest of his work, though not forgotten, is comparatively secondary to this pleasantly rambling collection, in fifteen inexhaustibly fluent hexameter Books averaging more than eight hundred lines apiece, of the mythological stories still perennially familiar. The title, which means *Transformations*, indicates its only pretence to unity. Beginning with the miraculous transformation of chaos to order, proceeding with carelessly easy transition to the miraculous transformation of stones thrown behind them by Deucalion and Pyrrha into men and women, and so to the miraculous transformation of Daphne into a laurel-tree no longer alluring to the desires of Apollo, it goes on through numberless tales of miraculous transformation, each told with spirit and grace, until at the close of the Fifteenth Book it relates how Julius Cæsar was miraculously transformed into a star, and complacently ends

Quaque patet domitis Romana potentia terris,
Ore legar populi perque omnia sæcula fama,
Siquid habent veri vatum præsagia, vivam.

(Wherever Roman power rules the world,
If poets say true, read by the lips of men
Throughout all time I shall live on in fame.)

Beside the similar words of Horace, "Exegi
monumentum ære perennius" and "Non omnis
moriar," [1] these lines look trivial. The contrast
implies the difference not only between the two
men, but also between the earlier phase of Augustan poetry and the later. In fact, however, the
two predictions have proved equally true. Long
ago,[2] we reminded ourselves how the pretty stories
of Hawthorne's Wonder Book and his Tanglewood Tales come mostly if not wholly straight
from Ovid. So do almost all the images of mythologic antiquity familiar to us through the masterpieces of Italian painting. So indeed do by far
the greater number of impressions, distinct or
misty, which still make people feel as if they knew,
or ought to know but cannot quite remember, who
the creatures of immemorial Greek and Latin
mythology were and what they did. Wherever
you open the Metamorphoses and fall to reading a story or two, you will probably have the
double pleasure of surprise to find the story told
with such graceful animation, and of subtly complacent satisfaction that you were so well informed
as to have a bowing acquaintance with it already.
If you are learned enough, meanwhile, to play
with the original lines, you may very likely find a
distinct difference between the impression they
make and the impression made by an equal amount
of Horace or of Virgil. In either of these greater
poets you will incessantly come across long-since

[1] *Cf.* p. 256.   [2] *Cf.* p. 12.

proverbial phrases, which have so passed into tradition that you knew the words without remembering where they were originally used. "Facilis descensus Averno,"[1] for example—"the downward path is easy" roughly expresses what this means—will be recognised again and again by men who might be at pains to tell you much about the interview of Æneas with the Cumæan Sibyl; and thousands have known the words "Integer vitæ"[2] without the slightest notion that when first used they were not meant seriously. With Ovid, on the other hand, you will more probably feel that, while each of his tales is familiar yet perennially fresh, the copious words in which he tells them have nothing like so often lingered in traditional memory. Admirably felicitous, at least, they have proved less enduringly salient. Only one phrase of his instantly comes to mind completely apart from its context. When Apollo hesitantly allows Phaethon to take his place as driver of the Sun, he warns him against the dangers of going too high and thus getting cremated, and of going too low and thus getting smashed; and utters the prudent counsel "Medio tutissimus ibis."[3] ("You will go safest in the middle.") The wisdom of this advice has proved separately enduring. So, no doubt, have other bits of Ovid: "Conscia mens recti,"[4] for example, which means "a clear conscience," and is usually misquoted "Mens conscia recti"; or "Tacitisque senescimus annis,"[5] which means "we grow old in the silent years," a pretty way of saying "without knowing it." But in the poems

---

[1] Æn., VI, 126.   [2] Cf. p. 25.   [3] Met., II, 137,

[4] Fast., IV, 311.   [5] Fast., VI, 771,

of Ovid such more or less familiar expressions are
far less obvious than the familiarity of the stories
where they occur.

As a light story-teller, indeed, Ovid is unsurpassed. Those who know their languages best
often liken his temper to that of Ariosto, which is
most nearly approached in English by the comparatively ponderous and acrid Don Juan[1] of
Byron. The Fasti, or Holidays, which came
later than the Metamorphoses, has been less
popular; written in elegiacs, it is a calendar of
Roman festivals, arranged month by month and
celebrating with occasional narratives these frequent incidents of the Roman year, which were
something like the Saints' Days of our ancestral Church. Without the Metamorphoses, the
Fasti, only half of which has been preserved,
might hardly have lasted very long; those who
have read it, however, do not grudge their time.
A cursory but adequate summary of both poems
may be found in Church's little monograph on
Ovid.[2] To get any fair impression of why these
innumerable retellings of Greek legend in the
prettily and fantastically modernised terms of
Augustan Rome have stayed alive through almost
two thousand years, you must read them, at least
here and there, as they were written. This was
the highest form of contemporary poetry when
our Christian Era began.

The later works of Ovid concern his exile from
Rome. In various ways his elegiac letters—the

---

[1] Incidentally, as Byron rhymes Don *Juan* with *true one* and *new one*,
those learned moderns clearly err who pronounce this title "Whän," after
the Spanish fashion.
[2] Ancient Classics for English Readers: 1876.

Tristia and the Letters from the Pontus—are memorable; they contain many passages which imply the history of his time, and many others which express his haplessly unheroic yet not unamiable self. The last lines of the last letter from the Pontus[1] go far to summarise his lamentations through eight despairing years:

> Omnia perdididimus[2]: tantummodo vita relicta est,
> Præbeat ut sensum materiamque mali.
> Quid juvat extinctos ferrum demittere in artus?
> Non habet in nobis jam nova plaga locum.
>
> (I have lost[2] everything: nothing but life is left me,
> So that mind and body still may feel their woe.
> Why plunge the sword again into veins that are dry
> with bleeding?
> There is no spot in me where a wound can now
> be new.)

By themselves, at the same time, these prolonged though by no means unreasonable laments could hardly have given Ovid more traditional importance than he would have if he had written only the naughty elegiacs of his gay and fashionable youth. The beginning of his work and the end may never be neglected by those who would study the last twenty years of the reign of Augustus. What makes him enduring, however, and almost if not quite great, is the exhaustless animation with which he retold for his own times and thus for all future time the pretty mythologic tales already immemorially antique when he told them.

[1] Ep. ex Ponto: IV, XVI, 49–52.
[2] Latin literary idiom allowed the plural for the singular in the first person, much as English now requires it in the second.

XI

LIVY

Virgil and Horace belong to the first half of the reign of Augustus, and so do Tibullus and Propertius. Ovid, who wrote mostly in the second half of the reign, has carried us beyond the end of it, and also beyond the limit of the Century when it began; as he was past forty years old, however, when our chronology shifts we may fairly call him a man of the First Century before Christ. This is even more the case with Livy, the only important writer of Augustan prose. Though he died within a year or so of Ovid, he was hardly ten years younger than Virgil, and he was busy with his colossal work from long before the Æneid was published until well after the Tristia drifted moaning back from the Pontus. No other considerable Augustan writer could remember both the death of Cæsar and the accession of Tiberius. To find another example of memorable work contemporary at once with the rise and with the decline of the period where it belongs we must wait for sixteen hundred years. In this respect, the relation of Livy to Augustan literature resembles that of Shakspere, contemporary alike with Marlowe and with John Webster, to the Elizabethan drama.

Livy, to be sure, was nowise Shaksperean in range, in imagination, or in creative power. In two ways, however, his huge history—of which during some forty years he produced no less than one hundred and forty-two consecutive Books—distantly resembles the historical plays of Shakspere: it put hitherto more or less dry records into a form so acceptable that though by no means authoritative it became and has remained a permanent source of historical tradition; and the sentiment of it throughout is contagiously patriotic. Ab Urbe Condita Libri (Books from the Founding of the City) is the title now given it. Beginning with a compact but fluent summary of events and sovereigns from the time of Æneas to that of Numitor, Amulius, and Rhea Sylvia, it gets in the fourth section of the First Book to the twins, Romulus and Remus, brought forth by this legendary Vestal, and to the wolf who suckled them. From this point it proceeds, or rather it proceeded, with the story of Rome until the death of Drusus, adopted son of Augustus, and brother of the Emperor Tiberius, in the year 9 Before Christ. Livy is thought to have had in view eight more Books, bringing the whole number to a complete hundred and fifty, and carrying the story of Rome to the death of Augustus. If so, he died, past seventy-five years old, a little prematurely. Since this regrettable event, besides, more than a hundred of the Books he actually produced have been lost. What we now possess are only two fragments of the whole, the first ten Books, and a group of twenty-five others, beginning with the Twenty-first and ending with the Forty-fifth. Apart from these, we know him only from compact summaries of the lost Books made while they were still intact. The first ten Books carry the story of Rome from the legendary period of Romulus to the year 293, when Rome was beginning to master all the neighbouring Italian regions. The

twenty-first Book begins with the year 218, when
Hannibal was sweeping on to Italy; the thirtieth
Book ends with 201, when the triumph of Scipio
concluded the Second Punic War; the remaining
fifteen Books cover about thirty-five years, to the
year 167, when Roman power had begun to extend in every direction—to Spain, to Gaul, to
Syria, and to Macedon, for example. By that
time, Plautus was dead and the work of Terence
was beginning.

The very mention of these names may remind
us of how much the loss of Livy's later Books, and
almost a full hundred of them, may mean. Livy
himself was a gentleman of Padua, born in the
year 59, who came to Rome like Virgil full of such
patriotic feeling as was more fervent among the
newly constituted citizens of the Northern provinces than it then remained at the heart of the Empire. He began to write his history almost at
the time when the sovereignty of Augustus was
finally established. He kept on throughout the
reign, of more than forty years. As his compact
but fluent Preface indicates, his notions of history were by no means like those now prevalent.
He regarded its function as chiefly moral. "This
is the great advantage," writes his leisurely English translator, "to be derived from the study of
history; indeed the only one which can make it
answer any profitable and salutary purpose: for,
being abundantly furnished with clear and distinct examples of every kind of conduct, we may
select for ourselves, and for the state to which we
belong, such as are worthy of imitation; and carefully noting such as being dishonourable in their
principles are equally so in their effects, learn to

avoid them."[1] With this edifying purpose, he
was by no means careful in scrutinising the authorities on which he happened to light. So, his
first ten Books, particularly the first of all, which
deals with the Seven Kings, are of little historical
as distinguished from traditional value. When
he tells of the Second Punic War, to be sure, he
relies mostly on Polybius, a careful and intelligent Greek writer who was born a few years before the war ended, and personally knew the surviving Roman heroes of it.[2] Here Livy is consequently more nearly trustworthy; but we must
remember, at the same time, that even here he is
writing about events which occurred more than a
century before he came into the world. When,
somewhere about his seventieth Book, he came to
the Social War, and then to the conflicts between
Marius and Sylla, he was on firmer ground; for
he was old enough to have known old men who
could remember the times he dealt with. And his
last thirty or thirty-five Books concerned matters
within his own memory. He was fifty years old
at the point where his history stopped. Not a
line survives to show us how he could set forth
affairs concerning which he was himself an increasingly contemporary authority.

It has often been supposed, accordingly, that
if his later Books should ever be recovered they
would flood with light nooks and corners of the

[1] Tr. George Baker (Philadelphia, 1823): I, 3. The original is far less
diffuse: Hoc illud est præcipue in cognitione rerum salubre ac frugiferum,
omnis te exempli documenta in illustri posita monumenta intueri; inde tibi
tuæque reipublicæ quod imitere capias, inde fœdum inceptu, fœdum exitu
quod vites.

[2] There is an admirably spirited Eighteenth Century translation of Polybius by James Hampton. The most recent translation, Shuckburgh's,
though more accurate, is nowhere near so readable.

First Century which without them remain obscure. Perhaps they would. More probably, however, they might disappoint us. His moral view of history was generally accepted by his contemporaries, who were apt to class history with oratory, as a kind of literature whose prime purpose was to influence conduct. And his general opinion of his own times is implied in the passage of his Preface immediately following that on which we have just touched:[1] "Now, either partiality to the subject of my intended work misleads me, or there was never any state either greater, or of purer morals, or richer in good examples, than this of Rome; nor was there ever any city into which avarice and luxury made their entrance so late, or where poverty and frugality were so highly and so long held in honour; men contracting their desires in proportion to the narrowness of their circumstances. Of late years, indeed, opulence has introduced a greediness for gain, and the boundless variety of dissolute pleasures has created, in many, a passion for ruining themselves, and all around them. But let us, in the first stage at least of this undertaking, avoid gloomy reflections, which, when perhaps unavoidable, will not, even then, be agreeable." He had a deep sense of the past grandeur of Rome, of the fundamental unity of Roman history, and of the

---

[1] Tr. Baker, I, 3–4. Here is the original: Ceterum aut me amor negotii suscepti fallit, aut nulla unquam respublica nec major nec sanctior nec bonis exemplis ditior fuit, nec in quam civitatem tam seræ avaritia luxuriaque immigraverint, nec ubi tantus ac tam diu paupertati ac parsimoniæ honos fuerit: adeo quanto rerum minus, tanto minus cupiditatis erat. Nuper divitiæ avaritiam et abundantes voluptates desiderium per luxum atque libidinem pereundi perdendique omnia invexere. Sed querellæ, ne tum quidem gratæ futuræ, cum forsitan necessariæ erunt, ab initio certæ tantæ ordiendæ rei absint.

superb ideal of Roman Empire. This did not
blind him to decadent aspects of the period when
he began as the prose rival of Virgil and Horace,
and ended as that of Ovid. As a moralist, therefore, he might have been the original of a fragment
of Horace's Art of Poetry often quoted without
the context which would distort the portrait:

> Laudator temporis acti,
> Se puero, castigator censorque minorum.[1]
>
> (A praiser of old times when he was young,
> A scathing critic of his juniors now.)

Thus, although by no means disposed to proclaim
all right with the world, he was doubly acceptable
to Augustus, who at once desired to emphasise
the colossal unity of the Roman State from the
very beginning and in spite of personal aberra-
tions appears sincerely to have wished that Roman
character and conduct might be restored to something like the traditional austerity of the past.
So Livy, in his own day, set forth what people
generally assumed that history ought to be; and
there was never a period when people were more
profoundly disposed to think what ought to be
preferable to hard and ugly fact. Except incidentally, therefore, his account of his own times may
have been rather moralised than authoritative.

His traditional eminence is nevertheless deserved. He was not only the single writer of Augustan prose who could claim anything like such
distinction as that of his contemporary poets,
Virgil, Horace, and Ovid. He was a great master
of narrative, too, a story-teller remarkable for the
skill with which he told his stories. He was a mas-

---

[1] Horace: Ars Poetica: 173–174.

ter of literary oratory, as well; the speeches which occur throughout his work, though now variously old-fashioned, were originally among the passages most genuinely admired. More signally still, he was accepted by his own times, and indeed almost until ours, as the standard authority on Roman history; the tradition of the Roman Republic, through the centuries of European literature, has been based on what Livy wrote about it. And what Rome thought of him when he had hardly faded from living memory is best told in the words of Quintilian, the most eminent critic of literature under the Flavian emperors. Admitting Homer the first of poets, Quintilian asserts Virgil to be the second, and nearer the first than the third.[1] In elegiacs, he proceeds, Latin has rivalled Greek:[2] of this form he holds Tibullus the chief master, but he admits that some prefer Propertius; Ovid he finds too lewd, and Gallus too harsh. Satire[3] he says is wholly Roman; and the best satirist is not Lucilius but Horace.[4] "In history, too," he goes on a little later,[5] "I would hardly yield to the Greeks, nor fear to compare Sallust with Thucydides. And Herodotus will not object if we call Titus Livius his equal for matchless eloquence, not only in wonderfully pleasant and excellently hon-

[1] Quintilian: Inst. Orator, X, 1. 86: Secundus est Virgilius . . . propior tamen primo quam tertio.

[2] Ibid., 93: Elegia quoque Græcos provocamus.

[3] Ibid.: Satira quidem tota nostra est.

[4] Ibid., 94. Multo est tersior ac purus magis Horatius, et ad notandos hominum mores præcipuus.

[5] Ibid., 101. "At non historia cesserim Græcis, nec opponere Thucydidi Sallustium verear. Neque indignetur sibi Herodotus æquari Titum Livium, cum in narrando miræ jucunditatis clarissimique candoris tum in concionibus, supra quam enarrari potest eloquentem: ita quæ dicuntur omnia cum rebus tum personis accommodata sunt. Affectus quidem, præcipue eos qui sunt dulciores, ut parcissime dicam, nemo historicorum commendavit magis."

est narrative but also in speeches. Everything he says is thoroughly adapted both to his subjects and to his characters. No historian, in short, has ever more appealed to sympathies, particularly of the best kind."

Like Ovid, Livy outlived Augustus and the Century when Roman Empire was finally established. Even more distinctly than Ovid, too, he was a man of that epoch. At the time of the Christian Era Ovid was not yet forty-five years old, and Livy was almost sixty. They were the only important writers then surviving from the Century which had also added to the traditions of European literature the names of Cicero, of Cæsar, of Lucretius, of Catullus, of Virgil, and of Horace. When the Century began, enduring Latin literature hardly existed. When it ended, the greatest works of Latin literature had been produced. Tradition has been right in placing there the Golden Age of Rome.

CHAPTER III

THE FIRST CENTURY OF THE CHRISTIAN ERA

I

HISTORICAL TRADITIONS

At the date conventionally assigned to the birth
of Christ, the name Cæsar was that of a family
which had produced two dominantly great men:
Julius, already forty-four years dead, who had
virtually established imperial sovereignty on the
ruins of the Republic; and his nephew Augustus,
who for some thirty years had actually exercised
increasingly acknowledged imperial sovereignty
throughout the dominions of Rome. The change
which had come over the name Cæsar a hundred
years later is the chief historical tradition left us
by the First Century of the Christian Era. From
a family name it had developed into an imperial
title; and though the first twelve men who bore
it may not yet have been set apart, as they were
later, in a distinct group, we may confidently describe the Century, for our purposes, as that of the
Twelve Cæsars.

No other tradition of it, through time then to
come, gathers quite so portentous as this. The
names of the Cæsars have never been forgotten;
even though we can hardly know what manner of
human beings they really were, there have collected
about each of their names more or less distinct char-

acteristics which nothing can ever quite dispel;
and their portrait busts, calm now as if their lives
had been, have kept their very features familiar.
They were men, of course; but men whom the
course of history had placed in something more
like superhuman power than had ever before
tempted European humanity. Tradition is probably right in attributing to them as a group unspeakable crimes and excesses. Yet at the same
time their position was one which justified their
own times in paying to them even when alive honours which by the year 100 had become hardly
distinguishable from those paid by antiquity to its
ancestral gods. Once dead, they became deities.
Strange as this may seem now, something very
like it is true at this moment of the Japanese emperors; and to come nearer home, there is more
than a trace of it in such American moods as in-
sist that our Revolutionary demagogues were
pure of heart or that we must all ritually celebrate
the Stars and Stripes. Whatever else, the Cæsars
incarnated the imperial sovereignty of Rome.

Even though the Twelve Cæsars are thus half-
legendary, the legends of them are based on recorded fact. When Julius Cæsar was murdered
there was no constitution for the new form of
government in which he had become practically
sovereign. The natural tendency of personal
sovereignty has always been hereditary. Cæsar
had no legitimate son, and the paternity of Cæsarion, who was probably his son by Cleopatra, was
not undisputed. When Octavian, whose mother
was a sister of Cæsar, conquered Egypt, he was
nevertheless prudent enough to have Cæsarion,
technically the last of the Ptolemies, put to death.

So his final mastery of what already was virtually
an imperial throne had some colour of dynastic
right.   If his forty years of sovereignty as Augustus had been domestically fortunate he might then
have established hereditary succession.   His only
legitimate child, however, was a daughter, Julia,
whose conduct was far other than matronly.   Marcellus, her first husband, a nephew of Augustus
and formally adopted by the emperor, died at the
age of twenty, and has been remembered mostly
by reason of the beautiful lines in which Virgil
mourns his fate.[1]   Julia's two sons by another
husband, Agrippa, died as children.   After certain
other bereavements, Augustus adopted as his heir
Tiberius, son of his empress Livia by her first
husband, Tiberius Claudius Nero.

When Tiberius succeeded to the sovereignty, accordingly, the imperial inheritance of the Cæsars
passed to a male line of the great Claudian family,
noble and traditionally unpopular since before
those remote times when a legendary Appius
Claudius was heroically foiled in his attempt to
possess the hapless maiden Virginia.[2]   Concerning
the Emperor Tiberius record and tradition disagree.   There is no question that for many years
he seemingly tried both to govern and to behave
well, that the tendency of government was beneficent in the provinces but tyrannical at Rome, that
at one time he was extremely influenced by a
favourite minister named Sejanus, ultimately overthrown and put to death, or that in old age he retired to the island of Capri.   There, hidden from
general view in a vast palace, of which grim tra-

[1] Æn., VI, 860–886.
[2] The story is familiar in Macaulay's Lays of Ancient Rome.

ditions haunt the lovely region to this day, he is said
to have abandoned himself, when past the age of
seventy, to unspeakable excesses both sensuous
and cruel.   Rumour said, when he died there, that
he had consequently been smothered by treacherous attendants.   Under him the Crucifixion had
occurred unremarked, in a rather remote province.

Like Julius and Augustus before him, Tiberius
left no son.   He was succeeded by his grand-
nephew, a man of about twenty-five, in childhood
nicknamed Caligula, or "Little Boots," whose
mother, Agrippina, was a granddaughter of the
great Augustus.   Caligula, who reigned only four
years, probably became mad; at all events he
soon conducted himself so recklessly and abominably that nobody pretended to regret his murder
by his own guards in a subterranean corridor of his
palace on the Palatine Hill.   As he, too, was childless, there was a moment, but little more, when
the succession was in doubt.

The story goes that some soldiers, taking advantage of the confusion to explore and perhaps loot
the palace, found a terrified elderly uncle of Caligula
trying to hide in a remote room.   They dragged him
out; and instead of killing him on the spot, as he
fully expected, they hailed him Emperor.   Thus
Claudius became for thirteen years lord of all.
Though given to scholarship, he is thought to have
been stupid; he was clumsily awkward; but he seems
to have been good-natured and on the whole more
nearly respectable than might have been expected.
Maritally, however, he was an object of ridicule.
The reported conduct of his wife, the Empress Messalina, has made her rightly or wrongly the classical European type of what a sovereign woman ought

not to be. At last she outdid even herself, by publicly going through the form of marriage with one of her lovers. This led at once to her own end and ultimately to the exclusion from the succession of her son Britannicus, whose paternity she had attributed to the Emperor. Soon after bereaving himself of Messalina, Claudius married his niece, the younger Agrippina, a sister of Caligula and a niece of the younger Julia, whose friendship had cost Ovid so dear. By a previous husband, Domitius Ahenobarbus, Agrippina had a son, whom she persuaded the clumsy Emperor to adopt as heir under the Claudian name of Nero, and whose education was placed considerably in the charge of the celebrated philosopher Seneca. Having thus fulfilled her notions of maternal duty, she found less allurement in conjugal; she was believed to have ordered the dish of mushrooms on which the sexagenarian Claudius abundantly feasted, "and thereafter ate no more."[1]

So, at the age of seventeen, in the year 54, Nero became the sixth of the Twelve Cæsars. His reign of fourteen years has never been forgotten by tradition. It began with renewed Augustan promise; it ended with excesses which paled those of Caligula or Messalina. Through his mother, his grandmother, and his great-grandmother—the two Agrippinas and Julia—he was great-great-grandson of Augustus, nephew of Julius Cæsar. His title, therefore, had some faint colour of legitimacy, which was permanently to disappear with him. His good beginnings have not been traditionally remembered. Truly

[1] See Juvenal, V, 146–148.

or not he has remained, almost from his own time, the arch-type in European history of arbitrary, monstrous, and fantastic tyranny. Though the empire magnificently persisted, both property and life were worthless anywhere near the Emperor. Among his victims were thought to be both Britannicus, the disinherited son of Claudius, and his own beautiful mother, Agrippina, with whom scandal accused him of incest. Among them were certainly Seneca and Lucan, who were probably concerned in a conspiracy against him. There is no doubt that he supposed himself a poet, an actor, and a singer, of genius; or that he consequently appeared on the public stage, in his time as disreputable as it has ever been anywhere. Legend has associated this propensity with the most widely remembered episode in his career. He took it into his head to build a palace, the Golden House, which should surpass in scale and magnificence anything previously known, and of which a central feature should be a colossal statue of himself. The name of this effigy, by the way, survives in that of the Coliseum, built a little later on the site of his pleasure grounds. The closely built city of Rome presented obstacles to his plans. An unprecedented fire thereupon cleared it from his way; and a report arose that while Rome was burning he looked on as if the spectacle had been arranged for his amusement, and entertained those about him by singing verses of his own about the destruction of Troy. This rumour naturally gave rise to another that the city had been set on fire by his orders. Even he found the suspicion inconvenient. He therefore seized the occasion publicly to throw the blame on the new, obscure, and unpopular sect of Christians. With various refinements of torture many of them were put to death; some, fastened on poles and drenched with oil, were burned alive at night in his gardens, and are called the Living Torches of Nero; and to this persecution are traditionally assigned the crucifixion head-downward of St. Peter, the first Bishop of Rome, and the beheading of St. Paul. It all came to an end when Nero was little more than thirty years old. Movements against him occurred in the army,—in Spain, in Gaul, and in Germany; his imperial guards at Rome proved treasonable; he was denounced as a public enemy; and as the story runs, he tried to escape almost alone, and being pursued took his own life, with the words: "Qualis artifex pereo!" ("What an artist I am who die!") This occurred in the year 68, after he had reigned some fourteen years. He was the last of the Cæsars who could make any pretension to dynastic succession from Julius. The legitimate dynasty, if one may venture to call it so, consists of Julius, Augustus, Tiberius, Caligula, Claudius, and Nero.[1]

So far as sovereignty goes, the next year and a half were a nightmare of recurrent revolution. Before Nero's death, an old, austere man named Galba, governor of a Spanish province, had been proclaimed emperor by his army and others; he made his way to Rome, was recognised as emperor for some six months, and was finally dragged from his litter in the Forum and there murdered by his own guards. They had already proclaimed in his place Otho, a fashionable courtier of Nero, and

---

[1] The popular novel Quo Vadis, translated from the Polish, gives a brilliant picture of Neronic Rome.

therefore—though of easy morals—much more popular than the grave and seemingly penurious old usurper whom he had for a while pretended to support. His reign lasted less than three months. Vitellius, a fat general, had already been proclaimed emperor by the troops in Germany, and was marching towards Rome. Otho went out to meet him, was defeated in battle, and thereupon killed himself, with something like antique Roman dignity. So, by the middle of July, 69, Vitellius was recognised as emperor at the capital. Already, however, another emperor, Vespasian, had been proclaimed in the East, where with his son Titus he had been conducting vigorous campaigns against the rebellious Jews. The armies of his adherents proceeded to attack and to capture Rome, thus exposed to horrors unknown there since the time of Sylla. Vitellius, not allowed to abdicate, was seized and beaten to death. And before the end of 69 Vespasian was recognised as the successor of the Cæsars.

The last thirty years of the Century recapitulated its earlier story. Vespasian, about sixty years of age at his accession, was a successful soldier who owed his rise not to distinguished origin, but to work and skill. He had two sons, Titus and Domitian, already mature men, and highly trained. Titus, left in command of the army in Palestine, captured Jerusalem and destroyed the lately rebuilt Temple. He presently returned to Rome, and in company with his now imperial father celebrated the triumph commemorated by the arch of which the ruin in the Forum still bears his name; everybody knows the sculptured relief within it, where victorious Romans carry on their shoulders the sacred seven-branched candlestick of the Jews. Domitian, a man of less military experience but more accomplishment, was given high civil office. Something like general peace ensued for a while. Titus, the elder son of the Emperor, was the more closely associated with him during the ten years of his reign. So the accession of Titus when Vespasian died made little change in the government, except that as emperor Titus appears to have been unexpectedly magnanimous. A new dynasty had begun, called from their hitherto obscure family name the Flavian. Rome breathed more freely. As had been the case earlier, however, this respite was not to persist. Titus reigned only two years— during which, to be sure, at least two memorable events occurred: the cities of Herculaneum and Pompeii were overwhelmed by an eruption of Vesuvius; and the Flavian amphitheatre—the Coliseum—was opened for public games on the site of the gardens of Nero. The premature death of Titus was attributed by scandal to the designs of his brother Domitian. Though there is no proof of the charge, the career of Domitian as emperor tended to give it colour. He was luxurious, cruel, and suspicious; and in the fifteen years of his reign he managed to win a traditional reputation comparable for tyranny, sensuousness, and murder with those of Nero and of Caligula. Like them, he met a violent end; he was assassinated in the year 96 by one of his household. Thus the short-lived Flavian dynasty followed from life into record the Julian or Augustan.

Before the Century ended, the two years' reign of Nerva, an old Senator elected sovereign by his colleagues, had occurred; and he had been peaceably succeeded by his adopted heir Trajan. The reign of Trajan, however, more properly belongs to the Second Century than to the First; and that of Nerva groups itself rather with those which followed than with those at which we have glanced. In historical tradition, the First Century is beyond question that of the Twelve Cæsars. It found Julius, to be sure, already a tradition, and Augustus already sovereign for nearly thirty years. To their dynastic names it added those of Tiberius, Caligula, Claudius, and Nero; to this group it added the usurping names of Galba, Otho, and Vitellius; and the nine were made twelve by the usurping Flavian dynasty, Vespasian, Titus, and Domitian. By the year 100 they were all, personally and dynastically, things of the past. Ensuing time has grouped them together, the most tremendous company of sovereigns in all our traditional record. Evil men they are held on the whole, unable to bear the weight of a power which went far to justify their gradual assumption of divinity. They mostly met hapless ends, too. Julius was murdered; there were rumours that the death of Augustus was not natural; Tiberius was said to have been smothered or strangled; Caligula was assassinated; Claudius was probably poisoned; Nero virtually and perhaps actually took his own life; Galba was killed by a mob; Otho killed himself; Vitellius was torn to pieces; only Vespasian surely died in his bed, with the grim jest that at last he was to be a god; scandal whispered that Titus was put out of his path by Domitian; and Domitian was stabbed to death. Yet all the while the

Empire magnificently persisted, and with it something like a strengthening ideal of imperial sovereignty. This rather than they is what men think of in the presence of their marble busts.

As these portraits will remind us, the First Century was a period of by no means negligible fine art. This bore to the fine art of Greece a relation analogous to that borne to Greek literature by the literature of Rome. The most conspicuous feature of architecture which we owe to Rome itself is the arch, now immemorially familiar in the triumphal arches, the amphitheatres, and the aqueducts of which the ruins appear beyond all else to symbolise the colossal diuturnity of the Roman spirit. We are carelessly apt to think of them as coming from the whole Roman past. In fact, however, hardly any of them now recognisable antedates the reign of Augustus, and very few are so old as the First Century of the Christian Era. The Rome of our general imagination, the Rome of which the ruins are familiar in the picturesque fancies of Piranesi, is mostly the Rome which came into being between the accession of Vespasian and the fall of the Western Empire, not quite four hundred years later. We have already touched on the great Flavian monuments, the Arch of Titus and the Coliseum. We might have touched on the Aqueduct which bears the name of Claudius. We should be at pains to remember anything half so well known from the time of Augustus. His traditional saying, nevertheless, that he found Rome of brick and left it of marble, is essentially true. What Rome looked like before the Empire nobody but archæologists can now easily conceive. The image Rome stamped on the visual notions of posterity began with him, and never lost its massive dignity. While the Twelve Cæsars quivered alive, one after another, these traces of their empire were made wherever their empire extended, to outlast not only them, but the Empire which each in his tragic time momentarily embodied. In the reign of Nero, the bronze horses long placed on the west front of the Church of St. Mark, at Venice, probably surmounted, with their lost chariot, a triumphal arch of the Emperor. The story of their peregrinations has been memorably told of late in the imaginatively powerful "Can Grande's Castle" of Amy Lowell.[1] As we have reminded ourselves, too, chance has preserved for us one extraordinary relic of the Flavian times. The town of Pompeii, buried under volcanic ashes during the reign of Titus, has been excavated within the past two hundred years. It was an agreeable seaside place, of no considerable importance. It may be taken as an example of the surroundings commonplace in the First Century. As you grow to know it, you will come to feel a sense of the civilised and sometimes exquisite conditions of habit which it implies. This was the daily existence of the Rome surmounted by the maddening grandeurs of the Twelve Cæsars. Theirs was a tragic world to dominate, but a pleasant world, after all, to live in.

Its literature, too, was copious. Compared with the literature of the previous Century, however, it seems for a while almost if not quite decadent. There were writers under Tiberius, nevertheless, who have not been quite forgotten; under

---

[1] New York: 1918, 123–232.

Nero there were writers of distinctly more importance; and under the Flavian dynasty, from amid a group of writers more noteworthy still, there emerged at least four,—Martial, the younger Pliny, Tacitus, and Juvenal,—eminent enough for separate consideration even in a retrospect so cursory as ours. We must accordingly turn now to these three periods and these four men.

II

LITERATURE UNDER TIBERIUS

VELLEIUS PATERCULUS; VALERIUS MAXIMUS; PHÆDRUS

As we have already reminded ourselves, both Ovid and Livy survived the reign of Augustus. When they died at about the same time, probably in the third year of Tiberius, the great period of Latin literature was at an end. The literary conditions which ensued persisted throughout the Century, and longer. Of these, two or three deserve a passing word. Political conditions gave a new character to the still copious flood of Roman eloquence. Up to the time of Augustus, Latin orations—of which the most memorable examples are those of Cicero—were intended to influence public conduct, often in matters of politics. Under the strengthening Empire this kind of thing became politically dangerous and therefore extremely dangerous to the personal safety of any one disposed to indulge in it. There was a general tendency, accordingly, to avoid inconvenient topics, conventionally to eulogise those in power, and to depend for effect no longer on what was said but rather on the manner in which this was set forth. And this tendency was encouraged by many schools of ingenious but formal rhetoric. Such fashion and such education naturally gave increasing importance to public readings and the like for the purpose of entertaining hearers more eager for new turns of phrase than for anything so inconvenient as independent thought. Great houses often contained rooms built for these performances, where sometimes men of accomplishment and fortune would read works of their own, or again would allow some favoured client to bring his work to fashionable attention. On the whole, it was glittering, sonorous, and empty. Even if circumstance had been more free, something similar might probably have occurred. When, as in the preceding Century, any form of expression has reached excellence, the next generations must either conventionally repeat effects already achieved or by trying to avoid convention stray, as literature is apt to stray nowadays, into deliberate and conscious eccentricity.

The two prose writers under Tiberius who have not been quite forgotten imply these conditions. Though neither is much read or much worth reading, the names of both have traditionally survived. Velleius Paterculus wrote in two books —that is, on about one seventieth of Livy's scale —a swift, declamatory [1] abridgment of Roman history, which is said to be occasionally brilliant,

---

[1] A comical example of this tendency is faintly familiar. Touching on Pompey, Velleius Paterculus tells us (II, 53) that his fortunes were so various that the earth, which had lacked room for his victories, could not find room for his grave (ut cui modo ad victoriam terra defuerat deesset ad sepulturam).

never solid or trustworthy, and obsequiously
favourable to the powers that held sway. Valerius
Maximus at about the same time put together an
equally obsequious work which has been more
nearly popular through the centuries. It is an
undigested collection, arranged under numerous
headings themselves in no traceable order, of anecdotes and the like suitable for use in rhetorical
allusion. So whoever has later desired to look
learned has often done so most easily by selecting
from Valerius Maximus a character, an incident, or
an aphorism suitable to his purpose, and not mentioning where he found it. The book, in fact,
is a magnificent Roman prototype of those cheap
treasuries of apt stories and fine words said to have
bulged the pockets of unskilled after-dinner speakers during the Nineteenth Century. Compared
with Augustan literature or Republican, this kind
of thing is negligible.

The only poet who familiarly survives from the
time of Tiberius is more solid. Phædrus, traditionally said to be a freedman of Augustus, put
into Latin verse a considerable number of fables,
conventionally attributed to the legendary Greek
fabulist Æsop. He added others, some perhaps
of his own invention. Apart from his compactness, which is generally clear, the most salient
feature of his method is that he often begins with
the moral of a fable to which he appends the story,
much as conventional sermons are tagged on to
trite texts. Two circumstances have kept him
more or less alive. The first is the accident that
fables lend themselves as readily as the anecdotes
of Valerius Maximus to the frequent requirements
of rhetorical allusion. The second is that by put-

ting into Latin material previously expressed in Greek, he brought the substance of the fable— often a matter of prehistoric origin—into the permanent current of European literature. The first two lines of his versified preface imply this: they may freely be rendered

> The stuff that Æsop quarried I have smoothed
> In Latin verses.[1]

From his time to ours, European men of letters, often ignorant of Greek, have always been able to read him. So he is not only the source of almost every story now associated with the name of Æsop, but also the progenitor of such fables, more elaborately developed than his, as have been written in the languages of modern Europe. Without him, to go no further, French literature might have lacked the chiselled Fables of La Fontaine, and English literature the less firmly wrought but still remembered Fables of John Gay. Whatever his positive merit, accordingly, Phædrus has a certain importance, both traditional and historic. When we reflect, however, that nothing more important survives in literature from the reign of Tiberius, the story seems rather like that of English literature under the Commonwealth and the Protectorate. The subjects of Cromwell's tyranny, mostly born when Shakspere was at his best, added to the literature of our language only one surely permanent book—the Complete Angler of Izaak Walton.

[1] Æsopus auctor quam materiam repperit,
Hanc ego polivi versibus senariis.

III

LITERATURE UNDER NERO

SENECA; LUCAN; PETRONIUS; PERSIUS

By the middle of the Century, literature had strengthened. Under Nero at least four writers died whose work, for various reasons, has a certain claim to permanence.

Of these the oldest, the most eminent, and altogether the most important was Seneca. Historically, indeed, his importance remains considerable. Whoever would seriously study Roman atmosphere under the first and more or less legitimate dynasty of the Cæsars must know Seneca well; and the same is true of whoever would follow the course of ancient philosophy during the First Century. Son of a Spanish rhetorician long established at Rome, another son of whom was the Gallio familiar to Christian tradition as the magistrate who dealt summarily at Corinth with a complaint against the Apostle Paul,[1] he was already past ten years old when Augustus died. During the reigns of Tiberius and Caligula, he attained such distinction, official and fashionable, philosophic and literary, as made him at the accession of Claudius perhaps the most conspicuous intellectual personage of his time. Under Claudius he passed some years in exile, from which he was recalled to undertake the instruction of the boy who was soon to be the emperor Nero. The promise of better things with which the sovereignty of Nero began has been tradi-

---

[1] Acts xviii, 12–17.

tionally attributed to the influence of Seneca. Whatever happened, this influence did not last long; and in the year 65, Seneca, charged with complicity in a conspiracy against the Emperor, was graciously permitted, at the age of sixty-two, to end his life by comfortable Stoic suicide.

His writings had been copious. Such of his prose as now survives is mostly concerned with moral philosophy. In treatises and in letters alike, and even in his discussion of Natural Science, he incessantly sets forth eclectic but mostly Stoic opinions of how men ought to behave. These have now and again enough in common with the principles of Christianity to give some faint colour to the tradition that he was influenced in his later years by the preaching or the conversation of St. Paul. The frequent addiction of thoughtful men, between his time and ours, to formal moralising has combined with the meticulous finish of his style, which deliberately differed from the long and Hellenised periods made classical by Cicero, to keep him generally more nearly alive than he now happens to seem. Except for students of history or philosophy, his volumes at this moment grow respectably dusty.

So from our present point of view, his historical importance in the history of European literature is almost accidental. Tradition attributes to him a collection of nine or ten formal dramas which happen to be the only surviving specimens of antique Latin tragedy. He stands accordingly in just such relation to the revived tragedy of modern literature as that of Plautus and Terence to its comedy; for there were many centuries, we must remember, when men could read Latin but

not Greek. What ensued is clearly set forth in
Sir Philip Sidney's Apologie for Poetrie,[1] written less than ten years before both Marlowe and
Shakspere had produced masterpieces of Elizabethan drama. Yet Sidney held the lifeless
Gorboduc the only mentionable English tragedy,
"which notwithstanding as it is full of stately
speeches and well-sounding phrases, climbing to
the height of Seneca his style, and as full of nota-
ble morality which it doth most delightfully
teach, and so obtain the very end of poesie, yet
in troth it is very defectious in the circumstances,
which grieveth me because it might not remain an
exact model of all tragedies. For it is faulty
both in place and time, the two necessary companions of all corporal actions." Drama in English took a turn of its own; but the standard
tragedy of both France and Italy owes its form
and much else to the fact that the tragedies of
Seneca were long held absolute models of what
tragedy ought to be. Unhappily, however, they
are not true dramas. They are based on Greek
plays written for actual performance; four of them
on surviving tragedies of Euripides, two on surviving tragedies of Sophocles, one on the Agamemnon of Æschylus. They appear, however, to have
been written not for presentation on the stage, but
for public reading before audiences who so delighted
in elaborately artificial rhetoric as to welcome
moral commonplaces if ingeniously set forth. Their
consequent effect on modern literature has been
something like what might occur if poets of a
future civilisation should base their dramatic

[1] Sidney died in 1586; but this work was not published till 1595—two
years after the death of Marlowe.

methods on those of Robert Browning—in Pippa Passes for example, or even in the Ring and the Book. If Seneca had not thus chanced to be a permanent though distorting literary influence, he might hardly have been so highly esteemed by tradition.

Lucan, his nephew, was born like the uncle in their ancestral Spain. Coming young to Rome, he found himself by reason of Seneca's eminence in a socially important position. He was brilliant and precocious. He is said to have excited first the approval and then the artistic jealousy of Nero. There is no reason to doubt that he was concerned in the conspiracy which led to his condemnation as well as to that of Seneca. And, although, at the age of twenty-six, he killed himself in similar circumstance, it seems more than probable that he tried to save his life by far from heroic means. Young as he was he left a long, unfinished poem which at times has enjoyed an epic reputation second in Latin only to that of Virgil. It deals with the Civil Wars by which Cæsar came to imperial power; it was probably intended to end with the murder of Cæsar;[1] and the boldness with which it treats history historically, discarding the intervention of gods generally held from Homeric precedent essential to epic poetry, is a remarkable and sensible innovation. It contains many passages brilliant, sententious, and patriotically Roman, of which the most familiar is

Victrix causa deis placuit, sed victa Catoni.[2]
(The winning cause pleased Heaven, the losing Cato.)

[1] Lucan, Pharsalia, VII, 592–596.　　　　[2] Ibid., I, 127.

In all likelihood, no epic poem on recorded and recent history has ever been better; but there is still room for doubt whether recorded and recent history can possibly be treated with epic excellence. Of late Lucan has been rather less admired than he once was and may be again.

The earliest extant comment on Lucan is thought to have been contemporary. Though he is not named, a lengthy passage in the Satyricon of Petronius Arbiter[1] evidently concerns his poem, and by offering a conceivably ironical example of how such a subject ought regularly to be treated —with a flood of allusions, of interposing deities, and the like—undertakes to demonstrate his artistic errors. The work where this passage occurs is different from any on which we have as yet touched. It is a considerable though broken fragment of what must have been a very long and rambling story, such as might now be called a picaresque novel, attributed to the Petronius of whom Tacitus[2] has left us a strong portrait. Its prurient indecencies remain unsurpassed; but so do the facile graces of its excellently pure Latinity, the colloquial freedom of its often literal talk, the poised precision of its incidental criticisms, and the compact realism of its pictures from life. It could have been written only by a man of exceptional wit, fashion, and culture. Here and there it makes the world of Nero live as vividly as the London of George II lives in the prints of Hogarth. And nothing more clearly indicates Neronic conditions than the fact that conscientious Victorians are said sometimes to have dissembled the truth that they had read it. To

[1] 119–124 (Loeb pp. 252–274).   [2] Annals, XVI, 18–19.

scholars it must always remain variously and inexhaustibly curious; others than scholars may console their ignorance by assurance that any unprejudiced modern would probably find it both rambling and tedious. Whatever its virtues or vices, it seldom touches the springs of human nature. Of course, it was not unprecedented; no formally ripe work of art ever has been.   Its Greek models, however, have not survived, nor have any earlier imitations of them in Latin. And anyhow, what we now call fiction had no considerable place in European literature until Cervantes, a contemporary of Shakspere, made Spanish literature a permanent part of it by writing Don Quixote.

The fourth Latin writer who died under Nero seems, unlike the other three, to have known little of life, of fashion, or of public affairs. Born in comfortable circumstances at Volterra, Persius came to Rome as a boy, studied faithfully, occupied himself with somewhat desultory literary work, and closed his invalid and generally domestic life somewhere about the age of twenty-eight. His six short satires, posthumously published, gave him in literature a reputation never quite lost. They are often printed as a kind of appendix to those of Juvenal, in comparison with which they appear both weak and obscure.   Taken by themselves, they show how a studious, respectable, and never robust young man, whose knowledge came not from experience but from books, was disposed to think when Horatian urbanity was already classical, and the generally Stoic moral commonplaces of Seneca were the fashion. If it had not been for Juvenal, a generation later,

Persius might now look larger than he does. Even so he would probably have been held to mark rather a decline of satire from the studied ease of Horace[1] than a step in its progress. The truculent invective of Juvenal has chiefly influenced its later course.

Seneca, Lucan, Petronius, and Persius may be taken as typical of Roman literature under Nero. Compared with its condition under Tiberius, they indicate something like revival. But this falls so far short of the grandeur attained in the preceding Century—the Century of Cicero, Cæsar, Lucretius, Catullus, Virgil, Horace, Ovid, and Livy —that the story still seems principally decadent.

IV

LITERATURE UNDER THE FLAVIAN EMPERORS

PLINY THE ELDER; QUINTILIAN; SILIUS ITALICUS; VALERIUS FLACCUS; STATIUS

Between the accession of Vespasian and the death of Domitian literature became decidedly stronger. At least five names of men then held important though now little read survive, as against three from the time of Tiberius and four from that of Nero; and furthermore, the four men on whom we must still touch separately, though three of them did most of their extant work later, came to full maturity of experience under the Flavian Cæsars. Literary tradition tenaciously remembers the elder Pliny, Quintilian, Silius

---

[1] "Horatii curiosa felicitas" is the best-known critical dictum of Petronius (Satyricon, 118: Loeb, p. 250).

Italicus, Valerius Flaccus, and Statius. Latin literature, as we possess it, would be incomplete without the epigrams of Martial, the letters of the younger Pliny, the historical works of Tacitus, and the satires of Juvenal.

Three letters of the younger Pliny combine to give us a pretty clear notion of his uncle and adoptive father, Pliny the elder. One[1] recounts the literary work and habit of this enormously industrious student, whose punctilious concern with military and administrative affairs would more than have exhausted ordinary human energy; the others,[2] which contain our only full account of how Herculaneum and Pompeii were destroyed, describe the spirit with which, unwieldy and elderly, he behaved when the tremendous eruption of Vesuvius surprised him. Urged by both administrative duty and scientific curiosity, he had himself carried from safety to danger; at a moment of hesitation he quoted the still familiar saw of Terence, "Fortune favours the brave,"[3] and went ahead; hard of breathing anyway, he was suffocated in sleep; and they found his body, like that which left its mould for modern plaster in the ashes of Pompeii, looking not lifeless but rather at rest.[4] His copious historical writings were among the authorities of Tacitus. Both these, and his treatises on grammar, oratory, and other matters have long since perished; but his huge encyclopædic work in thirty-seven Books on Natural History—a term used so comprehensively as to include among

---

[1] III, 5.   [2] VI, 16, 20.
[3] "Fortes Fortuna adjuvat": Phormio I, IV, 26.
[4] Habitus corporis quiescenti quam defuncto similior.—Ep., VI, 16.

other topics medicine and the plastic arts—remains to console us for the loss. Though doubtless accumulated earlier, it was published under Vespasian and dedicated to Titus; so we may fairly group Pliny as we know him with the Flavian writers. And, except for the light he throws on Flavian conditions of what would now be science, he has shrunk into little more than an indomitable collector of such curious odds and ends as to this day occasionally amuse desultory English readers in Burton's Anatomy of Melancholy.

Quintilian, a Spanish master of rhetoric, came to his own under Vespasian, who endowed the school he had opened at Rome. After twenty years as chief corrector of vagrant youthful minds there,[1] he retired from his active teaching, and produced the twelve Books on the Principles of Oratory, with some incidental criticism, which remain on the whole our standard Latin authority about such matters. His taste and perhaps the inherent mutability of fashion led him to condemn the elaborate ingenuities of Seneca and to prefer the larger and more ingenuous artificialities of Cicero. In substance, he was a sound teacher, searching all things and holding fast that which is good. But books about books and how to make them can hardly be quite living books themselves.

Contemporary with these two secondary writers of prose were three secondary epic poets. Two, though their extant work is extensive, have long been little more than names. Silius Italicus, after having made a rather disreputable fortune under Nero, devoted his comfortable and polite later

---

[1] Quintiliane, vagæ moderator summe juventæ,
    Gloria Romanæ, Quintiliane, togæ.—Martial, II, 90, 1-2.

years to the composition of seventeen hexameter
Books, with plenty of conventional deities and
the like, on the Punic Wars. He survived the
Century, dying at a ripe age under Trajan. Those
who have read his poem are unanimous in pro-
nouncing it the dullest they have ever come across;
but perhaps by reason of the sanction implied
in his wealth and fashion it has happened, like his
name, to survive intact. A similar fortune or misfortune has befallen the unfinished Argonautics of
Valerius Flaccus, who appears to have died under
Domitian. It is said to be mostly derived from
the Alexandrian epic on the same subject by
Apollonius Rhodius, and to reveal sympathetic
study of Virgil. Those who have read it do not
always think their time wasted. Those who have
not, and even among devotees of the classics they
have been far more numerous, have never consequently been held illiterate. One vaguely wonders whether it might not have got lost if the
first of this poet's names had not happened to co-
incide with the first name of the popular Valerius
Maximus, and his second with the last name of
Horace himself.

Statius, the third epic poet of this period, was
held in his own time the most eminent, and is held
so still. Professor Reid's article on him in the
Encyclopædia Britannica is a model of what such
things ought to be and seldom are; and the more
admiring introduction to Professor Slater's translation of the Silvæ[1] proves how deeply Statius can
even now appeal to a sympathetic reader. Were
all else lacking, too, the tenderly and almost
playfully beautiful account in the Twenty-first

[1] Oxford, 1908.

Canto of Dante's Purgatorio of how the redeemed
spirit of Statius recognises the doomed spirit of
Virgil—whose influence had unwittingly led him
to salvation—would combine with all that follows
there about Statius to keep him among the permanent traditions of European literature. Positively,
perhaps, he is not so important as he thus appears. The closing lines of his Thebaid deprecate
comparison with Virgil:[1]

> Shalt thou endure, read when thy poet is gone,
> Thebaid, nursed by me through twice six years?
>
> . . . .
>
> Live on, I pray, but never claim to be
> Like the divine Æneid. Following that,
> Reverence its lightest foot-print from afar. . . .

Amid the revived politeness of Flavian literature,
Statius, who appears to have been under Domitian the most fashionable court poet, retold in
something like Virgilian manner, the primal story
of Thebes on which so much of our extant Greek
tragedy is based. During the ages when Western
Europe had forgotten the Greek language, these
legends were read mostly as he wrote them.
Æschylus and Sophocles have now long supplanted him, but not so rudely as ever to let
him be quite forgotten. And through centuries he
had been reverently esteemed for a lofty beauty of
sentiment which gave colour to the tradition that
he had secretly embraced Christianity.

[1] Theb., XII, 810 *seq.*
> Durabisne procul dominoque legere superstes,
> O mihi bissenos multum vigilata per annos
> Thebai? . . .
> Vive, precor; nec tu divinam Æneida tempta,
> Sed longe sequere et vestigia semper adora. . . .

For seven or eight hundred years he was known, as Dante knew him, only by his completed Thebaid, and by the beginning of an epic poem concerning Achilles which he never lived to carry beyond the first lines of the Second Book. Scholars now and then remembered, however, that he had also written occasional poems, much more hastily composed. Early in the Fifteenth Century, these were discovered. The Silvæ, as they are called,—the word means *woods* or *thicket*, and implies unpruned luxuriance of growth,[1]—comprise thirty-two poems, mostly in hexameter, but now and then in other metres less firmly mastered. Some of them, notably the first, flatter Domitian monstrously; some describe in detail sumptuously delightful houses, temples, and the like; some are personal—laments for the dead, for example, and an epithalamium; one[2] concerns Lucan, and incidentally refers to the crimes of Nero which even in Domitian's time were conventionally painted very dark in contrast with the bright serenity of benign Flavian sovereignty; and so on. If we lacked other documents on the passing life of Rome under that dynasty, the recesses of the Silvæ might seem less dim. Even as it is, any student of the period must explore them and will not find his pains wasted. But in literature, as well as traditionally, they are incomparably surpassed by the epigrams of his contemporary Martial.

[1] The Preface of Ben Jonson's Underwoods touches on the term: With the same leave the ancients called that kind of body Sylva . . . in which there were works of divers nature, and matter congested, as the multitude call timber-trees, promiscuously growing, a wood or forest, so am I bold to entitle these lesser poems of later growth by this of Underwood, out of the analogy they hold to the Forest, in my former book.

[2] II, 7.

V

MARTIAL

The four writers to whom we now come have more than one claim to our attention. All were in full maturity of life, if not of work, under Domitian; all, far more strongly than any other Romans later than the Augustans, remain distinct and individual figures in European literature; two of them, Martial and Juvenal, brought hitherto secondary forms of expression into permanent literary importance; and when Juvenal died, who outlived the other three, the literary production of European antiquity was virtually complete. Until the time of Dante, some twelve hundred years later, no subsequent European writer achieved anything like their eminence, not to speak of that attained by the greater men, Roman and Greek, who were already safe in tradition when these last considerable makers of Latin literature were alive.

Of the four only Martial fully belongs to the period where for our purposes we may most conveniently consider them all. The younger Pliny, Tacitus, and Juvenal probably wrote most of their work, as their contemporary Plutarch probably wrote most of his, not under Domitian but under Trajan. The literary revival which they crown, however, had fully developed before the end of the First Century; all four may very likely have known not only one another but also the elder Pliny, and Quintilian, and Silius Italicus, and Valerius Flaccus, and Statius. Martial, indeed, addresses epigrams to Pliny the younger,[1] to Quinti-

----

[1] X, 19.

lian,[1] to Silius Italicus no less than five times,[2] and
to Valerius Flaccus[3]; as well as more than one to
Juvenal.[4] The fact that he and Statius never
mention each other has been held evidence of
their mutual jealousy. And the letters of the
younger Pliny demonstrate the intimacy of his
relations not only with his uncle, but with Tacitus, to whom he addressed the celebrated letters
concerning his uncle's death.[5] All these men may
clearly be considered as a contemporary group,
subject to the sovereignty of the Flavian emperors.

So far as extant work goes, Martial wrote mostly
under Domitian. What is commonly thought to
be his earliest extant poem consists of four elegiac
couplets[6] concerning the Coliseum, written for its
public opening under Titus or perhaps for its
completion under his brother. Either way, it
fixes the poet and his times in traditional
memory as contemporary with the most stupendous remaining monument of imperial Rome.
Like Seneca, Lucan, Quintilian, and the Emperor
Trajan, he was by birth not Italian but Spanish.
Unlike them he was neither born in prosperous
circumstances nor ever in a very favourable social

[1] II, 90.   [2] IV, 14; VII, 63; IX, 86; XI, 48, 49.
[3] IX, 55.   [4] VII, 91; XII, 18.
[5] Ep., VI, 16, 20; cf. p. 301.
[6] Here are the first and the fourth of them:
 Barbara pyramidum sileat miracula Memphis,
  Assyrius jactet nec Babylona labor; . . .
 Omnis Cæsareo cedit labor Amphitheatro;
  Unum pro cunctis fama loquetur opus. (De Spectaculis, 1.)
An old translation (1695) renders these lines:
 Egypt, forbear thy pyramids to praise, . . .
 Let Babylon cease incessant toil to prize, . . .
 All works to Cæsar's theatre give place;
 This wonder Fame above the rest does grace.

position. He came to Rome during the reign of
Nero; he supported himself there by his wits for
almost thirty-five years; and he finally went
back to Spain, whence the news of his death
evoked a kindly though supercilious comment
from one of his numerous patrons, the younger
Pliny.[1] The tone of this combines with the number of the laudatory verses he addressed to the
rich but dull Silius Italicus to imply his un-
enviable condition. The Fifth and the Seventh
Satires of Juvenal give a probably overcharged
and certainly resentful account of how literary
clients were treated by First Century Romans;
in comparison the Grub Street of Eighteenth Century London seems a fortress of affluent self-
respect. That Martial, so circumstanced, often
kept his temper is to his credit.

On the whole, he may be counted among the few
men of letters who have achieved something like
greatness by completely understanding their limitations. He never attempted what he could not
do well, and what he did was always well done.
Only one of his fourteen hundred and fifty epigrams reaches fifty lines;[2] only one other exceeds
forty;[3] few contain more than a dozen, many only
two. Within these limits he used language very
adroitly. Up to his time, it is hardly too much
to say that the word *epigram* retained something
like its original Greek meaning of *inscription*.
Any short poem which might conveniently be cut
in stone was properly so described. This appears
to have been the nature of the epigrams of Callimachus. More than any one else Martial gave
the word its later and permanent meaning, which

[1] Ep., III, 21.   [2] III, 58.   [3] I, 49.

implies keen wit and sharp point, such as cut into memory and stick there. The substance of his epigrams is widely various. Some, like those addressed to Silius Italicus and Pliny, and his frequent adulations of Domitian, are elaborate pieces of flattery, for which he was probably well paid; many, which are extremely and often obscenely abusive, would look like deliberate blackmail if we did not accept his assurance that he never published the real names of persons thus lampooned or attacked; the most memorable—and they are numerous—are inimitable snap-shots of daily life at Rome;[1] and a few, though probably made to order, are exquisitely tender. There are nowhere lovelier elegiacs than he wrote in memory of a little girl whom he calls Erotion:[2]

> Hanc tibi, Fronto pater, genetrix Flaccilla, puellam
> Oscula commendo deliciasque meas.
> Parvula ne nigras horrescat Erotion umbras
> Oraque Tartarei prodigiosa canis.
> Impletura fuit sextæ modo frigora brumæ,
> Vixisset totidem ni minus illa dies.
> Inter tam veteres ludat lasciva patronos
> Et nomen blæso garriat ore meum.
> Mollia non rigidus cæspes tegat ossa; nec illi,
> Terra, gravis fueris; non fuit illa tibi.

(To thee, father Fronto, and to my mother Flaccilla too, I send this girl, my pet and darling. Do not let little Erotion be frightened by the dark or by the dreadful bark of the watch-dog below. She would have known the full chill of a sixth winter, if she had lived only six days more. May she play now with you dear old friends, and lisp my name in her baby voice. May hard clods not touch her soft bones; and, Earth, lie not heavy on her; she never was to thee.)

[1] A pleasant impression of these may be had from the fluent English versions in Paul Nixon's A Roman Wit: Boston, 1911.
[2] V, 34.

Ben Jonson's lines, On My First Daughter,[1] named Mary, echo this Flavian Latin:

> . . . At six months' end she parted hence
> With safety of her innocence;
> Whose soul Heaven's queen, whose name she bears,
> In comfort of her mother's tears,
> Hath placed amongst her virgin-train;
> Where, while that sever'd doth remain,
> The grave partakes the fleshly birth,
> Which cover lightly, gentle Earth.

The collection of Epigrams where Jonson published these pretty lines in 1616 is easily accessible in any edition of his works or poems. Though never slavishly translated from Martial, the verses are throughout saturated with his spirit—none more so than the quatrain addressed to his Ghost:[2]

> Martial, thou gav'st far nobler epigrams
> To thy Domitian than I can my James:[3]
> But in my royal subject I pass thee,
> Thou flattered'st thine, mine cannot flattered be.

Glance at the epigrams of Jonson; then glance at the Hesperides of Robert Herrick, published thirty years later and as much more charming in their light grace as they are less robust; and, combining your impressions, you will have found in lasting English something very like what delighted Flavian Rome in Martial's epigrams. That Herrick could not have existed without Jonson is evident; no more could Jonson have existed without Martial—nor for that matter could any European writer of epigrams from the

[1] Jonson: Epigrams, XXII.   [2] Jonson: Epigrams, XXXVI.
[3] King James the First.

reign of Domitian to this day. The mould in
which he cast wit remains unbroken. One perplexing result follows. Even Herrick, and still
more Jonson, permits himself a degree of ob-
scenity, of coarseness, and of vituperation which
any one who knows Seventeenth Century England—the England of the Pilgrims and the Puritans, of the Authorised Version of the Bible
and of Oliver Cromwell—must instantly perceive
to give a distorted or at best a very incomplete
notion of the world they wrote in. An obvious
reason for this is that writing at a time with a
great future before it they modelled their work
on Martial's, produced when imperial antiquity
was on the verge of its decadence. Classic now
for eighteen hundred years, Martial has been traditionally held more certainly authoritative. But
quite apart from his own countless passages which
are free from evil, there is fair reason to doubt
whether even Flavian Rome was quite so black as
he often seems to paint it.

VI

THE YOUNGER PLINY

To correct or modify a too vile impression of
Roman society under the Flavian emperors, one
need only turn to the Letters of the younger
Pliny.[1] Compared with their models, the far
more numerous and less meticulously revised letters of Cicero, they doubtless have a secondary
aspect of studious artificiality. Taken by them-

---

[1] Melmoth's admirably sympathetic translation, of 1746, is happily reprinted in the Loeb Classic edition of the Letters. No translation of Cicero's letters is anywhere near so good.

selves they give a remarkably wide survey of life and character from the standpoint of a cultivated and prosperous Flavian gentleman. In this aspect as well as in the fact that each letter is politely confined to a single subject, they have a certain analogy to the English essays of Steele and of Addison. Like these, too, they present in a new light the conditions about them. If we knew England from 1675 to 1725 only through what may broadly be called the Comedy of the Restoration, we might hardly suspect that it contained such men as Sir Roger de Coverley. If we knew Flavian Rome only from the flashing sketches of Martial and the lurid memories of Juvenal, we might never dream that such men as Corellius Rufus[1] and Spurinna,[2] or such women as Arria[3] and the little daughter of Fundanus,[4] were no less part of it than rascals like Regulus[5] or the brutal slaves who played the devil with Larcius Macedo.[6] The difference between the Tatler or the Spectator and the Letters of Pliny is that the former present life under the guise of fiction and that the latter touch on it directly. But so, to take another English example, does Swift's Journal to Stella; and, to ramble on through the later Eighteenth Century, the Letters of Horace Walpole, the anecdotes in Boswell's Life of Johnson, and the Journals of John Wesley are contemporary.

The Letters of Pliny may here and there remind us of any or all of these, except that they are revised in detail with something like Horatian assiduity. You can hardly avoid the notion that

[1] Ep., I, 12.   [2] Ep., III, 1.   [3] Ep., III, 16.
[4] Ep., V, 16.   [5] Ep., I, 5; IV, 2, 7; VI, 2.   [6] Ep., III, 14.

when it came to style this excellent man attempted to out-Cicero Cicero, and therefore came nowhere near the comparatively free manner which often makes the letters of Cicero seem the best thing he left behind him. Apart from this polished hardness of surface, Pliny stays good reading still, particularly if you approach him, as you should always approach good reading, not too seriously. Turn his pages carelessly, as you might turn those of the Queen Anne essayists; read when the mood seizes you; and before long you will find, without knowing how, that he has given you a distinct notion not only of his amiable and accomplished character, but of the not yet desperate Roman world where he managed to keep out of serious trouble. His Greek philosopher, Euphrates,[1] for example, resembles Plutarch rather than the "Græculus esuriens"—which may be rendered in colloquial American terms "hungry little Dago"—of Juvenal.[2] His descriptions of country houses,[3] of natural curiosities,[4] of works of art,[5] and of literary pursuits[6] are very pleasant. His clear and interesting accounts of legal matters[7] deserve prayerful study by English and American lawyers who may prefer not to annoy their readers. And his Tenth Book, which consists wholly of his correspondence while a provincial governor with the Emperor Trajan, and appears not to have been

[1] Ep.. I, 10.
[2] Juvenal, III, 78. The well-known passage (58–80) where this occurs is worth comparing with Pliny's letter about Euphrates. Which seems more nearly true any one is at liberty to decide.
[3] E. g., Ep., I, 3; II, 17; V, 6; IX, 36, 40.
[4] E. g., Ep., IV, 30; VIII, 20; IX, 33.
[5] E. g., Ep., III, 6; IX, 39.
[6] E. g., Ep., I, 8; VI, 21; VII, 4, 17.
[7] E. g., Ep., I, 20; II, 11, 14; IV, 9; VIII, 14.

elaborately revised for literary effect, has preserved an excellent model of what conscientious administration ought to be.

Like the uncle who adopted him, he was born a gentleman of Como, and passed most of his life in high official and social condition at Rome. Like many kindly men so circumstanced throughout history, he never forgot or neglected his native place, partly perhaps because there are few more innocent joys than being recurrently welcomed home and heartily celebrated there as a successful favourite son. Apart from his letters about the destruction of Herculaneum and Pompeii, on which we have already touched,[1] his most widely remembered are that concerning ghosts,[2] and those which he exchanged with Trajan when not quite sure how to deal with the uncompromising behaviour of Christians in a world previously blest with religious toleration.[3] Even these, we may fully admit, do not reveal him as exactly a great man. If he had been, he could hardly be accepted as beyond peradventure a typical man of his time. The great must always be few and solitary, rising constantly larger through the perspective of the centuries. But only a time still great could have bred so great a gentleman as we come to know when we come to know the younger Pliny.

VII

TACITUS

Whoever even begins to know the works of Tacitus must instantly recognise him, too, as a

---

[1] *Cf.* p. 301. [2] Ep., VII, 27. [3] Ep., X, 96, 97.

great gentleman. At the same time he reveals himself, at least in literature, as a great man. The facts of his life are little known. We have glimpses of him in a dozen or more of Pliny's Letters,[1] one of which, addressed to him, begins "I predict, and I am apt to be right, that your histories will last."[2] They were evidently intimate friends, sympathetic too as officials and as men of letters. His wife was a daughter of Agricola, whose career, as he has recorded it, was among the most wholesomely distinguished of the First Century of the Cæsars. But where he was born, who were his ancestors, and when he died nobody now knows. His grandeur therefore, strongly individual though he be, has a touch of half-Homeric impersonality.

A few things about him are nevertheless clear. Probably born under Claudius, he was undoubtedly old enough to remember the worst years of Nero and the revolutionary horrors of the year 69. Under Vespasian, he was already in office. He was fully mature under Titus and Domitian; and if he outlived Trajan, under whose beneficent rule his principal works were written, it cannot have been for more than a little while. His later years were passed, to be sure, not in the dark days of the First Century, but in the brighter days of the Second. His personal memories, however, included the most ominous threatenings of the rising deluge which before very long was to submerge antique civilisation. And as he wrote only of times within the memory of men whom he

---

[1] Duly specified, for a wonder, in the scanty index of the Loeb Classic edition.

[2] Auguror, nec me fallit augurium, historias tuas immortales futuras. Pliny, Ep., VII, 33.

knew well, if not within his own, the final effect
of his work is like that of a grim epilogue to the
world-tragedy whose buoyant prologue was written a thousand years before in the Iliad and the
Odyssey.

His literary manner—style if you prefer the
word—has the conscious oddity of a time when
ingenious phrase-making had long been the fashion.   He could master, however, a tendency which
masters most men.   The power of his compact
words more than redeems their artifice; they defy
at once forgetfulness and alteration.   To take a
few examples, of widely different kinds, try as
long as you like to put into English an aphorism
imbedded in the noble paragraph which closes
his life of Agricola:[1] "Is verus honos, ea conjunc-
tissimi cujusque pietas."   What it means is clear
enough: "True honor is the loving respect of all
who are nearest";   but this gives hardly more
notion of what Tacitus has said than if the words
meant different things.   Or take his statements of
a healthy virtue and of an insidious vice observa-
ble among the German Barbarians: "Sera juvenum
Venus," he writes,[2] "eoque inexhausta pubertas"
("Their animal passions come late, so they breed
with full vigour");   and again,[3] "Sine apparatu,
sine blandimentis expellunt famem; adversus sitim
non eadem temperantia."   ("Without sauce or
ceremony they get rid of hunger; in combatting
thirst they are less moderate.")   These English
words tell what he means but not how he put it;
you would be at pains to imprison in any other
terms than his the implicit sarcasm with which
he calls to mind the juvenile lasciviousness of

[1] Agricola, 46.   [2] Germania, 20.   [3] Germania, 23.

imperial Rome, and the profligate extravagances
of Roman feasting. Passages from his historical
work are still more characteristic. His narrative
is too trenchant for disguise even by translation.
Whoever has read of Galba's end,[1] and Otho's,[2]
and that of Vitellius,[3] can hardly forget how the
surging mob in the Forum overwhelmed the
stern old man for a little while imperial, or how
nothing in the life of the usurping Neronic deb-
auchee became him like the leaving it, or how the
Roman populace watched as they would watch a
show the last attempt to withstand the victorious troops of Vespasian on behalf of the fat sovereign whose end was too ugly to be pitied. "De-
formitas exitus misericordiam abstulerat"[4]—are
the four words which those last eight feebly try
to represent in English. It is just as useless to
attempt translation of the eight Latin words in
which Tacitus tells how when the terrified Vitellius
was beaten to death the crowd abused him as
vilely as they had fawned on him when he was
alive: "Vulgus eadem pravitate insectabatur inter-
fectum qua foverat viventem."[5] No other words
than his own can quite reproduce the power with
which Tacitus makes one feel the momentary thrill
of horror when frightened lookers-on suddenly perceived that Galba—the first fleeting incarnation
of Cæsar who could nowise claim kinship with the
mighty Julius,—was falling before their very eyes:
"Neque populi aut plebis ulla vox."[6] ("Neither
gentle nor simple uttered a single sound.") We
need his own very syllables fully to marvel at the
tremendous antithesis with which he contrasts the

---

[1] History, I, 39–41. [2] Ib., II, 46–49. [3] Ib., III, 82–86.
[4] Ib., III, 84. [5] Ib., III, 85. [6] Ib., I, 40.

opinions concerning Otho and Vitellius entertained
by Romans uncertain as to which must presently
be their sovereign: "Vitellius ventre et gula sibi
inhonestus, Otho luxu sævitia audacia reipublicæ
exitiosior ducebatur."[1] ("The belly and gullet
of Vitellius were held damaging to himself; the
lechery, cruelty, and recklessness of Otho more
threatening to the State.") And, memorable
though the passage be in any form, none but
those who have compared translations with the
original Latin can ever fully appreciate the firm
strokes of Tacitus when he records how the stanch
Helvidius Priscus behaved in the Senate on the
accession of Vespasian.[2]

Apart, however, from a style so individual that
if it fail to dominate it may repel, Tacitus has
qualities which no translation can obscure. He is
the last of the four great antique writers of history—the form of literature least damaged by
rendering into other languages.[3] He bears to
Livy, so far as Livy now survives, a relation analogous to that borne by Thucydides to Herodotus.
That Livy is less powerful than Herodotus is
pretty clear; that Tacitus can hold his own beside Thucydides is a tenable opinion. He lacks,
no doubt, the large primality of Greece; but no
subject comparable in range with the imperial
dominion of Rome could possibly have tested the
strength of a Fifth Century Athenian. And this
imperial dominion Tacitus exhibits to us in three
distinct aspects. His Life of Agricola presents
it as on the whole it must have appeared to those

---

[1] *Ib.*, II, 31.   [2] *Ib.*, IV, 4–8; and *cf.* **43.**
[3] And the translations of his History and his Annals by Church and
Brodribb are admirably readable.

beyond its range; here at last was an organised system which could reduce the warring world to wholesome and orderly peace, capable too of embodiment in commanders as imposing for their virtues as for their discipline of what otherwise might have been only colossal brute force. His book about Germany presents, as nothing else comes near presenting, the barbarian vigour constantly and everywhere threatening the Roman frontiers. The task of Roman Empire was not only to bring order out of chaos within its bounds; it must also resist incessant external pressure, urged on by obscure forces—remote, shadowy, exhaustless—which were ultimately to prove insuperable. If Tacitus had written only these two monographs, he would have left us a uniquely distinct record of how Rome was conditioned throughout the first Century of the Cæsars. Yet, even when considered together, the monographs appear of only secondary importance beside his two greater works. His History originally recounted the story of Rome from the accession of Galba until the death of Domitian; his Annals, a vast preface written later, begins with the accession of Tiberius and originally extended to the death of Nero. Though a great part of each has been lost, enough remains tremendously to indicate the disease already fixed upon the Roman state. To survive, Rome had need of health superb as her strength; and she was stricken with a sickness beyond all medicine. Thus trebly presented, the Empire resembles a clear-skinned giant overawing enemies while cancer gnaws at his vitals.

Whether the story be altogether and positively true is another question. That he meant it to be we can hardly doubt; nor yet that his treatment of it went far to fix in tradition the view of it which has generally prevailed. A familiar passage from the Annals[1] will serve at once to illustrate this and to suggest his limitations as an authority. It tells of the great fire at Rome under Nero, and how the Emperor thought well to hold the Christians responsible for the disaster. It speaks of them as generally "hated for outrageous misconduct,"[2] and as an example of such moral filth as pours into a capital, "where from far and wide abominable and shameful things of all kinds gather together and are welcomed."[3] It implies that guilty or not they were on hateful terms with humanity.[4] His compact account of their martyrdom, to be sure, which immediately follows, would hardly displease John Foxe himself. Nobody, however, would dream these outcasts to be professors of the principles of the Gospel, and parishioners of Peter and of Paul; and nobody can deny that the historian who thus misconceived them is the same on whom we must chiefly depend for our belief in the abominations of Nero. Yet, right or wrong, that belief has been rooted in European posterity. The truth or the falsity of it need not concern us now. Our business is with the traditions of European literature. When we come to these we may well stay uncertain whether any writer of history has ever been greater than Tacitus, the last great historian of classical antiquity. A period which could produce, amid all its confusions, a figure such as his was not yet altogether decadent.

[1] Annals, XV. 38–44.   [2] Per flagitia invisos: XV. 44.
[3] Quo cuncta undique atrocia aut pudenda confluunt celebranturque: Ib.
[4] Haud perinde in crimine incendii quam odio humani generis convicti sunt: Ib.

VIII

JUVENAL

The last unquestionably great Latin writer
lived at this time still great; thus chance, perhaps,
has assured his greatness. Though little is definitely known about Juvenal, there can be no
doubt that under Domitian he was a contemporary of Martial, of Pliny, and of Tacitus; that
his relations with persons of condition were less
cordial or less pliant than those of his friend Martial; or that he outlived the others. One tradition has it that, exiled in Egypt, he died there at
eighty some two years after Antoninus had succeeded Hadrian as emperor. Though he chiefly
wrote, however, in the freer days of the Second
Century, his opinions of the world had become
fixed in the First. The Fourth Satire, which bur-
lesques Domitian by pretending that he summoned
his Privy Council to decide how the largest turbot
ever caught should be cooked, happens to be fixed
in historic time; and substantially the lines which
fix it apply to the other fifteen Satires as well.
All are based on what existed

> When the last Flavian flayed the fainting world,
> And Rome still cowered before a bald-head Nero.[1]

During that period, to be sure, Juvenal appears prudently to have occupied himself not with
satire but with the far safer pursuit of rhetoric,
then used mostly as an elaborate exhibition of
ingenuity. Our nearest approach to it nowadays

[1] Sat., IV, 37–38:
> Cum jam semianimum laceraret Flavius orbem
> Ultimus, et calvo serviret Roma Neroni.

is probably a conventional debate for a prize where, whatever the issue, the affirmative and negative sides are assigned by lot. Practice of such performances, though often leading to skill in popular appeal, is favourable neither to judicial opinions of life nor to sensitive personal sincerity. If you win your point, you have done your job; if you have done your job, you are noisily commended; and if you are thus commended for work well done, it is hard, at least for you, to avoid the conclusion that you are an unusually weighty moralist. This is particularly the case when you happen, in the turmoil of this world, to find yourself an under dog or even only to sympathise with such luckless animals. Juvenal was apparently beset by both of these insidious temptations. His Fifth Satire and his Seventh describe the plight of penniless literary Romans in terms generally thought to be personally reminiscent; and if any great European writer has ever assumed more incessantly than he that whatever prevails is therefore all wrong, the fact remains unremarked.

The form of satire, which he finally chose to set forth his views and of which he has proved the most influential exponent, is generally held the chief contribution of Latin to the tradition of world-literature. Every other form used by the lasting Roman writers—from Plautus to Tacitus— was more or less modelled on primal Greek masterpieces. No Latin imitation of Aristophanes, however, if indeed any ever amounted to much, has been preserved. The kind of discontent which animated Fifth Century Greek comedy developed in Latin a comparatively independent variety of expression. Even Lucilius, to be sure, who first

brought satire into literature during the Second
Century before Christ, so far yielded to Greek
allurements as ultimately to abandon all metres
but the originally Greek hexameter, thereafter accepted as the regular satirical vehicle of Rome;
but the Greeks seem never to have used it for precisely such purpose as, by Juvenal's time, was
already classical among the Romans. The principal satirists before Juvenal were the now lost
Lucilius and the still extant Horace and Persius.
Whether they would have sufficed to make satire
more than a minor form of European literature
may be disputed. When Juvenal had done his
work, he had not only obscured his predecessors
for all future time; he had made formal satire as
important as most forms of literature brought
into being by the Greeks.

Without troubling ourselves to define it, for
nothing is much more futile than to attempt precise definition of artistic matters and then worry
whether a given work comes within the limits,
we should probably agree that satire, as we know
it, is apt to be an appeal to dormant or dominant
prejudice. It assumes something, anything, or
things in general to be wrong or ridiculous. It
assumes itself, and anybody who will sympathetically listen, to be intellectually and often morally
superior. It exaggerates and denounces; it is
often clever and trenchant; it is sometimes fervid but seldom kindly. When it does not make you
resentful it grins or shames you into acquiescence.
It permits itself excursive liberties of structure;
whatever comes to mind at any moment may pop
out if to the point. Formal satire, to be sure,
is not at present the fashion; nowadays men find

any too firmly precedented artistic traditions life-
lessly formal.   But nothing can ever suppress the
most powerful piece of satirical writing in our English language—the Gulliver of Swift.   This exhibits
individual man first as a giant among pygmies who
can subdue him by their countless numbers;   next
as a pygmy among giants, the stupidest and
pettiest of whom has enough brute strength and
careless thoughtlessness to frustrate his best wits;
then as sane in a world of madmen;   and finally as
foul amid the clean simplicities of beasts.   "Sæva
indignatio" (raging wrath) are the words chosen
by Swift to describe in his epitaph how he writhed
under the whips and scorns of time.   With less
lifelong meaning they might equally be applied to
the political mood of James Russell Lowell when
he threw off the Biglow Papers—the most nearly
lasting expression of satiric temper as yet produced in the United States of America.

A frequent though not necessary phase of such
temper is implied in the dialect made familiar by
the stinging lines of Lowell.   It purports to be
the speech of plain folks as distinguished from those
who have been trained in polite amenities, of the
simple as distinguished from the gently nurtured,
of your every-day hard-headed Yankee.   A
healthy fashion used to describe such men as the
common people, thereby recognised as the source
of common-sense.   Nowadays we are apt to leave
out the adjective, to use the word *people* not as
Lincoln used it, including all sorts and conditions of
men, but as if only the lowly could rightly claim
rights.   One consequent difficulty met us a little
while ago;[1] when Tacitus described the thrill of

[1] *Cf.* p. 317.

horror in the Forum as the crowd saw Galba toppling, he used the words "Neque populi aut plebis
ulla vox"; we now have no terms exactly to define
his distinction. We clumsily contented ourselves
with an inadequate translation: "Neither gentle
nor simple uttered a single sound." Both *populus*
and *plebs* we might carelessly have translated by
the same word, *people*. But *populus* implies responsibility, meaning people of the better sort;
and *plebs* implies irresponsibility such as we now
associate with people of the lower sort, sometimes
described by our comparatively new word *mob*.
The compilers of Sir James Murray's New English
Dictionary have discovered no earlier use of this
now established word than an evidently slangy one
in 1688, the last year of King James II; and they
note a comparatively familiar deprecation of it by
Addison in 1711.[1] It is really a contraction to a
single syllable—something like that of *bus* from
omnibus—of the Latin words *mobile vulgus*, which
mean the *unstable crowd*, such as Shakspere shows
us in Julius Cæsar and in Coriolanus. Its classical origin may be a line from the Tristia of Ovid,[2]
where after mentioning how shadows evident in
sunlight disappear when clouds gather he goes on

> *Mobile* sic sequitur fortunæ lumina *vulgus*.
> (So fickle crowds follow the rays of chance.)

That fickle crowds are not ill disposed, the scene
where Coriolanus presents himself as candidate
for the consulship[3] reminds us quite as clearly as
it exposes their fickleness; and that all the fault is
not theirs duly appears in the scene which follows.[4]

[1] Spectator, 135.
[2] Ovid: Tristia, I, 9, 11.
[3] Coriolanus, II, 3.
[4] Coriolanus, III, 1.

But they are not to be depended on for anything more than community of crude human emotion. This was memorably expounded some years ago by Monsieur Lebon, whose "Psychologie des Foules" has been at once summarised and anglicised by the playful translation of its title as the Psychology of Fools. The French word *foule* means very nearly what is meant by the Latin word *vulgus;* we have no exact English equivalent signifying numbers and implying a humanly fallible tendency to unreason and other imperfections of refinement. And by this time, our plunge into a mist of words and allusions may well have seemed to distract us from Juvenal. He has none the less been in mind all the time. Until we can feel with the mob, and welcome the dialect of Hosea Biglow, we can never understand either the pervasive subconsciousness of humanity or how uncompromisingly this underlies all trenchant satire. Classic though Juvenal's hexameters look, they are so saturated with springs of popular prejudice that their aroma has flavoured all the subsequent satire of Europe. And to describe the nature of this contagiously unamiable temper, our English language affords us no other word than what without our plunge, and perhaps despite it, would be the misleading term *vulgar.*

Unlike almost all the other lasting writers of classical antiquity, Greek or Roman, Juvenal was neither a person of quality nor disposed to gratify his betters. It is not from his temper but rather from his manner and his style—accidents of the period when he wrote—that we derive our impression of his grandeur. Compared with Tacitus and Pliny, he may sometimes remind us of Piers Plow-

man when compared with the Canterbury Tales.
To know him you must doubtless turn all his pages
more than once, and linger over phrase after phrase
which has persisted through the ages: "Frontis
nulla fides," [1] for example (You can't trust looks);
or

> Haud facile emergunt quorum virtutibus obstat
> Res angusta domi. [2]
> (It's hard for those to struggle up whose strength
> Is sapped in narrow homes);

or

> Sed quis custodiet ipsos
> Custodes? [3]
> (But who shall guard the guardians themselves?)

Standard English literature will nevertheless give
you some impression of him. Truewit's comments
on women in the Silent Woman of Ben Jonson[4]
are an admirably free, and decently expurgated,
translation into racy Jacobean English of passages
from the Sixth Satire of Juvenal—itself the most
unbridled denunciation of womanly misconduct
in all the literature of Europe. And the two principal poems of Dr. Samuel Johnson—London and
the Vanity of Human Wishes—are excellently lasting adaptations, by an Eighteenth Century English
churchman, at the time a literary hack, of the
Third Satire of Juvenal, which denounces Rome,
and of his Tenth, which slashes rather than pricks
the bubble of vanity.

As to the influence of Juvenal on our literature,
you will find the Satires of Donne, although re-
pellently crabbed and thus unlike him in style,

---

[1] Sat., II, 8.
[3] Sat., VI, 347.
[2] Sat., III, 164–165.
[4] Act II, Scene 1.

constantly inspired with his spirit and sometimes approaching his power. Without him Dryden could hardly have written Absalom and Achitophel, nor Pope when pretending to imitate Horace have been so bitterly un-Horatian. His temper underlies much of Byron's invective, such as occurs in English Bards and Scotch Reviewers. And the distorted perspective in which Juvenal sees the better classes of imperial Rome has been likened to that in which the far more sympathetic Dickens observes the better classes of Victorian England. He is rhetorical, he distorts and exaggerates; but he is fervid, and if not always and indisputably a sincere moralist he is at least sincere in his moral pretense; writing at a period still great, he writes in the grand style of classical antiquity; and while he thus appeals to the fastidious taste of culture, he veils under his grand manner a kind of feeling which those who would praise it will call popular, and those who would rather appraise it may more truly call vulgar. He speaks, perhaps, to the favoured few; but he speaks for the human, uncritical, suffering, and distorted many.

Another epilogue, if you like, you may find his work to the world-tragedy of which Homer made the prologue. He was contemporary with Tacitus. Both lived and wrote long after the year 100, but by the year 100 both were in full maturity of life and experience. We may best think of them, and of those who made literature about them, as then grouped together. As a group these men are secondary among the Latins only to the greater group which made the First Century before Christ the Golden Age of Latin Literature. Plutarch lectured and wrote in Greek for the same public which Martial, and the younger Pliny, and Tacitus, and Juvenal addressed in Latin. And the great literature of European antiquity ends with this Silver Age of Rome.

CHAPTER IV

THE SECOND CENTURY OF THE CHRISTIAN ERA

I

HISTORICAL TRADITIONS

As we have already seen, the memorable writers who came to maturity under the Flavians lived on and wrote long into the Second Century. Though they record or imply impressions and memories of terribly ominous and troublous times, they therefore survived to know something of what Gibbon summarised in his familiar sentence: "If a man were called to fix the period in the history of the world during which the condition of the human race was most happy and prosperous, he would, without hesitation, name that which elapsed from the death of Domitian to the accession of Commodus." [1]

Gibbon's Decline and Fall of the Roman Empire begins with an account of its condition during these halcyon days, and then tells its history from the death of Marcus Aurelius until the last trace of the Eastern Empire vanished when Constantinople fell before the Turks more than twelve hundred years later. The book is among the most remarkable ever written. The first volume appeared in 1776, the year of the American Declaration of Independence; the last in 1788, the year before the Constitution of the United States went

[1] Decline and Fall: chap. III (ed. Bury, I, 78).

into operation. Professor Bury's introduction to what is now the standard edition[1] clearly specifies various aspects in which the colossal work is no longer quite authoritative. The marvel is that it remains on the whole what it probably will always remain—so comprehensive and so firmly outlined a record of European history through a dozen centuries that for any who wish to see in perspective the period between antiquity and modernity it can hardly be superseded. Furthermore it is a work of admirably readable literature. Its prejudice against Christianity no doubt makes its treatment of the religion which has long dominated Europe misleadingly unsympathetic;[2] but, to go no further, its accounts of two facts immeasurably important both traditionally and historically —Mahometanism[3] and the Crusades[4]—are probably the best ever written, at least for such purposes as ours. We cannot too often remind ourselves that our concern is not primarily with history or even with literature, but rather with the traditions assumed as familiar throughout the growing literature of Europe. The fact that Gibbon's work is itself a great traditional fact in English literature would alone bring it within our scope. And, quite apart from this, it so records the general traditions of European history from the Second Century to the Fifteenth, that whoever wishes to remind himself of them should always have it at hand.

The first three chapters of Gibbon[5] summarise the condition of the Roman Empire during the

---

[1] Seven volumes: London, 1900.

[2] The famous chapters on this point are XV and XVI (Bury, II, 1–139).

[3] Chapter L (Bury, V, 311–396). Chapters LI and LII continue the story (Bury, V, 397–494; VI, 1–61).

[4] Chapters LVIII, LIX (Bury, VI, 259–365).   [5] Bury, I, 1–82.

Second Century, which he generally calls "the age of the Antonines." For us the chief tradition derived from this period may rather be called that of the Five Good Emperors who succeeded the first Twelve Cæsars. From the accession of Nerva, in 96, to the death of Marcus Aurelius in 180, the Empire enjoyed a succession of sovereigns who, whatever their personal failings, so conducted affairs of state that they seemed to realise the imperial dreams already classically recorded in the Æneid.[1] Though Nerva, to be sure, lived only two years, and died before the Second Century had quite begun, his beneficent policy was continued and developed by his adopted heir Trajan, the first Cæsar not of Italian birth. Born in Spain, somewhere near what is now Cordova, Trajan was already in the second year of his sovereignty, and well past the age of forty-five, by the year 100. The details of his life and reign need not concern us now. He left behind him a tradition so excellent that, although he was pagan, Dante preserves the legend of how his soul, permitted the grace of momentary infantile reincarnation, was duly baptised and thus admitted to Paradise;[2] and the column which commemorated him in his own Forum still stands at Rome less mutilated than any other monument now so old there. He had no son, and probably adopted as heir the kinsman who succeeded him, Hadrian.

Under Hadrian the boundaries of Roman power were for a few years at their widest; and something like personal memories of him traditionally linger. That his presence left his name in such diverse parts of the Empire as Britain, where he built the

[1] *Cf.* pp. 188, 201; Æn., VI, 679–901.   [2] Paradiso, XX, 103–117.

first Roman wall, and Athens, where the ruins of his buildings are almost as apparent as those of his stupendous villa at Tivoli, and Egyptian Thebes, where an inscription on the singing Memnon is said still to record the fact of his visit, proves how widely he surveyed his dominions. The Castle of San Angelo at Rome was originally his domed tomb. The lovely images of Antinous combine with the tender legend of this favourite's fate to soften the mood in which we might judge his infirmities. And the lines which he is believed to have composed as a farewell to life are lastingly and sweetly human:[1]

> Animula vagula, blandula,
> Hospes comesque corporis,
> Quæ nunc abibis in loca,
> Pallida, rigida, nudula,
> Nec ut soles dabis jocos?
>
> (Gentle breathlet, ever fresh,
> Guest and comrade of the flesh,
> Whither goest thou now away,
> Pale and stiff, unclothed of clay,
> Laughing no more, no more at play?)

His adopted heir, Antoninus Pius, was emperor through more than twenty years. No reign ever more justified the saying that periods of happiness are without history; in tradition Antoninus hovers indistinct but benignant. His adopted heir and successor, Marcus Aurelius, was as good a man. Walter Pater's Marius the Epicurean introduces him in a story, itself almost if not quite literature, full of the spirit of his time. Though he con-

---

[1] See Spectator, No. 532 (10 Nov., 1712); and Elwyn and Courthope's edition of Pope (London, 1871), VI, 187, 393, 397.

scientiously opposed as revolutionary the conduct
of the Christians, his Meditations, which he jotted
down in Greek, prove him at heart to have been
something like a Stoic saint.   The column raised
in his memory at Rome remains there the only
rival of the column of Trajan; and his equestrian
statue, now long placed on the Capitol hill, has
never been overthrown.   With him ended the
period of imperial beneficence begun by Nerva;
it had lasted almost eighty-five years.

Justly or not, tradition represents the wives
of Antoninus and of Marcus Aurelius, both named
Faustina, as luxuriously corrupt.   The elder Faustina left no son; the younger bore to Marcus
Aurelius the son who succeeded him, the Emperor
Commodus.   His reign of thirteen years resembled those of Nero and of Domitian.   Debauchery
and tyranny led to his murder.   Then ensued
a brief parody of the appalling year 69, more
than a century before, when Galba, Otho, and
Vitellius had quivered momentarily imperial
between the last of the Julian dynasty and the
first of the Flavian.   For some three months
Pertinax—traditionally only a cloudy name—
was emperor; he was killed by his own guards,
who are said thereupon to have sold the sovereignty to the highest bidder, Didius Julianus.
Three months later they had murdered him, too;
and the succession of the Cæsars had passed to
an able general of African birth, Septimius Severus.
In the year 200 he had been emperor for seven
years; he lived for more than ten years longer.
Among the shapeless ruins on the Palatine Hill,
those of his palace are perhaps the largest—they
say it was once seven stories high; and his

triumphal arch is the only monument of the Forum now imaginably recognisable by eyes that saw Rome in its splendour.

As we shall remind ourselves by and by, other Cæsars have lingered in tradition; but no subsequent line of imperial succession is anywhere near so distinct as the Twelve Cæsars of the First Century and the Five Good Emperors of the Second. Something of what impended may be felt by any who will call to mind again the works of art on which we have casually touched. The column of Trajan has something like Augustan dignity; the portraits of Antinous despite their beauty are sentimental; the column of Marcus Aurelius and still more his bronze statue appear in comparison almost rude; and the sculpture which frets the triumphal arch of Septimius Severus looks rather barbaric than classic. Gibbon was right in beginning with the accession of Commodus his tremendous narrative of the decline and fall of the Roman Empire; and we may believe ourselves equally right in summarising the Second Century of the Christian Era, the last full century of classical and purely European antiquity, as the Century which added to the historical traditions of Europe the stately line of the Five Good Emperors—Nerva, Trajan, Hadrian, Antoninus, and Aurelius.

II

LITERARY TRADITIONS

SUETONIUS, APULEIUS, PERVIGILIUM VENERIS; LUCIAN, GALEN

Compared with the two First Centuries, before and after Christ, during which almost all the great extant writers of Latin literature came into existence, the Second Century is nowhere. In the year 100, to be sure, many of the writers grown to mature years under the Flavian emperors had not yet produced the works which make them enduring. But if we ask for names virtually unknown when the Second Century began, recognised when it ended, and still in some kind of existence, we shall find them surprisingly few and impressively unimportant. Suetonius and Apuleius are the most memorable Latin authors; whether the anonymous Pervigilium Veneris, which here and there may remind one of the lines attributed to Hadrian, was written under the Antonines or a century or two later may never be quite settled. Apart from these, our literary traditions from the Second Century are not Latin, but at least in language Greek. We have already touched on Plutarch, a full contemporary of the writers whom we have grouped as Flavian, and on the Greek Meditations of the last of the Good Emperors, Marcus Aurelius. When we were concerned with the First Century, we may remember, we mentioned nothing Greek at all; that period, indeed, was so rich in Latin that we did not even glance at Vitruvius, whose famous Latin treatise on architecture was written under Augustus, any more than when concerned with the great centuries

of Greece we had found place to touch on the
medical tradition of Hippocrates. In the Second
Century, Latin literature so subsided that we can
hardly help noticing, together with the Greek
dialogues of Lucian, the Greek medical works
of Galen.

None of the men of letters who came into
existence during the Century is comparable in
scale with their predecessors. Historically the
most considerable is probably Suetonius. He
was a younger friend of the younger Pliny; he
was more or less of an official, at one time a sort
of private secretary to the emperor Hadrian;
some indiscretion is thought to have caused his
retirement from public life; and almost throughout the reign of Antoninus Pius, he devoted his
later years to industrious literary leisure. Much
of the fruit of this is lost. The work by which he
is permanently known is his anecdotic biographies,
in eight Books, of the Twelve Cæsars. The six
emperors of the Julian line are given a Book apiece;
Galba, Otho, and Vitellius are put together in
the Seventh Book, and the three Flavians in the
Eighth. The new succession of Good Emperors,
under whom these accounts of their predecessors
were written are left untouched, much as Shakspere in his plays concerning English history
wrote nothing about the Tudors until, well after
the Stuarts had succeeded them, he had a hand
in Henry VIII. And it may be that the traditional group of the Twelve Cæsars originated
in the fact that these and only these were recorded
by Suetonius. For just his task he had more than
one qualification. He liked gossip; he was by
way of hearing court gossip concerning both
present and past under Trajan and Hadrian; and

at least in Hadrian's time he probably had access to the long-since lost private archives of the Cæsars. For many details about them, some not scandalous, he has always been the principal authority; he is a principal source, as well, of the most abominable traditions about them indelibly fixed in European memory. That he wrote under what was virtually a new dynasty may rouse our suspicion when we consider him as a serious historical authority. Nothing can avert his importance in anecdotic tradition. And there can be little question that he is the most important historical writer of the Century succeeding that which began when Livy was still at work and ended when Tacitus, though not yet a great author, was already mature.

Apuleius, the other Latin writer of the Second Century who has indisputably survived, was an African rhetorician and philosopher, little and inconspicuously at Rome. Whoever desires light on his life and character may find it pleasantly shed in Mr. H. E. Butler's translation of his Apologia,[1] and the adequate introduction prefixed to it. This Apologia, to be sure, an elaborate speech in his own defense, is interesting mostly as an example of what had happened, by the Second Century, to such forensic eloquence as we find in Cicero and in Demosthenes. Their rhetorical devices look fresh as nature when compared with the vivacious but extremely conventionalised artifices of Apuleius. His importance in literary tradition is wholly due to another piece of his work—the fantastic tale which he called Metamorphoses but which has long been nicknamed the Golden Ass. The story, modelled

[1] Oxford, 1909.

like that of Petronius on a now lost Greek phase
of fiction developed at Miletus in Asia Minor,
tells how a by no means austere young man is
magically changed into an ass, and after many—
often unmentionable—adventures as a beast of
burden is at last restored to human form. Here
and there it may still be found faintly amusing;
it contains incidental descriptions of daily life
interesting to students of history; and some of
its excursions into philosophy and the like are
said to be very useful to those who would know
how the Second Century was disposed to speculate. So far as Apuleius distinctly survives, however, it is only by reason of the skill with which
he retells, as a long episodic story, the world-old
legend of Cupid and Psyche.[1] Walter Pater's
version of this is perhaps the most surely delightful passage in Marius the Epicurean.[2] The tale
is charmingly pretty; for all its sentimentality
it has not only sweetness but significance; yet it
is further even than Suetonius from what still suffused the writings of Tacitus and of Juvenal—
the grandeur that was Rome.

So too, if indeed it belong to this period at all,
is the anonymous Pervigilium Veneris, with what
Marcus Dimsdale[3] calls "its haunting refrain":

Loveless, mayst thou love to-morrow; loving, still to-
morrow love.

This translation has the unusual merit of preserving not only the meaning but the exact rhythm
of the original Latin line:

Cras amet qui nunquam amavit; quique amavit cras amet.

---

[1] It runs from Book IV, 28 to Book VI, 24 (Loeb, 185–285).
[2] Part I, chap. 5.   [3] Latin Literature (1915), p. 528.

The poem where it recurs is a kind of pagan hymn, probably composed for some festival of Venus. Though it may possibly be as late as the Fourth Century, it may have been written during the Age of the Antonines. Compared with anything on which we have as yet touched, except the five lines of Hadrian, it has for modern ears the quickening charm of a lyric movement half-way between those of our own times and the strangely different lyric measures of the Greeks. It has beauties, too, which make one always glad that it has not been lost. But it is neither primal, like the beautiful works of Greece, nor grand, like the enduring works of Rome.

And this is all that in the perspective of time now stays surely visible of what Latin literature brought to birth during the Second Century of the Christian Era.

The introduction to Fowler's translation of Lucian[1] clearly tells all that is known about the most ingenious and most nearly popular Greek writer of this period. He was a Syrian, probably born under Hadrian and dead after Commodus. During the first half or more of his life he seems to have travelled widely, as a rhetorician and a lawyer; and it is noteworthy that, although he tarried and probably practised for some time in Italy and even in Gaul, he is thought never to have found need of mastering the Latin language.[2] His copious work during his later years, when he had turned from rhetoric and law to philosophy, took the form of animated, witty, and pregnant

[1] Oxford, 1905 (four volumes).
[2] This, we may remember, was the case with Plutarch; cf. p. 162. As for Lucian, see A Slip of the Tongue: Fowler, II, 34.

dialogues. Whoever has been able to read Greek has generally found them both entertaining and stimulating. At least two of our enduring literary traditions have proceeded from them: Shakspere's Timon of Athens is remotely derived from Lucian's Timon, or the Misanthropist,[1] and Swift's Gulliver from Lucian's True History.[2] Any student of his times should know him well. But the fact that he wrote only in Greek kept him a sealed book in Western Europe for hundreds of years; and in Greek literature he can never have quite such dignity as marked it when from Homer to Theocritus it was not only the primal but the only expression of the spirit later to be European.

Among the translations in the Loeb Classical Library, Doctor Brock's version of Galen's treatise on the Natural Faculties stands out as at once clear and readable. His introduction gives a compactly summarised account of Galen's position in the history of medicine. This evidently takes us pretty far afield. The name of Galen has always remained traditional. Precisely what he wrote is not generally remembered, nor is the fact —incidentally not indexed in Bury's edition of Gibbon—that he lived during the Age of the Antonines and is said to have been consulted by Marcus Aurelius. That no Latin work nor any considerable work of pure literature distracts from him now such cursory eyes as ours, throws light or shadow, as you will, on the condition of European literature when the Second Century came to an end. The great literature of Rome was also a thing of the past.

[1] Fowler, I, 31.   [2] Fowler, II, 136.

CHAPTER V

THE ROMAN TRADITION

Though by the year 200, classical Latin literature, like Greek before it, was already classic, there was no cessation of writings in the Latin language. As the official language of the Roman Empire, this was used and more or less understood for centuries throughout the civilised world. Except for the prevalence of French since the reign of Louis XIV, it has never been even remotely approached as a vehicle of communication among Europeans whose native languages were different. Until something like modern times, it stayed everywhere the standard language of law, of learning, and of serious literature. The Divine Comedy of Dante, written after 1300, is the first great and enduring European poem ever composed in any modern tongue. Even in the Nineteenth Century, any educated European could be assumed able to decipher a Latin letter. And to this day, as everybody knows, Latin remains the world-wide language of the ancestral Catholic Church. In one sense, therefore, it has never died.

Its history as a still living language, however, differs from that of Greek. There has never been a time since the days of Homer when Greek was not a language in which living men habitually thought and talked, and they do so still; there has hardly been a time for more than a thousand years when Latin was not, even among

those who knew it best, a foreign language learned
at school, just as it is now. In this sense, Latin
has long ceased to be humanly idiomatic. There
is some reason, too, for believing that classical
literary Latin was never humanly idiomatic at all.
The classical Greek writers, believing everybody but
Greeks barbarian, had before them only the simple
problem of expressing what they had to say in the
language which to them was native. When Romans
attempted to make literature they were aware
that admirable literature already existed in Greek.
Their problem was to rival this in a language held
by the Greeks comparatively barbarous. What
is more, for all its sententiousness, it really was a
far less flexible and sensitive means of communication. To improve it, at least from times before
Cicero, they laboriously tried to make it as like
Greek as they could. The more nearly they succeeded, the less it resembled the thoughtless dialect
of their daily life.

At its best, accordingly, literary Latin was ele-
gantly artificial; and all the while men were using
with careless freedom such colloquial Latin as occasionally appears in the fragments of Petronius. One
sometimes wonders whether the monkish Latin of
the Middle Ages may not be about as like the
every-day talk of imperial Rome as the speeches
and essays of Cicero are, or the studied classics
of the Augustans and the Flavians. Beyond
question, this barbarous Latin of the times between antiquity and modernity served two purposes: as we have already seen, it was a useful
international language; and whoever could easily
use it had learned in the process to read currently
not only classical Latin literature but also the

numberless important works composed in Latin long after ancient Rome was dead and gone. To take a single random example of these, the Principia of Isaac Newton, which in 1687 set forth the doctrine of gravitation, was written in Latin as a matter of course. One curious result of the disuse of Latin since the Eighteenth Century has been futile effort to invent completely artificial languages, like Esperanto, for accepted international use; and one reason why worthy people persevere in such effort ingenuously revealed itself a few years ago. An ardent French advocate of Esperanto, setting forth its merits to an American friend, was nowise disturbed by the suggestion that a simpler plan would be to revive the old international language, current Latin, which had long served its purpose and already had a priceless literature. To this apparently wise plan, he said, there is an insuperable objection: no doubt Latin has proved admirable both for international communication and for literary purposes—"*mais, monsieur, c'est la langue de l'Eglise*" ("but, sir, it is the language of the Church"). All who deplore the influence of Christianity, should therefore do all they can to suppress Latin. At present the tendency of popular education appears to be in their favour. The prospects of Esperanto nevertheless look hardly auroral; and as long as the Church persists, Latin will considerably survive.

Evidently, at the same time, this modern phase of Latin has in common with almost everything written since the Second Century a feature which marks it as different from Latin literature and tradition before that period. We need hardly remind ourselves that even more than when we were touching on the traditions of Greece[1] we have left unnoticed much that would demand the attention of serious students, nor that we shall have to neglect more still, as we proceed to later times. All we can attempt is to call clearly to mind, century by century, what now seem the chief things added by each Century to European tradition. Thus regarded, we found that up to the Second Century before Christ European tradition, so far as it came to literary expression, was only Greek. To this Greek tradition the next four hundred years added that of imperial Rome, different, nearer to us in other aspects than mere time, assuming the primal traditions of Greece and unwittingly interposing itself between them and the future, but still—so far as we have yet considered it—purely European. Thus, in such perspective as ours, the traditions of classical Rome group themselves with those of Greece, clearly distinct from any later. For classical antiquity was pagan, and later Europe has been Christian, and Christianity—whatever else—is not of purely European origin.

Hereafter, Christian tradition becomes for our purposes increasingly important. Before long it had so blended the other than European traditions of the Jews with the traditions of Greece and of Rome that European tradition has never since been quite free from Asiatic. Our next business is evidently to consider Christianity. Before doing so we have only to define our impression of the condition in which it found the antique traditions of Europe.

[1] *Cf.* p. 153.

In the first place, as we have already reminded ourselves again and again, the secondary traditions of Rome, assuming and appropriating the primal traditions of Greece, had not supplanted these but had so mingled with them that only the critical scholarship of recent times has restored them in anything like their original lustre to the general knowledge of Europe. Even still we are carelessly apt to think of Greece not as it was, but rather as it looked for centuries on centuries through the interposed veil of Rome. Secondly, the Romans, nowhere near the Greeks in intelligence or in artistic perception, were decidedly their superiors in common-sense. Their language has never been surpassed for sententious wisdom; nor their conduct for practical administrative and military organisation. In the third place, although they adapted and modified the primal types of literary expression originated by the Greeks, they added to them nothing more important than the stinging ends of Martial's epigrams or the formal satire which culminated in Juvenal. But, finally, their genius for government had fully developed, after centuries of legal and political experience, the colossal ideal of Roman Empire—of a world kept at peace by the righteous power of an all-embracing sovereignty. This ideal, no doubt, has never been fully realised nor often long approached. But we of the Twentieth Century need only watch how men are trying to establish a League of Nations to be sure that, in altered form, this ideal is living still. The genius of Greece tended to diversity; that of Rome to unity; and we of America cherish no ideal more clearly than our national ideal of Union.

One great tradition, the while, neither Rome nor Greece had ever originated. What most clearly groups them as purely European is that, like all subsequent Europe, they never brought into being an enduringly potent religion.

BOOK III

THE TRADITIONS OF CHRISTIANITY

CHAPTER I

RELIGION AND EMPIRE

For more than fifteen hundred years, as every one knows, Christianity has been the accepted religion of Europe. If our concern were with its history, its principles, or its truth our task now would be not only colossal, but perilous and endless. Approaching it as we do, however, and considering it only as the origin of traditions which although unknown to classical antiquity saturate later European literature, we may treat it even more summarily than we have treated the traditions of Greece and of Rome. The very sacredness with which it has been cherished by generations on generations of our ancestors has for ages given its traditions, as distinguished from its precise story and doctrines, a unique unity. For our purposes, it has long since generalised itself.

Religion is a hard word to define. The phase of human perception it concerns, however, is both elementary and everlasting. In human life, everywhere transitory, there has always been and there must always be, a vast and increasing mass of experiences closely related to our bodily existence and to the material conditions about us. These we become aware of, at first in confusion, mostly through what we call our senses; and what we call our reason gets them here and there into something more or less like manageable system and order. A convenient generalisation is nowadays apt to group our conjectures about them as capable of verification or disproof by observation, like the subjects of astronomic study, or by experiment, like the matters presented for the study of chemistry. The very process of scientific study, however, involves limitation of the field it concerns. Your astronomer is not an authority on poisons, nor your chemist on the dreary laws of grammar. No phase of earthly experience can be more uncompromisingly incessant than the environment of your knowledge, however extensive, by things you know nothing about. The more you scrutinise these, the more illimitably they reveal themselves. Before long, you must grow aware that what is thus true of any given man is no less true of all humanity. Beyond what we know must always and everywhere extend fathomless depths, variously affecting ourselves and our knowledge, but completely beyond the range of any "observation or experiment which may verify or disprove our opinions about them. Though modern science, no doubt, has considerably extended the bounds of ascertained knowledge, it has made no appreciable advance into the unknown infinities; nor is there any reason to suppose that the science of the future will be more fortunate. Intercommunication throughout the stellar universe might very possibly result in extensive modification of our economic and social perplexities; it could hardly bring us a step nearer either Heaven or Hell.

These dogmatic names might here give rise to debate as to whether there are any such places at all. Alluring as this discussion would be, it is just now none of our business. Everybody knows

what the words indicate, and furthermore that for
many hundreds of years innumerable millions of
European Christians have lived and died in the
firm faith that they must finally find abode in one
or the other. To maintain that they have known
this grimly solemn fact, nevertheless, at least in
any such sense of the word *know* as would assure
them that they must eat to live, that a burnt child
dreads the fire, or that twice two is four, would
be a mistake. They have accepted it as true,
not because it could ever be verified or disproved
by observation or experiment, but for the very
reason that, as it could not be, it was evidently
a matter for a more congenial phase of human
opinion than any knowledge can ever be: namely,
belief. There is a vast and limitless range of
human perception utterly beyond the limit of any
scientific investigation. Concerning this boundless immensity human beings have always been
disposed to make more or less credible conjectures;
and when these conjectures crystallise into anything like system they are apt to become what we
call religions. Superstitions they often seem to
those who do not accept them; but there are few
more illuminating pleasantries than that which
has described a superstition as a religion in which
you do not happen to believe.

Considered so generally as this, no doubt, the
line between religion and philosophy is indistinct.
When the human mind begins to soar above things
earthly, it almost always tends to recognise the
existence of something infinitely transcending all
limitation whatsoever. Fate you may call this
in philosophic moods, or Nature, or whatever
else; in the moods more characteristically religious

men call it Divinity, and throughout the course
of human record they have believed it to be personified, sometimes—like every-day Greeks—in
many diverse and separate forms; more seldom—
like orthodox Christians—in the form of a single
omnipotent, omniscient, omnipresent God. Once
thus personified, either through human conjecture
or by means of divine self-revelation to human
seekers for divine and transcendental truth, the
gods or God become objects of worship. And the
many religions, more or less enduring, which have
marked the course of human history are all based
on dogmatic belief in one or another Deity or
group of deities, who, whatever their peculiar features, are generally believed to enjoy a durability
of existence vastly beyond human experience.

Now although, at least to us, the European
mind appears inexhaustibly fertile in philosophic
speculations and in scientific aptitudes, pure and
applied, it has never displayed commanding religious power. To put the matter most simply,
there are at this moment three different systems
of religion which appeal, each in its own way, to
countless millions of our fellow beings: Buddhism,
Christianity, and Mahometanism. Whatever
their divergencies, all three have in common the
faculty of commending themselves, far and wide,
to men widely different in every way from those
who originated them,—of being taught and accepted as eternally and immutably true; and all
three were first formulated not in Europe but in
Asia. We need hardly go further to assure ourselves that, just as clearly as the genius of Europe
is philosophic and scientific, the genius of Asia
is religious.

Of the three great religious systems still potent,
one—the Buddhist—was physically so remote
from the Roman Empire that it could have little
obvious or direct effect on our ancestral Europe;
it has never prevailed, indeed, except in what we
may broadly call the Far East. A second—Mahometanism—did not come into existence until
the Seventh Century of the Christian Era. Just
here, therefore, only Christianity can historically
concern us. How inevitably it does so is clear,
if we stop to think, from no more than the fact
that for many centuries our whole European
chronology has been based on the date when Jesus
Christ is assumed to have been born. At that time,
as we have reminded ourselves, the Roman Empire was already established; born under Augustus,
he preached and taught in the reign of the Emperor
Tiberius. During his earthly life, his preachings
and teachings could hardly have impressed any
Romans who happened to hear of them as either
unusual or important. They appeared to be only
a kind of religious revival addressed to a far from
cordial sect, or whatever you choose to call the Jews
from an imperial point of view, in a rather troublesome easterly province; and if we may accept the
Gospel narratives, they were opposed not by the
imperial authorities, but principally by the Jews
themselves. Otherwise Barabbas would regularly
have come to grief. As for Rome, it was extraordinarily tolerant in matters of religion. When
the Empire extended, the Roman power came to
subdue many and various regions which had long
had more or less local gods of their own. The
Roman policy in general was not to suppress or
to ignore these previously hostile divinities, but

unless they were politically, socially, or morally
mischievous to adopt them with prudent politeness. Thus, you might evidently placate their
worshippers; and if by chance the divinities
should be genuine you might at the same time
placate and conciliate them too. And, at least
after hospitably receiving the gods of Greece,
Rome had so many gods already that occasional
new ones could hardly complicate the religious
situation. All Rome asked, in return for this
religious liberality, was mutual consideration:
if Rome duly respected the gods of other people,
it seemed only fair to expect other people duly
to respect the gods earlier or later recognised by
Rome.

When Augustan empire was established, this
convenient practice found itself, at least theoreti-
cally, in a new situation. Whether anybody was
then aware of the fact we need not inquire; at this
distance, everybody can see for himself that a political power claiming universal earthly dominion
happened to be provided with no god of indisputably more than local authority. The natural
consequence of this deficiency was a tendency to
supply it by the recognition of new deities more
general in scope than had hitherto been usual.
Temples dedicated to Augustus and Rome presently resulted, at first in the East; and long
before the last of the Twelve Cæsars had quivered
out of his feverish splendours a number of them
had already been set up as permanent imperial divinities. The practice of ritually worshipping an
emperor while still alive had meanwhile declared itself, as an obvious method of pledging
allegiance to the established state. What is

more, this was far from unreasonable; whatever the personal infirmities of the emperor as a human being, his power and his surroundings—the circumstance of his office—gave him as a magistrate something like superhuman dignity. This form of imperial religion, however, was hardly in accordance with ancestral Roman tradition; and besides the disadvantage of evident novelty it was burdened with at least two others: as the emperors followed one another on the throne they began to swell the possible number of imperial divinities at a disconcerting rate, and meanwhile their conduct in the flesh was often such as uncomfortably to deprive them, even when deified, of the moral regard inspired by personal respectability. A rapidly increasing group of imperfectly reputable gods is an unpromising basis for a not yet firmly established system of devout catholic worship.

Quite apart from any deeply religious consideration, accordingly, there was bound to be religious disturbance before very long. Imperial principle was hardly to be satisfied by prolonged practice of recurrent apotheosis; for superhuman sanction, universal dominion required a universal god. The general faith of Christian Europe has later been apt to hold this condition of earthly affairs due to inscrutable divine purpose. Things were making ready for final acceptance of the supreme truth revealed to mankind by one who in the flesh was a Jewish peasant, born under Augustus and crucified under Pontius Pilate, Procurator of Judæa under the Emperor Tiberius.

The history of the Jews had been in two ways the very antithesis of the history of the Romans.

As a political power they had never long or considerably prevailed over their adversaries; but throughout their national existence they had tended to find increasingly certain spiritual consolation for material adversity in the justice and mercy of the deity whom their ancestral religion proclaimed to be the one and only true and universal God. Other gods might very likely be malignant spirits suffered to punish the sins of mankind; even so, when in His own good time the Lord should choose to shine in His glory the most potent of them must shrivel into cinders. Unrecognised by others, the religion of the Jews like the government of Rome was in principle imperial.

In its Christian version this religion has now prevailed so long, wherever the influence of Europe has extended, that a bit to realise how it appeared to the imperial authorities of Rome demands imagination. To them it was only one of a great many alien religions which at different times came under their political dominion. They were prepared to treat it as cordially as they had treated any other, expecting only that it would be equally accommodating to them. When it declined to be, they were both perplexed and displeased. They had no idea either of its imperial principle or of its spiritual efficacy. They were not conciliated, at the same time, by the racial peculiarities of the Jews, which have never been sympathetic to Gentiles. As has lately been said, there are three distinguishable aspects of Jewish character: the Hebraic, sublimely spiritual; the Jewish, penetratingly intelligent; and the Jewy, trickily slippery. They commingle in Shylock; and the tenacious loyalty of Jewish affection has often made all three hang confusingly together. Jewish dominion, accordingly, none but Jews have ever contentedly accepted; even among themselves, too, they have often been turbulent; meanwhile, the amazing instinct for self-preservation evident throughout Jewish record has always made them repellent antagonists. Nothing was less to be expected than that the religious doctrine of such a people as this should presently appeal to anybody else, particularly when it demanded as a condition of its acceptance that every other religion should be renounced as false.

A few lines of Juvenal[1] incidentally indicate how a casual observer in Flavian Rome regarded the Jews, at that time making occasional converts from paganism. Their observance of the Sabbath amounts to neglecting work for idleness every seventh day; they make mysteries of their fantastic rites and sacred volumes, and they have no such thing as a reasonably imaginable god:

> Nil præter nubes et cæli numen adorant.[2]
> (They worship only clouds and wilful sky.)

Hardly any words could imply at once more invincible ignorance of what has made originally Jewish religion world-wide and more ingenuous though blind recognition of what through all the later centuries of Europe has given it unapproached spiritual efficacy. Dealing with it as we are dealing now, considering it not as a question of doctrinal truth or mortal error, but only as an incomparably important tradition, we cannot fail to

[1] Sat., XIV, 96–106. [2] Ib., 97.

see that faith in it has sustained and comforted the weakness and the suffering of humanity beyond anything else in our ancestral history. Human life is inexorably tragic—a struggle of sentient beings with an environment certain to annihilate them in every aspect of their bodily and earthly form. The law of material existence decrees not only that all men must die; so must all races of men, of beasts, of things that swim, and fly, and crawl, and palpitate; so, in due course of that immensity which we call astronomic time, must earth itself, sun and moon and stars, and all the sensible universe. Thus conceived, human experience can truly express itself only in one vast, re-echoing cry of despair. And gods in organic form cannot help much or long; even though you grant them existence, the very fact of their form is itself a limitation which groups them with things local and transitory, not omnipresent and everlasting. The fact of limitation, at the same time, involves another fact—that something probably exists beyond any limit which we can imaginably fix. Grant this, believe in it, believe it for all its ineffable mystery just and yet merciful, and you will find your spirit newly irradiate. Death and sorrow, sin and pain shrink into nothing, if your faith be fixed in a righteous, omnipotent, and eternal spiritual God, prefigured even to such as craved graven images by nothing baser than the fathomless purity of the skies.

We stray, most likely, as far as Juvenal himself, from any formal orthodoxy, Jewish or Christian. There can be no doubt, however, that the imperial principle and the spiritual efficacy inherent in the ancestral religion of the Jews were destined to become, for centuries on centuries, the most profound and sacred fact in the later traditions of Europe. There can be no doubt that their Asiatic origin, beyond anything else, gave Christian Europe a quality distinctly different from that of purely European classical antiquity. And there can be no doubt that the sacredness with which Christian Europe has cherished its religious traditions has so generalised them that we should go further astray still if we tried to examine them in detail. Our present business is only to give ourselves some account of the traditions of Christianity as they had gathered by the end of the Second Century of the Christian Era. We may summarily do so under three heads: the Old Testament, the New Testament, and the Church.

CHAPTER II

THE OLD TESTAMENT

For some fifty or seventy-five years past, the Bible has been so critically studied that many good moderns fail to remember how long it was for almost all Europeans a sacrosanct object of faith. Pretty lately, for example, an unregenerate old-fashioned American, sinfully lamenting the drab approach of constitutional prohibition, found comfort in the twenty-fourth Chapter of Isaiah, which gloomily predicts this kind of joylessness. A friend to whom he read it presently brought him to pause by eagerly inquiring whether the passage was written by the first Isaiah or the second,— which evidently implied the friend, a man accomplished in recent literature, to be more instantly familiar with such writers as the lamented Matthew Arnold than with orthodox tradition of the Holy Scriptures. Now if any one wishes to understand just what these historically are, he cannot too diligently devote himself to the Higher Criticism. But whoever, like us at this moment, wants to recall what they traditionally have been may best for the while neglect the Higher Criticism altogether.

Neglecting this advantage of modern enlightenment, we may find the Old Testament as a matter of tradition pretty distinct. In substance, it is a classic collection of the classic literature of the Hebrews—the ancestral Jews. Thus regarded, it resembles a book which should comprise all extant Greek literature from Homer to Theocritus, or all Latin from Plautus to Juvenal. Furthermore, nobody ever questioned that every word of it was written by human beings; tradition, for example, attributed the first five Books to Moses, the Psalms to David, the Proverbs to Solomon, and the various Books of prophecy to the prophets whose names they bear. These men were believed actually to have lived, at various times in the historic past; and in point of fact, it is now thought that, whether they wrote what has been credited to them or not, David and Solomon may be regarded, for general purposes, as contemporary with Homer, and the last of the now orthodox prophets as flourishing somewhere about the Age of Pericles. Whatever their historic dates, they were all venerably in the past long before the Christian Era began. For at least two other reasons, also, they were tremendously venerable to the Jews: their writings taken as a whole displayed a constant sense both of the existence of God and of the consequent relation between God and man; and, at a time when even primal Greek poetry was still often assumed to be superhumanly inspired,—the first line of the Iliad simply and probably sincerely invokes the goddess, or muse, to sing of the wrath of Achilles,—the words of Scripture were believed by the faithful to have been inspired by God Himself, and accordingly to be a direct revelation through human mediums of the will of supreme Divinity. Humanly a classic literature compendiously collected, the Old Testament, accepted by believers as the word of God, became traditionally a divine unit.

This phase of it, incomparably surpassing any other, led to various traditional results. The utterances of God must of course have an authority beside which any utterance of humanity shrinks into nothing. They become themselves objects of something like worship. The least of them may enshrine unsuspected truth, true throughout the heavens above, and the earth beneath, and the waters under the earth, and all time that has been, and all that shall be, world without end. Your pagans thought the cryptic ravings of their oracles authoritative; your true believer, despising such superstition, must reverently listen to every syllable vouchsafed him by the God who created heaven and earth, the sea and all that in them is. The divine unit of Scripture accordingly tended to become an exhaustless treasury of oracular sayings, proceeding straight from the wisdom of Divinity.

Now nothing can be much more evident to the devout, through all the ages, than that God works in a mysterious way His wonders to perform; and, although His words throw light on the mystery of His conduct, they neither completely explain it nor always prove such as uninstructed man can fully understand. Misunderstanding of them, the while, is perilous. They need interpreters, who must be devout, learned, and skilful, much as legislation when carried into practice needs to be interpreted by competent courts. The official interpreters of divinity are priests, who tend to sink their individuality in the common and perdurable identity of their priesthood. And in any priesthood, where human beings with all their infirmities are required to become in many aspects the ministers of superhuman Divinity, there is a tendency, if only of accumulating precedent, to let the fire of divine truth smoulder into the life-lessness of formal orthodoxy. According to the traditions everywhere accepted by Christians, something of this kind had happened among the Jews well before the Christian Era dawned. Among the Jews themselves, far and wide, not to speak of peoples not yet blest with any revelation of divine truth, there was consequent need of a new dispensation. We can hardly be mistaken in believing that, at least from the time of Theoc-ritus, when Rome had not yet interposed its veil between primal Europe and the Europe of the future, the religion of the Jews, as later Europe was to conceive it, had begun to sink into little more than a great accumulation of oracular sayings ob-scured rather than illuminated by the theologic subtleties and ritual formalisms of priestly ortho-doxy.

To the Jews themselves, however, then as ever since, this opinion has appeared abominably false. Until Christianity began to spread, their holy traditions were little known to others than them-selves, any more than modern Christians know much of anything about the religious tenets of Confucian Chinese or the Shinto rituals of Japan, or than pious Catholic Christians, Roman or Anglican, are critically familiar with the Book of Mormon, or with the apostolic teaching of Mrs. Mary Baker Eddy. The Jews themselves, the while, however distracted by sectarian disputes, were not only fervently devoted to every detail of their already immemorial laws and ceremonies, but incidentally apt to be familiar with the very

letter of their sacred writings. They remain so
to this day. There are few more poignant stories
than that of the sick rabbi who, not long ago, in
an American city, finding himself too feeble with
age ritually to adjust some priestly ornament,
turned his face to the wall, and, with Yiddish words
which meant "Now I can no longer be a Jew; now
I will die," gave up the ghost. Such a man as
this would abhor the Higher Criticism with all his
loyally passionate heart; but both he and his disciples could tell you more instantly than the highest of critics just what words have been traditionally cherished through the Jewish and Christian
ages as orthodox Scripture.

In a general way, neglecting numberless and intricate questions of detail occasionally disputed
by the godly and the godless alike, we may agree
that these traditional words, familiar in the time
of Augustus to all good Jews but not yet to anybody else, present their divine truth under more
than one distinguishable aspect. The most popular of these is, of course, the narrative. It begins
with the story of Creation, of Adam and Eve, and
of their temptation and fall; it lingers for a chapter
over Cain and Abel, and then swiftly proceeds
to the time when the sins of mankind were punished
by the Deluge, from which none were saved but
Noah and his family, with a great many attendant
animals, in the ark which rested at last on the
mountains of Ararat. It goes on to tell of the
confusion of tongues generations later at Babel.
Then comes the more leisurely story of the patri-
archs Abraham, Isaac, and Jacob, and the detailed
account of how Joseph, sold into Egypt by his
brethren, made asylum there not only for himself,

but for all these other children of Israel. The ultimate oppression of their offspring by the Pharaohs follows, and the prolonged history of how under the tremendous leadership of Moses they escaped and made their way after years of wandering in the desert to the sight of their promised land, whither Moses was not suffered to go in the flesh. The conquest of it was achieved by Joshua. Then came the period covered by the Book of Judges, in the midst of which occurs the story of Samson, and at the end of which appears the tender story of Ruth. On this follows that of Samuel, which leads straight to the brilliant history of David and of Solomon, when the earthly power of the Jews was most splendid. And so the narrative goes on, through a succession of kings good and evil, until their accumulated sins brought upon the Jews the heavy penalty of Babylonian captivity. To indicate the story further, or in any detail, or to point out its occasional interruption by those elaborate statements of Law which the Jews held its most signal feature, is needless here. Whoever desires to know it, or to refresh his memory of it, may best ask his spiritual adviser what version may most prudently be consulted. Those who neglect spiritual advice will find in the Authorised Version of the English Bible—the text of 1611—an admirable work of literature which for some three hundred years was accepted as uniquely orthodox by English-speaking Protestants, and beside which any sensitive ear must probably feel illiterate the clarifying revisions proposed by pious and learned Protestant scholars of the Nineteenth Century. Any version will serve to remind anybody of countless names and incidents immemorially known both to Jewish tradition and to that of Christian Europe, but totally strange to European antiquity.

Any complete copy of the old English Bible, too, such as used to be venerated in American families and enriched with Yankee genealogical records, will be found to contain certain Books which English Protestants have held uninspired, but admitted to be edifying. Some of the stories recorded in these writings, commonly called apocryphal, have persisted in European tradition,—that of Judith, for example, or that of Tobit. They have hardly the traditional importance, however, of those believed equally sacred by all Jews and all manner of Christians alike.

A second aspect of Scripture may be found in the lyric passages, of which the most obvious example is the Book of Psalms, traditionally ascribed to King David. The use of the Psalms as exceptionally consecrated hymns by almost all sorts and conditions of Christian worship has made them, and the devoutly distinct lyric moods which they express,—magnificently Hebraic, and totally strange to classical antiquity,—immemorially familiar among Europeans of later than classic times. To a less degree, this is true as well of a third aspect of Scripture—the books and passages of aphoristic wisdom, of which the most salient example is the Book of Proverbs, attributed by tradition and its own first words to Solomon.

More characteristic still, or at least more widely different from anything purely European, are the Books of the Prophets, each attributed to some antique Jewish worthy specially irradiated with the spirit of God and thus able to utter with his human tongue the actual words of mysterious and omniscient Divinity—to understand the past, to judge the present, and to foretell the future. Here and there in these books are imbedded familiar stories, such as those of Daniel in the lions' den and of Jonah's misadventures when he would rather not obey the word of the Lord and go to Nineveh. In general, however, the words of the prophets are less comprehensible. They often profess to be uttered in moments of vision, of inspiration, of what we may call possession by the spirit of God. They denounce the sins of men, they dwell on the punishments which these have brought on the sinners and all about them, they predict deeper sorrow and suffering still for those who persevere in iniquity, and yet they promise victory and consolation to them that will serve God with all their hearts. They tremendously preach a morality unlike that of any mere philosophy however noble, for essentially it is a morality not of the flesh or of the mind, or of any aspect of the body, but rather of the ineffable spirit. For this they claim the authority of eternally divine sanction; they are the conduits of the spoken will of God. Nothing can exceed the grandeur of their solemnity; nothing can avert the pitilessly just penalties of sin, accumulating vast material and earthly misery among the godly as well as among the godless. But those who dwell in the spirit need never despair; nothing can quell the souls of the righteous; nothing can abate the flood of consolation forever surging from the boundless infinitude of God. And in God's good time, His will shall finally prevail. A Mes-

siah—an Anointed one[1]—shall work the wonder.
The term is not clearly defined in the Old Testament; but what it signifies is mysteriously set
forth in such glowings as these of

Rapt Isaiah's wild, prophetic fire:[2]

For unto us a child is born, unto us a son is given: and
the government shall be upon his shoulder: and his name
shall be called Wonderful, Counsellor, The mighty God,
The everlasting Father, The Prince of Peace.[3] . . .

And there shall come forth a rod out of the stem of Jesse,
and a Branch shall grow out of his roots: and the spirit of
the Lord shall rest upon him, the spirit of wisdom and
understanding, the spirit of counsel and might, the spirit
of knowledge and of the fear of the Lord.[4] . . .

And righteousness shall be the girdle of his loins, and
faithfulness the girdle of his reins. The wolf also shall
dwell with the lamb, and the leopard shall lie down with the
kid; and the calf and the young lion and the fatling together; and a little child shall lead them.[5]

Again, and more than before, we may well be
straying from both sound scholarship and formal
orthodoxy. Even so, as our concern is with the
traditions of European literature, we need not hold
ourselves all wrong. We have attempted only to
perceive how Europe has supposed the Old Testament, itself accepted as divinely inspired, to have
presented itself to the Jews before the time of
Christ. It contained the classic version of their
national history, as the chosen people of God,
from the Creation of the World to a time later
than that of the brightest glory of Greece. It

---

[1] This is the literal meaning of the Greek word *Christos*, now commonly
supposed to be a personal name of Jesus.
[2] Burns: Cotters' Saturday Night, XIV.
[3] Isaiah 9 : 6 (Authorised Version). [4] Isaiah 11 : 1, 2. [5] *Ibid.*, 5, 6.

comprised the statement of the Divine Law which they must reverently and submissively obey. It treasured for them divinely sacred poetry, and words of wisdom sanctioned by the omniscience of Divinity. Its prophecies denounced their sins, promised spiritual consolation for all material adversity, and foretold righteous triumph to come. It was at once mystically sacred and altogether their own. The Jewish priesthood officially interpreted it. Every faithful Jew knew and reverenced it. Nobody else knew much of anything about it; and few cared to know.

CHAPTER III

THE NEW TESTAMENT

Our concern with the New Testament, as with the Old, has nothing to do either with its original history or with its truth; so, once again, we may let alone all questions of theology or of the Higher Criticism. Traditionally the volume has been accepted by Christians as the record of how, during the First Century of the Christian Era, their religion, which still dominates Europe, came into existence. They have consequently been apt to regard it, even more than the Old Testament, as a divinely sanctioned unit; and for them its relation to the earlier Scripture has resembled the relation of Roman tradition to Greek. The traditions of Rome, as we have seen, interposed themselves like a veil between those of primal Greece and subsequent Europe; in much the same way the New Testament has interposed itself between Christian Europe and the primal Jewish antiquity recorded in the Old. Both together, too, treasured by Christians as together a unit, have combined with the traditions of the Church to interpose a second and a deeply venerable traditional veil between Christian Europe and all classical antiquity.

At this point, of course, Jewish tradition abruptly separates from that of Christianity. Both would agree that New Testament record begins with an account of how, during the reigns of Augustus and of Tiberius, there appeared among

372

the Jews a great prophetic preacher, addressing himself chiefly to hearers profoundly familiar with Jewish tradition, and professing to irradiate this with new revelations of truth. To the Jews in general He seemed no genuine prophet, but only an obnoxious and heretical revivalist. To those who believed in his teaching, as to Christians ever since, He seemed miraculously and marvellously to fulfil the inspired prophecies of the Messiah. The humility of His circumstance combined with the unshaken confidence of His spirit to excite the angry contempt of the Jewish priesthood. His followers, through the centuries which have believed Him the one and only Incarnation of God, have held the more fervently that His divinity is most wondrously attested by the fact that His kingdom is not of this world,[1] but is the everlasting kingdom of our Lord and Saviour Jesus Christ.[2] The fact that in the course of the ages it has acquired considerable and various material and earthly power may be regarded as a transitory incident; nothing can affect for them the spiritual changelessness of its divine eternity.

The story of His life, of His death by crucifixion, and of His resurrection from the dead is told in four separate and parallel accounts, with which the New Testament opens. To these is given the special name of Gospels; and the writers to whom they are attributed—Matthew, Mark, Luke, and John—are called the Evangelists, which means the bearers of good tidings. In the Authorised Versions of the Bible, Latin and English alike, Mark[3] and Luke[4] briefly mention His ascension

---

[1] John 18 : 36.
[3] Mark 16 : 19.
[2] II Peter 1 : 11.
[4] Luke 24 : 51.

into heaven, more fully set forth in the Book of Acts,[1] the fifth and the last narrative book of the New Testament. The full name of this book in English is the Acts of the Apostles. Originally there had been twelve of these chosen vessels of the Lord, His immediate and constant personal followers, specially called by Him to prosecute His mission. One, Judas Iscariot, had proved faithless and had betrayed Him. Presently after the ascension, the remaining eleven gathered together and after devout prayer filled by lot the vacant place, and the lot fell upon Matthias.[2] On the ensuing day of Pentecost, when they were all with one accord in one place,

there came a sound from heaven as of a rushing mighty wind, and it filled all the house where they were sitting. And there appeared unto them cloven tongues like as of fire, and it sat upon each of them. And they were all filled with the Holy Ghost, and began to speak with other tongues, as the Spirit gave them utterance.[3]

From this point the book proceeds to tell of the nature and the spread of apostolic teaching; and the apostolic teacher of whom it gives by far the most full and circumstantial account was not one of the original twelve, but Paul, whose miraculous conversion is related in the Ninth Chapter, and who is traditionally remembered beyond the rest as especially the apostle to the Gentiles. At the end of the book, he had come safe to Rome, where he

dwelt two whole years in his own hired house, and received all that came in unto him, preaching the kingdom of God,

[1] Acts 1 : 9–11.   [2] Acts 1 : 15–26.
[3] Acts 2 : 1–4. The whole chapter is well worth reading, as the orthodox account of a primal incident in the Apostolic Church.

and teaching those things which concern the Lord Jesus Christ, with all confidence, no man forbidding him.[1]

With these words, New Testament narrative closes. The traditional belief of Christians has been that both Paul and Peter, the first bishop of Rome, suffered for their faith under Nero—that Peter was crucified head downward, and that Paul was beheaded.

After the five narrative Books of the New Testament come twenty-one separate Epistles, of which fourteen are attributed to Paul, and seven to four of the Twelve Apostles. In general, these writings may be described as pastoral letters, some addressed to special bodies of Christians, some to all the faithful, a few to individuals, but all accepted by Christian tradition as inspired examples of apostolic teaching at a period when living apostles could still remember the Lord in the flesh. And, although all have thus been traditionally held equally holy, there can be no doubt that those most instantly remembered are those which Paul is believed to have written. The Thirteenth Chapter of the First Epistle to the Corinthians, for instance, is a masterpiece of Christian doctrine; and so is that solemn passage from the Fifteenth Chapter, beginning at the Twentieth Verse and proceeding to the end, re-echoingly familiar among all who have listened to the ritual with which the Church of England buries the dead.

The last Book of the New Testament is different from anything else well-known to the literary traditions of Europe. Its title in the Authorised Version is the Revelation of St. John the Divine,

[1] Acts 28: 30–31.

a term often misunderstood by English readers.
They are apt to suppose that the word *Divine* is
an adjective, celebrating the heavenly qualities
of the saint. It is really a noun—the original
Greek words literally mean "the Theologian"—indicating that the writer, like the "grave divines,
God's conduits,"[1] of John Donne, was entitled
to the respect due to regular holy orders. And
the Greek word *Apocalypsis* translated by the
Latin term *Revelation* literally means *uncover-
ing;* the book, indeed, is now and then called the
Apocalypse. As an apocalypse it is not unique.
In the books of prophecy of the Old Testament
you will find passages of the kind; the First Chapter of Ezekiel, for example, sets forth a mysterious
vision, from which appear to be originally derived
the classic symbols of the Evangelists in Christian
art—the angel of St. Matthew, the lion of St.
Mark, the ox of St. Luke, and the eagle of St.
John;[2] and similar visions are described in the
Seventh and Eighth Chapters of Daniel. Among
writings never accepted as inspired, there seems
to have been a considerable and earnestly devout
literature in this form, of which a typical specimen
may be found in the Book of Enoch, well translated and edited by R. H. Charles.[3] In general,
however, writings of this kind, except as they occur
among those of the regular prophets, have not
survived as literature; when known at all, for
centuries on centuries, they have been known only
to initiates or scholars. So the one accepted

---

[1] Quoting from memory, I find that I have reversed the order of these
two phrases from Donne's First Satire, l. 5.

[2] They occur again in Revelation 4 : 6–7.

[3] The Book of Enoch: Oxford: 1893.

Christian apocalypse has long seemed like a tremendously solitary instance of symbolic inspiration. It purports to have been written by John, who has traditionally been held identical with John the Apostle and John the Evangelist. After all eleven other Apostles had been martyred for the faith, he is believed when very old to have been sent into exile in the isle that is called Patmos,[1] and there, the last survivor of those who had known and followed Jesus Christ in the flesh, and thereafter on the Day of Pentecost had been filled with the Holy Ghost, to have been vouchsafed this marvellous vision of all things which were to be. What these were and what they are we cannot inquire now; it is enough to say that they are an important basis of Christian tradition concerning the Last Judgment. We may solemnly agree that hardly a passage in the whole book of this Revelation can surely be understood without interpretation. Symbol piles on symbol, glory outdazzles glory. All that is clear is that evil is to pass away and the Will of God as revealed through our Lord and Saviour Jesus Christ is finally to triumph, world without end. There shall be pain and sorrow and sin in abundance; but the wages of sin is death, and the reward of Christian faithfulness is everlasting life. Despite its appalling prophecies of Judgment, its final note is of supreme, ecstatic, certain hope for those who will believe and believing will obey.

Tradition has it that St. John, the last of the Apostles and the only one to meet a natural death, slept in the Lord under the emperor Domitian, the last of the Twelve Cæsars. The complete record

[1] Rev. 1 : 9.

of the New Testament is accordingly believed to belong to the First Century of the Christian Era; and even the most sceptical would agree that everything mentioned there as historical falls within this period. Concerned only with the traditions of literature, we may confidently so think of it. So thinking, two reflections may be worth our while. The contrast between the Old Testament tradition, which purports to cover four or five thousand years, and that of the New Testament, embraced within the limits of a single long natural life-time, is stupendous. And the Century which added to the traditions of Europe the sovereign group of the Twelve Cæsars, embodying earthly empire, added to them too, though at the time almost unobserved, the glorious company of the Twelve Apostles, destined to embody the supreme sovereignty of God.

CHAPTER IV

THE CHURCH

In Christian history, everybody will admit, the First Century stands alone. For thirty years or more of it Christ moved among men, to all appearance like other human beings. After the crucifixion, the resurrection, and the ascension, His visible presence on earth was no longer habitual; but for sixty or seventy years men who had known Him, or who had seen or heard Him, still lingered alive. By the year 100 almost all of these were dead, and among them every one of the Twelve Apostles. Thenceforth, the Christian story became a matter not of living memory but of record or tradition.

So far as record goes, there is not much, after the Book of Acts, until a later period than yet concerns us. Traditions generally believed by the Christian centuries of Europe supply the lack. Even doubters, disposed to dispute their authenticity, must keep them in mind; otherwise no one can understand the traditions of European literature which they suffuse. There can be no reasonable doubt, either, that they were in existence by the year 200, when Septimius Severus was emperor and beyond which we have not yet considered the traditions of Rome.

Whoever has been at Rome can hardly forget the most holy shrine of Catholic Christianity, where never-quenched lamps gleam around the

tomb believed to contain the relics of the Apostle
Peter. Above it rises the great dome of his Cathedral Church; and within the base of the dome, inscribed in vast mosaic letters on a golden ground,
are the words:

> Tu es Petrus et super hanc petram ædificabo ecclesiam
> meam et tibi dabo claves regni cœlorum.

This is a literal translation into Latin of the words
in the Greek New Testament rendered by the
Authorised Version of the English Bible as follows:

> "Thou art Peter, and upon this rock I will build my
> church; . . . and I will give unto thee the keys of the king-
> dom of heaven." [1]

Our language does not permit, as Latin does, re-
production of the original Greek play on the words
Petros, the apostle's name, and *petra*, which means
a rock. They were spoken at Cæsarea Philippi,
when Jesus had asked:

> Whom say ye that I am? And Simon Peter answered
> and said, Thou art the Christ, the Son of the living God. [2]

Though the lists of the Apostles in the New
Testament[3] do not superficially quite agree, particularly in the order of their names, they all assert
that there were twelve of these,[4] and they all name
Simon Peter first. All four Gospels, too, lay
special emphasis on the calling of Peter; [5] and in
the Book of Acts it is Peter who, after the ascension, first directs the others.[6] On the ensuing

---

[1] Matt. 16 : 18–19. [2] *Ibid.*, 15–16.
[3] Matt. 10 : 2–4; Mark 3 : 13–19; Luke 6 : 14–16; Acts 1 : 13.
[4] *Cf.* Rev. 21 : 14.
[5] Matt. 4 : 18–20; Mark 1 : 16–18; Luke 5 : 1–11; John 1 : 35–42.
[6] Acts 1 : 15–22.

day of Pentecost, no doubt, the eleven survivors of the original twelve, and Matthias too, appear equally to have been filled with the Holy Ghost;[1] but presently Peter again takes the lead.[2] We need go no farther to assure ourselves that there is abundant scriptural authority for holding him first among his fellows, all divinely charged with the Christian mission. The doctrine of the ancestral Church maintains, in effect, that on the day of Pentecost valid holy orders were miraculously conferred on the twelve; that they and they alone could transmit these orders by certain rites to others, thus enabled in turn and in succession to transmit them through the centuries; that all men so made sacredly official— whatever their personal failings—are duly commissioned ministers of God; and that none others may pretend to be. The tradition of the Church agrees with the Book of Acts in asserting, as historical fact, that the Twelve Apostles by and by separated, carrying their glad tidings of the gospel far and wide; with it, of course, they must have carried their power of conferring holy orders. In Church tradition, however, Peter remains first; he is believed to have made his way to Rome, the imperial capital of the world, to have become the first Bishop of Rome, to have been recognised by Christians as their special leader, and to have died there for the faith in the persecution decreed by Nero. It is held that his body lies to this day at or near the spot where he was martyred; and that the scriptural words at the base of the dome now soaring above him pro-

---

[1] Acts 2 : 1-13. [2] *Ibid.*, 14-40.

claim, from the lips of Christ Himself, that here is the corner-stone of Christendom.

From Peter's time forth, tradition holds,—and before long it begins to be supported by extant record,—Rome has always had her bishop. As the lineal successor of St. Peter he has been held by the great majority of professing Christians, who as long as the Roman Cæsars lasted were their loyal subjects, the divinely official head of the Church. For centuries on centuries he has been specially called the Pope, or the Holy Father. That his authority has again and again been disputed or denied is beyond question; heresies and schisms are humanly inevitable; at times, too, there have been rival claimants to the papacy. As we look back on the Christian centuries, however, from our place in the beginning of the twentieth, their general belief appears to have been that the Church was established by Christ; that, although in human hands, it has remained the visible earthly body of His spiritual kingdom; that the holy orders miraculously conferred on the Apostles and by them and their successors transmitted to others through the ages remain holy,— even though now and again the men through whom the orders are transmitted may prove personally unworthy;—and that the official heads of the catholic and apostolic Church, the Church true everywhere and for all men by reason of the virtue unbrokenly continuous in it from the days of the Apostles, have been the men who in succession to St. Peter have been duly consecrated Bishops of the still spiritually imperial city of Rome. Just when and how this belief came into being is no concern of ours now, any more than theological details are. Whether it be true or mistaken, indeed, makes for us here no difference. Without fully recognising its existence, and furthermore admitting that—whatever the human infirmities of the men who have officially sustained it—the belief has been through the centuries a source of unspeakable spiritual consolation, we cannot in the least understand the literary traditions of Europe.

In what precise condition the year 200 found the history and the traditions of Christianity is a question for scholars and divines immeasurably more learned than we. One or two facts about this history and tradition even then, however, seem indisputable. The growth of Christianity at Rome, as well as in various parts of the Roman Empire, and the conscientious refusal of Christians everywhere to pay formal respect to Roman gods whom they believed false, had combined to bring upon them legal penalties now and again so sweeping as to be called persecutions. We have already touched incidentally on one or two such matters, as when Tacitus mentions the persecution by Nero,[1] and Pliny consults Trajan about how Christian obstinacy may best be handled by a judicious magistrate.[2] Particularly in periods of acute persecution, great numbers of the early Christians were more or less legally put to death. As we have seen, for example, it is believed that eleven of the Twelve Apostles and St. Paul too had thus suffered before the end of the First Century. Almost from the beginning those who died for the faith were called *martyrs*. The original Greek word seems to have meant neither more nor less

[1] *Cf.* p. 320.　　　　　　　　　　[2] *Cf.* p. 314.

than witnesses; a martyr was anybody who gave testimony in legal proceedings, or even less formally asserted some special knowledge of fact. A Christian martyr[1] was one who testified to the truth of the faith and sealed his testimony with his life-blood. And in Rome alone, by the year 200, the noble army of martyrs has been believed already to have comprised many eager thousands. As a matter of course, the memory of all who had died for the faith was especially venerated. So far as might be in their human power, they had followed the example of Christ to the very agony of the Cross. They must probably have possessed or acquired a holiness beyond that of every-day believers, however devout. From some such beginnings as this probably came their recognition as what Christians have immemorially denominated saints. These beings who had suffered in the body were nowise dead, but deathlessly happy in the eternity of Paradise. Even there they could not have lost their sympathy with the troubles and perplexities, the temptations and the sorrows, of the flesh. Nothing was more reasonable than to think of them as intercessors, who could be addressed in the terms of earth and could pitifully translate these into the terms of heaven. At once human and made holy, they were the special ministers of the immortal church invisible.

Again, no doubt, we stray into regions where only orthodox doctrine can keep the vagrant safe from error. We cannot too often remind ourselves that, although for the moment we are forced to

---

[1] The Authorised Version thus translates the word as used by Paul concerning Stephen in Acts 22 : 20. In Rev. 20 : 4, the Greek word *martyrian* is translated *witness*.

touch on matters believed through all the Christian centuries vital or mortal to the future of every living man, we are here attempting only to feel, in a general way, how the Church probably presented itself to believers when Septimius Severus was emperor. By that time believers were more numerous than unbelievers have been apt to suppose. It has been estimated that the Christian burials actually to be counted in the catacombs of Rome alone amount to several millions,[1] a large part of which may be referred to the First and Second Centuries; and these by no means comprise all the Christians who had then lived and died there. A clause in the Apologeticus of Tertullian, a work attributed to about the year 200,[2] has lingered distorted in Christian memory. "Semen est sanguis Christianorum,"[3] he wrote ("The blood of Christians is seed"); and few words are more familiar now among the faithful than those which have sprung from his: "The blood of the martyrs is the seed of the church." Every drop of it was capable of spiritual fatherhood. Compared with this, the empire of the Cæsars—the last masters of pure and antique Europe—was sterile. Theirs was not the standard which was presently to conquer, even on earth.

This Tertullian, though his name is not very important in literary tradition and his lapse into heresy deprives him of place among the most venerated fathers of the Church, is worth a glance now. In some ways his character and career re-

---

[1] I have mislaid my reference for this; but I think the statement may be found somewhere in the regrettably unindexed works of Gaston Boissier.

[2] Hall: Companion to Latin Studies: Cambridge, 1910: p. 142.

[3] Tertullian: Apol., 50, near the end.

semble those of Milton. Both were men of the
highest accomplishment; both found conscientious
reason for conversion to religious views other than
they had been born to; both were eager controver-
sialists; both were consummate masters of language and imperfect masters of temper; and both
were ultimately led to headstrong break with orthodoxies which they had once enthusiastically accepted. Tertullian, an African gentleman, appears
to have been a rhetorician and a lawyer, skilled
in literature and philosophy. When converted to
Christianity he became, in his day, its most pow-
erfully passionate advocate. His works, like the
prose works of Milton, are generally matters
for students rather of controversy and of history
than of literature. But anybody who desires a
vivid impression of Christian feeling at the end of
the Second Century will do well to turn the pages
of his earlier works—his Ad Martyres, for example,
his De Spectaculis, and his Apologeticus.[1] What
is more, such readers will probably be somewhat
less bored than they expected.

We have now dwelt enough for our purpose on
the traditions of Christianity up to the year 200—
the period to which we carried our glances at the
traditions of Rome. The Church was then already the official interpreter of all scripture; and
the remoter scriptural traditions of the Old Testament were seen by the Church only as they appeared through the intervening veil of the New.
Here is clearly an analogy to the manner in which
the traditions of Greece were by that time veiled
from the future by those of Rome. The Greek

[1] The writings of Tertullian have been readably translated by Roberts
and Donaldson (3 vols.: Edinburgh, 1869).

and Roman traditions were already beginning to combine, as they combined through many subsequent centuries, in the single tradition of classical antiquity. As yet, however, the traditions of Christianity were generally familiar only to Christians. The time was not yet come when they were themselves to be the sacred veil through which, for generation after generation, Europe was to see the traditions of its own separate past.

BOOK IV

THE TRADITIONS OF CHRISTENDOM

Between the beginning of the Third Century and the end of the Tenth there are far fewer traditions for us to record than either earlier or later. In 200 the Empire of the Cæsars still seemed durable; by 1000 Europe was at one only in acknowledging Christ as Lord of All. Over these eight centuries, when the past was retreating and the future still indefinite, we must now hasten. Glancing at them one by one, and one after another, we may perhaps come to feel something of how the European dominion of imperial Rome grew to be Christendom.

CHAPTER I

THE THIRD CENTURY

I

HISTORICAL TRADITIONS

Under Septimius Severus, and indeed throughout the Third Century, the bounds of the Roman Empire remained virtually unaltered. If we take it to include the Mediterranean Sea, which was completely surrounded by Roman provinces, the imperial city was about in the centre. Rome was sovereign over Britain, which comprised what are now England and Wales but not Ireland or northern Scotland. On the continent she was sovereign everywhere to the west of the Rhine and to the south of the Danube. In Asia she was sovereign throughout what we now generally call the Near East—roughly speaking, Asia Minor and Syria; in Africa over Egypt and the whole northern coast, westward as far as the Straits of Gibraltar and southward to the verge of the desert. Within these limits, the dominion of the Cæsars, though not always undisputed, was regularly recognised as supreme.

It was threatened, however, from both without and within. All along its northerly boundaries it was increasingly menaced by rude but vigorous barbarians; and to the eastward it was pressed by the colossal and diuturnal force of little-known, immemorial Asia. Within the limits of the Empire, meanwhile, the growth of Christianity was so constant that, as we can now see, there had arisen an irrepressible conflict for the dominion of subsequent Europe between the great temporal tradition of the First Century—the tradition of the Twelve Cæsars—and its great spiritual tradition of the Twelve Apostles.

The number of Third Century emperors, if we include Septimius Severus at the beginning and Diocletian at the end, was no less than twenty-eight. Of these, however, few are remembered by tradition. The huge ruins of the Baths of Caracalla combine with the unpleasant ferocity of his portrait-busts to make him vaguely monstrous. The fantastic name of Elagabalus, or Heliogabalus, is associated with indistinct memories of his fantastic Oriental excesses. There may persist a faint notion that Alexander Severus was comparatively decent, partly because he is reported prudently to have worshipped Christ among other exotic deities in his private chapel. Compared with the Twelve Cæsars and the Five Good Emperors, these names look shadowy; and they were all in the shadow of the past by 235. Decius, who flickered on the throne for two or three years in the middle of the Century, has not been quite forgotten, by reason of the severity with which he persecuted the Christians; it is said, incidentally, that his is the last sovereign Roman name to occur among the hieroglyphic inscriptions of Egypt. Twenty-five years or so later came Aurelian, of whom no personal anecdote is familiar; his name lingers, though, for under him were built or at least begun the fortified walls of Rome

still in ruinous existence.   When we stop to think
that these imply need of defense in the very heart
of the empire, they become portentously significant.   It was he, too, who overcame Zenobia,
queen of Palmyra, for a little while victorious in
Egypt itself.   Then come fresh confusion and
bloodshed, from which at last emerges the greater
figure of Diocletian.   A self-made soldier, apparently of Dalmatian origin, and said to have
been, like Horace three hundred years before, the
son of a freed slave, his military gifts combined
with his administrative to make him, after almost
a century of threatened anarchy, so conspicuous a
restorer of order that he has been called a second
Augustus.   The ruins of his Baths at Rome rival
those of the Baths of Caracalla.   The relics of
his palace at Spalato, where he passed some restful
years after his abdication, are memorable in the
history of architecture as preserving almost if
not quite the first extant example of arches springing from columns—the fundamental feature of
the great later styles known as Romanesque and
Gothic.   It is remembered, as well, that his persecution of the Christians was violent, and that
among other administrative reforms he first divided
the Empire into two parts—the Eastern, which
was to survive for more than a thousand years,
and the Western, which was to perish in the Fifth
Century.   Rough, powerful, magnificent, he somehow seems, and not happy.

For, as we have reminded ourselves, the Empire
was threatened not only by increasing insurgent
disputes for the sovereignty but also by hostile
forces at work both without and within.   To those
pressing from without the general name of Bar-

barian is given. The fate of some of the emperors we have glanced at implies the growing danger of this menace. Septimius Severus died in Britain, where he went to oppose Barbarian attacks from the North; Decius perished on the Danube, where hordes of Goths were advancing; Aurelian, after defeating Barbarian invaders of Italy, and fortifying Rome, and overcoming Zenobia of Palmyra, was murdered in Thrace. No great Barbarian personages, to be sure, have traditionally survived from this Century; but tribal names destined to linger in later Europe begin to appear. We have just mentioned that of the Goths. Among others recorded in the accounts of these times are those of the Alamanni and of the Germans, already possessed of regions now called Germany; of the Franks, who by Diocletian's reign were settled somewhere in Gaul; and of the Burgundians, of the Saxons, and of the Vandals. In Europe, before long, such enemies were to be irresistible.

So was the internal growth of Christianity. The blood of the martyrs was bearing harvests the richer for each recurrent persecution. Their names are not familiar. Of the sixteen popes believed to have lived in the Third Century, more than one martyred, and all—like all their predecessors—recognised as saints, none is distinctly remembered as a personal tradition. But there is a general notion, right or wrong makes no difference now, that this was a time when the faithful could be depended on to die for the faith.

Compared with the Second Century, the century of the Five Good Emperors, this next seems indistinct, and still more so when we compare it with the First Century, the century of the Twelve

Cæsars—not to speak of the First Century before Christ, the century of Julius Cæsar himself. It was as long, though, as any of them. In the time of Diocletian, Septimius Severus was as much a thing of the past as Trajan was in the time of Septimius Severus, or Augustus in the time of Trajan, or Caius Marius in the time of Augustus; and in the time of Caius Marius the age of Pericles was almost as remote as the age of Caius Marius was in the time of Diocletian. Traditionally, however, as we shall soon come to feel, the sterile centuries far outnumber the prolific. And if we ask ourselves what the Third Century added to historical tradition, besides vague imperial names like those of Caracalla, Heliogabalus, Decius, Aurelian, and Diocletian, we can hardly find more precise answer than that the tottering Empire was threatened at once by Barbarian aggression and by surgent Christianity. As constellations, the Twelve Cæsars were setting and the Twelve Apostles rising clear.

II

LITERARY TRADITIONS

To general literary tradition, the Third Century added hardly anything. Names, no doubt, like that of Tertullian at the beginning, will always be important for students of religion and of philosophy. One is that of Origen, who has been called the greatest scholar and the most original thinker of the Church. This was the century of Longinus, too, philosopher and critic, counsellor of Zenobia, and put to death by Aurelian. It was the century when Plotinus made Neo-Platonic philosophy permanently important in the history of thought, not least because of its influence a hundred years later on the doctrine of St. Augustine. It was the century of Porphyry, disciple of Plotinus, and himself author of a now lost attack on Christianity. It was the century when Eusebius grew up, who lived to be eminent at the Council of Nicæa, and who is called the "Father of Church History." It was the century, too, when Lactantius was born, who has been called "the Christian Cicero." But if anybody can tell you without reference to authority which of these wrote Greek and which Latin, you may hold him wiser than most mere men of letters. It is fair to add that some refer the Pervigilium Veneris[1] to the Third Century and others to the Fourth; but the most learned nowadays incline to place it in the Second.

[1] *Cf.* p. 339.

CHAPTER II
THE FOURTH CENTURY

I

HISTORICAL TRADITIONS

Though so far as historical detail goes the Fourth Century may be almost as shadowy in traditional memory as the Third, it includes far and obviously more important names and facts. Of these the most memorable is the conversion to Christianity of the Emperor Constantine. His father was a soldier who under Diocletian had been advanced to imperial rank. His mother, Helena, seems to have been of humble origin and to have had marital experiences not unlike those of Josephine with Napoleon; as was the case with Josephine, however, the passing of the sovereign power to her descendants confirmed her imperial dignity, and furthermore the piety of Helena presently made her a saint. On the death of his father at York, Constantine was proclaimed emperor there. His title was disputed. A period of anarchically rival Cæsars ensued, during which Constantine boldly marched on Rome itself. As a very old legend has it, he perceived on the way a miraculous vision of a flaming cross in the sky, surrounded by the words "In hoc signo vinces" ("With this standard thou shalt conquer"). Duly impressed by the heavenly mandate, he put the Christian emblem on his banners. To this obe-

dience was attributed the victory at the Milvian
Bridge, near Rome, which made him master of
the imperial city and thereafter of the world.
From that moment, although his formal baptism
was long delayed, tradition dates the Christian
sovereignty of Europe.

His triumphal arch at Rome, near the ruined
Coliseum, singularly implies the condition of his
time. Its form has all the grandeur of Roman tradition; but its decoration proves on inspection to
be largely made up of spoils from monuments of
earlier emperors, particularly Trajan and Marcus
Aurelius. In two hundred years the art of sculpture had so declined that even if they had waited
for time to make new ornaments for this new structure they could hardly have produced better effects
than that of the few original reliefs which they
added to it. Not even undeniable decorative
splendour can prevent these from looking barbari-
cally rude.

Yet Rome was still imperial, and in view of the
future never more so than when Constantine, as
Emperor, presided over the famous Church council
at Nicæa, in Asia Minor. The cause of this meeting and the matters disputed there would take us
into regions of theology and of Church history far
beyond our present scope. Even tradition, however, remembers the names of Arius, whose views
were held heretical, and of Athanasius, which has
become a synonym for uncompromising orthodoxy. The dogmatic and minatory Creed called
by his name, though not historically traceable to
him, has persisted in the Prayer Book even of the
Church of England. To this day, the Creed attributed to the Council of Nicæa is professed as basic

not only by the older Churches, but by both the Church of England and the Protestant Episcopal Church of the United States. At least two less assured Christian traditions have also been associated during many centuries with the period of Constantine. One, now pronounced historically mistaken even by the Catholic Encyclopædia, concerns the Donation of Constantine, a document by which the Emperor was believed to have conferred on the Pope certain temporal gifts and rights. Whether he actually did so may still be disputed; there is no longer doubt that the document purporting to proceed from him is not genuine. How thoroughly it was long believed to be, however, appears—to go no farther—from the passionate exclamation of Dante:[1]

> Ahi, Constantin, di quanto mal fu madre
> Non la tua conversion, ma quella dote
> Che da te prese il primo ricco padre!
> (Ah, Constantine, of how much ill was mother
> Not thy conversion, but that dower of goods
> The first rich Holy Father took from thee!)

The second legendary tradition of this period concerns the pious pilgrimage to the Holy Land of the empress-mother, St. Helena. There she is said miraculously to have discovered the True Cross, and other peculiarly sacred relics, such as the lance with which the side of Christ was pierced; and thence to have brought them back to Christian Europe.

The most enduring imperial monument of Constantine is of another kind than his arch at Rome, his conversion, or his relations with the Church.

[1] Inferno, XIX, 115–117.

As we have seen, Diocletian, for administrative convenience, had temporarily divided the Empire into two separate parts—the Eastern and the Western. Although this division did not become permanent until the death of the Emperor Theodosius in 395, it was greatly emphasised by the transfer of the capital in 330 from Rome to Byzantium, thenceforth to this day called Constantinople—the City of Constantine. Rome fell before the end of the Fifth Century; but until 1453, when the Turks conquered the city which they have held ever since, the emperors at Constantinople remained something like successors to the sovereignty of Constantine and therefore of the Cæsars.

One reason for this removal of the capital was probably the commanding commercial situation of Constantinople, still among the most important in the world. Another was its equally commanding military strength, peculiarly desirable at a time when, as the walls of Aurelian at Rome had implied some fifty years earlier, the Empire was compelled to be on the defensive. When the Roman Empire had possessed itself of Western Europe,—the regions now known as England, France, and Spain,—the Virgilian ideal of Roman peace was still paramount. Though the frontiers had always been more or less guarded, as the walls erected in Britain by Hadrian and the Antonines may remind us, there had been little care for fortification within them. Considerable regions which had enjoyed the comforts and the wealth of Roman civilisation for a period about as long as has now elapsed since Columbus discovered America were consequently far more open, in the Fourth Century, to the danger of Barbarian invasion than they were apt to suppose. An extraordinarily clear notion of the situation in Britain may be derived from three interesting stories by Rudyard Kipling: "A Centurion of the Thirtieth," "On the Great Wall," and "The Winged Hats." [1] Picts, Scots, and Northern invaders from across the sea are what threatened there, while the internal structure of the government was breaking down. On the continent, particularly to the eastward, the Empire was threatened by Barbarians whose name has always remained traditionally more portentous —the Goths. Not the least part of the danger from them lay in their power of assimilation. Under Constantine himself they were already in some degree allied with Rome. Before the end of the Century, they had learned the art of Roman warfare in the Danubian legions. It was there that the Gothic conqueror, Alaric, at the beginning of his power in 400, studied his lessons of generalship; and, though as an Arian peculiarly detestable to the orthodox catholicism of Rome, he professed Christianity.

During the Fourth Century no less than nineteen emperors—some, to be sure, rivals or contemporary sharers of the government—are recorded. Apart from Constantine, however, only two or three linger distinct in tradition. Of these the least forgotten is Julian. He reigned for only two or three years, falling young during a campaign against the Persians in 363; but his idealistic attempt to restore the old religions of the declining Empire, won him for the future the detested name of Apostate:

> Perfidus ille Deo, quamvis non perfidus urbi,
> (Faithless to God, but loyal to the State,)

[1] Puck of Pook's Hill. Works, Outward Bound Edition, XXIII (New York: 1906), 139–224.

a Christian poet, Roman to the core, is reported
to have written of him.[1] Though Julian, as the
last pagan Cæsar, is generally remembered, no
incident of his life is anything like so clear in tradition as one in that of Theodosius, the last Western sovereign of the undivided Empire, who came
to the throne about fifteen years later. In the
course of his reign he authorised a treacherous
massacre in the seditious city of Thessalonica; as
a punishment for this guilt he was compelled to
do penance by St. Ambrose, Bishop of Milan; and
those who visit Milan are shown to this day the
spot where the gates of the church now dedicated
to St. Ambrose are said to have been closed by
the successor of the Apostles against the crowned
successor of the Cæsars. When Theodosius died
in 395, the division between the Western Empire
and the Eastern became permanent. One of his
sons, Arcadius, succeeded him at Constantinople;
another, Honorius, in the West. Honorius, however, made his capital, not at Rome, but at the
safer city of Ravenna; and the story goes that
when they brought him the news that Rome was
lost, he took it to mean that something had happened to a favorite chicken, named for the ancestral city of his toppling empire. The daughter of
Theodosius, and sister of both Eastern and Western Emperors, Galla Placidia,[2] was a little later to
be the wife of a Gothic prince, Adolphus. She
lived far into the Fifth Century, married Constan-
tius, and was mother of the dissolute Valentinian

---

[1] This line, quoted from memory by a classically accomplished friend, he
believes to be from Prudentius. I have not verified it.

[2] Her story, which belongs mostly to the Fifth Century, may be found
in Gibbon.

III. At her tomb in Ravenna they show you not only her sarcophagus, but others which are said to have contained the bodies of her brother Honorius, and of her son Valentinian, the only Western Cæsars believed to have lain for centuries where they were laid first. All three receptacles are empty now; none may be authentic; but they tell us that none has ever been displaced.

In the year 400, Alaric was invading Italy on a scale unexampled since the time of Hannibal, six hundred years before. While the Empire was thus crumbling, the Church persisted. Tradition has commonly held, indeed, that it grew a good deal stronger—a notion later fostered by the long-general belief that the Donation of Constantine conferred on Sylvester, the Pope, and all his successors, temporal sovereignty over the imperial city and regions about it. In point of fact, ten sainted popes are said to have succeeded during the Fourth Century to the throne of St. Peter. The names of none remain widely familiar, unless the beautifully cut inscriptions with which Damasus marked holy places in the Catacombs may have kept him faintly unforgotten. All the more, the Church as an unbroken institution seems greater than the passing men who one after another embodied its authority; and among the churchmen of the Fourth Century were at least three who remain in tradition, and rightly, greater than any pope since St. Peter until a much later time. These are the long-since sainted Fathers and Doctors, Ambrose, Jerome, and Augustine. Ambrose lived all his life within the Century. Jerome seems to have been past fifty when it ended, and Augustine past forty-five. Though both sur-

vived a good while longer, we may accordingly
best consider them here; for, like the Flavian writers, they were men rather of the Century when
they were born than of that when their eyes closed.

Any study of Fourth Century Christianity
would lead us into endless details of Church history and heresies. In the perspective of time,
however, it is clear that what was to be the
dominant Church of Europe persisted, and now
seems to have persisted the more vigorously, at
Rome for the reason that Rome was ceasing to
be the imperial capital. The tradition of the
Twelve Cæsars was no longer unrivalled in sovereign splendour. The tradition of the Twelve
Apostles, adopted by the Empire itself when the
Empire became Christian, grew slowly but steadily
dominant. Barbarians and Romans alike, gentle
and simple, learned and ignorant, increasingly
tended to acknowledge the supremacy of the Cross.
Always imperial in principle, the religion first revealed to the Jews and extended by Christianity
to all mankind was at last becoming imperial in
fact. So we may think of the Fourth Century of
the Christian Era as the first traditional century
of Christianity imperial.

II

AUSONIUS; THE FATHERS OF THE CHURCH

There is hardly need to remind ourselves that
neither Latin literature nor Greek has ever quite
stopped. By the Fourth Century, however, the
perpetual masterpieces of both had long been classic. So we should waste time by lingering over

such accomplished but secondary poets as Ausonius and Claudian—the first originally of Bordeaux, the second of Alexandria. One curious chance of English literature may nevertheless be worth a word. At the end of the Rosæ of Ausonius[1] occurs the line

Collige, virgo, rosas, dum flos novus, et nova pubes.
(Pluck roses, girl, in bud, whilst thou art young.)

Tasso read this as the Renaissance read all ancient poetry,—as one of the countless beauties of the Classics, to be parodied at reverent will. He played with it in his Gerusalemme Liberata;[2] and Spenser in his Faerie Queene[3] prettily translated the singing lines of Tasso. And, under King Charles I, Robert Herrick, knowing his Ausonius or remembering his Spenser, brought the thought into English words hardly to be surpassed:

Gather ye rosebuds while ye may,
Old Time is still a-flying;
And this same flower that smiles to-day
To-morrow will be dying.[4]

To Latin Literature, however, the Fourth Century, like those which followed, added nothing new, unless, indeed, we find germs of novelty in the Mosella of Ausonius, declared by some careful students to indicate genuine observation of Nature. By this time, for our purposes, the classics of antiquity were complete.

By this time, however, another kind of tradition than classic was already coming into lasting

[1] Eidyll., XIV, 49. [2] XVI, xv. [3] II: XII, lxxv.
[4] Hesperides: To the Virgins, to Make Much of Time.

existence. Though not primarily literary in character, and indeed so hallowed by subsequent reverence that at first thought they may seem hardly literary at all, the forms of Christian expression subsequent to the New Testament have so suffused the later literature of Europe that without some note of them its temper cannot be understood. On one important phase of them we have already touched.[1] Vagrant tendencies of Christian doctrine by this time demanded control. The danger of heretical error was the most profound which had ever confronted the imagination of Europe. The philosophies and earthly loyalties of antiquity could hardly lead to anything worse than mischievous blunder; but among the Christians any deviation from the Will of God as set forth by His revelation and interpreted by the Church was held to involve the pitifully just penalty of eternal damnation. No such deviation could be more abominable than mistaken belief. From needs like this probably arose those fundamental and official statements of true doctrine which in English we call creeds. A tradition nowadays common attributes the shortest and most popular of orthodox Creeds to the Apostles themselves, by whose name it is conventionally called. Though there appears to be no historical basis for this tradition,—and, indeed, the terms of our usual Apostles' Creed are not clearly recorded until much later,—some such formulas were probably in immemorial existence as early as the Third Century. As we have seen, too, the more studied Creed authorised under Constantine by the Council of Nicæa remains, in an amended

[1] *Cf.* p. 398.

form, liturgically alive;[1] and the tremendously Trinitarian and grimly damnatory Creed called by the name of Athanasius has been generally, though perhaps mistakenly, attributed to about the same period. Of one thing there can be no doubt. From this time forth, doctrinal Creeds, to stray from which involved perdition, were a fully recognised part of Christian teaching; and conflicts of creed, or of interpretation thereof, were a recurrent tragedy in Christian history. Of all sins, the spiritual sin of heresy has generally been held most mortal by the faithful.

By the Fourth Century, too, another and a less portentous phase of Christian expression had assumed more or less permanent form. Though not lately of impressive literary importance, it has never been more copious than during the Nineteenth Century. The classical Greek word *hymn* signified such choral song in honour of some god or hero as is now best exemplified by the hymns attributed to Homer. The Septuagint translators into Greek of Hebrew Scripture used the term to describe the lyric passages there which celebrated the true and living God. Thence it gradually passed so deeply into Christian tradition that one is at pains now to think of it without some notion of the rhymed doggerel more or less piously shouted out at Sunday-schools and revivalist meetings. In the Fourth Century, so far as we can tell from what now remains, Christian hymns, already in excellent existence, remained free from anything

---

[1] The current English versions of the Apostles' Creed and of the Nicene may be found in the Prayer Books of the Church of England and of the American Episcopal Church. In the former the Athanasian Creed also appears.

like their later vulgarities. They were fervid and solemn chants, such as still make impressive the regular offices of the ancestral Church and of the Church of England. Of these the most generally familiar now is probably that which is commonly called by its first two Latin words: "Te Deum." "We praise Thee, O God; we acknowledge Thee to be the Lord," it begins in English. Its precise origin appears not to be certainly known; for centuries a venerable tradition attributed it to something like a joint inspiration of St. Ambrose and St. Augustine, chanting alternate verses in the church of St. Ambrose at Milan on the occasion of the younger Saint's conversion or baptism.

These names bring us back to the three great Christian Fathers and Doctors who were certainly alive in the second half of the Fourth Century, of whom there is much historical record, and whose works have been preserved in huge folio volumes. Ambrose, Jerome, and Augustine—roughly speaking, men who lived more than a century later than Tertullian—were all three not only ardent Christians, but accustomed to good society, scholars by training and persons of remarkable intellectual power. Ambrose and Jerome came of families already Christian, at least in traditional sympathy; Augustine, son of a pagan father and a Christian mother, was converted when well grown up. None of the three was Roman or even Italian by birth. Ambrose, of higher rank than the others, has been thought a native of Treves, Jerome is said to have been born in Dalmatia, Augustine was African. All three, however, were much in Italy. Ambrose was long Bishop of Milan—a dignity to which he is said to have been miracu-

lously called by the voice of a little child, who when
succession to the vacant see was in high dispute
uttered the words "Ambrose is Bishop." Jerome, after serving among other duties as secretary to the pope, finally betook himself to Palestine, and there died in solitary monkish retirement at Bethlehem, ministered to—as legend tells
—by a friendly lion, his immemorial companion
in pictures. Augustine became bishop of Hippo,
in Africa, where—as we shall remind ourselves a
little later—he died at a time when besieging Barbarians were under the very walls of his city,
presently to fall into their hands; not a vestige
of it remains. Two or three things, deeply characteristic of their time, seem true of all three. At
a period when the temporal power of the Roman
Empire was finally collapsing, all these potent
supporters of the imperial religion which was to
persist and strengthen appear to have been not
only advocates of the cause which the course of
the centuries proved triumphant but also, in almost all respects, personally and positively superior to both doctrinal and other opponents—
heretics and supporters of pagan religion or philosophy, clerics and laymen. In social origin, indeed, as well as in culture, they were better men
than most if not all of the quivering Third and
Fourth Century Cæsars themselves. Any glance
at the ponderous bulk of their works will serve
to remind anybody that all three were much en-
gaged in doctrinal controversies, now matters
only or chiefly for students of Church history, and
that all brought to this the full strength resident
in the best rhetorical and literary training of their
age. The greater part of the stupendous work of

each has long ceased to have much more than
historical existence, far beneath the surface of
conscious literary tradition. At the same time,
something from the work of each has traditionally
survived.

Although, as we have seen, a share in the Te
Deum is attributed to St. Ambrose only by tradition, there is no reason to question that he wrote
some of the hymns regularly included in his works.
An example of the metrical form he usually preferred may be found in the versions of the Gloria
Patri with which most of his hymns close. The
regular words of the lesser Doxology in the Latin
ritual—

Gloria Patri et Filio et Spiritui Sancto; sicut erat in
principio, et nunc, et semper, in sæcula sæculorum—

are rendered in the English Prayer Book:

Glory be to the Father, and to the Son, and to the Holy
Ghost; as it was in the beginning, is now, and ever shall
be, world without end.

Rhyming parodies of this, to suit various metres,
regularly occur, under the title of Doxology, in most
Nineteenth Century hymn-books. At the end of
the first Hymn of St. Ambrose he turns it into the
simple iambics—capable of strongly stressed emphasis on the second, fourth, and sixth syllables—
which he appears to have found generally most
convenient for Christian lyric purpose:

Deó Patrí sit glória,
Ejúsque sóli Fílio,
Cum Spíritú paráclito,
Et núnc et ín perpétuum.

A more free version, perhaps more suitable for chanting, and at any rate more frequently repeated, occurs at the end of his second Hymn:

> Præsta, Pater piissime,
> Patrique compar unice,
> Cum Spiritu paraclito,
> Regnans per omne sæculum.

What St. Ambrose most clearly contributed to the traditions of European literature is probably this newly classic form of the Christian hymn, simply stressed, surgently rhythmic, and instinct with sound Trinitarian doctrine. That he invented it nobody will pretend;[1] that he made it perpetual we can hardly deny—just as Horace made perpetual in later Europe the lyric melodies of Greece.

The most learned of the Fourth Century Fathers was St. Jerome. Most of his copious work—the Paris edition of 1846 comprises eleven quarto volumes—is beyond our scope, who are concerned only with literary tradition. One part of it, however, though often forgotten to be his, has had as enduring an influence on literature as anything that ever was written. When we touched, a little while ago, on the words inscribed in mosaic at the base of St. Peter's dome,[2] and placed beside them the translation sanctioned by the Authorised Version of the New Testament, we can hardly have helped perceiving a singular likeness of rhythm between languages generally so dissimilar as Latin and English. This is not accidental. For many centuries the words of Scripture were familiar to

---

[1] Some of the hymns of his contemporary Prudentius have never been quite forgotten, for instance.

[2] *Cf.* p. 380.

Europe only in their Latin form. Thus immemorially read aloud, the surges and cadences of their movement came to seem part of them, lingering in the ears of those who finally rendered them into our vulgar tongues. One deep phase of the style we now associate with the Bible is accordingly the liturgical Latinity of its movement. Any one to whom English and Latin are equally strange would hardly recognise which was which, when the words of Scripture are solemnly read in the offices of the Church. The Latin rhythm, at the same time, is not that of classical antiquity; it has, rather, a peculiar quality of its own, which anybody can perceive and no one need analyse. On the whole, we may pretty confidently attribute this quality to St. Jerome himself. The Old Testament, as he found it, existed in the original Hebrew, and in the Hellenistic Greek version, known as the Septuagint, produced by scholars of Ptolemaic Alexandria; the New Testament, as he found it, existed in what was believed to be the original Hellenistic Greek. Neither Hebrew nor Greek was intelligible to men who thought and spoke in Fourth Century Latin. At the same time, the current Latin renderings of Scriptural text were apt to be rude and unlettered. To avoid this indignity, St. Jerome rendered into standard Latin form the greater part of all the Bible; and those who completed his work did so after his manner. This is the basis of the Biblical text commonly known as the Vulgate and sanctioned throughout the later history of the ancestral Church. The words

Tu es Petrus et super hanc petram ædificabo ecclesiam meam,

for example, are given as St. Jerome's own in the Paris edition of his works.[1] They are exactly those which now hover above the tomb of St. Peter; and the words

Thou art Peter, and upon this rock I will build my church

—even though the ancient play on the words be lost —re-echo them wherever the English Bible is read. We need go no farther to acknowledge how much those who find in the Bible their message of salvation owe to the second of the three great Fourth Century Fathers.[2] It seems more than probable, as well, that the influence of his Scriptural work has greatly affected the style and the rhythm immemorially associated, in all languages, with Christian prayer.

Great as the importance of hymns has been in literary tradition, and great as that of scriptural style and of public prayer, neither seems quite so definite as two or three traditions traceable to St. Augustine. For one thing, he wrote a book which not only has lasted as literature but may fairly be held the first of its inexhaustible kind in the lasting literature of Europe. The purpose of his Confessions[3] is doubtless altogether devout; he candidly confesses to God his errors and his spiritual troubles, and describes his conversion and the ecstatic peace of spirit thereby vouchsafed him. All this might well seem of interest only to the

[1] 1846. Vol. X, p. 565.

[2] It is perhaps fair to add that the Latin Psalter, the most widely used of all Christian hymnals, is not Jerome's final version, but a revision of an earlier.

[3] The text of this book, with Watts's translation (1631), is most accessible in the Loeb Classical Library (1912). Pusey's translation (1838) may almost be held an English classic.

godly. His manner of telling it, however, is excellently and originally human. Avoiding at once any self-obtrusion and any conventional reluctance to reveal himself, he writes, with masterly freedom from morbid self-consciousness, not only of his inner life, but of such circumstance about him as impeded or helped his spiritual development. The result is admirable autobiography—the true story of a human being in true historical surroundings. His unwitting picture of the Fourth Century accordingly rivals that of Flavian Rome which we find in the Letters of Pliny, and that of the last days of the Republic which we find in the Letters of Cicero. His incidental sketches of character, particularly of St. Ambrose[1] and of St. Monica,[2] are enduring portraits. His account of the moment of his conversion[3] is a classic case of religious psychology. And so on. The ancient world was falling to pieces about him; no one knew this better than he. But any of us who should fancy that the manners of life had yet followed politics and fine art into barbarism, will waste none of the time he gives to the pleasant task of reading what St. Augustine writes about men and things, and skipping at pleasure those longer passages of which the interest is chiefly philosophic or spiritual. In all European literature you can hardly find a lady of gentler breeding than St. Monica, as her son describes her. If St. Augustine had left no other work than this, he would always be not only a great saint and a great thinker, but also a great gentleman and a great man of letters.

Most of his extant writings, even more copious than those of St. Ambrose, are matters only for

[1] E. g., VI, III.　　[2] IX, VIII-XIII.　　[3] VIII, XII.

students of religious history and philosophy; but one, commonly held his masterpiece, survives beyond the rest. "De Civitate Dei," the name by which its twenty-two Books are commonly known, means something like "Concerning the Polity of God." Well on to five hundred years after Lucretius, the world was again crashing, this time beyond recovery. The earthly hope of Augustan Empire was finally disappointed. The Christian Doctor, however, who strove in something like Lucretian spirit to generalise all things, was not like Lucretius despairing. Lucretius thought in terms of Nature; Augustine eagerly and devoutly recognised the supremely just sovereignty of the Christian God. In his colossal book, writes a French historian of Latin Literature,[1] "there is everything: a philosophy of history, an apology for Christianity, a system of metaphysics, a system of ethics, and a proof of Providence, all based on a mass of historical facts, of learned recollections profane and sacred, set forth in a style of prodigious strength and animation, sometimes melancholy when it describes the woes of this world, sometimes enthusiastic when it chants the triumph of religion and cheers the soul with heavenly hopes." The book has been called, among other things, the first Christian attempt to philosophise history. St. Augustine, in his opening words, undertakes to defend[2] "the most glori-

[1] René Pichon: Histoire de la Littérature Latine (7th edition), 1919, p. 869.
[2] Gloriosissimam civitatem Dei, sive in hoc temporum cursu, cum inter impios peregrinatur ex fide vivens (*Habac. ii, 4*), sive in illa stabilitate sedis æternæ, quam nunc expectat per patientiam (*Rom. viii, 25*), quoadusque justitia convertatur in judicium (*Psal. xciii, 15*), deinceps adeptura per excellentiam victoria ultima et pace perfecta . . . defendere . . . suscepi. Preface.

ous polity of God, whether in this temporal state where among the wicked the just shall live by faith (Habak. ii, 4), or in that changelessness of eternal order which now we with patience wait for (Rom. viii, 25), and where judgment shall return unto righteousness (Ps. xciv, 15),[1] and at last excellence shall bring us final victory and peace made perfect." To follow him through his hundreds of pages would clearly be far beyond our present scope. But the words with which he closes the book may be placed beside those with which he begins it: In that final Sabbath, he writes, which shall have no twilight, "we shall be freed from care and see; we shall see and love; we shall love and give praise. That shall be endless in the end. For what else is our end than to pass into that kingdom which hath no end? And so, by the help of the Lord, I think I have completed this huge work. Let those for whom it may prove too little, or too much, take no thought of me; let those for whom it may suffice give happy thanks not to me but to God who has been with me."[2]

Though, of course, the details of his theology and philosophy would take us too far afield, we can hardly even here neglect one general phase of it which has had incalculable influence on all the Christian future. Among the persistent tenden-

---

[1] In the Authorised Version of the English Bible, the Psalm numbered xciii in St. Jerome's version is numbered xciv.

[2] Ibi vacabimus, et videmus; videmus, et amabimus; amabimus, et laudabimus. Ecce quod erit in fine sine fine. Nam quis alius noster est finis, nisi pervenire ad regnum, cujus nullus est finis? Videor mihi debitum ingentis hujus operis, adjuvante Domino, reddidisse. Quibus parum, vel quibus nimium est, mihi ignoscant: quibus autem satis est, non mihi, sed Deo mecum gratias congratulantes agant: De Civitate Dei, XXII, xxx, 5, 6.

cies of the human mind has always been a complacent aptitude to assume human nature at heart healthy, and consequently to attribute social or other evils to nothing more profound than human blunder. Against any such views, at a time when Rome itself had fallen before a Barbarian conqueror, St. Augustine protested, loving God with all his heart, with all his soul, and with all his mind. Man he believed essentially sinful, by reason of the fall of Adam; the just penalty of sin could be averted only by the grace of God, through the mediation of the crucified Christ, persistent in the Church; and grace was granted only to those whom God should be pleased to save. Such, at least, seems roughly like what those who best know his opinions declare them to be. The subtleties of theology are more than enough to exhaust the study of life-times. Between the time of St. Augustine and ours armies of martyrs have suffered for his views and for those to which he was opposed. Eternal doom has been believed to turn on the splitting of hairs. But whoever knows the inner history of New England can hardly fail to see that the impulse which drove Pilgrims and Puritans to the deserts of an American wilderness came originally, even though perhaps distorted, from the African Father of the Church who gave up the ghost when Vandals were besieging his episcopal city of Hippo:

Calvin had taught them in their earlier home,
As grim Augustine taught imperial Rome,
How God disdained, with justly endless wrath,
The seed of Adam, scattered by the path
Where they must totter on and still revere
His Majesty, in consecrated fear.[1]

[1] See my Literary History of America (1900), pp. 15–17

Without St. Augustine, and the thought which
from him has persisted through the centuries,
we might have lacked not only countless tenets
of orthodox Catholic theology, insisting the sacrifice of Christ essential to salvation, but also the
heresies, as Catholics believe, which inspired the
lives of Calvin and of Jonathan Edwards, and have
lain deep in the spiritual heart of American Prot-
estantism.

Whoever can feel this will not think that we
have here lingered too long over the Fourth Century Fathers of the Church. St. Ambrose gave
us Christian hymns; St. Jerome gave us Christian Scripture, and those phases of Christian
prayer which depend upon Scriptural rhythm;
St. Augustine, human beyond the others, poured
forth springs of orthodox Christian thought and
faith. All this doubtless is not literature; but
without it the traditions of European literature
could never have taken the form in which, orthodox or vagrant, we historically know them.

CHAPTER III

THE FIFTH CENTURY

I

HISTORICAL TRADITIONS

In the year 400, as we have seen, Alaric the Goth already threatened the Roman Empire. Ten years later he had besieged and captured the imperial city of Rome. This is a typical beginning for the traditions left us by the Fifth Century. Kingsley's Hypatia, a medicated novel widely popular when muscular Christianity was the fashion, gives an animated impression of what life was like in those agonising days of the antique world; incidentally, the lectures and the opinions of Hypatia may serve to give us a popular notion of how Neo-Platonic philosophy tended a century or so after the time of Plotinus; and the fall of the Eternal City is said to have impelled St. Augustine to compose his great defense of the Polity of God. When he lay dying at Hippo, the Vandals had already swept down through Gaul and Spain, and were pressing eastward along the African coast. By that time St. Ambrose had been dead at Milan for more than thirty years, Alaric had lain for some twenty in his unmarked grave beneath a river turned from its course to receive his body, and St. Jerome had ceased for ten or so to trouble his ministering lion at Bethlehem. A Century of final confusion for antique Europe was well begun.

To tell the story here, except in confusion, would

be to disguise the tradition of it. After Honorius, who somehow pretended for a good many years to be imperial at Ravenna, there were ten shadowy Western Cæsars. The last, a puppet-child called Romulus Augustulus, was deposed by Barbarians in the year 476. The Empire of Augustus had lasted for just about five hundred years. For a thousand more the successors of Constantine were to preserve the Eastern semblance of it at Constantinople; except in name, however, the Byzantine Empire was never, like the antique Empire of Rome, a full part of general European tradition. Whatever their pretensions through the centuries, the Eastern emperors presented themselves to later Europe only as the recognised sovereigns of regions pretty far away. Like their last feeble fellows in the West, too, they were powerless in the Fifth Century to protect the ancient capital.

As we have seen already, Alaric the Goth captured Rome well before St. Augustine died. In the middle of the century it was threatened by the fierce Barbarian whose ravages have been traditionally remembered as the most appalling in history. Attila, the Hun, devastated the northerly regions of the Empire, far and wide, after a fashion unsurpassed until in our Twentieth Century the Germans put him to the blush in Northern France. Among the incidents of his descent on Italy was the destruction of Aquileia, a city near the head of the Adriatic Sea; some of the inhabitants managed to take refuge in inaccessible islands among the neighbouring lagoons; from them by and by sprang the marvellous city of Venice. At the time of Attila's invasion, the nearest approach to sovereignty at Rome, the time-honoured cradle of the Empire and the seat of the primal bishopric of St. Peter, seems to have passed into the hands of the Pope. Of the twelve Fifth Century popes, the one best remembered by tradition apart from his office is Leo, who chanced then to be on his throne. Partly, perhaps, by reason of the confusion about him, but to no small degree because of his commanding ability, he so strengthened the papal power that he has rightly been called the Great. His personal intercession, combining with the dignity of his presence and the sanctity of his office, was later believed to have dissuaded Attila from sacking the Eternal City, now become immemorially holy. A little later, however, even these failed to protect it from a raid by Vandals, who had possessed themselves of Northern Africa, and surged up to Rome from the mouth of the Tiber. On the fall of Romulus Augustulus, Italy fell to a Barbarian general called Odoacer. He seems to have restored comparative order there for twelve or fifteen years, nominally in some sort of subordinate relation to the Byzantine successors of the Cæsars. But he only made ready the way for his own conqueror, the Gothic king Theodoric. In the year 500 Theodoric was sovereign at Ravenna, whence he was to govern Italy through the prosperous first quarter of the next Century. By way of defending it from northern invasion, he greatly strengthened the city of Verona, and went there whenever things looked dangerous. In German tradition he was consequently remembered under the name of Dietrich of Bern (Theodoric of Verona). German traditions, however, more gracious than Germans themselves, have been apt to stay harmlessly at home.

To trace with any detail what had meanwhile happened to the northerly and westerly provinces of the Empire would be only to confuse our confusion. Repeated waves of Barbarian invasion had done their disintegrating work. No longer kept in Roman peace by a serenely and sternly just imperial sovereignty, Europe was already broken into some such pieces as have troubled its peace ever since. In Gaul and in Spain, civic and social vestiges of Roman civilisation considerably persisted, and for a good while longer. With Britain, never entirely subjected to Roman authority and singularly open to attack by sea, the case was less—or more—fortunate. Barbarian invasions of Gaul had completely cut off the island from central and southern Europe; and the Roman garrisons had been gradually withdrawn. Thus left to care for itself, a region which had been both civilised and Christian found itself at the mercy of rude heathen invaders. A few names linger in tradition to imply the story. This was the century of Hengist and Horsa; by the year 500 Angles and Saxons were already planted in the regions which still bear their name—East Anglia, for example, Essex, and Sussex. If there ever was a living King Arthur, either the end of this Century or the beginning of the next was the time when he vainly strove to defend against these inroads the civilisation implanted but no longer protected by Rome. Historically, too, this Fifth Century was the century of St. Patrick, who made Ireland Christian at just the time when England became heathen once more. Cut off from the rest of the world, Irish Christianity and Irish culture thenceforth flourished for a while as never thereafter. From times so far away as these conceivably spring the traditions of defiant hostility which even in the year 1920 still threaten the union of the British Empire and the peace of the English-speaking world.

A good part of Gaul, meanwhile, was already in possession of the Franks, whose name persists in that of France just as the name of the Angles persists in that of England. Their king, Clovis, was baptised at Rheims before the Fifth Century ended; his name, in its modernised form of Louis, or Lewis, has been the most persistently royal among French kings. In the year 500, too, Burgundians were already settled in the region popularly called Burgundy ever since. Spain was already a Gothic kingdom, and to stay so until more than two hundred years later it fell mostly into the hands of Mahometan invaders from across the Straits of Gibraltar. And, as we have already seen, Vandals were sovereign in Northern Africa.

In the year 400, the empire of Theodosius, divided between his sons Honorius and Arcadius, could still pretend to fancy itself intact. In the year 500, the Western half of it had vanished and the Eastern was none too safe. The Empire which Virgil had foretold was a thing of the past; but the successor of the Twelve Apostles still claimed authority throughout Western Europe, where the successor of the Twelve Cæsars had become only a memory.

II

LITERARY TRADITIONS

Amid the confusions of the Fifth Century, nothing of importance was added to the lasting traditions of European literature. The works of Leo the Great, at least as compared with those of St. Ambrose, St. Jerome, and St. Augustine, are matters only for students of history and theology. Though St. Jerome and St. Augustine, as we have seen, wrote memorably in the first years of the Fifth Century, both were men who had reached their full maturity before the end of the Fourth. And Orosius, a universal historian and a disciple of St. Augustine, has survived as a name mostly because King Alfred translated him, or had him translated, into Anglo-Saxon four or five hundred years later. In the year 500, to be sure, two men —St. Benedict and Boethius—on whom we must a little touch were already alive. Like Theodoric himself, however, they belong for our purposes not so much to the Fifth Century as to the Sixth.

CHAPTER IV

THE SIXTH CENTURY

I

HISTORICAL TRADITIONS

As we reminded ourselves a little while ago,[1] they still show you at Ravenna the sarcophagus of Galla Placidia, and beside it the stone coffins believed to have contained the bodies of her brother Honorius and of her son Valentinian. The heavy arches and the domed roof of the rather small mausoleum where they lie are decorated with mosaics on a deep-blue ground. Whether in the year 500 this ponderous yet not graceless structure was at all what it is now only archæologists know. By that time, however, Galla Placidia had been dead for some fifty years and Honorius for about seventy-five. Like the Western Empire and the fleeting sovereignty of Odoacer they were already memories, swiftly vanishing into the greater past behind them. At Ravenna, and virtually in all Italy, Theodoric the Goth—a Barbarian but no disdainer of Roman civilisation, a Christian but an Arian—was king; and such a king that he has sometimes been called the Great.

They show you at Ravenna, too, a ruinous wall which is traditionally called that of his palace. An authentic relic of him there is the heavy circular stone tomb, with its huge monolith of a dome, where for a while his body rested, after he had

---

[1] *Cf.* p. 403.

reigned more than thirty years. It was not destined to lie in peace so long; its fate was something like that of Oliver Cromwell's. By the middle of the Century, a good part of Italy had been reconquered by the arms of the great Eastern emperor Justinian; and, if we may believe tradition, the dust of the Arian heretic Theodoric had been scattered by the command of the orthodox imperial general Belisarius. Since then the tomb of the Gothic king has been empty.

Among the names of the Eastern Emperors that of Justinian, by whose forces the kingdom of Theodoric was destroyed, stands traditionally alone, and on the whole rightly. None before him and none afterwards came so near to reviving, with its centre at Constantinople, a European dominion which should equal that of the true Roman Cæsars. When Theodoric died, the actual dominions of the Roman Empire stopped at the southeast end of the Adriatic Sea. Italy, the Dalmatian coast and everything north to the Danube, Switzerland, and the regions later called Provence, or Southern France, were included in the kingdom of Theodoric; another Gothic kingdom dominated almost all of the Spanish peninsula; Northern Africa, Corsica, and Sardinia were under the rule of the Vandals; and what had been Gaul was mostly subject to the Frankish kings traditionally called Merovingian. In France and Spain the conquests of Justinian made little progress; elsewhere, however, they reduced to his imperial power virtually all the Mediterranean coasts except those of Northeastern Spain and of Southern France; they commanded the Adriatic, Sicily, Corsica, Sardinia, and the Straits of Gibraltar; and their actual, if not always their nominal capital in Italy was not the antique city of Rome, but the more accessible and more securely defensible city of Ravenna, where Honorius and his shadowy successors had taken refuge.

In the Sixth Century Ravenna, still a seaport, had already been a seat of sovereignty for something like a hundred years. Almost from that time, it fell into decay; its later unimportance has kept from complete ruin the churches which still remain monuments of its greatness. None of these is very large; none in their own day pretended to rival the great churches of Rome and of Constantinople. But Rome has been devastated, and quarried, and rebuilt again and again; and ever since the Turkish conquest in the Fifteenth Century the splendours of the Cathedral church of Santa Sophia at Constantinople have been veiled by the iconoclastic piety of the Mahometans. So the churches of Ravenna are now unique. Two of their interior features, quite unlike anything now extant from Roman or Greek antiquity, must instantly impress us: the first, particularly evident in the naves of the churches dedicated to St. Apollinaris, is the surmounting of the marble columns by capitals strong in outline, rudely rich with exuberant decoration utterly foreign to the Greek orders, and supporting round arches on which the upper walls rest; the second is that the walls are everywhere incrusted with mosaics, often pictorial, always splendid, but so remote from the reproductive skill of classical fine art that they seem magnificently barbarous. Remember, for example, the portrait-statue of Sophocles, which was about a thousand years old when Justinian was Emperor;

remember the imperial statue of Augustus, five hundred years old by that time. Beside them the mosaic portraits of Justinian and of his empress Theodora in the choir of the octagonal church of San Vitale at Ravenna look almost prehistorically primitive.

To tell the story of Justinian, nephew of a self-made Emperor who began life a man of the people, and of Theodora, whose earlier life is said to have been lower still, would delay us too long. The curious may find it in Gibbon, and if not there satisfied may explore the scandalous court-gossip of Procopius. Two enduring things remain to attest the traditionally Roman greatness of his Byzantine sovereignty. Disguised though it has been for more than five hundred years, his great Cathedral Church at Constantinople is in substance intact; and, though Mahometan worship deeply differs from Christian, prayer has ascended thence to the same God ever since Justinian was on the throne. The second monument of Justinian is to be found in the massive volumes where by his command the whole body of Roman Law was digested. No other system of the principles on which all stable society must rest has ever surpassed the Roman for practical wisdom; none, in all likelihood, ever will surpass it. And wherever men enjoy its benefits, they may rightly give thanks to the memory of the Byzantine Cæsar whose wide-eyed image, sovereign amid his stiffly staring priests and courtiers, still surveys his wide-eyed empress on the mosaic walls of San Vitale at Ravenna. The Mediterranean empire of Justinian outlasted him, but not much longer than the Sixth Century.

During this Century, two eminent saints greatly strengthened the church. The story of the first is excellently told in Cuthbert Butler's Benedictine Monachism.[1] Before this time, monastic tendencies had been evident, but mostly in the East. It was reserved for Benedict, who came to his maturity in times when the Arian heresy of the Barbarian Theodoric threatened alike the traditions of the Apostles and of the Cæsars, to establish in Italy the monastic Rule from which, in one way or another, all the later monastic orders of Western Europe may be said to have sprung. Whatever we may think of monks now, there can be no question that for centuries, above all men else, they perpetuated the traditions of European civilisation and learning. Among other things, their schools of diligent copyists preserved for modern times almost all our surviving texts of the ancient classics.

The second great Saint of the Sixth Century was the pope who had been ten years on his throne in 600—Gregory the Great. Before his elevation to the papacy he had been a monk, probably accepting the Rule of St. Benedict. Tradition holds him the Fourth Father and Doctor of the Roman Church; the other three were St. Ambrose, St. Jerome, and St. Augustine, contemporary some two hundred years before him. Like them, as his traditional title shows, he wrote gravely and copiously. In tradition, however, he is mostly remembered for other things than this—for his firm and wise assertion of centralised ecclesiastical power at a time when cen-

---

[1] 1919. And for the swift growth of legend about St. Benedict see the Second Book of the Dialogues of St. Gregory.

tralised temporal power was wavering, for his insistence on disciplinary matters such as the celibacy of the clergy, for that careful attention to the public ceremonies of the church which still associates his name with the grave solemnity of Gregorian chants, and above all for his missionary zeal.

At least to English-speaking people, the most familiar instance of this is his concern with the conversion of Anglo-Saxon Britain to the true faith. The story is told in the Venerable Bede's Ecclesiastical History of the English Nation,[1] written in the earlier part of the Eighth Century. Almost at the end of the chapter which recounts the life of St. Gregory,[2] he records the tradition of how, before Gregory was Pope, his attention was called to Britain and its spiritual needs by the sight of certain captive boys, "their bodies, white, their countenances beautiful, and their hair very fine," offered for sale as slaves at Rome. He asked questions about them, and being of ready though devout wit made plays on words in commenting on the answers. Being told that they were called Angles, "'Right,' said he, 'for they have an angelic face, and it becomes such to be coheirs with the angels in heaven.'"[3] The form which these words have taken in careless tradition is "Non Angli sed Angeli sunt" (They are not Angles but Angels). Whoever cares to know his other holy pleasantries will not grudge the time required for

[1] I, xxiii to II, i. The original Latin text, with an excellent translation by J. A. Giles, may be found in the Second Volume of Bede's Works: London: 1843.

[2] II, i.

[3] "'Bene,' inquit, 'nam et angelicam habent faciem, et tales Angelorum in cœlis decet esse coheredes'": ed. Giles, II, 170.

a glance at Bede. This venerable historian of
English Christianity tells how when Gregory was
Pope he despatched a devoted missionary named
Augustine to convert the English. By 600, they
tell us, this other St. Augustine was already
archbishop of Canterbury. His successors in that
see have been the primates, or chief priests, of all
England ever since; and at Canterbury you may
still see the little church of St. Martin, of which
the walls are partly Roman, where St. Augustine
of Canterbury is believed, in the ruins of a rude
Christian chapel, first to have celebrated the renewed Mass, beginning for the centuries then to
come the Christian history of England.

Think of the Cathedral Church of Justinian at
Constantinople; recall the churches of Ravenna;
and then remember this tiny structure where the
first Archbishop of Canterbury ministered as a
missionary to English heathen. So you may come
to feel the traditions of the Sixth Century.

II

BOETHIUS

Neither the Rule of St. Benedict nor most of
the abundant Works of Gregory the Great belong
exactly to literature, even so much as the hymns
of St. Ambrose do, or the Bible of St. Jerome, or
the Confessions of St. Augustine. Just imaginably the Dialogues of St. Gregory are vaguely remembered as a treasury of legendary miracle, or if
you prefer of guileless superstition. But, very
surely, the solemn intonation of Gregorian chants
is a matter not of literature but of history. In

purely literary tradition, we may fairly say, the Sixth Century has left us only the name of Boethius.

Unimportant now, this was long held in an esteem which at present appears either accidental or excessive. Boethius,[1] a Roman gentleman of the highest contemporary accomplishment, was born at just about the time when the Western Empire fell. He grew up in the reign of Odoacer, and under Theodoric he was advanced to high offices of state. In those days eminence was even more than usually perilous. Somewhere about the age of forty-five he came to grief; a year or two before Theodoric died, he was thrown into prison and ultimately put to death, on suspicion of treason. It is said that his ambition had been to translate into new Latin all the works of Plato and of Aristotle, and incidentally to reconcile these apparently divergent masters of philosophy, already distorted by superstitious veneration into fantastic oracles. His work of this kind, if any of it survives, is now a matter only for students; and so, indeed, may be called everything he wrote but the very last. This consists of five Books concerning the Consolation of Philosophy. Interspersing his prose with occasional passages of verse, in various metres, he tells how, miserably imprisoned, "methought I saw a woman stand above my head, having a grave countenance, glistening clear eye, and of quicker sight than commonly Nature doth afford";[2] and so on. This miraculous visitant proves to be Philosophy,

---

[1] Hugh Fraser Stewart's Boethius (Edinburgh and London: 1891) is an admirably literate study.

[2] I, i; Tr. Stewart and Rand: Loeb Classics (1919), p. 131.

who presently proceeds to console him for his misfortunes in a manner remotely reminding one of analogous discussions in the Book of Job.

It is remarkable that, spiritual as much of this consolation is, nobody can now make quite sure whether Boethius was Christian or not. Though a good deal of his feeling is undoubtedly so, he never expresses it in formally Christian terms. One reason for this was perhaps prudence. If Christian, Boethius may have been disposed to Roman orthodoxy, at a time when the religious opinions of the Arian Theodoric were temporally the stronger. In such case, he may have thought it wise to avoid either insincerity or dangerously precise statement of doctrine unwelcome to the civil authorities. He has been called both the last of antique writers and the first of modern; he has been grouped both with the philosophers of antiquity and with the scholastic philosophers of the Middle Ages. The one sure thing is that for centuries thoughtful men thought him seriously important, and that no work anywhere near so much respected was produced in later Europe until modern literatures began. As we shall see, for example, King Alfred held this book worth translating into Anglo-Saxon; a Fourteenth Century translation into English was made by Chaucer; and Sixteenth Century "Englishings" of it are attributed to Queen Elizabeth herself. Stewart's Boethius describes no less than sixteen "ancient" translations of it into modern languages well before her time. Thus, though neglected nowadays, Boethius beyond almost any one else bridged the gap between ancient times and modern.

A neglected example of how well he was once

known appears in a passage to which Stewart[1] incidentally calls attention. In the Consolation of Philosophy occurs the sentence "In omni adversitate fortunæ infelicissimum est genus infortunii fuisse felicem."[2]   (In all adversity of fortune it is the most unhappy kind of misfortune to have been happy.)   Remembering this, Dante rendered it:

> Nessun maggior dolore
> Che ricordarsi del tempo felice
> Nella miseria.[3]
>
> (There is no greater sorrow
> Than to be mindful of the happy time
> In misery.—Tr. Longfellow.)

Boethius wrote his words in prison; Dante puts his into the mouth of Francesca, clinging to her lover in the Hell to which overmastering love has doomed them unparted.   And how incomparable Dante's are we can feel when we put beside them Tennyson's jingling parody of the passage:

Comfort? comfort scorned of devils! this is truth the poet sings,
That a sorrow's crown of sorrow is remembering happier things.[4]

In literary tradition Boethius long made the earlier years of the Sixth Century faintly alive.   He was the last memorable writer whose native language was Latin.

One trace of the later years of the Sixth Century

---

[1] P. 60.

[2] II, iv—near the beginning: ed. Loeb, p. 188.   Chaucer's version of this may be worth glancing at, to remind us how far away from us Boethius is in time: "In alle adversitie of fortune, the most unsely kind of contrarious fortune is to have ben weleful."   This was written years after Dante died.

[3] Inf., V, 121-3.   [4] Locksley Hall.

has also survived, familiar at least to all who are
acquainted with the services of the ancestral
Church.   When relics of the True Cross were received at a church in France, they were welcomed
by a hymn beginning

> Vexilla regis prodeunt,
> Fulget crucis mysterium,
> Quo carne carnis conditor
> Suspensus est patibulo.
>
> (The Royal banners forward go;
> The Cross shines forth in mystic glow;
> Where he in flesh, our flesh who made,
> Our sentence bore, our ransom paid.)[1]

Dante parodies the first line, with tremendous
effect, at the beginning of the last canto of the
Inferno.[2]   In his time it was known to all good
Catholics; and the Catholic Encyclopædia will
tell you the history of its processional use throughout the centuries.

[1] The Seven Great Hymns of the Mediæval Church (1867), 122.
[2] Inf., XXXIV, 1.   *Vexilla regis prodeunt Inferni.*
   (The banners of the King of Hell lead on.)

CHAPTER V

THE SEVENTH CENTURY

I

HISTORICAL TRADITIONS

Though the historical traditions of the Seventh Century are misty in detail, their general outline is almost startlingly distinct. In the year 600, as we have seen, the Mediterranean, the historic centre of the antique world, was nominally under the dominion of the Byzantine Emperors, and thus, after Barbarian episodes, again nominally Roman. What is more, the later course of history has long merged the blood and the traditions of the Barbarians who had destroyed the Western Empire with those derived from the Empire itself. Modern Europe, like old Christendom, includes as part of itself not only descendants of the Romans but descendants of Goths and Vandals, of Germans, of Franks, of Saxons, of Burgundians, and of many more such tribes or peoples, whose first incursion seemed utterly destructive to European civilisation.

At the beginning of the Seventh Century, accordingly, a Mediterranean sailor who wished to proceed from the Straits of Gibraltar—still the Pillars of Hercules—to the imperial capital at Constantinople need only keep fairly near the African coast until past Carthage to find himself throughout in waters as Roman as they had be-

come when Carthage was conquered in the Third
Punic War, some eight hundred years before.   To
starboard and to port alike, the nearest coasts—
Africa, Egypt, Syria, and Asia Minor; Southern
Spain, Sardinia, Sicily, Greece, and Thrace—
were all subject to the successors of Justinian,
and the sea power of the Byzantine Cæsars was
as yet little affected by the northerly Barbarian
powers destined to increase and to strengthen.
These were busy enough on shore.   Throughout
the Seventh Century the Anglo-Saxon kingdoms
traditionally called the Heptarchy were flourishing
and quarrelling in England; in France the Merovingian kings were at the greatest extent of their
power, and before the Century ended Pepin, father
of Charles Martel and great-grandfather of Charlemagne, had risen to more power than that of the
puppet sovereigns whom he pretended to serve;
in Spain the Visigothic kingdom came to control
the whole peninsula; in Italy Lombards established a considerable power to the north of Rome,—
their name is traditionally said to be an Italian
corruption of German words very like our English
"Long Beards,"—and at the head of the Adriatic
Venice was so growing that before 700 the first of
the Doges was chosen—a line to continue unbroken until the Venetian Republic fell before
Napoleon eleven hundred years later.   Already,
too, these powers were mostly Christian, as the
Empire was and as all Europe was destined to be
and nominally to remain.

In 650, a Mediterranean sailor on the same
voyage would have found the coasts to starboard,
from Tunis to Asia Minor,—including Egypt and
Syria,—in possession of a new sort of Barbarian,

permanently alien to Europe. In 700, this power controlled virtually the whole north coast of Africa, and had by no means reached the limit of its conquests. Substantially, indeed, it has held many of them until our own times. For more than a thousand years after 700, a Mediterranean sailor proceeding from the Straits of Gibraltar to Constantinople would generally have found Barbary to starboard and by and by, as he got eastward, to port as well; and Christendom meanwhile was only for a time to port. And no American can much need to be reminded that one of the first exploits of the United States Navy was the bearding of Barbary pirates in their North African den.

This Barbary of the centuries, too, was permanently alien to Europe not only in race but in civilisation and religion. As we reminded ourselves when we first touched on the historical traditions of the Second Century, five hundred years before the period with which we are now concerned, the story of Mahomet and of Mahometan conquests is classically told by Gibbon.[1] To tell it here in detail would at once exceed our limits and carry us into regions rather of history than of tradition. Traditionally, the name of Mahomet was unknown at the beginning of the Seventh Century, when he was somewhere about thirty years old and had made no particular impression even in his native Arabia. He was fifty or so, indeed, when his flight from Mecca to Medina, commonly called the Hegira, began in 622 the Era by which his followers to this day reckon the years. When he died, not much past sixty, his principles were

[1] Chapters L–LII.

already prevalent throughout Arabia, and Mecca was already what it has ever since remained—the Holy City of a faith relentlessly hostile to that of the Christians.

The details of this new faith, again, are clearly beyond our province. Two or three facts about it are nevertheless both historically and traditionally clear. Like Buddhism and Christianity, it was evidently not of European but of Asiatic origin. Buddhism has chiefly appealed to the more easterly and southerly parts of Asia itself; Christianity, adopted and developed by the civilisation of the Roman Empire, had already proved itself the general religion of Europe; Mahometanism, singularly acceptable to those parts of Asia and of Africa which come under Mediterranean influence, has never made perceptible appeal to Europeans. One reason for this may perhaps be found in its persistent zeal to propagate by the sword—a zeal which in later times became pitilessly ferocious. When Mahomet died it was virtually confined to Arabia. Fifty years later, it was in full possession of Persia, in Mahomet's time a dangerous enemy of the Eastern emperors; and it had twice attacked their imperial capital of Constantinople. It was in full possession, as well, of Syria and Palestine, including Jerusalem, the Holy City of the Christians; and of immemorial Egypt, where a probably mistaken tradition pretends that, by burning the books of the Alexandrian library to heat their baths, Mahometan conquerors permanently and wantonly destroyed a great part of the literature of classical antiquity. It was surging westward along the north coast of Africa, too. Before the end of the Century, it had con-

quered Carthage, and extended itself almost if
not quite to the Straits of Gibraltar. And of all
names abhorrent to Christians that of Mahomet
was already the most detestably fearful.

For, according to the tradition of his creed, there
is but one God and Mahomet is His Prophet. He
recognised, no doubt, something like inspiration
in Jewish tradition and Scripture; he recognised
it in the traditions and utterances of Christ; but
only as preliminary to the fuller truth divinely
imparted to himself. Not an incarnation of God,
he professed himself to be God's last and ultimate
spokesman to humanity; and the will of God made
him and his successors supreme at once religiously
and temporally, in Church and State. Simpler
than any orthodox Christian belief involved with
Trinitarian mystery, and recognising little if any
official difference between temporal and spiritual
power, his doctrine for that very reason appeared
damnably monstrous to all Christians. Nothing
could have been more insidiously tempting to
uninstructed minds. The temptation was increased, at the same time, by the robustly practical
simplicity of his far from ideal moral teachings.
And the peoples who yielded to these temptations,
willingly or at the point of the sword, found themselves in a condition of enthusiastic and intolerant
missionary union, just at a time when, whatever
the spiritual union of European Christendom, its
temporal condition was most bewilderingly unstable. This, in brief, is the great historical tradition of the Seventh Century: that Century found
the European world in some broken semblance
of antique imperial communion; when it ended,
the great opposing forces of Barbary and Chris-

tendom were clearly defined, and for a while the Mahometan force of Barbary was the stronger.

II

LITERARY TRADITIONS

To the literary traditions of Europe, the Seventh Century added nothing that has generally been remembered. The only book of the period which has traditionally survived has never been familiar to Europeans. Its name, however, is known to everybody. From the time of Mahomet to this day, the Koran—the sacred volume of successive revelations in which he set forth what Christians have held his impious parodies of divine truth— has been regarded by his followers with a veneration exceeding, if so may be, that with which English and New English Puritans cherished the text of the Bible.

CHAPTER VI

THE EIGHTH CENTURY

I

HISTORICAL TRADITIONS

A long blank-verse poem by Southey—Roderick, the Last of the Goths—recounts in a manner lately popular and still readable the traditional story of how the Eighth Century began. The Gothic king of Spain is said to have violated the daughter of Count Julian, an eminent noble. In revenge, Julian is said to have plotted against him with Mahometan conquerors of Northern Africa —in later Spanish and European tradition called Moors. They made their way into Europe across the straits between the Pillars of Hercules, the traditional limits of the antique known waters; and the hill near which they landed has ever since borne the name of their general. If we may believe Gibbon, at least, Gibraltar is only a popular corruption of the words Gebel al Tarik (the Hill of Tarik). Southey tells how Roderick fled before his conquerors, and finally, after vain though brave struggle, died in indistinct obscurity. For a longer time than had then elapsed since the Christian Era began, the Moorish Mahometans were to maintain in Spain more or less of the power —in all aspects alien to Europe—which at first swept all over the Peninsula, and surging across the Pyrenees threatened to overwhelm France as well. In 732—just a thousand years before George Washington was born—they were checked and driven back at Tours by forces under the Frankish general Charles Martel, son of Pepin and grandfather of Charlemagne. At least in tradition, his victory saved European Christendom; for a good while, though, Spain was lost.

In the middle of the Century came the dynastic change which has most profoundly influenced later European tradition. For generations the Merovingian kings had been weaklings; the power nominally theirs had been exercised by their principal officers. The second Pepin, son of Charles Martel, put an end to the pretense. He deposed the Merovingian Childéric, assumed the sovereignty, and within a few years acquired new and something like divine authority for his claims by receiving anointment at the hands of the Pope. A little later, he conferred on the Pope the temporal sovereignty of the exarchate of Ravenna—the last capital of the Western Cæsars three hundred years before, and the capital, too, of Odoacer, of Theodoric, and of the Byzantine successors of Justinian. As for Childéric, only accident has revived his traditional memory. He was buried, they say, in a long-since vanished church of the old Merovingian capital, Tournai. Centuries afterwards, repairs in the cellar of a mediæval house there brought to light a tomb believed to be his. At all events, it contained bones and the vestiges of a splendid mantle which had been ornamented with golden bees. These were assumed to be the insignia of Merovingian sovereignty; and when Napoleon became French Emperor they were chosen as the special badge of the Bonapartes, to replace the lilies of the Bourbons with an even more venerable emblem of French sovereignty.

The reign of Pepin lasted fifteen or twenty years. His son Charles, generally called Charlemagne, or Charles the Great, was alone on the throne for some thirty years in the Eighth Century, and some fifteen in the Ninth. By a chronological accident fortunate for weak memories, the year 800 marks the change in the nature of his sovereignty which has made his traditional name greater than that of any other European but Julius Cæsar. At his accession, his dominions included France and the Netherlands, the whole region of the Rhine, Southern Germany, and most of what is now Switzerland and of what have lately been the southwestern parts of the Austrian Empire. The principal authority concerning his life and reign is Eginhard, an accomplished man of high official rank, on whom we shall touch again when we come to consider the traditions of the Ninth Century. His Life of Charlemagne and his Annals of the Franks from 741 to 829[1] combine to remind us that the career of Charlemagne was tempestuous from beginning to end. Conditions, within his dominions as well as without, looked desperately chaotic. Instead of discouraging him they seem rather to have stimulated his determination that Europe must be reduced to imperial order.

Again, we must not allow ourselves to be lured into matters of historical detail. Only one military incident of his reign has conspicuously survived in literary tradition. This, itself of no great im-

[1] An excellent two-volume edition of the Works of Eginhard (ed. A. Teulet), with French translations, was published under the auspices of the Société de l'Histoire de France (1840–1843).

portance, occurred before he had been ten years on the throne. As Eginhard tells the story,[1] the Frankish king crossed the Pyrenees and conquered that strip of country to the South of them which historical maps of the period call the Spanish March, thus made a buffer frontier between Christendom and Barbary. Having received the submission of all the cities and castles before which he appeared, he withdrew his troops beyond the mountains again, with no loss except to his rear-guard. This was attacked in a narrow valley by some treacherous and brigandish Gascons, who wished to pillage the baggage of the army; and the heavily armed Frankish soldiers suffered a good deal at the hands of their light-armed enemies, descending on them from the heights. "In this action," writes Eginhard, "Eggihard, the king's chief steward, Anselm, a high officer of the palace, and Roland, prefect of the marches of Brittany, with a good many more were killed."[2] The defile where this took place is called Roncevaux—a name now as memorable in literary tradition as that of Thermopylæ; and the casual mention of Roland in that sentence concerning those who there fell is said to be the only known historical record of him. When we touch on him later, however, we shall find him traditionally grown to be an almost Homeric hero, and Roncevaux transformed into the spot where Christendom finally held back Barbary.

The account of the year 800 in Eginhard's Annals tells how Charles left his capital at Aix-

---

[1] Life of Charlemagne, IX.

[2] In quo prælio Eggihardus regiæ mensæ præpositus, Anselmus comes palatii, et Hruodlandus Britannici limitis præfectus, cum aliis compluribus interficiuntur. (Ed. Teulet, I, 32.)

la-Chapelle about the beginning of March, got together a fleet to protect his coasts from piratical Northmen,[1] lost his wife[2] at Tours, returned to Aix, went to Mayence early in August, and presently started with an army for Italy. He stopped for a few days at Ravenna, started to invade Southern Italy, and leaving the campaign there to his son proceeded from Ancona to Rome, where about the beginning of December he reinstated Pope Leo III, who had been deposed by sedition. What ensued may best be told in Eginhard's own words:[3]

When on the most holy day of our Lord's Nativity, the king had entered the church of St. Peter to attend the solemn celebration of the Mass, and had knelt in prayer before the altar, Pope Leo placed a crown on his head, while the whole people of Rome joined in the shout: *"To Charles Augustus, crowned by God, great and peace-making Emperor of the Romans, long life and victory."* After this salute, honour was rendered him by the Pope himself after the fashion in which honour was rendered to the princes of olden time, and thereafter, dropping the title of Patrician,[4] he was called Emperor and Augustus.

---

[1] Eginhard calls them "Nortmannici."

[2] Although, according to Eginhard's Life (XXVI), Charlemagne "practised the Christian religion, in which he had been steeped from infancy, most holily and with the greatest fervour," the same work respectfully credits him (XVIII) with four wives and five acknowledged concubines, the name of one of whom has escaped Eginhard's memory.

[3] 801 (the year then began on Christmas Day). Ipse autem cum die sacratissima Natalis Domini ad missarum solemnia celebranda basilicum beati Petri apostoli fuisset ingressus, et coram altari, ubi ad orationem se inclinaverat, assisteret, Leo papa coronam capiti ejus imposuit, cuncto Romanorum populo acclamante: *Karolo Augusto, a Deo coronato, magno et pacifico imperatori Romanorum, vita et victoria!* Post quas laudes ab eodem pontifice more antiquorum principum adoratus est, ac deinde, omisso Patricii nomine, Imperator et Augustus appellatus. (Ed. Teulet, I, 248.)

[4] This title, originally conferred by Constantine, apparently implied subordination to the Roman sovereign. The Pope had conferred it on Pepin.

Thus began the new Empire of the West, to grow into the never realised ideal of the Holy Roman Empire,[1] and to last, with greatly fluctuating fortunes, until it was abolished by Napoleon in 1806. For a thousand years, Europe was once more to have a titular successor of the Cæsars. The revived Empire, however, had a different character from that of Augustan sovereignty. From its beginning it claimed more than human authority; its ultimate head was not the Emperor but God, just as God and not the Pope was the ultimate head of the Church. Full conception of its principle was doubtless of slow growth, and any attempt to expound it simply must be open to the derision of the learned. Without some notion of it, however, we can come nowhere near understanding the great poem which, five hundred years after Charlemagne's time, was to enrich the lasting literature of Europe—the Divine Comedy of Dante. Here, accordingly, we may best consider, at the moment when the Holy Roman Empire began, something of what, as the generations passed, Western Europe came to believe it.

God is sovereign everywhere. On earth His sovereignty has two aspects, temporal and spiritual. It is concerned both with the affairs of the body, in all their transitory mutability, and with the affairs of the soul, on which depend the eternal destinies of men. God is pleased to confide the earthly conduct of His sovereignty to human lieutenants,—nowise freed thereby from human frailties, and individually as responsible for their

---

[1] Lord Bryce's admirable and frequently republished monograph on the Holy Roman Empire began, in 1864, a career now for nearly sixty years equally distinguished in historical literature and in public service.

sins as are the humblest of their subjects. Even though the officers are human, however, the authority of their office remains divine. Personal excellence on their part cannot increase nor personal sinfulness impair it. The temporal Vicar of God is the Emperor—the human vehicle of His authority—and the spiritual Vicar of God is the Pope. Together and in concert they summarise His authority through the fleeting years; all subordinate authority here below must be derived from Him through them.

The very circumstances of the coronation of Charlemagne indicate a practical difficulty from which this apparently simple scheme of earthly government was never long free. The Pope, as Vicar of God, crowned the Emperor as his fellow Vicar, and then proceeded to do him such honour as was done by Roman citizens to the Cæsars of antiquity. Only a few weeks earlier, the armed force of Charlemagne had reinstated the temporarily deposed Pope. Was the Pope a higher official of God than the Emperor, or the Emperor than the Pope? The question was never fully decided; we need not linger on it here. But a line of Dante's Paradiso excellently implies what for centuries men held true of Pope and Emperor alike. In Heaven the poet meets a blessed spirit who tells him

> Cesare fui, e son Giustiniano.[1]
> (Cæsar I was, I am Justinian.)

Justinian had been a man; as a man he had become Cæsar, the Emperor, the temporal Vicar of God; as a man he had so borne himself as to merit sal-

[1] Paradiso, VI, 10.

vation; and his blissful spirit, no longer Cæsar,—
for the essence of imperial office was that it should
be administered by a responsible human being
still in the flesh,—was only the spirit which had
animated the man Justinian. Put beside this the
passage in the Inferno,[1] where Dante shows a Pope
writhing in Hell and awaiting the man who was
Pope when the lines purport to have been written;[2]
not even the spiritual Vicarhood of God could
protect men, as men, from the penalty of their
sins. The divine authority of the Holy Roman
Empire gave no impunity to its colossally responsible human agents.

As we have seen, there were always two of these,
often at odds with each other. The Mahometan
world was in theory more fortunate; there, broadly
speaking, the temporal sovereignty and the spiritual combined in the successor of the Prophet. In
practice, however, like the Roman Empire, it had
for hundreds of years two centres, Eastern and
Western. The capital of the Eastern Caliphate,
acknowledged as the superior, was at Bagdad in
Mesopotamia; that of the Western was at Cordova
in Spain. In the time of Charlemagne both already existed. No Spanish Caliph is distinctly remembered by general European tradition; but at
least since a version of the Arabian Nights became
familiar to Europe in the Eighteenth Century the
name of one Caliph of Bagdad has been known to

---

[1] Inferno, XIX.

[2] *Ib.*, 53. We need hardly remind ourselves that the first line of the
Divine Comedy—

> Nel mezzo del cammin di nostra vita
>
> (Just midway in the journey of our life)—

fixes the assumed date of the action in the year when Dante was thirty-five,
that is, in 1300.

everybody. This was Haroun al Raschid, at the
height of his power in the year 800, when Leo
III crowned Charlemagne, Emperor of the Romans.

II

LITERARY TRADITIONS

Though no important work of European literature was produced anywhere near these times, a
single name of the period faintly survives in
English tradition.   In the Galilee Chapel of Durham Cathedral, beneath Norman arches lighter
than you would have believed that Norman build-
ers could dream of, is a plain old tomb bearing the
inscription

> Hac sunt in fossa
> Beadæ Venerabilis ossa.
> (In this grave are Venerable Bede's bones.)

These words, the guide-books tell us, are supposed
to date from the first quarter of the Eleventh
Century, when the remains of the venerated but
never formally sainted worthy were taken by
force from their original resting-place to Durham.
At that time he had been dead for about three
hundred years.   He was past twenty-five in 700;
he outlived the Moorish conquest of Spain and the
victory of Charles Martel at Tours.

Of his copious writings[1] only one has ever been
much read—his Ecclesiastical History of the English Nation[2] from the beginning to the year 731.

[1] The edition of his Miscellaneous Works, with English translations, by
J. A. Giles (London, 1843) fills twelve good-sized volumes.
[2] Ed. Giles, vols. II and III.

At the end of it is an autobiographical note,[1] with a portentous list of his works, closing with the words

And now I beseech thee, good Jesus, that to him whom thou hast graciously permitted sweetly to partake of the words of thy wisdom and knowlege, thou wilt also vouchsafe that he may some time or other come to thee, the fountain of all wisdom, and always to appear before thy face, who livest and reignest world without end. Amen.[2]

He passed his whole life, from the age of seven, in a monastery at Jarrow. Something of his temper may be felt in that last sentence of his History. Those who wish to know the mood of England at the beginning of the Eighth Century will find his pages gently pleasant to turn; those who have patience only for a short passage may accept as characteristic his account of St. Cuthbert,[3] which may perhaps allure them to glance at his poem on the Miracles of St. Cuthbert,[4] in forty-six short chapters of by no means Augustan hexameters. These passages will take any one into the spirit of his time. If you do not care for the excursion, you may rest assured that, except for his name, Bede and his time have long been traditionally forgotten.

[1] Ed. Giles, III, 312-9.
[2] Tr. Giles, III, 319. Here is the original: Teque deprecor, bone Jesu, ut cui propitius donasti verba tuæ sapientiæ vel scientiæ dulciter haurire, dones etiam benignus aliquando ad te, fontem omnis sapientiæ, pervenire, et parere semper ante faciem tuam, qui vivis et regnas Deus per omnia sæcula sæculorum. Amen.
[3] Book IV, Chapters XXVII-XXXII.
[4] Ed. Giles, I, 1-34.

CHAPTER VII

THE NINTH CENTURY

I

HISTORICAL TRADITIONS

Charlemagne was Emperor for fourteen years. His grandeur in tradition has rather grown than lessened with the centuries. Indistinct though he may often seem, there can be little doubt that Europe has habitually assumed him second only to Julius Cæsar. If you are curious to know how his contemporaries admired him you will find the story pleasantly told in his Life by Eginhard. Written not long after he died, this gives a vivid picture of him during his imperial years:

In body he was large and strong, in height tall, but not excessively—for he was just seven times the length of his feet,—his head was round, his eyes large and bright, his nose a little long, his hair beautifully white, his face cheerful and pleasant. . . . Though his neck was short and thick, and his belly protuberant, he was so well proportioned that you never noticed it. His walk was firm, and the whole carriage of his body masculine; but his voice though clear was weaker than quite suited his appearance.[1]

[1] Life of Charlemagne, XXII: Corpore fuit amplo atque robusto, statura eminenti, quæ tamen justam non excederet—nam septem suorum pedum proceritatem ejus constat habuisse mensuram,—apice capitis rotundo, oculis prægrandibus ac vegetis, naso paululum mediocritatem excedenti, canitie pulchra, facie læta et hilari. . . . Quamquam cervix obesa et brevior, venterque projectior, videretur, tamen hæc cæterorum membrorum celabat æqualitas. Incessu firmo, totaque corporis habitudine virili, voce clara quidem, sed quæ minus corporis formæ conveniret.

Teulet's notes (I, 72) show that many of the words here used are taken from Suetonius.

And so on. He was rarely ill. He loved roast meat. He swam remarkably well. One of his reasons for settling at Aix was because the natural hot springs there were so abundant that he could summon a hundred friends to bathe with him at once. He dressed after the fashion of the Franks, putting on fine clothes only for state occasions. He was remarkably temperate in the matter of drink. He liked to be read to at meals, particularly enjoying St. Augustine on the Polity of God. After his midday dinner he undressed and went to bed for two or three hours. At night he was apt to be wakeful, and when awake to do business. He studied hard, especially languages; Latin he spoke perfectly, but he understood Greek better than he pronounced it. He was good at rhetoric, dialectics, astronomy, and mathematics; but, although he kept tablets by his bedside, to practise when time served, he could never learn to write very well, because he began too late.[1]

If you wish details of his reign and his policies, you will find them in Eginhard. For a little while, it was hoped and believed that he would renew the imperial unity and civilisation of antique Europe. On all their borders he extended his dominions; between his accession and his death, they came to include not only the Spanish March, Northern Germany, Bohemia, much to the eastward, and a good part of the Dalmatian Coast, but also, excepting Venice, all Northern and Central Italy, stopping about half-way between Rome and Naples. And when he died, at the age of seventy-two, he was buried in the Cathedral Church of Aix-la-Chapelle; his mon-

[1] Life of Charlemagne, XXII–XXV.

ument is gone, but on the pavement above where he is thought to lie imperial you may still read the inlaid letters *Carolus Magnus*.

Unlike Augustan empire, however, that of Charlemagne was not sovereignly to persist. Before he had been thirty years dead, three of his grandsons had divided it between them. One took the greater part of France; another the greater part of Germany; the third, Lothair, took with the title of Emperor a long and comparatively narrow territory between them, extending from the Netherlands and the mouth of the Elbe to Burgundy, Provence, the northerly coast of Dalmatia and all the imperial dominions in Italy. France and Germany have existed, with very various fluctuations, ever since; the dominions of Lothair soon broke to pieces, but something of his memory and vestiges of the disputes for the regions he once governed survive to this day in the name *Lorraine*, which roughly means the country of Lothair.

Apart from these long-dim traditions, which make the reign of Charlemagne seem like a false dawn, the Ninth Century has left us memories only of bewildering confusion. The northern coasts of France were recurrently vexed by Northmen, who began to possess themselves of the region a little later called Normandy—the country of the Northmen; before the Century ended their first remembered leader, Rollo, was already active. In England, meanwhile, one great name emerged. The life of Alfred lasted from 849 to 901; his career accordingly belongs to the last quarter of the century. Traditionally it is distorted by much legend, such as that of how he forgot to watch the cooking cakes. In general, he is rightly remembered as the first great national hero of the English, for he successfully opposed Danish invasion threatening to overwhelm the Anglo-Saxons much as they themselves had overwhelmed Roman Britain four or five hundred years earlier. He is remembered, also, as a sovereign who hoped to revive civilisation in his dominions as ardently and as fruitlessly as Charlemagne had hoped on the continent a generation or two before Alfred was born. In these times, Mahometan affairs looked more prosperous than those of Christendom. The Moors possessed all but the extreme north and northwest of Spain; and the Saracens, as their more easterly fellows began to be called, infested the Central and Eastern Mediterranean, and among other things established themselves in Sicily, a good deal as Carthaginians had done before the Punic Wars—by that time some twelve hundred years ago.

II

LITERARY TRADITIONS

Like the Eighth Century and the Tenth, this murky Ninth Century contributed nothing important to the traditions of European literature. As we have seen, Eginhard wrote in the first quarter or third of it; and by and by there arose a pretty legend of how he had wooed and won Emma, thought to be a daughter of Charlemagne. His wife was really named Emma; if she was of imperial blood, though, the fact is not recorded and probably was discreetly dissembled. Eginhard's writings are still readable; those on which we have touched tell almost all that is known of Charlemagne as a human being; and the History of the Translation of the Blessed Martyrs of Christ, Marcellinus and Peter,[1] is interesting not only for its artless Ninth Century mingling of piety and rascality, but also both for its vivid glimpses of life and for its accurate statement of hysterical symptoms then supposed to be miraculous cures. It has not survived as literature, however; nor has the Oath of Strasbourg, sworn to a little after Eginhard's time, and reprinted in modern works on philology as the first written example of the dialect which was to develop into French, the most exquisitely finished language of modern Europe. Late in the Century, King Alfred translated, or directed to be translated, into Anglo-Saxon four more or less compendious works with which he hoped to civilise his unlettered subjects. For this purpose he chose from the Fifth Century the History of Orosius, from the Sixth the Consolation of Philosophy of Boethius and certain writings of Gregory the Great, and from the Seventh Bede's Ecclesiastical History of England. Compare these names with those of Greek and Roman antiquity, and you will taste the savour of Ninth Century culture. As for Anglo-Saxon, patriotic and linguistic enthusiasts have tried to revive a reading knowledge of it; but most of us can discern there only material rich in fossil roots.

[1] Ed. Teulet (Paris, 1843): II, 175-377.

CHAPTER VIII

THE TENTH CENTURY

I

HISTORICAL TRADITIONS

Shadowy beyond almost all others, such historical names of the Tenth Century as have at all survived somehow group themselves. In France this was the Century when the Northman Rollo became Duke of Normandy and was duly baptised; when the founding of the Abbey at Cluny began what was to be the most memorable monastic establishment of Western Europe; and when, at last, the feeble descendants of Charlemagne were supplanted as kings by Hugh Capet —much as their ancestor Pepin had supplanted the Merovingians two hundred years before. Lines descended from Hugh Capet were thereafter kings of France until the French Revolution; it was as the "Widow Capet" that Marie Antoinette was condemned to the guillotine. In Germany, though the names are even less familiar, one can discern something similar. This was the century of Henry the Fowler, revived in European tradition by his appearance in the Nineteenth Century opera Lohengrin; and of his imperial descendants named Otto, or Otho. Under them the Holy Roman Empire was newly established; and from their time as long as it lasted this nominal succession to the Western authority of the

457

Cæsars was almost always German and sometimes amounted to little more than a formal overlordship of Germany. Indistinctly one begins to feel something like an emergence from chaos of modern Europe. Though there was as yet no clear sense of nationality, the origins of France and the origins of Germany were arising, more or less hostile, from amid the ruins of the Empire of Charlemagne, already become grandly legendary. England, meanwhile, was isolated, and harried by Danes; the one English name of the period at all generally known is that of Dunstan. He was really an able ecclesiastic, Archbishop of Canterbury some three hundred and fifty years after Augustine had founded the see, and like Augustine duly sainted. So far as he is commonly remembered, however, it is because of a fantastic and parodied legend that on one occasion, when approached by the Devil, he drove off the enemy of our souls by nipping at him with red-hot tongs.

A social fact is perhaps worth touching on here. From the time when the Roman Republic became firmly established, nothing was more characteristic of Roman civilisation than the family, and its inheritances of tradition and of property. Nothing has been more characteristic of strongly established societies in modern times. But in the year 1000, it is said, not a vestige of any Roman family or its property survived, whether of republican origin or imperial; and it is equally said that hardly any family or property known in our own times can trace its origin so far back as that period. If even approximately true, this indicates how far Christian Europe had fallen away from the stability of civilisation. And all the while Mahometans were flourishing. This Tenth Century is reputed that when the Spanish Caliphs were most prosperous. Among the records of their Eastern fellows there is said to be a mention of stories concerning A Thousand and One Nights. And the celebrated Persian physician Avicenna was about twenty years old in the year 1000.

II

LITERARY TRADITIONS

In Europe, the Tenth Century produced nothing which has been generally remembered as literature or in it.

CHAPTER IX

THE TRADITION OF THE DARK AGES

The year 1000, an easy date to remember, is a point where we may do well to pause and take breath. So doing, we shall find ourselves in an atmosphere very unlike that which surrounded us when we similarly surveyed the Roman tradition, in the Second Century of the Christian Era, or the Greek, some four hundred years earlier. Together, we can now perceive more clearly than ever, these comprised the first great period of European civilisation, distinctly European and free from conscious infusion of other than European tradition. By the year 1000 they were as remote in the past as that year itself is at the beginning of the Twentieth Century. They must then have seemed, too, even more remote than they seem at the present day; for, on the whole, we fancy our own times orderly, and, as we look back at the eight hundred years through which we have just been hastening, there can be little doubt that the general course of them looks like a steady decline from order to chaos.

A familiar tradition of a tradition implies that they looked so as the year 1000 approached. A general opinion of Christianity has been that the evils of this world will persist until Our Lord comes again in His Glory. Though hopes for this new dispensation have been recurrently disappointed, they have sometimes run so high as to believe it near at hand; and they are said never to have been much more confident than at the period where we have now arrived. Things in heaven, of course, always go right; and by the year 1000 things on earth had so long been going wrong that they could not rationally be expected to do so much longer. The completion of a thousand years from the birth of Christ was evidently a convenient moment for the final and righteous change. There is good reason to suppose that it was generally thought to be imminent.

In any case Europe had fallen desperately far from the comforts and graces of civilisation, and meanwhile had never enjoyed any compensating prospect of earthly peace and good-will. What had once been open countries, in free and orderly communication over admirably maintained Roman roads, were often pathless regions, infested by brigands and wolves, and dotted with rude but often strong protective fortifications—walled towns and castles, as well as monasteries and churches prepared at once to nurture the life of the spirit and to defend themselves with the arms of the flesh. Only the clergy preserved any vestige of learning. They had forgotten Greek; but, although they everywhere thought and spoke in dialects presently to develop into the various languages of modern Europe, they had all been trained in the once imperial and still general language of Latin. No longer exactly living, this was by no means dead; it was the only vehicle of serious thought; it was the official medium of the Church—as it still remains; and reading and writing were concerned with little if anything else. Persistent monkish copying of manuscripts, century after century, is the only thing which has preserved for later times, refreshed in critical intelligence, the records and the literature of classical antiquity.

At this far-off civilisation men of the Tenth Century looked, when they looked at it at all, through a dense mist of Christian tradition. Quivering films of wonder—saintly, devilish, miraculous, villainous, heroic—hovered confused between their eyes and the great things, temporal and spiritual, of the past. Somewhere to the eastward—already for them more like what the future was to call Oriental than like anything European—were Emperors who vaguely maintained in localised power a last claim to the traditional succession of the Cæsars. Somewhere in Germany was a Holy Roman Emperor who pretended to something like the temporal authority once really imposed by the Cæsars on Western Europe. At Rome the Pope maintained the spiritual authority conferred on the Church when St. Peter was its first head. But even Emperors and Popes were often at pains to sustain themselves and quite as often at odds with each other. Nothing was clear but confusion, and the then long traditional belief that there must be such a thing as ultimate spiritual truth. So far as this world went, life was a constant, perilous, and far from hygienic struggle for existence. The struggle, too, was not only within the bounds of Christendom. To the southward, almost from the Pyrenees, and along the whole African coast of the Mediterranean, and to the eastward, including the Holy Land itself, the regions united only in loyalty to the Christian faith were environed and threatened by Mahometan infidels more nearly blessed with civilised conditions—if we may trust monuments and records

—than the European Christians whom they menaced.

And even the England of Alfred had been dead and gone for a hundred years; it was two hundred years since the Pope had crowned Charlemagne as he knelt before the altar in the Basilica of St. Peter; it was three hundred years since the Mahometan Moors had begun to threaten Christian Spain; it was four hundred years and more since Justinian had restored imperial control of the Mediterranean from Constantinople; it was more than five hundred years since the Western Empire had fallen before repeated Barbarian invasions; it was more than six hundred years since Constantine had been converted to the true faith; it was seven hundred years since the great persecutions had marked the last struggle for supremacy between the tradition of the Twelve Cæsars and that of the Twelve Apostles; it was eight hundred years since the reign of Septimius Severus, and nine hundred years since the reign of Trajan, and a full thousand years since Christ was born to this world under Cæsar Augustus. Those thousand years had enriched European literature hardly so much as it had been enriched by Virgil, Horace, Ovid, and Livy during the reign of Augustus alone. At the end of them, this age of Augustus must have appeared more inexorably antique than it appears to us now.

Yet almost from that year 1000, European civilisation was to revive, and to grow into what we call modernity. To our eyes the period where we have a little while lingered accordingly seems so dim that we are apt vaguely to call it the depth of the Dark Ages.

BOOK V

THE TRADITIONS OF THE MIDDLE AGES

CHAPTER I

THE ELEVENTH CENTURY

I

HISTORICAL TRADITIONS

To us, concerned only with traditions of literature, the first half of the Eleventh Century may
at first look almost as obscure as the Tenth.
The Danes were now at their height in England,
and Canute is legendarily reported to have been
sobered by discovering that for all his power the
tide would not obey his command not to rise.
Before 1050, to be sure, Edward the Confessor had
come to the English throne. Before 1050, too,
Norman adventurers had gained footing in parts
of Southern Italy never reduced to the Empire of
Charlemagne and exposed, like Sicily, to Saracen
attacks by sea. A more noteworthy fact for us
is that during these fifty years four or five men
were born whom we cannot neglect. That half-
century may perhaps be best remembered, for
our purposes, as the time when Hildebrand, who
was to be Pope Gregory VII, and Robert Guiscard,
and William the Conqueror grew up, and when the
Emperor Henry IV and Peter the Hermit came
into this world.

The moment we reflect on these names we must
remark what is probably the most distinctive
feature of Eleventh Century tradition. Before
the year 1000, the Normans appear hardly more
conspicuous than many other barbarians of the

past who had surged down through the centuries on regions richer and more comfortable than they came from, and before very long had mostly been absorbed therein. By 1100, they began to look imperially dominant as a race. With no loss of their original vigour they had proved so sensitive to the influence of what remnants of culture existed as quite to have forgotten their Northern language. Wherever they went they managed to take command; and we need hardly remind ourselves of how firmly they took it in England. From that day to this, except for the revolutionary tyranny of Cromwell, the sovereign of England has been descended from the Norman conqueror, William. The persistence of his line has disposed English tradition to assume that in his own time he was the only Norman of remarkably high importance. This is by no means the case; for a while the Normans looked equally portentous far and wide. Whoever desires a clear view of their story may find it in a book prevented by the World War from attracting the attention it deserves: Haskins's Normans in European History[1] is one of those unconsciously ripe works, usually disdained by their authors, which make the fruits of scholarship digestible for human beings.

The Norman Conquest of England, at least in general tradition the point where the modern history of England begins, took place in 1066. Before that time, only students have much if any notion of what had taken place there since the large apparition of Alfred. There had been a good deal of internal dispute; for a while, Danes had been in the ascendant; and the English prince Edward,

[1] Boston, 1915.

later to be saintedly known as Edward the Confessor, had passed his youth in his mother's country, Normandy. His royalty accordingly seems a little like that of Charles II, six centuries later; when Edward became king, his personal experience and sympathy were rather Norman than English. At this time, Norman vigour was at its freshest. Legend has it that the Norman Duke Robert—the same who was revived for Nineteenth Century Europe by Meyerbeer's opera Robert le Diable—looking down from a window of his castle at Falaise observed a particularly pretty peasant girl washing clothes at a spring or fountain below. He sovereignly summoned her to his presence; and in the fulness of time, when Duke Robert's soul went to its good or evil due, their bastard son William came to reign in his place. Edward the Confessor was childless. At his death,—he was presently laid in his Abbey church at Westminster, thereafter to grow into the most illustrious place of sepulture among all English-speaking races,—his Norman kinsman, Duke William, claimed his throne. The most nearly contemporary record of the story is pictured in the quaint tapestry traditionally stitched by William's wife Matilda and still preserved at Bayeux. The English set up as king one of their greatest nobles, Harold. With a retinue of Norman knights and followers, William invaded England. Harold fell before him at the Battle of Hastings; and for more than twenty years William was sovereign in England as well as in Normandy. During these years, the ascendancy of his Norman aristocracy was established throughout the kingdom. Traces of its monumental remains exist

far and wide—most evidently, perhaps, in the
square keep of the Tower of London, where the
chapel of St. John has been restored to its original
form. Norman architecture, military and religious, sprang up everywhere. Norman French
became the language of the court and of the
ruling class. For some three hundred years English appeared hardly more than the dialect of a
subjugated race. No more signal evidence of all
this can be imagined than that the early records
of our English Common Law from which have
sprung all the liberties of England and of America,
when not written in corrupt Latin, are written in
a corrupt surviving form of the language habitually spoken by William and his followers. For
hundreds of years before his time England had been
anarchic; ever since his time, it has been on the
whole the region where law has most nearly prevailed. And from that time when the bastard
Duke of Normandy established himself King of
England, every successive English king has been
one of his legitimate descendants. Though by
no means all the line have sat on the throne, George
V is his descendant in the twenty-seventh generation.[1]

William died from an accident in 1087. Tradition has it that he was hurt by his horse, leaping
away from a firebrand while they were sacking a
rebellious Norman town. He was laid in an
Abbey church at Caen. Like Charlemagne's, his
monument is gone; and they say that revolutions
have scattered his relics. As is true still of Charle-

---

[1] His actually reigning ancestors in this line were Edward VII, Victoria,
George III, George II, George I, James I, Henry VII, Edward III, Edward
II, Edward I, Henry III, John, Henry II, and Henry I—the Conqueror's
son.

magne too, though, a simple name in the church-pavement solemnly reminds you that here once lay a king too great ever to be forgotten.

For the remaining thirteen years of the Eleventh Century William Rufus—William the Red, the Conqueror's son,—was King of England. Traditionally he was a bad man and a tyrant. In the New Forest there still exists a stone said to mark the spot where in 1100 one Purkis, a charcoal-burn-er, found his body, pierced by a perhaps acciden-tal arrow. The living peasant carted the dead king to the Cathedral of Winchester. There they show you his grave to this day. To all English-speaking peoples these traditions of the Norman Conquest must always be the most instantly familiar of Eleventh Century history. Before 1066, England had been repeatedly conquered by invaders; Roman, Saxon, and Danish are the best remembered. Thereafter, it has never been conquered again. The England of modern his-tory developed from the fusion, under Norman sovereigns, of their own race with the races of which the successive conquests had been tradi-tionally begun by the landing in Britain of Julius Cæsar himself.

Apart from the great English tradition of the Norman Conquest, the last quarter of the Eleventh Century was marked by two more. The first, though comparatively indistinct, concerns con-tinental Europe, in the time of William the Con-queror. We have touched on the sublime theory of the Holy Roman Empire[1]—the sovereignty of God, whose temporal Vicar was the Emperor and whose spiritual Vicar was the Pope; we have

[1] *Cf.* p. 447.

touched as well on the never settled question of which, if either, was the superior of the other; and we have intimated that neither office could in any way protect its holder from sin or other infirmities of the flesh. Another perplexity beset both of these divinely commissioned dignities. For a good while, it was by no means clear how God intended them to be conferred. The final settlement that the Pope must be regularly chosen by the College of Cardinals was chiefly due to Hildebrand, himself Pope Gregory VII, the greatest ecclesiastic of the Eleventh Century and one of the greatest of all. It was not until a later time that the election of the Emperor was vested in certain German princes, lay and ecclesiastical, and thereby made as German as the papacy has been Roman, or at least Italian. Both of these measures were evidently, to a considerable degree, matters of reform.

Reform was never more needed than in the dark period over which we have been lingering and from which we now begin to emerge. However divine the sanction of authority, its human representatives, both ecclesiastical and temporal, had often been far from admirable in their personal conduct. True even of popes and emperors, this had been more deeply so of their subordinates. There has never been a time when affairs of this world seemed more hopelessly the prey of corruption and violence; and there has hardly ever been a more confusing tale of corruption and violence rife on all sides than you will find if you try to understand the story of the Emperor Henry IV. All detail of it we must leave to students of history. The one fact about him which survives in tradition is that when he desired to assert supreme imperial authority he was confronted by Gregory VII, who had already gone far to suppress incontinency and simony among the clergy. Two incidents of the long conflict between Gregory and Henry have never been forgotten. The first occurred in 1077, eleven years after the Battle of Hastings. Though at that time Henry had not yet been crowned Emperor, tradition assumes that he was already imperial when excommunicated by the Pope. He was compelled to do penance far more humiliating than that to which St. Ambrose had subjected Theodosius seven hundred years before: at the gates of the Castle of Canossa he is reported to have stood for three days —barefoot in the snow some of the time—before the sovereign Pontiff would admit him to the Papal presence. Seven years later, and three before William the Conqueror died, the tables were turned. Henry had somehow acquired more power than Gregory, had set up an antipope, had captured the very city of Rome, and was besieging his great antagonist, whose last stronghold was the Castle of San Angelo—the fortified structure which had once been the Mausoleum of Hadrian. The Pope summoned to his aid the Norman adventurer, Robert Guiscard, who had by that time made himself the most powerful military personage in Southern Italy. He not only drove back the forces of the Emperor, but having recaptured the city proceeded to plunder it as it had never been plundered before. Just at the moment when the Normans were laying the foundations of a future imperial law in England, they were completing the ruin of the imperial and holy city from which the law of antiquity had been derived. At about the same time they were founding in Sicily a kingdom of which the broken monuments are far more splendid than any ever raised in England; but England survives to this day, and for centuries Norman Sicily has been only a memory.

It was during the reign of William Rufus that the last great event of the Eleventh Century took place. At least in tradition this is impressively different from any at which we have glanced for a long time. Though the First Crusade started in France, and though the two personages whom it brought into most familiar tradition came from a region so near Normandy that one may almost fancy them to have caught something of the Norman vigour, nobody generally thinks of it now as either Norman or French; rightly or wrongly we imagine the movement to have been, almost in the modern sense of the word, European. If readers of English will remember that Gibbon's Eighteenth Century prejudice was anticlerical, they may still find the story most accessibly told in his always literate pages.[1]

During the four hundred years which had passed since Mahometans captured Palestine, a fairly friendly state of things had arisen there. European Christians naturally wished to visit the places made holy, centuries before, by the earthly presence of Christ; and the Mahometan masters of Palestine found it evidently convenient to let them do so provided that they paid for the privilege and behaved peaceably. Something at once like the modern practice of pious touring and like Mahometan pilgrimages to Mecca had resulted.

[1] Decline and Fall, etc.; Chapters LVIII, LIX. (Ed. Bury, VI, 259-365.)

This was disturbed, at just about the time when Gregory VII humiliated Henry IV at Canossa, by a new conquest of Jerusalem. The cradle of Christianity fell into the hands of Turks, Mahometan but by no means so affably disposed as their originally Arabian fellow believers whom they had overcome. Before long Europeans who wished to make pilgrimage became generally and indignantly aware that the holy places of their Catholic faith were in possession of infidels. It is said that Gregory VII purposed an organised Christian attempt to retake them by force. His later troubles with Henry IV prevented this project from coming to anything; his regular successor in the papacy lived for less than two years; and Urban II, a Frenchman, who then succeeded to the throne of St. Peter, found himself for a time involved in all manner of confusion with the Emperor, with an antipope, with the King of France, and more. Modern authorities, however, tend to agree that the final impulse to the First Crusade was given by Urban himself at the Council of Clermont in 1095. Tradition has been apt to ascribe the enthusiasm there aroused to the stirring and fanatical eloquence of Peter the Hermit, a native of Amiens, who certainly fanned the flame when once lighted. In 1096, the Crusade began: its principal military leader was Godfrey of Bouillon, or Boulogne; but there were others, mostly French, or of the Italian branch of the Normans—among them Tancred. The Crusaders passed through Constantinople, where they came to some sort of understanding with the Eastern Emperor; they made their way overland through Asia Minor; in 1099 they captured Jerusalem, where they put to death great numbers of Mahometans and Jews; and setting up a Christian kingdom there they made Godfrey king. The sovereignty thus begun lasted about ninety years. Urban II, instigator of the Crusade, never knew of its success; he died in Italy almost at the moment when Godfrey of Bouillon was taking the walls of Jerusalem by storm. This was about a year before the charcoal-burner Purkis found William Rufus shot to death in the New Forest.

By the end of the Eleventh Century, which had begun so dimly in tradition, we thus emerge at last into something like light again. Of course the passing days of life were then, as they always have been and always will be, full of trouble and confusion. The difference between the times where we have now arrived and those through which we have lately been groping is that henceforth a sometimes mistaken but always tenacious tradition has remembered, much as it clearly remembers things from Roman antiquity and from Greek, men and events thus raised above the belittling confusion of reality. They were historical facts; they are living names, by the chance of survival purified and simplified into heroic semblance. The First Crusade, for example, was no doubt as deeply intermingled with intrigue and treachery, cruelty and all manner of human baseness, as any other military adventure of the times. For hundreds of years, however, it has been vaguely and generally imagined to have been a marvellous exhibition of devoted self-sacrifice for the sake of the Lord and Saviour who a thousand years before had offered Himself as the one supreme sacrifice for sinful mankind. We of America may sadly

or humourously remark the likeness of this transformation to those which have already overtaken
cherished incidents of our own short national existence, such as the American Revolution and the
Civil War. However instructive, though, these
considerations are hardly to our present purpose.
If we began here to scrutinise the facts of history,
we should soon be distracted from the equally
persistent fact of tradition. This nobody can forget who will ponder for a moment over the word
Crusade. From childhood it has meant for us
all not what the last five years of the Eleventh
Century really were, but what the generations
have long since come to fancy that olden time to
have been.

Even in tradition, too, less distinct memories
gather near. We have lingered a little over the
Norman Conquest of England, Canossa, and the
Crusading victory at Jerusalem. We have reminded ourselves, the while, that Turks had just
then been upsetting the originally Arabic Mahometan sovereignty in the East. Put beside
this the first heroic name of later Spanish tradition; the Cid lived in that same Eleventh Century. Historically, he seems to have been an
able mercenary soldier, prepared when duly paid
to fight impartially for either Moors or Christians.
Traditionally he is the stainless champion of the
Cross against no longer crescent Mahometan
power. He died, they say, in the very year when,
at the other end of the Mediterranean, the Crusaders mastered Jerusalem. East and West, traditional Christendom begins to look no longer defensive but aggressive. At just about this time,
too, a new monastic order was founded: the Cath-

olic Encyclopædia dates the origin in France of
the Cistercians from the year 1099. Fifteen years
earlier, in 1084, Robert Guiscard had come to
the rescue of Gregory VII besieged at Rome by
the forces of the Emperor, and incidentally had
sacked the city. To this very year they refer the
foundation in France of the Carthusians. Just
what either order was we need not now inquire.
One thing appears beyond dispute. Any such
fact as the institution of either implies on the
part of earnest men a passionate desire to reform
the evils of this world—to make mankind better. The foundation of both within hardly more
than fifteen years implies, like the name of Gregory VII and the name of the Crusades, a refreshed
vigour of Christian impulse—and in those days
Christianity had long been immemorially believed
identical with the Church. That both of these
monastic orders, like Cluny a little earlier, were
largely French means much, too. So was the Norman Conquest; so were the Normans in Southern
Italy and Sicily; so were Peter the Hermit and
Godfrey of Bouillon. There is monumental record, too, of this newly awakened French vitality.
In the year 1000 the round-arched Romanesque
churches of France and the Norman churches of
England were hardly in existence; by the year
1200 almost all of them were finished. The time
of the First Crusade, when the Norman succession
to the English throne was already secure, was the
time as well of the first great architectural expression of the Middle Ages. All these things cluster
about the year 1100.

II

THE SONG OF ROLAND

Just about here Henry Adams's Mont-Saint-Michel and Chartres[1] begins; and for two or three centuries it takes one marvellously into the heart of awakening and awakened Europe. Though it cannot be read carelessly, it cannot fail animatingly to reward whoever will stop to feel what it means; and, quite apart from all else, it contains much remarkably sensitive translation. Most of these translations are from the Old French—a literature for a while exuberantly alive and then so neglected by revived reverence for the ancient classics that it was long both disdained and forgotten. So, even when they are known, the names of its masters have never grown familiar again, if indeed they ever were; and their work, though Nineteenth Century erudition has now made it accessible, is apt to seem a subject rather for laborious research than for human edification. Yet the more you come to know them, the more variously vital they prove; at once ingenious and spontaneous, they expressed the sentiment of the Crusading centuries as genuinely as it was expressed by the equally unremembered church-builders—first Norman and later Gothic—whose history is summarised in the title of Henry Adams's book. What is more, even though for a long time later Europe hardly recognised their existence, their influence in later European literature has been constant.

[1] Boston, 1913.

The second chapter of Adams's book discusses the Song of Roland so compactly and yet so fully that whoever would approach the story may best do so there. There you will find it starting from an episode of the Battle of Hastings recounted, in still singing lines, by the Twelfth Century Norman poet, Wace:

> Taillefer qui moult bien chantout
> Sor un cheval qui tost alout
> Devant le duc alout chantant
> De Karlemaigne et de Rollant
> E d'Oliver e des vassals
> Qui morurent en Roncevals.[1]
>
> (Taillefer who was famed for song,
> Mounted on a charger strong,
> Rode on before the Duke, and sang
> Of Roland and of Charlemagne,
> Oliver and the vassals all
> Who fell in fight at Roncevals.—Tr. Adams.)

Adams goes on with more of the story as Wace tells it. Even this, however, is enough to remind us that by the time when William the Norman won England, Roland, the Prefect of the Marches of Brittany who had fallen before Gascon brigands three hundred years before, had become a traditional arch-type of Christian knighthood warring against Mahometan infidels.

How and when the story had developed nobody surely knows. Its origin is briefly recorded in the passage from Eginhard's Life of Charlemagne which we set down[2] a little while ago. When we meet it here again it seems complete. Charlemagne, the Christian Emperor, had triumphed in

---

[1] Wace: Roman de Rou, 8035–40. (Ed. H. Andresen, 1877.)
[2] *Cf.* p. 445.

Spain, and led his victorious army back across the
Pyrenees. A traitor, Ganelon, betrayed his rear
to the Moorish enemy. Attacked at Roncevaux,
they made stand, like the Greeks at Thermopylæ;
among them were renowned heroes—Roland,
Oliver, Archbishop Turpin of Rheims, and more;
they fell to a man; the horn of Roland, summon-
ing back the Emperor, sounded too late; even in
defeat, though, they were victorious; nobly dying, they saved Charlemagne and with him Christendom. And the heroic song which records
them, primitive though it be beyond anything left
us by the ancients, has a large epic simplicity
almost Homeric.

The Song of Roland, as we possess it, is thought
to be later than the Battle of Hastings. We may
assume it, however, as Adams assumes it, substantially like what the minstrel Taillefer sang
there when he led the Norman charge against the
English. It takes us into a world different from
any of which we have had glimpse before—a
world that was never quite real, but a world such
as the awakened Eleventh Century fancied a
not very olden time to have been. To feel its
full atmosphere, you must turn the pages—no
great task, for up to the death of Roland there
are only two hundred and six stanzas, 2396 lines
in all. They are full of the spirit of Christian war,
magnificently masculine; here is no place for love
or dalliance, but here are men glad bravely to
answer the call of duty. For all the rudeness of
their lives and their tasks, too, they are gentle,
instinct with honour and courtesy; so, for example,
a passage chosen and translated by Adams shows
them, when Oliver, blinded by wounds, strikes

Roland unawares and is not rebuked.[1]   They know
themselves sinners, as well, like all mankind enabled to attain unmerited salvation only through
the grace of God.   Adams gives and translates the
stanza concerning Roland's death:[2] Roland throws
himself down beneath a pine, turns his face from
Spain, and gives his last moments to memory—of
the lands that he had conquered, of pleasant
France, of his lineage, and of Charlemagne, who
had nurtured him.   Then he prays God for grace:

> Veire paterne ki unkes ne mentis
> Seint Lazarun de mort resurrexis
> E Daniel des liuns guaresis
> Guaris de mei l'anme de tuz perils
> Pur les pecchiez que en ma vie fis.
>
> (O God the Father who has never lied,
> Who raised up Saint Lazarus from death,
> And Daniel from the lions saved,
> Save my soul from all the perils
> For the sins that in my life I did.—Tr. Adams.)

And he proffers his right glove to God, and St.
Gabriel takes it from his hand, and

> Desur sun bras teneit le chief enclin
> Jointes ses mains est alez a sa fin.
> Deus li tramist sun angle cherubin
> E Saint Michel de la mer del peril
> Ensemble od els Seinz Gabriel i vint
> L'anme del cunte portent en pareis.
>
> (Upon his arm he held his head inclined,
> Folding his hands he passed to his end.
> God sent to him his angel cherubim
> And Saint Michael of the Sea in Peril,
> Together with them came Saint Gabriel.
> The soul of the Count they bear to paradise.
> —Tr. Adams.)

[1] Stanza CLXXVI (lines 1989–2009).
[2] Stanza CCVI (lines 2375–2396).

"God," writes Adams, "was the feudal seigneur, who raised Lazarus—his baron or vassal—from the grave, and freed Daniel, as an evidence of his power and loyalty; a seigneur who never lied, or was false to his word. . . . To this seigneur, Roland in dying proffered . . . his . . . gauntlet. Death was an act of homage. God sent down his Archangel Gabriel as his representative to accept the homage and receive the glove."

It is all in a world as different from ours as the old French words are from any we read or hear to-day; more different still, if so may be, from classical antiquity. Yet without classical antiquity it could not have been itself. The very first line of the Song of Roland sounds the key-note of his earthly loyalty:

> Carles li Reis, nostre emperere magnes.
> (Charles the King, our great Emperor.)

The title, Emperor, which asserts imperial sovereignty greater than royal, could never have had its meaning if it had not been borne by the Cæsars. The Cæsars bore it because it had been borne by Cæsar; and to make Cæsar needed all the antique intelligence of Greece and all the antique common sense of Rome. In the Eleventh Century, no doubt, antiquity lurked dim behind the intervening veil of Christian tradition, thickening all through what we call the age of darkness. Without antiquity, nevertheless, the world of Roland could not have existed; and without that world of Roland, itself now seemingly more remote than Rome or Greece, our own world could not be quite what it is.

In one way, as the lines may indicate which
we have set down in old French, the epic verse
of the Eleventh Century seems almost modern.
Just how any classical Latin lines originally sounded
we can never be quite sure; and the question is
more perplexing still when we come to the original sound of lines in classical Greek. One or two
things, however, are clear about both. Both
considerably depended on what is called length of
vowels and syllables; it is often said, for example,
that a long vowel or syllable required for pro-
nunciation twice as much time as a short. Again,
neither seems to have held stress on syllables a
very important metrical feature; that the lines
can be read with stress, and thus made easier for
modern ears, does not prove that they were meant
to be read so. And neither Latin nor Greek ever
paid much if any attention to regular rhymes.
Just how the old French sounded eight or nine hundred years ago may doubtless be held as uncertain
as any such question about the ancient languages.
You need only read aloud, however, the eleven
lines quoted a page or two ago from the Song of
Roland to assure yourself that whoever made
them had an ear very like ours. Stress every
second syllable and they will fall into primitive
semblance of lines habitually written in French
or English now. Again, though the lines do not
rhyme like modern rhyming verse, they have one
principal feature of modern rhymes: all end with
the same vowel-sound—in this case the letter *i*.
Ingenuity, indeed, might conceivably translate
them into eleven consecutive rhymes. Such
leashes of rhyme, as they are called, occur in every
stanza of the Song of Roland. Though not yet

modern, the form of poetry is well on its way to modernity.

This is clearer still if we turn to the verse which was making at about the same time in Provence. On the place of Provence in European literature we shall touch more decidedly when we come to the Twelfth Century. Here it is enough to glance at four lines of a Prayer to the Virgin, attributed by Bartsch to the Eleventh:[1]

> O Maria, deu maire,
> Deus t'es e fils e paire:
> Domna, preja per nos
> To fil lo glorios.

> (Mary, thou of God the mother,
> God to thee is son and father:
> Lady, say a prayer for us
> To thy Son, the Glorious.)

The rhythm and the rhyme of that off-hand translation almost if not quite reproduce those of the original verse; yet, so far as rhyme and rhythm go, those four English lines are almost such as might be written to-day.

[1] Chrestomathie Provençale (Elberfeld, 1868), p. 18.

CHAPTER II

THE TWELFTH CENTURY

I

HISTORICAL TRADITIONS

At this point our historical tradition takes on a new aspect. English-speaking people generally know the names of the English kings from the time of William Rufus to the present day. Though little informed about serious history, they may accordingly be apt to recognise four Twelfth Century names: Henry I, who reigned thirty-five years; Stephen, who disputedly reigned for nineteen; Henry II, who reigned for thirty-five; and Richard I, "Cœur de Lion," who reigned for ten. The story of John, who succeeded in 1199, belongs not to the Twelfth Century but to the Thirteenth. Neglecting him, we may conveniently consider Twelfth Century traditions as they accumulated under his four predecessors.

Henry I, the younger brother of William Rufus, though generally remembered as an accomplished and able man, nicknamed "Beauclerc," and important both as a soldier and as a statesman, stays traditionally distinct mostly because of the bereavement after which he is said never to have smiled again. The "White Ship," while carrying his only legitimate son from Normandy to England, ran on a rock; the prince was drowned, and with

him the male line of succession from his grandfather, the Conqueror, to the English throne came
to an end. When Henry died, fifteen years later,
he expected to be succeeded by his daughter,
Maud or Matilda, widow of an Emperor and wife
of Geoffrey of Anjou, who was called Plantagenet;
but before Henry was in his grave, the English
had set up in her stead his nephew, a grandson of
the Conqueror, Stephen of Blois.

The moment we ask ourselves what continental
traditions arose in these first thirty-five years of
the Twelfth Century, we shall feel a double difference. Though even less familiar, perhaps, than
the names of Henry Beauclerc and of the White
Ship, those to which we now come look and indeed are variously more important. For our
present purposes a very few will serve. This
reign of Henry I was the time when Abelard
flourished in France. His name must instantly
suggest two others: Heloise and Bernard of Clairvaux. The love-story of Abelard and Heloise has
never been forgotten; the not surely authentic
letters on which it is partly based are worth a
glance—and more, if you like. Those who wish
a deeper impression of his life, his character, and
his surroundings will do well to ponder over the
careful study of him in Henry Adams's Mont
Saint Michel and Chartres. This will take them
straight into the presence of St. Bernard of Clairvaux, and into the heart of the revived Christian
enthusiasm of the time, in passionate dispute
with its reawakened philosophy. Remember that
in these same years two great orders of knighthood
were founded under the impulses which had lately
established the Crusading kingdom of Jerusalem:

the Templars, who were to be tragically suppressed
—particularly in France—about two hundred
years later, but whose name and tradition has survived far and wide; and the Hospitallers, who were
to develop into the Knights of Malta. Already
you must feel the stormy surge of that crusading
world—whatever else, amid all its confusions,
no longer waking but awake.

King Stephen is not so distinct. Grandson of
the Conqueror through his daughter Adela, who
married the Count of Blois, Stephen found his title
disputed by his cousin Matilda, or Maud. The
period, so far as England goes, looks dim again—
confused, anarchic, with an amiable king unable
to master things. In his time, indeed, continental
tradition grows not only more important but more
clear. He was on the throne when St. Bernard
of Clairvaux, in the height of his power and after
Abelard was dead, gave its final impulse to the
Second Crusade. Of all the Seven, this is traditionally the least distinct. Its chief leaders were
the Emperor Conrad III and King Louis VII, of
France. It came to grief. For us, perhaps, the
most evident memory of it is that Louis's queen
was Eleanor of Guienne, or Aquitaine, herself
sovereign throughout much of Western and Southwestern France. You will find her alive in
Adams's Mont Saint Michel and Chartres; and
otherwise alive, when very old, fifty years later
than the Second Crusade, in the King John of
Shakspere. For us just now it is enough to remember that if she ever sinned

With some black-bearded Saracen, long since
Gone to his lying Prophet,

it was when her French husband was a chief soldier
of the Cross; that she was divorced from this
crusading king; and that before King Stephen died
she had married Henry, son of Geoffrey of Anjou
and of the Matilda who had previously been
Empress. This Henry, traditionally called by his
father's nickname Plantagenet, was to succeed
Stephen on the English throne; his marriage with
Eleanor made him partly sovereign, too, over her
extensive dominions in France.

The reign of Henry II lasted from 1154 to 1189;
his heirs male regularly succeeded to the English
throne until Richard II was deposed two hundred
and ten years later. Even then, they were replaced—and have been replaced to this day—only
by other lines descending from Richard's grandfather, Edward III; and tradition still associates
all English kings until the accession of the Tudors
with the name of Plantagenet, thus originated in
the Twelfth Century. In many other and more
profound aspects than this firm establishment of
the succession, the reign of Henry II is historically
important; our present concern, however, is not
with history. Traditionally the reign is best remembered as the source of two familiar stories,
one probably legendary, the other based on fully
recorded fact. The first is that of Fair Rosamond, the pretty mistress of the king, thought
safe in her Bower at Woodstock, near Oxford,
but there followed by the jealous elderly Queen
Eleanor and given only the choice of steel or poison
to end her daintily sinful days. The second story
is that of Thomas Becket, the swiftly sainted
Archbishop of Canterbury, whose shrine there,
from the reign of Henry II to the Reformation,

was among the most popular centres of pilgrimage in Western Europe. A brilliant and able man, he had risen to influence and importance under an Archbishop of Canterbury before Henry came to the throne. Henry made him Lord Chancellor, an office in which he both greatly strengthened the state and so commended himself to the king as to become a prime favourite. Among the incidents of the reign were violent disputes about the relations and the limits of royal and ecclesiastical power. Naturally enough, when the see of Canterbury became vacant, King Henry managed that it should be given to Becket, his most acceptable public servant. Once Archbishop, however, Becket proved the ablest ecclesiastical antagonist whom Henry, as King, had ever had to meet. As the story goes, the King, occupied in Normandy, was so enraged by news of some new assertion of the Archbishop's independence that he uttered an exclamation which sounded like a wish to be delivered from the proud priest. Certain knights who overheard him took it literally. They made haste to England, broke into Becket's episcopal palace at Canterbury, pursued him through cloisters to the Cathedral, and there cut him down on the steps of an altar. Within three or four years, a papal bull had canonised him; and Henry did barefoot homage to his relics. Before long, the Cathedral of Canterbury, where he lay, became the richest of English shrines; and, two centuries later, the Canterbury Tales of Chaucer added to the glories of the "holy, blissful martyr." Apart from these two familiar stories, the chief traditional memory of Henry's reign is that his sons, when they grew up, were on turbulent terms both with their parents and with one another.

During these thirty-five years, English traditions are for us far more distinct than anything continental. The principal continental name which then came into lasting existence is that of the Emperor Frederic Barbarossa. Historically he is in many ways memorable—not least for his devastating destruction of the rebellious city of Milan, where nine hundred years earlier the tradition of the Twelve Apostles, embodied in St. Ambrose, had asserted its power over that of the Twelve Cæsars, embodied in Theodosius. Traditionally, Barbarossa is the colossal sovereign who started on the Third Crusade, never to return, but who for ages was expected to emerge from a German cavern where, his red beard grown through the stone table before him, he sat asleep, awaiting the moment to awake and restore the warring world to the order of imperial dominion.

The Third Crusade, on his way to which Frederic Barbarossa was accidentally drowned, began in the year 1189, when Richard Cœur de Lion succeeded his father as King of England. Richard's name is among the most familiar in all English tradition; he seems really to have made so deep a popular impression that it has never been forgotten. A contemporary account describes him as tall and lithe, very strong and very courteous, with reddish hair and masterful bearing—brave as Hector, too, magnanimous as Achilles, manly as Alexander or Roland, generous as Titus, wise as Nestor, and prudent as Ulysses.[1] These personal advantages were enhanced by the circumstances of

[1] Archer: The Crusade of Richard I (1888), 6–7.

his restless and romantic story. A little before his
accession, Jerusalem had been retaken from the
Christians by the Saracens under Saladin.   Christendom was aflame to repossess the Holy City.
In the Crusade which ensued, Richard led the
English, and was not on confident terms with King
Philip Augustus, who led the French; the times
were tricky, and neither of them relished difference
of opinion. They failed to recover Jerusalem;
they came to terms with Saladin; Richard seized
the Island of Cyprus from the Byzantine Emperor,
and gave it to the dispossessed King of Jerusalem,
whose successors held it for two or three hundred
years; and on his way back to England the Lion-
Hearted King was captured and imprisoned by
the Duke of Austria.   Thus for a while, like Barbarossa before him, he was out of sight.   Unlike
Barbarossa, to be sure, he was soon discovered
alive, and presently was ransomed.   In England,
however, these incidents gave chance for notions
to get root something like those which made later
Germany fancy a righteous Barbarossa not dead
but sleeping.   While Richard was away his brother
John—a deeply unpopular person—had been virtually regent.   Whatever went wrong was attributed to him; when the hearty king should return to his own all might go right again.   This
general condition is assumed in Scott's Ivan-
hoe, which together with his Talisman made
the Third Crusade very familiar to English readers
of the Nineteenth Century.   And Richard had
the good fortune to be in England so little as never
seriously to disturb John's unpopularity by much
unwelcome behaviour of his own.   He met his
death in Normandy, when a year or two past

forty, from a wound received in an unimportant action but beyond the skill of Twelfth Century surgeons. In 1200 John was King.

During the Century then ended, the traditions gathering in Southern Europe are for us more vague than the northerly group on which we have touched. In Italy, amid what generally seems bewildering confusion and all manner of local and civic intrigue, two facts emerge: the vigour of the great mercantile Republic of Venice; and the fairly definite appearance, throughout the local disturbances, of the famous antagonistic parties —the Guelphs and the Ghibellines. To explain what these factions were at this time, or at any other, would tax the learning of the best historian. It has been conveniently said that the Guelphs, whose name in English has only one syllable, held the monosyllabic Pope superior to the Emperor, and that the trisyllabic Ghibellines similarly preferred the Emperor's contentions to the Pope's. In Spain, where the famous Moorish scholar Averroes flourished during the Twelfth Century, and greatly enhanced the authority of Aristotle, Christian powers were beginning finally to press back the Mahometans; at the time of the Third Crusade, the kingdoms of Aragon, Navarre, Castile, Leon, and Portugal possessed the whole peninsula to the north of the Tagus, and a considerable central region to the south of it.

The names on which we have touched—England, France, Germany, Italy, and Spain—of course impress any modern mind as national. By our Twentieth Century each of them has had a long and distinct national history of its own. In the Twelfth, however, no modern sense of distinct

nationality appears yet to have developed. Local
regions everywhere had their distinct customs and
dialects, and often an alert sense of independence,
or at least of impatience with anybody who tried
to meddle with them. Various systems of hereditary and disputed sovereignty had arisen, and
persisted or vanished, right and left. In general,
these may be said to have been based on the opinion that everybody owed some sort of allegiance
to a lord above him until you got to the Pope or the
King, and that in a vague way the Emperor had
a shadowy claim to the allegiance of a good many
Kings, just as some Kings had one to that of
others. The two things unquestionably common to
all Christendom were the Church and its language
—the Latin by that time at once dead and living;
both retained, as indeed they still do, something
of the traditionally universal authority which
they had first enjoyed under the original Empire
of Rome. Latin, too, was the language not only
of the Church but of learning, then almost wholly
monopolised by the clergy. By the middle of
the Twelfth Century, the older universities of
modern Europe were in prosperous existence:
Bologna, for example, already old; Padua, lately
founded; Paris, the most intensely animated of
all; Oxford and Cambridge.

Some notion of how the ancient classics then
looked in perspective may be gathered from an
interesting manuscript lately studied in the library of Caius College.[1] It advises that after
learning the alphabet, and reading some elementary books, a student turn to satire and history,

[1] C. H. Haskins: A List of Text-Books from the Close of the Twelfth
Century: Harvard Studies in Classical Philology, XX, 75–94 (1909).

to Statius, the "divine Æneid," and Lucan. Then it mentions among other things which should be read, Juvenal, Horace, Ovid, the Bucolics of Virgil, Sallust, Cicero, Martial, Petronius, Suetonius, Livy, Seneca, Aristotle, Apuleius, Quintilian, Boethius, Euclid, Hippocrates, Galen, the Code of Justinian, and almost every book of the Bible—of course in Latin. In the Middle Ages, no doubt, scholars had no scientific knowledge of Latin; but the worst of them could make shift to read, write, and speak it. A familiar local name in Paris, probably quite as old as the Twelfth Century, implies what then existed at all centres of learning. To this day the part of Paris near the university is popularly called the Latin Quarter. What the term really means, few stop to think; it goes back to this period when students from all over Europe flocked to well-known professors, and for want of any other common language not only pursued their studies, but talked among themselves—often riotously enough—in Latin. This long remained the general vehicle of communication throughout the European world.[1]

Adams's Mont Saint Michel and Chartres excellently tells of the architectural vigour which at this same period was changing the whole face of Northern Europe. His method, not severely chronological, may perhaps appear at first sight bewildering. But remember that in 1100 the round arch was virtually the only form used by church-builders, and that by 1200 the pointed arch—Gothic, as we are apt to call it—was lift-

[1] As the story goes, it was barbarously spoken, when they talked together, by George I, who knew no English, and Sir Robert Walpole, who knew no German; both finding it easier than French.

ing itself, in its earlier form, wherever French influence extended. Turn to what he has to say about this change; then read his chapter on "Twelfth Century Glass," and come to understand that this was the moment when the jewelled windows of the French churches glowed into their most glorious splendour. Without knowing quite how, you will find that he has saturated you with a feeling not exactly like any other, before or since; and you may rest content that you have been led unawares into the surgent heart of this olden time. This was the Century, too, when the wondrous church of St. Mark at Venice grew into the form which makes its interior still seem, in certain moods, the most magnificent sanctuary of Western Europe.

There is one other phase of the Twelfth Century on which we must touch. A little while ago, we put beside some lines from the Song of Roland a stanza from a Hymn to the Virgin thought to have been made in Eleventh Century Provence. The contrast between the poetry of Northern France and that of Southern was evident. Comparatively the Song of Roland seems primitively rude, and the Provençal hymn gracefully polished. The regions, like their dialects, or better their languages, were really different. In Southern France—the place to which the name Provence is vaguely applied even still—there had somehow arisen a civilisation more nearly and more delicately mature than had anywhere else existed in Europe since Roman antiquity had declined into barbarous ruin. It was not destined to last. Early in the Thirteenth Century, Provence came to such grief that, at least from 1400

to times almost our own, its language lived on
only as a popular local dialect. In 1200, however,
that pleasant Southern country still promised to
be the most exquisitely cultivated garden of reviving European culture. At least in literature,
what bloomed elsewhere seemed comparatively
wild. So far as general tradition goes, only one
word has survived the devastation then close at
hand; and few know just what that word
troubadour means. It was the Provençal term
for the French *trouvère*, or *finder;* it was applied
to a distinct kind of poet, who flourished most
luxuriantly in the Twelfth Century. The word
poet, we may remember, originally meant *maker*—
of beautiful literature. That the Provençal term
implied an ideal existence of beautiful things,
which men might rather find than make, is in
itself evidence of the perhaps fantastically ideal
quality of Provençal culture. Fantastic or not,
however, the Troubadours, as we shall see before
long, have influenced European sentiment even
to this day. Without their long-since faded
Twelfth Century graces, we of the Twentieth Century could never have been quite what we are.

II

LITERARY TRADITIONS

We come now to a period of literary expression
distinctly unlike either antiquity, the centuries
between the decline of the Roman Empire and the
Crusades, or the centuries after 1300. Before
1100, the most recent fully acknowledged masterpiece of surviving European literature was the

Satires of Juvenal, then a thousand years old.
Since 1300, all the literatures of Europe have produced, in their various languages, what are now
generally accepted as masterpieces of their own.
Between 1100 and 1300, amid the conditions of
reawakened activity expressed by the Crusades
and by the great cathedrals of England and
France, there came into existence a copious and
varied vernacular literature, both courtly and
popular. At least two circumstances, however,
combined to make it long seem ephemeral and unimportant: while it was at its richest, particularly
in France and England, all scholarly writing and
indeed all intended for more than local purposes
was regularly done as a matter of course only in
Latin; and the subsequent effort of all Europe to
revive the cultural manners of civilised antiquity
—the movement generally called the Renaissance
—resulted in centuries of conventional disdain
for any methods of expression obviously different
from those of Rome and Greece.

A familiar English word implies the story.
The masterpieces of mediæval architecture we
regularly call *Gothic*. Now, when you stop to
think, this has nothing to do with the Goths of
history; it concerns only the tradition they left
as Barbarian invaders of imperial Roman civilisation. In other words, it is a special term for *barbarous*. The notions it implies prevailed so lately
as when Louis XVI was crowned in the Cathedral of Rheims, a little before the American Revolution. If you have the curiosity to hunt up
a picture of this ceremony, you will find that the
Gothic glories of a sanctuary almost intact until
it lately was ravaged by the Barbarians of Germany

were then politely masked with large temporary screens in the pretty style of Eighteenth Century France. A Europe which through five hundred years could thus regard the aspiring achievements of Gothic architecture would of course neglect still more the works of Gothic literature, sealed books to all who cannot read mediæval dialects. The first poet in any modern language who has commanded and retained general European respect was Dante.

Yet without the full vitality of literature during the Twelfth and Thirteenth Centuries neither the substance of Dante nor his form could have been the stupendous masterpieces that they are. Even for no other reason we should have to linger over "Gothic" literature longer than we have now lingered over any since the Flavian period. The revival of interest in mediæval expression during the Nineteenth Century would also compel us to do so. The literature of the Middle Ages has now been freshly and enthusiastically explored and celebrated. At present, indeed, there are signs of such reaction in its favour that without due care we might be tempted to overrate its positive as distinguished from its historical importance. It was genuine; though its luxuriance was unlike anything classic, much of it had almost Greek spontaneity; it developed, like all real things, swiftly and strongly; it recorded countless phases of tradition ever since as familiar, and quite as potent, as any derived from antiquity; but at least until the time of Dante it produced no great masters who have been remembered by any means so distinctly as the writers of classical antiquity or even as the Fourth Century Fathers of the Church.

The single fact most clearly characteristic of it is perhaps one which off-hand might seem only formal. Broadly speaking, we may say that hardly any kind of metrical expression produced in Europe before 1100 sounds to a modern ear quite like those we use nowadays. The quantitative measures of Greek and Roman antiquity must now be learned at school, like the languages in which they are written. Exquisitely idiomatic, they record a poetic idiom different from ours. Compared with them, no doubt, the lines of the Song of Roland sound very like lines which we might ourselves have made; but taken alone the lines of Roland often sound almost as archaic as the words of which they are composed. In 1100, too, such verses as we glanced at from the Provençal were local and exceptional. Two hundred years later, all this had almost insensibly changed. Broadly speaking, we may say with equal confidence that by 1300 every poetical form familiar to later Europe was already in excellent existence. From that time until we come to extravagances contemporary with ourselves, the poetic idioms of Europe have demanded no new measures. And something similar seems true of the tunes which the uninitiate still imagine to lie at the heart of music. So far as we know, the songs of Europe before 1100 were archaically different from what are sung nowadays; but many among those sung by 1300 might almost be mistaken for bits from Italian opera of the Nineteenth Century.

If we now attempted to disentangle all this, we should stray from our mists of tradition into the clearer light of history. Yet without some lingering over literature in the Twelfth and Thirteenth

Centuries we might be tempted to suppose Dante even more of a miracle than he is. Our simplest plan will be mostly to neglect, as tradition has neglected, names and other such details; but to remind ourselves of a few characteristic ways in which during these two hundred years modern literatures began their still unended course. So doing, we may meanwhile try, if we can, to distinguish the tendencies of these literatures in the Twelfth Century from their tendencies in the Thirteenth.

III

ROMANTIC EPICS:

"CHANSONS DE GESTE," AND "ROMANS"

During the Twelfth Century, there came into existence a great number of heroic narrative poems, of which the earlier are commonly called *Chansons de Geste*, or Songs of Deeds, and the later *Romans*—a term which any English or American eye might easily mistake for Romans as the name of a people. The most frequent English translation of the old French word *Roman* is *Romance;* but this has the disadvantage of being to the eye indistinguishable from the old French word *Romance*—the name, as we shall soon see, of a less considerable phase of Twelfth Century poetry. What the term *Roman* originally meant may perhaps be most nearly indicated by the paraphrase *Romantic Epic*. This, to be sure, is open to evident objections: it is not only sometimes used as a technical name for the later form of literature most familiar in the work of Ariosto and of Tasso; it is

itself by no means definite, for the word *romantic*
has never yet been satisfactorily defined, and the
word *epic* has been virtually appropriated by classical antiquity and the imitators thereof. Even
the untutored can nevertheless perceive that we
generally use the word *romantic* to describe a
temper hardly perceptible in Greek literature or in
Roman but deeply characteristic of the Middle
Ages, and that the word *epic* may defensibly be
used to describe any heroic story heroically told.

Now there can be no doubt that both *Chansons
de Geste* and *Romans*, though no more like the epics
of Rome and Greece than a Gothic cathedral is
like an Athenian temple, had epic characteristics.
As has been believed true of the Greek epics themselves, they most probably developed from ballads and the like, made to celebrate local heroes,
worthies, and traditions, and tending to associate
their more or less unfamiliar subjects with the
great central facts of tradition as tradition existed
when they were made. Their measures, too, like
those of antique epics, were generally such, or at
least resembled such, as minstrels at one time
actually sung. What distinguishes the form of
Romantic Epics from anything Greek or Latin are
its invariable use of rhyme and the fact that it
moves unrestrained by any troublesome consciousness of classical or standard form.

The best-known *Chansons de Geste* and *Romans*
are in Twelfth Century French—then the language
of the courts in France and in England alike;
until well after 1300, indeed, it is doubtful whether
any Norman king of England could so much as
understand the English language. And two lines
now often quoted from Bodel, a poet of the

Thirteenth Century, conveniently summarise the groups or cycles into which Romantic Epics tended to fall:

Ne sunt que trois matières à nul hom entendant—
De France, de Bretaigne et de Rome la Grant.[1]
(There are only three subjects for a poet who knows his
    task—
France, Britain, and Rome the Great.)

The central figure of the Matter of France was Charlemagne; that of the Matter of Britain was Arthur; the Matter of Rome included all antiquity —not only Rome itself, but Alexander, who was distinctly popular, and the heroes of the Trojan War.

On the Matter of France we have already touched, when we glanced at the Song of Roland. To dwell on lesser French heroes than Roland— William of Orange, for example, or Huon of Bordeaux—would only distract us from the main currents of tradition. So, having seen how in three hundred years the Charlemagne and the Roland of history had become superhuman creatures of romantic fancy, we may perhaps do best to wander into legendary and later offshoots of the story, such as that which pretended that Eginhard, overtaken by a snow-storm one night when he had been admitted to the chamber of Charlemagne's daughter Emma was carried on her shoulders across the courtyard, to hide telltale footprints, and was seen in the process, forgiven, and permitted to marry his dauntless mistress, by her sympathetic though sovereign father. Another legend has grown and lingered on the Rhine, where the name

---

[1] Bodel: Chanson des Saxons, 7–8.

of Rolandseck revived the hero asserted by both Eginhard and the Song of Roland to have fallen at Roncevaux. The story goes that when he went to the Spanish wars he left behind a betrothed lady, who was induced by the rumour of his death to become a nun; that he by and by returned to find her a bride of Christ; and that he thereupon built himself an abiding-place on the spot still called after him, whence for the rest of his days he longingly looked at the walls of the convent of Nönnenwerth, within which she lovingly awaited the joy of their reunion in Paradise. The robustly masculine Song of Roland contains no such sentimental episodes as these; at least to the point where the angels bear the soul of the Count to Paradise it hardly mentions women or love at all. Its primitive strength has not only made it the chief poem concerning the Matter of France but has made anything later seem comparatively weak. Historically its position is like that of a not fully developed Homer almost smothered by a swiftly luxuriant aftergrowth. The nature of that aftergrowth, which finally decayed into romantic sentimentality, appears more distinctly when we turn to the Matter of Britain.

This Matter of Britain was hardly in literary existence before the Twelfth Century. During the first half of the Century,—in the reigns of Henry I and Stephen,—an English ecclesiastic, Geoffrey of Monmouth, writing in readable Latin prose about the History of England, brought into literary notice and embellished with many inventions two bodies of legend which immediately appealed to the imagination of poets. The first, no longer generally familiar, pretends that royalty was

founded in Britain by a Trojan prince called Brut
or Brutus, from whose name that of Britain was
derived. The story is evidently developed from
the story of Æneas—when or how we need not now
inquire; among other successors of Brutus it
tells of King Lear, later to be brought into world-
literature by Shakspere. The second body of
legend thus introduced to Twelfth Century poetry
has remained important ever since; in the Nineteenth Century it kindled memorable work by
men so different as Tennyson and Wagner. Before
1100 King Arthur was little more than a hero of
popular tradition; by 1200 he was already the
centre of a cycle of poems destined popularly to
eclipse those concerning Charlemagne.[1]

Just how this body of legend and tradition thus
gathered, and how it later developed are questions
for students more special than we. For us it must
be enough here to remind ourselves of a few characteristic episodes and personages nowadays carelessly assumed always to have clustered together.
The Round Table one first thinks of, and the
knights proved worthy of seat there; among these
knights, none more instantly comes to mind than
Lancelot, loyal in every impulse and yet, like the
queen, Guinevere, disloyal to their stainless sovereign by tragic reason of the mutual loyalty of their
forbidden love. Love leads us straight to the
kindred story of Tristan and Isolde, at first separate, but later merged with legends we call Arthur-
ian. Already we are in a world of passion and of
mystery unlike anything we have hitherto found in
the literatures of Europe.

[1] For an admirable account of how the story of King Arthur has grown,
see Howard Maynadier: The Arthur of the English Poets: Boston: 1907.

Of all the mysteries none is more pervasive and elusive than that of the Grail. Without further waiting we may glance at its apparition in the Perceval, or Le Conte du Graal, of the Twelfth Century court poet Créstien de Troies. The poem has almost 46,000 lines, recounting endless episodes: early among them[1] is the passage given by Henry Adams, in his chapter on the "Three Queens." The youthful Perceval has been admitted to a strange castle. There, as he is seated in the hall, a mysterious procession unexpectedly enters. First comes a squire bearing a white lance, from the point of which a drop of fresh blood runs down the haft. Then

> A tant dui autre vaslet vindrent
> Qui chandeliers an lors mains tindrent
> De fin or ovrez a neel.
> Li vaslet estoient moult bel
> Qui les chandeliers aportoient.
> An chacun chandelier ardoient
> Dous chandoiles a tot le mains.
> Un graal antre ses dous mains
> Une demoiselle tenoit,
> Qui avec les vaslets venoit,
> Bele et gente et bien acesmee.
> Quant ele fu leans antree
> Atot le graal qu'ele tint
> Une si granz clartez i vint
> Qu'ausi perdirent les chandoiles
> Lor clarte come les estoiles
> Quant li solauz luist et la lune;
> (Presently came two more squires,
> In their hands two chandeliers
> Of fine gold in enamel wrought.
> Each squire that the candle brought
> Was a handsome chevalier.

[1] Ed. Ch. Potvin: Mons: 1866: lines 4365–4423.

There burned in every chandelier
Two lighted candles at the least.
A damsel, graceful and well dressed,
Behind the squires followed fast
Who carried in her hands a graal;
And as she came within the hall
With the graal there came a light
So brilliant that the candles all
Lost clearness, as the stars at night
When moon shines, or in day the sun;
　　　　　　—Tr. Adams.)

and so on.　Perceval, astonished at what he sees, neglects to ask what it means.　Those who care to know what subsequently and consequently happened may follow him in and out through more than forty thousand lines of this fluent old French—as easy to read, when you once get used to it, as the English of Chaucer.[1]　For us now it is enough to notice the swift rhythm of those graceful lines, their easy and varied rhyme, their modernity when you compare them with the passages we glanced at from the Song of Roland[2] about a hundred years older, and the atmosphere of romantic mystery in which they are enveloped—so utterly different from the large simplicity of Roland's end.　As for the Grail, legend says that it was the cup from which Our Lord drank with the Apostles at the Last Supper.　Joseph of Arimathea somehow possessed himself of it, and in it piously caught the blood of the Crucified dripping from the Cross. Then, partly by miraculous means, Joseph made his way, bearing the Grail as a pricelessly holy relic, across sea and land till he came to England and rested at Glastonbury.　There the story of the Grail lingered on until the Reformation ruined

[1] *Cf.* p. 153.　　　　　　　　　　[2] *Cf.* p. 482.

the mighty Abbey, and Whiting, the last Abbot, was hanged on the hill above it, in Henry VIII's time. And at Glastonbury, tradition has pretended, the monks had meanwhile discovered and lost again a venerable tombstone bearing the words

> Hic jacet Rex Arturus,
> Rex quondam, rex futurus.
> (Here lies Arthur royally,
> King that was, and king to be.)

Confused and inconsistent as all this must seem, it somehow takes us into a world of fancy where new ideals hover—ideals undreamt of by antiquity and yet for us still hovering in their iridescent distance. It was distance even in the Twelfth Century. No one then stopped to wonder quite how long ago Arthur might have lived his heroic and hapless life—destined to return again, like Barbarossa, when time should ripen for better days than men have known in the flesh. The sure thing was that in his olden time good men had been courteous and honourable and brave through all the temptations of their conflict with Evil, and that good women had been beautifully worshipful. These creatures of the Matter of Britain belong to the Age when throughout France and England the cathedrals were soaring, the luxuriance of Gothic sculpture clustering like flowers about their portals, and their windows glowing with such splendours as never before had made light more marvellous than itself.

Less familiar nowadays than the Matter of Britain or even than the Matter of France, the third chief division of Twelfth Century epic story

is for us perhaps more instructive than either.
What Bodel calls the Matter of Rome the Great
embraced all stories of classical antiquity, as the
Twelfth Century thought of them. By that
time, the whole past had merged in a temporary
unity of its own. Charlemagne was historical,
and had lived less than four hundred years before.
Arthur may have been historical and have struggled for righteousness, less than four hundred
years before Charlemagne. Already, however,
both had become virtual contemporaries in days
greater and more heroic than any that ever were
actual. Centuries behind them, dimmer only
by reason of distance, was imperial Rome, itself
at once veiling primal Greece and so merging with
it that seen through the prismatic veil of French
legend and British they not only intermingled
but merged with the legends of both Charlemagne
and Arthur in a far-off world where all things
were nobly alike in their grand unlikeness to the
sordid facts of reality. So Cæsar and Alexander,
Æneas and Hector appeared as knights who
might have ridden on in indistinguishable pageant
with Charlemagne and Arthur, Roland and Lancelot.

Here, for example, is how a Twelfth Century
poet, Beneoit de Saint More, wrote of Andromache:

> Andromacha apelloit l'om
> La feme Hector par son droit nom,
> Gent dame de haut parage,
> Franche, courtoise, proz e sage.
> Molt est leäus vers son seignor
> E molt l'ama de grant amor.[1]

[1] Bartsch: Chrestomathie: ed. 1875: 127. The lines read themselves;
but, if you have not patience to decipher them, this is what they mean:
"Andromache they called the wife of Hector by her right name, a gentle

And the same poet gives us an interview between Lavinia and her mother in which they discuss Æneas and Turnus[1] after a fashion reminding us now of Lady Capulet and now of the Nurse when similarly closeted with Juliet; except for the names, you would never dream that this passage had anything to do with the Æneid.

The Roman d'Alexandre,—the Romance of Alexander,—which was among the better-known of these long narrative poems about antiquity, has happened to leave deeper trace than any of the others. How remote the story is from anything classic, how completely in the spirit of the Twelfth Century, a few lines taken almost at random will show.[2] During his journey across the desert Alexander comes to an enchanted forest:

> En icele forest, dont vous m'oez conter,
> Nesune male chose ne puet laianz entrer.
> Li homes ne les bestes n'i ozent converser.
> Onques en nesun tans ne vit hon yverner.
> Ne trop froit ne trop chaut ne neger ne geler.
> Ce conte l'escripture que hom n'i doit entrer
> Se il nen at talent de conquerre ou d'amer.

> (In that same wood, of which you hear me tell,
> No evil thing can ever enter in.
> Nor men nor beasts dare linger there at all.
> Never throughout all time was winter there,
> Nor chill, nor heat, nor snow, nor biting frost.
> And scriptures say that no man there may come
> Unless he be a conqueror, or love.)

lady of high birth, frank, courteous, brave and wise. She was very loyal to her lord, and loved him much with great love."

Incidentally, the poet mentions Dares as his authority. By this time Homer was a mere tradition; and the Fourth or Fifth Century Latin fictions attributed to Dares and Dictys were supposed to be contemporary chronicles of the Trojan War.

[1] Bartsch, 117 *seq.*

[2] I have not gone farther for these than Bartsch, 175 *seq.*

And so on.   Alexander enters the forest, and there
has adventures which need not distract us until
he feels need of advice:

Alixandres apele les viellars, ses conjure
Par ce deu ki forma trestoute creature,
Si lor a demandé "Par come faite aventure
Sunt en cel bos ces femmes?   Est çou lois ou droiture?"[1]

and so on once more.   Even so few lines as these
are enough to exhale the atmosphere of a poem
where as a matter of course the Macedonian conqueror, surrounded by enchantments, invokes
the Scriptural God who in the beginning created
the heaven and the earth.   They also show us
that the verses collect in leashes of rhyme something like those we found in the Song of Roland.
The rhythm of these later lines, however,—their
measure,—is different from any other on which we
have yet touched; and by and by it proved particularly congenial to the idiomatic rhythm of
the French language, much as the hexameter
proved to that of Greek and of Latin, and the
blank-verse line to that of English.   Ultimately,
with a rhyming arrangement by which couplets
ending with masculine rhymes alternate with
couplets whose rhymes are feminine,—that is,
have a final *e*,—it became the chief standard measure of serious French poetry.   It remains so to
this day, and to this day it is called Alexandrine.
Even though the substance of Twelfth Century
Matter of Rome is mostly forgotten by tradition,

---

[1] These lines, which resist offhand metrical translation, evidently mean:
"Alexander calls the old men (sworn his fellows by the God who created all
living things) and asks them 'By what manner of chance are these women
in this wood?   Is it right or just?'"

the traditional influence of its form has accordingly persisted.

Glancing back at it, and with it at the Matter of Britain gathering about the central figure of Arthur and at the Matter of France gathering about that of Charlemagne, we can hardly help feeling that here was a great outburst of traditional utterance, wildly luxuriant yet imaginably capable of development into a masterpiece of new epic narrative. No such masterpiece appeared. The poems of Walter Scott, in the early part of the Nineteenth Century, are perhaps the nearest indication of what such a masterpiece might formally have been; Tennyson's Idylls of the King and Wagner's Parsifal similarly indicate something of what might have been its spirit. None of these moderns came anywhere near being Homeric, Dantesque, or Shaksperean. Yet compared even with Scott and Tennyson and Wagner the narrative poets of the Twelfth Century seem exuberantly and fluently monotonous, almost to the degree of childishness. In their Romantic Epics, we must nevertheless grant, they poured forth an inexhaustible flood of still living tradition; and their measures did much to establish the poetic idioms of later Europe.

IV

MINOR FORMS OF POETRY

The long narrative poems on which we have now touched as much as we can were by no means the only form of Twelfth Century literature. For one thing, there were short narrative songs,

telling of pretty little episodes, and so tripping in
measure that as you read them you can almost
hear the chords of the lutes they were sung to.
In eighteen lines, for example, one such ditty tells
of how twin sisters—Gay and Goldie, their names
appear to mean—went to bathe at a spring;
how Childe Gerard riding back from a tournament
found them there, and ran away with Gay, to
Goldie's dismay; but how he made everybody
happy by marrying her as soon as he got home.
It is in six rhymed triplets, with a refrain at the
end of each:

> Vante l'ore et li raim crollent:
> Ki s'antraimment soweif dorment.[1]
> (The wind blows and the boughs creak:
> Those who love sleep sweet.)

Romances they called these trifles, as distinguished from the long epic *Romans*, for which we
have hit upon no better English name than Romantic Epics. If you want another example,
you may look at a longer and later one by Audefroi
le Bastart,[2] telling how Isabel was married against
her will to an old lord; how her lover Gerard consequently went crusading and came home safe;
how the old lord on discovering the state of his
wife's affections had the tact to die of displeasure;
and how the lovers were united by the Holy Church.
"Et joie atent Gerars" is the refrain of twelve
stanzas; at the end of the thirteenth and last it
changes to "Or a joie Gerars." Gerard has the
joy he waited for; and though the tune be lost you
can still hear the echo of it in that lilting line.

There were ruder and more popular narrative

---

[1] Bartsch, 50.   [2] Bartsch, 218.

songs at the same time. *Fabliaux* is the name of them; and the nature of them may be inferred by the curious from occasional passages in the Decameron, or from one or two of the Canterbury Tales discreetly neglected by coeducational students of Chaucer. There were Fables, too, in the old sense of the word, harking back to the traditions of Phædrus and of Æsop, and tending toward what La Fontaine wrote in the France of Louis XIV, and John Gay in the England of George II. More characteristic of the time were works at once encyclopædic and fantastic, like the popular treatises on science of which a typical example is the Bestiary of Philippe de Thaun.[1]

This long piece of tripping doggerel undertakes at once to describe animals and to explain what they mean. Here, for instance, is a little of what it says about the Unicorn, perhaps confused with the Rhinoceros:

> Monosceros est beste,
> Un corn ad en la teste,
> Pur çeo ad si a nun.
> De buc ele a façun.
> Par pucele est prise,
> Or oëz en quel guise.[2]

When men want to take him, the doggerel proceeds, they go to his haunts with a girl, who exposes one

---

[1] Bartsch, 75.

[2] To make a rhyming translation would be hard; any one can read the rhythm, and the lines mean

> The unicorn is a beast,
> It has one horn on its head,
> For which it is so named.
> It is rather like a buck.
> It is taken by a virgin,
> You shall now hear in what manner.

of her breasts. Attracted by the perfume, the
unicorn appears, kisses the breast, presently falls
asleep, and is then killed with no trouble.   Now all
this, the poet—if we may so describe him—gravely
explains, has much significance: the beast signifies God, the virgin signifies Mary, her breast evidently signifies the Church, the death in sleep signifies the crucifixion of Christ, thereafter not incarnate. His destruction was our redemption,
deceiving the Devil:

> Ame e corps sunt un,
> Issi fud dés et hum,
> E içeo signefie
> Beste de tel baillie.[1]

This passage is followed by one about the Panther:

> Pantere est une beste
> De mult precius estre;
> Et oëz de sun nun
> Signeficatiun:
> *Pan* en griu *trestut* est;[2]

and so on.   He is many-coloured, gently disposed,
and beloved by all other animals except dragons—
in brief he signifies the Son of Mary, detested only
by the wicked.   Pseudo-science and fable inextrica-
bly intermingle; but the long morals of the fables
wander from the common sense of antiquity and

---

[1] Soul and body are one,
As He was God and man.
And this is what means
A beast of such sort.

[2] The panther is a beast
Of very precious kind;
Now hear of his name
The meaning.
Pan in Greek is *everything;*

of futurity into the wildest fancies of Twelfth
Century symbolism. Yet somehow the puerile
stuff has a quality of quaint charm.

A far more delicate charm may be found in a
collection of courtly stories which used to be attributed to the Thirteenth Century, but are now
thought to have been written under Henry II.
Who Marie de France was, where she found the
material for her Lays, and why and where she
wrote them we may leave to the learned; the
Lays exist, for all who care to read them without
wandering from their prettiness into thickets of
surrounding erudition. They are mostly love-
stories, gracefully rhymed. That of the Honeysuckle (Chevrefoil), which you will find in Bartsch,[1]
tells how Tristan, banished to Wales, came secretly back to a forest near Tintagel, where the
queen would soon ride by. There he cut on a
hazel-branch, untwined from honeysuckle, lines
that should meet her eye. When you part hazel
and honeysuckle, they say, both presently die:

> Bele amie, si est de nus:
> Ne vous sanz mei ne mei sanz vus.
> (Lovely friend, so languish we,—
> I without you, You without me.)

The sign catches her eye. She slips into the
wood where he awaits her; the interview consoles
him during the short remainder of his banishment;
and being skilled in song, he records his joy in a
lay about the honeysuckle:

> Gotlef[2] l'apelent en Engleis,
> Chevrefoil le nument Franceis.

[1] Chrestomathie, 257.

[2] Offhand this literal translation looks rather like the Portuguese Grammar; but it may be Twelfth Century English, if anybody cares to inquire.

(Goatleaf they call it in English,
Chêvrefeuille the French name it.)

We are back again in the world of Gay and
Goldie and their Gerard, and of the other Gerard,
whose loves with Isabel, interrupted by crusading
adventure, were sung by Audefroi le Bastart.

This world of the Lays, where hearts are true
and lovers apt to get their way, despite vexatious
enemies, is perhaps most pleasantly accessible in a
story lately grown more or less familiar again. It
is delightfully set forth in Henry Adams's chapter
on "Nicolette and Marion"; and good English
translations of it are not hard to find. Aucassin and Nicolette they call it. Most probably
it was written after the end of the Twelfth Century, but by some one who was well grown up
when the Thirteenth began. It is partly in prose,
which was read aloud or recited, and partly in
leashes of short-lined rhyme, which were more
probably sung; to the eye, it therefore looks
a little like the Consolation of Philosophy of
Boethius, by that time eight hundred years old.
In substance it is as ingenuously romantic as the
substance of Boethius is reminiscently classic.
It tells, with much adventurous episode, but with
no touch of coarseness, how Aucassin, highborn
son of the Count of Beaucaire, fell in love with
Nicolette, a charming girl of unknown origin
rescued from captivity among the Saracens; and
how both were consequently imprisoned, and both
escaped, and after many adventures—prettily
pastoral here and there—came together; and so
on. The scene, which pretends to be in Southern
France, is really in a pleasant nowhere whence,

three or four hundred years later, one might imaginably have journeyed to the somewhat more plausible nowheres of the Merchant of Venice, of As You Like It, or of the Winter's Tale— Belmont, the Forest of Arden, or the seacoast of Bohemia. Whoever can enjoy these regions of Elizabethan fancy will be glad to stray for himself through the country where, in 1200 or thereabouts, Aucassin and Nicolette wandered, delighting men and women about whom the Cathedrals were rising to send forth and welcome home the consecrated warriors of the Crusades.

Crusades, cathedrals, and all are now past— no longer actualities but only monuments and traditions. We have lingered as long as we can over a few of the dreamy fancies alive when they were the daily facts of waking life. Songs of Deeds and Romantic Epics were musical in the air, when you wanted heroics; rhymed love-stories and the like for lighter moments, still somehow singing. Even fables and coarse tales of full-throated laughter often took prettily lyric form, and so did the catalogues which made believe that half-legendary beasts were created to symbolise orthodox truths. Amid this confused luxuriance of romantic fancy one deep common fact seems to be an unthinking recognition or assumption that things other than reality are everywhere close at hand. Life, no doubt, was terribly real, but just beyond it brighter objects of faith or of fancy gleamed almost visible, to console the pains and the sorrows and the perplexities of the human generations.

V

LATIN LYRICS

This consciousness of ideals, only just beyond the poignant limits of earthly reality, clearly appears in a Latin poem, of which a translated fragment still survives as a familiar English hymn:

> Jerusalem the Golden,
> With milk and honey blest,
> Beneath thy contemplation
> Sink heart and voice oppressed.
> I know not, O I know not
> What social joys are there!
> What radiancy of Glory,
> What Light beyond compare![1]

The original Latin, at once so fluent and so complicated in rhyme that the writer is said to have believed miraculous his sustaining of the measure through three thousand lines, runs thus:

> Urbs Syon aurea, patria lactea, cive decora,
> Omne cor obvius, omnibus obstruis et cor et ora.
> Nescio, nescio, quæ jubilatio, lux tibi qualis,
> Quam socialia gaudia, gloria quam specialis.[2]

The passage occurs in a long poem De Contemptu Mundi (On Contempt of the World) made about the middle of the Twelfth Century by Bernard of Morlaix, a monk of Cluny. It begins with a few lines about the wickedness of the world, and the probable approach of the Last Judgment:

---

[1] The Seven Great Hymns of the Mediæval Church: New York: 1867: p. 23. For an Elizabethan hymn inspired by this older one, see the Oxford Book of Verse, 91.

[2] *Ib.*, 32.

Hora novissima, tempora pessima sunt, vigilemus.
Ecce minaciter imminet arbiter ille supremus.

(The world is very evil, the times are waxing late;
Be sober and keep vigil. The Judge is at the gate.
—Tr. Neale.)

It goes on with a contrasting picture of the celestial peace which awaits the righteous in Jerusalem the Golden. Just here we need follow it no farther; most of it, they say, bitterly expounds and satirises the sins of the times. The thing for us to notice is that, amid the ceaseless troubles of transitory earth, this monk of Cluny appears to imagine the joys of Heaven so vividly as to know them truly perdurable.

Though his poem is evidently not lyric in purpose, the chance that the surviving lines of it have become with hardly any change an ecstatic hymn implies the lyric virtue of his temper and of his style. Latin, we need hardly remind ourselves again, was the only vehicle used for serious expression by mediæval Europe. Thus, for clerical purposes and for lay as well, it was the only language of more than local range. The production of it was prodigious. Any careful student of history and of thought must read it indefatigably. Only one phase of it, however, has traditionally and familiarly endured—the rhyming lyric, most excellent in unsurpassed Christian hymns.

As we shall see by and by, they reached their best-remembered height not in the Twelfth Century but in the Thirteenth. One or two Twelfth Century stanzas, however, will remind us how wondrous hymns had already become by that time. The most easily accessible of these hymns are perhaps those dwelt on by Henry Adams in his chapter about the Virgin of Chartres. The first, by the great Saint Bernard of Clairvaux, the instigator of the Second Crusade, begins

> O salutaris Virgo, Stella Maris,
> Generans prolem, Æquitatis solem,
> Lucis auctorem, Retinens pudorem,
>   Suscipe laudem!
> (O saviour Virgin, Star of Sea,
> Who bore for child the Sun of Justice
> The source of Light, Virgin always,
>   Hear our praise!—Tr. Adams.)

At first sight, and still more when you first read them aloud, these rhyming lines look and sound completely different from anything we noticed in classical antiquity. A little comparison, however, will modify this impression. Turn, if you will, to any Sapphic stanza of Horace, such as

> Lenit albescens animos capillus,
> Litium et rixæ cupidos protervæ.
> Non ego hoc ferrem calidus juventa,
>   Consule Planco.[1]
> (Grizzling hair makes calm the heads beneath it,
> Eager of old for quarrels and contention.
> I'd not have borne this in the flush of youth, when
>   Plancus was Consul.)

The measure both of Horace's Latin and of our clumsy English attempt to reproduce it you will see to be the same which he used in the perhaps more familiar

> Integer vitæ scelerisque purus;[2]

and if our English parody of him be too vexatious, look back at Swinburne's attempt to reduce our

---

[1] Od., III, xiv, 25–8; and cf. p. 259, n.   [2] Od. I, xxii; cf. p. 251.

obstinate language to the beautiful shape best
wrought by Sappho in the flexible Greek she was
born to.[1]   Beside her, those who can hear her own
words tell us, even Horace's Latin sounds a little
barbarous.   To most Europeans it is the nearest
approach to her which they can ever make.   Some
of his lines linger with them always, none more
than that stanza beginning "Integer vitæ," still
sometimes chanted at funerals, and the like, to a
grave air which everybody remembers.   With this
air in your head, turn again to those four ecstatic
Christian lines of St. Bernard's hymn.   They
sing themselves to it, you may be surprised to
find, even more readily than the Horatian verse
by whose name we call it.   They differ, indeed,
from the Sapphic stanza of Latin only, or at
least mostly, in the facts that they depend for their
effect not on length of syllable, but on stress of
emphasis, and that the four lines are embellished—
or if you prefer bedizened—with no less than three
rhymes.   Then you may begin to wonder whether
the Twelfth Century Saint may not have supposed
himself only to be improving on the unrhymed
Sapphics of antiquity.   At least, you can hardly
help believing, he could not have done his own
poetic task without haunting consciousness of
what had been achieved in Latin by the Augustan
poet who brought the songs of Greece into the
verse of Italy and thus made gently boastful
triumph over both bronze and death.[2]

Adams quotes two more stanzas from St.
Bernard's hymn, fluent, ecstatic, and reverent.
Close to them he places three stanzas of a some-
what similar Twelfth Century hymn by Adam of

[1] *Cf.* p. 37.   [2] *Cf.* p. 256.

St. Victor, distinctly more modern in form. Here
is little vestige of the classics, except for the fact
that the words are Latin:

> Salve, Mater Salvatoris!
> Vas electum! Vas honoris!
> Vas cælestis Gratiæ!
> Ab eterno Vas provisum!
> Vas insigne! Vas excisum
> Manu sapientiæ!
> (Mother of our Saviour, hail!
> Chosen Vessel, sacred Grail!
> Font of celestial Grace!
> From eternity forethought!
> By the hand of Wisdom wrought!
> Precious, faultless Vase!—Tr. Adams.)

Even the two Twelfth Century stanzas at which
we have now glanced are enough to make us feel,
if we will, the wondrous ecstatic spontaneity of
the mediæval faith in Mary testified again by the
dedication to her of countless chapels, churches,
and cathedrals. On earth, twelve hundred years
before, she had been a pure girl of Palestine,
chosen by God to reach the second purity of motherhood without defilement of the flesh. Alone of
human beings she had been woman doubly holy—
at once maiden and mother. She had shared in
spirit the redeeming agony of her Divine Child;
and at last the Miracle of the Assumption had made
her almost one with the Triune God of whom here
below she had been the Chosen Vessel. Thenceforth, safe in the glory of Eternity, she lived and
reigned forever changeless—with the sweetness
of girlhood, with the tenderness of maternity, and
with the queenly courtesy of immortal sovereignty.
She had become what her Son had been made

through her, at once human and divine. The
difference, if Twentieth Century heretics may try
to define it, seems little more than that His
humanity had been only an episode in the course
of his infinite Divinity, and that before God had
made her divine her earthly origin had been closer
to that of other creatures. Whatever else, she
dwelt safe in Paradise, gentle, changeless, merciful,
and divinely imperial. And there in Paradise,
too, supremely, eternally, and righteously sovereign, was Christ, who had been made incarnate
and had suffered to redeem mankind from the
penalty of sin.

At least among Protestants, it has now long
been usual to think of Christ mostly as he is recorded in the Gospels, and seldom to remember
that divine though He there appears He appears
throughout amid earthly conditions both of short
time and of restricted space. Your most literal
Protestant, so long as he stays a bit orthodox,
would no doubt aver that Christ Above is forever
Lord of All; but nowadays a Protestant mind
would be less attracted by this mystery than by
the Passion, or preferably by the Sermon on the
Mount. At present, indeed, Protestant opinion is
apt to regard Christ rather as an example than as
the Saviour. So Protestant eyes, like most of
ours accustomed to American tradition, find something almost perplexing in the images of the
crowned Redeemer everywhere left us by the
Middle Ages—divinely, eternally, immutably, and
righteously sovereign in Heaven, whence in His
own good time He shall come again to judge the
quick and the dead, and to end the delusive ma-
terialities of this fleeting human world.

To the Twelfth Century, eternity seemed closer at hand than it mostly seems now; and if we lingered longer over the Latin hymns which tried to celebrate it, we should stray too far from the earthly conditions of their making. After all, that first line by Bernard of Morlaix will bring us back from the heights:

> Hora novissima, tempora pessima sunt, vigilemus.
> (The world is very evil, the times are waxing late.
> Be sober and keep vigil.—Tr. Neale.)

And if anybody wishes a notion of mediæval actuality, as it surrounded the students who thronged universities on their way to holy orders, he may find it admirably suggested in John Addington Symonds's Wine, Women, and Song.[1] Symonds skilfully translates some of the less ribald Latin verses in which they celebrated their amatory and convivial joys. This was not a period of unmingled and reverent devoutness. There is a burlesque ritual, for example,—Officium Lusorum, or Prayers of the Gamesters,[2]—where part of one of the petitions may be rendered as follows:

> Almighty and everlasting God, who hast been pleased to sow great misunderstanding between town and gown, grant we beseech Thee that we may enjoy the fruits of their labours and the persons of their wives.

A bit of rhyming advice to incautious and unwarlike students chants a variation on the same theme:[3]

[1] London, 1884. [2] Carmina Burana: Stuttgart: 1847: p. 248.

[3] Symonds, 19. He does not translate this doggerel, which means, line by line:

> When a clown gets drunk
> He does not think a student an armed soldier.
> So I clearly advise you to keep sober
> And never go into a tavern with clowns.

Rusticus dum se sentit ebriatum
Clericum non reputat militem armatum.
Vere plane consulo ut abstineatis
Nec unquam cum rusticis tabern'[am] ineatis.

"Goliardic" is the name commonly given to this
kind of song and verse, much of which purported
to come from a wandering order founded by a
legendary and by no means exemplary ecclesiastic
named Golias. Four lines of his Confession have
lingered almost as familiar as "Jerusalem the
Golden":

Meum est propositum in taberna mori,
Et vinum appositum sitienti ori,
Ut dicant cum venerit angelorum chori
Deus sit propitius isti potatori.[1]

Boys were naughty then as now, and men wicked,
and women what you look for. And song was
already such as we know it. "Gaudeamus igi-
tur"[2] is not so old as these times. Without
their spirit, though, it could hardly have come
to be, and still to be sung.

VI

FRENCH LYRICS

The rhythm and the rhymes of the Latin
songs we have glanced at, profane and holy, have

---

[1] Symonds's translation, in the original metre (p. 58), is a shade too literate. The lines mean

May I in a tavern die,
Drinking wine most thirstily,
So that when the angels come
Hymning from their heavenly home
They may mercifully say,
God forgive this toper's clay.

[2] "So let us joy while still we're young" roughly renders the first line of it.

a rather elementary simplicity—"childish jingle"
Henry Adams somewhere calls it. As we saw a
little before, too, the measures of the Romantic
Epics and of the pretty little episodic songs they
called Romances, of the doggerel Bestiary of Philippe de Thaun and even of the dainty Lays of
Marie de France have a charm, if you feel it at
all, rather of spontaneous artlessness than of subtle art. We may therefore have been tempted
to suppose this Twelfth Century a time when
lightly pretty music, such as the sophisticated
nowadays despise, was everywhere in the air, but
when anything like elaboration, deliberate artificiality, or ingenious convention had not yet gathered, to vex or to delight those who love the heart
of song.

Nothing could be farther from the truth; and
nothing can take us much nearer the truth than a
familiar legend probably untrue. When King
Richard Cœur de Lion, the story goes, on his way
home from Palestine, fell into the hands of the Duke
of Austria, he was imprisoned nobody knew where.
With the jaunty carelessness of their knightly
time, his great lords and their followers did not
trouble themselves to inquire, preferring to illustrate the adage that when the cat's away the
mice will play. Among his less illustrious re-
tainers, however, was one Blondel, an ingenious
minstrel with whom the king had sometimes
amused himself by matching skill in verse. Disguised as a wandering musician, this faithful fellow proceeded to travel about the Austrian dominions, and whenever he came to a castle sang
outside a song which King Richard knew. His
loyal search was at last rewarded by the voice of

Richard, who took up the song from inside a barred window. So the king was found, alive and safe; and presently his neglectful lords reclaimed and ransomed him. The story lingered on; and shortly before the French Revolution a popular opera based on it was produced in Paris. For a while everybody knew a song therein assigned to Blondel:

> O Richard, O mon roi,
> L'univers t'abandonne;
> Sur la terre il n'est que moi
> Qui m'intéresse à ta personne.[1]
> (O Richard, O my king,
> The world abandons thee;
> And no one now remains
> To deliver thee but me.)

How this appealed to some loyal but not quite sober officers of the Guard at Versailles under Louis XVI, how they sang it in an atmosphere before long to vibrate with the Marseillaise, and how royalty nowise benefited thereby you may find set forth, if you like, in Carlyle's prose Epic, the French Revolution.

Now, whether there be any truth in these legends or not, a poet named Blondel de Neele really lived in King Richard's time, and some of his poems are extant.[2] Though none of them is worth our special attention, one or two general impressions made by glancing through some twenty or twenty-five may help us to recall the period when he wrote. All the songs are concerned with love, which possesses the heart of the singer; none of

[1] Quoted from Larousse, where you will find Grétry's music, too.
[2] Brakelmann: Les Plus Anciens Chansonniers Français: Paris: 1870–1891: 140–192.

them names the lady who inspires the passion; all are lyrically fluent; and all have complicated schemes of admirably true rhyme. A typical example, contains six eight-lined stanzas with three rhymes in each stanza:

Cuer desiros apaie	(*a*)
Dolçors et confors:	(*b*)
Par joie d'amor vraie	(*a*)
Sui en baisant mors	(*b*)
S'encor ne m'est altres donez	(*c*)
Mar fui onques de li privez?	(*c*)
A morir sui livrez,	(*c*)
S'ele trop me delaie.	(*a*)

What this means you need not vex yourself to puzzle out; just here the rhymes and the rhythm are enough. These are repeated in the second stanza. The third and fourth stanzas, precisely preserving the measure, similarly repeat three new rhymes,—*istes*,—*er*,—and *is*, or (*d*), (*e*), and (*f*); and in the fifth and sixth stanzas the rhymes change to—*asse*,—*i*, and—*oir*. Observe the marked difference in length between the couplet made by the fifth and sixth lines and the four before it and the two after it; be assured that all this is a rather unusually simple specimen of the lyric versification fashionable in Twelfth Century France; and you will no longer be tempted to disdain that period as spontaneously artless. Its verse is often as intricate as any problem of Gothic vaulting.

Among the most memorable French lyrics of the Twelfth Century is one attributed to Richard himself, addressed from his prison to his sister, Mary of Champagne. You will find it, with an

admirable translation, in Henry Adams's chapter
on the "Three Queens." Here is half of the first
stanza and all of the second:

> Moult ai d'amins, mais povre sont li don;
> Honte en avront se por ma reänçon
>   Suix ces deus yvers pris.
>
> Ceu sevent bien mi home et mi baron
> Engleois, Normant, Poitevin et Gascon,
> Ke je n'avoie si povre compaignon
> Cui je laissasse por avoir an prison.
> Je nel di pas por nulle retraison,
>   Mais ancor suix je pris.
> (My friends are many but their gifts are naught:
> Shame will be theirs, if for my ransom here
>   I lie another year.
>
> They know this well my barons and my men,
> Normandy, England, Gascony, Poitou,
> That I had never follower so low
> Whom I would leave in prison to my gain.
> I say it not for a reproach to them,
>   But prisoner I am.—Tr. Adams.)

The masculine old leash of rhyme, which defies
even the translating skill of Henry Adams,
changes—like the rhymes of Blondel—with the
third and fourth stanzas, and again with the fifth
and sixth; but all six end not only with a short
unrhyming refrain but with the same word—*pris*,
which means taken, captive, or imprisoned. And
whether Richard really wrote this manly song or
not you feel sure that it is just such as he might
have written.

For like any great gentleman of his time he
was tolerably skilful in its arts; and if Blondel's
professional performance be more facile, Richard's
knightly utterance appears very much more genu-

ine. Neither could have come into existence except in a period of highly developed lyric song, not yet shackled by the conventions which it was fast forging. This courtly lyric we might go on to consider only in French. We shall find it, however, most characteristically grown to ripeness not in the north, but in Twelfth Century Provence.

VII

THE TROUBADOURS

Even those of us who can make something out of an old French text are puzzled by a Provençal. The languages are more different than English and Scotch—and for every-day Englishmen or Americans even the Scotch of Burns needs a good many notes. In a general way, though, one or two facts about Provençal poetry of the Twelfth Century must be evident to anybody who will take the trouble only to turn the pages of such a book as Bartsch's Chrestomathie Provençale.[1] A good deal of it takes rather short lyric form; these lyrics have a very careful regularity of their own, stanza corresponding with stanza like the strophes and antistrophes of Pindar; all are rhymed; and the rhyme-schemes are various and sometimes almost inconceivably ingenious. A lyric by Arnaut Daniel[2] goes perhaps to the extreme of this tendency. As printed by Bartsch it consists of six stanzas, each in seven lines; though the final words of these lines do not rhyme with one another, they are rhymingly repeated throughout the poem; all six stanzas are

[1] Elberfeld, 1868.   [2] Bartsch: Chrestomathie Provençale, 131.

composed of lines ending with the following seven consecutive sounds:—*utz*,—*oills*,—*encs*,—*ars*,—*ers*, —*aut*, and —*oma*. This would seem ingenious enough for anybody. Look a little closer, however, and you will see that within each stanza there are no less than ten other rhyme-words repeated through all six. Without bothering your wits about what the words mean, for example, look at the third line of the first stanza,

Els *letz becs* dels auzels ram*encs*,

and then at the third of the second,

Non *pretz necs* mans, don ai gon*encs*.

Here are three rhymes in eight syllables. As you read the poem aloud, they may not be instantly apparent, for they recur only in consecutive stanzas, after an interval of seven lines. They are repeated, however, in the four other stanzas; each of the six stanzas contains seventeen words duly rhymed in each of the other five; yet the total number of syllables in each stanza appears to be only sixty-three. Beside this marvellous example of Provençal ingenuity the French ingenuities of Blondel look like child's play and the leashed rhymes of Richard Cœur de Lion sound like five-finger exercises.

If, without understanding the lines, you will now try to read them aloud, or, indeed, if you will try to read aloud other Provençal poems of less amazing structure, you must presently be impressed by another evident fact. They all have a movement at once easy and exquisitely studied, such as we are used to in the sonnet lines of later Italy, and of the sonnets imitated from these in all modern literatures. Remember that the Provençal poems were actually sung,—that the traditional guitar of the Troubadours, though doubtless unlike instruments you nowadays find in shops, has historic basis. You can hardly help concluding that even though you have no idea what these verses mean they are clearly works of lyric art as conscientious as anything classic.

When we come to the question of what this exquisitely fine phase of literary art is concerned with, the opening words of a selection from Peirol, which in Bartsch follows a second from Arnaut Daniel, will help us to guess:

> Cora qu'amors volha
> Eu chan,

they run; and reference to a dictionary will inform you that they literally mean

> When love wills
> I sing.

Now a glance at the six stanzas thus begun will show you that if not so deliberately ingenious as Arnaut Daniel, the poet who made them was a good deal more so than Blondel. He could not have sung as he did without considerable forethought and careful subsequent polish. He ends his song, as incidentally Arnaut Daniel and all Twelfth Century poets were apt to, with a short "envoi," summing up his music; you can almost hear the chords he struck to the words

> Peirols fai fin e verai
> Lo sonet per amors,
> En sos cors estai totz jors.
> (Peirol really and truly made
> This song for love,
> It was in his heart always.)

Ingenious as you like, he pretended to be spontaneous; for he sang of love, and if love be not spontaneous it cannot be its own invincible self. Here is a convention of substance quite as evident as any convention or ingenuity of the style which sets it forth.

Conventional as you will, nevertheless, this Provençal song has in common with the French poetry of the Twelfth Century at which we have glanced one freshly spontaneous phase. It is not, like folk-song and the like, an offhand utterance of nobody knows whom, human and instinctive, and if skilful at all skilful only artlessly; it is as deliberately and as consciously studied as anything in the whole range of literature. The study it implies, however, is directed to an end hitherto disdained by Christian Europeans. There had been nothing like it since the poets of Rome tried to tame their rude Latin to semblance of Grecian grace. From that time for a thousand years, imperial Latin had been the only language held worthy of study throughout the generations of Europe. Meanwhile it had long ceased to be a language in which any uninstructed human being thought or spoke or lived. Now at last men were eagerly trying to make the languages they used in daily life serve also as vehicles for poetic art such as Rome learned from Greece.

If the chance of history had allowed Provence and its language to grow into full modernity—as France has grown, for example, and Italy, and England—nobody would ever have forgotten that this was the region where the form of modern poetry first developed into art incontestably fine. As we have already reminded ourselves,[1] however,

[1] *Cf.* p. 496.

Twelfth Century Provence was destined to an eclipse so swift and so long that only one word from it has remained familiar. More than probably, too, few of those who nowadays hear the word *troubadour* have any clear notion of what troubadours were, of where or when they flourished, of the ideals which they introduced into the subsequent habit of Europe, or indeed of much more than that a make-believe one of them—named Manrico—is the tenor hero of a delightfully tuneful opera by Verdi, now old-fashioned. Seriously to study them here would accordingly beguile us from tradition into history. Though we cannot altogether neglect them, we can prudently permit ourselves only a few general and far from scholarly observations.

The name troubadour was conventionally given to a kind of lyric poet greatly admired by Twelfth Century Provence, widely dispersed by the misfortunes of Provence in the Thirteenth Century, and thereafter a thing of the past.[1] The form and the substance of troubadour song was generally such as we have just been glancing at when we touched on Arnaut Daniel and Peirol; with exquisitely meticulous care for every dainty detail of lyric grace, these long-forgotten masters of a fleeting art concerned themselves with love. This they assumed to possess them; and the mistress who inspired it was in each case assumed to be a miracle of gently superhuman beauty and merit. Almost always, if not without exception, she was married to somebody else than the poet and

---

[1] Justin Harvey Smith's Troubadours at Home (New York: 1899) gives a rambling but sympathetic account of all this, interspersed with skilful translations.

furthermore of rank higher than his. This convention went so far and so deep that even great lords and princes, occasionally trying their lyric skill, regularly pretended to languish humbly at the feet of inaccessibly superior ladies. Under such circumstances, of course, nothing could be more imprudent or unprincipled than to allow the lady's true name to be revealed or even suspected. Yet, at once bold and honourably reticent, your troubadour must so express himself as both to excite general admiration and while distracting attention from the precise object of his affections and prayers to be clear as daylight for her. What was more, she was herself bound to hear, and having heard to reciprocate, the passion of her lover. A well-known line in the Divine Comedy will illustrate this. In the Fifth Canto of the Inferno, Francesca utters words which often perplex modern readers:

> Amor, che a nullo amato amar perdona.[1]
> (Love, who to none beloved pardons love.)

Everybody knows that, in point of fact, plenty of lovers, men and women alike, sigh and have sighed in vain. But when Dante wrote everybody also knew that the Law of Love, as expounded by the troubadours, decreed that whoever is truly loved must truly love in return.

Fantastic it all seems now, like the intricate rhymes in which the troubadours chanted it. Tradition has pretended that there were formal Courts of Love in Provence, where expert ladies judicially decided exactly what, in generally ad-

[1] Inferno, V, 103.

mitted circumstance, a lover and his mistress ought according to the Law of Love to do; and it is said that there were actual books of casuistry about such matters. Long-forgotten though these things be, we need go no farther than Dante to remind ourselves both of how living they once were and of how deeply the influence of them affects men still. Deep in Hell Dante finds a gentleman of Florence, Jacopo Rusticucci, who sadly asks him:

> Cortesia e valor di' se dimora
> Nella nostra città sì come suole?[1]
>
> (Courtesy and valor, tell me do they stay
> Still in our city, where of old they were?)

To which Dante grimly answers:

> La gente nuova, e i subiti guadagni,
> Orgoglio e dismisura han generata,
> Fiorenza, in te.[2]
>
> (The self-made people, with their ready wealth,
> Pride and disdain of order have begot,
> Florence, in thee.)

The virtues and the vices here named we still recognise. Men and women ought to be courteous, and men valorous; pride is unseemly and excess abominable. Dante seems to speak such words as are spoken to the present day. So he does, if you will; but when he spoke them six hundred years ago and more, he knew that they came to him straight from the code of the troubadours. Courtesy and valor were ideals which the troubadours celebrated, and so, to go no farther, was honour; pride and excess, like all other ignoble

---

[1] Inferno, XVI, 67-8.   [2] Ib., 72-5.

things, they condemned. And if you should be
tempted to doubt whether Dante knew that he
spoke in the spirit of the troubadours, turn to
the Twenty-Sixth Canto of the Purgatorio, and
see how he exchanges courtesies with Arnaut
Daniel, not yet quite purged by fire of the sin inherent in earthly love; linger a little over the lines[1]
where Arnaut Daniel sweetly petitions that prayer
be said for him while still detained in that inter-
mediate region,

> Dove poter peccar non è più nostro.
> (Wherein the power to sin is ours no more.)

And you will surely marvel over the worshipful
skill with which Dante puts into the lips of the
troubadour, now far on his way to Paradise, eight
gracious lines[2] of his own Provençal language.

It all may seem very far away; but come back
to earth. Even amid the clouds of Twentieth
Century American democracy, people are apt
sincerely and passionately to believe that ideal
women are pure and reverend, and consequently
to demand that men show them courtesies more
instant and more delicate than any man may
expect for himself. Consider what the word
courtesy originally means; and you will presently
find yourself remembering the courteous laws decreed by the Courts of Love, and the loving order
which makes glorious the imperial Court of God.
Then you will find yourself in an atmosphere
where the sweet monotonies of troubadour song
still faintly vibrate. And thence looking back
at the songs of France, at the singing Latin of

[1] 127-132.   [2] 140-147.

the Goliardic roysterers and of the ecstatic makers of hymns, at the Lays of Marie de France and the Bestiary of Philippe de Thaun, at the Romantic Epics of Alexander and of Arthur and of Charlemagne, you may begin to feel that, after all, the song of the troubadours was the finest flower of Twelfth Century utterance.

CHAPTER III

THE THIRTEENTH CENTURY

I

HISTORICAL TRADITIONS

During the Thirteenth Century there were
only three kings of England: John, who reigned
from 1199 to 1216; Henry III, who reigned until
1272; and Edward I, who reigned on until 1307.
In tradition the names of John and of Edward
are more distinct than that of Henry. As everybody knows, one of Shakspere's historical plays
concerns King John. He based it on an older
play; at that time such translations into dramatic
terms from the chronicles in which English history was accessible were so popular that a cycle
of them came into existence, covering the history
reign by reign. The greater number of those with
which Shakspere had to do concern the late Fourteenth Century and the Fifteenth, beginning with
Richard II, who was deposed in 1399, and carrying
on the story until Richard III fell, in 1485, at
Bosworth Field, making the Tudors royal. One
reason why he did not try to fill the gap between
John, who died in 1216, and Richard II, who came
to the throne in 1377, is that the gap was tolerably
filled already; there were plays about Edward I,
Edward II, and Edward III; and there was a
play about the reign of Henry III. This last, however, differed from the others by not bearing the

King's name; it was called "Friar Bacon and Friar Bungay." Of the direct line of Plantagenet kings Henry III is the least personally remembered. His position between his father John and his son Edward is nevertheless clear enough to warrant us in collecting the historical traditions of the Thirteenth Century as we collected those of the Twelfth, touching on them as they gathered during each English reign.

King John, of course, is best known to tradition from Shakspere's play. For theatrical purposes, this perhaps overemphasises the fact that his tenure of the throne was insecure until he got rid of his nephew Arthur, son of an elder brother. It is a good deal confused concerning his troubles with France, where he lost most of Normandy, and with the Pope, who excommunicated him and compelled his formal submission. It does not set forth his enforced granting to his barons at Runnymede of that Great Charter, Magna Charta, on which the subsequent liberties of England are traditionally based. But it strongly emphasises a popular notion that he was poisoned by a monk. In Elizabethan times, as any old folio of Foxe's Martyrs will remind you, this made him a kind of Protestant hero. Detested, and probably with justice, when alive, he thus became fleetingly popular some four hundred years after they had buried him in Worcester Cathedral.

For our purposes the tradition of his conflict with the Pope is at once the most important and that which leads us best to traditions then gathering elsewhere than in England. A dispute with Innocent III, centred by Shakspere on the question of which should appoint the Archbishop of

Canterbury, ran at last so high that the Pope
placed England under interdict—whatever that
means—and ultimately deposed the King, who had
meanwhile seized church property and treated
ecclesiastics roughly.   This brought John to terms;
he resigned the Crown to the Pope, and received it
back as a vassal of the successor of St. Peter,
thus for a while acknowledged by England as
temporally imperial.   The pontiff who then asserted something like the full sovereignty of the
Cæsars was among the greatest and most potent
in all papal history; and how active and wide-
spread he made the influence of the Church we
may feel when we remind ourselves of the most
familiar continental traditions from the time of
King John—broadly speaking, the first fifteen
years of the Thirteenth Century.
   Of these the first is that of the Fourth Crusade.
The circumstances of this extraordinary expedition
are recorded in the contemporary account of it by
Villehardouin, often called the earliest of French
historians.   The title of his book—the Conquest
of Constantinople—implies the story.   The Crusade had been instigated by the Pope; the Venetians had arranged to transport the Crusaders;
money troubles combined with the astute policy
of the blind Doge, Enrico Dandolo, to convert
the Holy War into a predatory expedition in the
interests of Venice.   The Crusading forces captured and sacked Constantinople, where Baldwin
of Flanders, their principal commander, was set
up as emperor; for more than fifty years Western or
"Latin" emperors, now faintly remembered, possessed Constantinople.   Though this diversion of
his crusade was by no means to the liking of In-

nocent III, he did his futile best to make it the beginning of a reconciliation between the Eastern and the Western Churches.

The state of emotion in Christendom which helped make Innocent III so potent is implied in the pathetic story of the Children's Crusade. At the very time when the Pope was subduing King John, tens of thousands of young people, aroused and led by enthusiastic men of God, somehow got together and started to destroy the infidel. Few came back; most who did not die ended their lives as slaves. Here you feel enthusiasm at its uncontrollable maddest. More normal phases of it were in the air. At about the same time the two first of the four great Thirteenth Century saints were laying the foundations of their still enduring work: Dominic was reviving the spirit of Catholic Christian doctrine, and Francis of Assisi that of ecstatic Christian charity. On them we shall touch again by and by. And we may perhaps touch again on the Albigensian Crusade in the region we have broadly called Provence. The civilisation expressed by the Troubadours was neither very peaceable nor at all docile. It was on the whole more amiable and perhaps more luxurious than strong. It strayed into heresies of its own, resenting orthodox authority. At last, overrun by Crusading forces directed not against infidelity but against heresy, it perished in blood and fire, considerably directed by the Catholic French soldier Simon de Montfort. And the dispersal of its pleasant centres drove ruined surviving troubadours and their culture to less harried regions, north and south. By a natural process of tradition, the Albigensians, as the people thus destroyed came generally to be called, were later venerated as Protestant martyrs. With Protestants, no doubt, they had in common an unforgiving hostility to the ecclesiastical authority of Rome. How little else these two enemies of the Pope really had in common you may conclude for yourself by comparing the love-songs of the troubadours with the Bay Psalm Book of Puritan Massachusetts.

King John and Innocent III died in the same year, 1216. Oddly enough, the most distinct personal tradition of Henry III is recorded in the Purgatorio of Dante:[1]

> Vedete il re della semplice vita
> Seder là solo, Arrigo d'Inghilterra.
> (See there the king who lived the simple life
> Sitting alone, Henry of England.)

In England, so far as he is remembered at all, his memory is less gentle. Like his father he was at odds with his barons; and the principles of these great feudal lords, like those of the aristocratic Whigs of the Eighteenth Century, had in them germs destined to develop into the democratic commonplaces confused at present with unchangeable truth. There were Civil Wars where another Simon de Montfort, son of the leader of the Albigensian Crusade and himself Earl of Leicester, is now imagined to have been not only a lordly but a popular leader. Henry himself at last confirmed the Magna Charta granted by his father. And so on.

After all, the most significant fact about him for us is what we have already touched on. Robert

[1] VII, 131-2.

Greene's Elizabethan play concerning his reign does not bear his name, but is called, "The Honorable Historie of Frier Bacon and Frier Bungay." How far this is from history may be inferred from the fact that, if we may believe casual books of reference, Bungay was not contemporary with Bacon, but lived under Edward IV about a century later. Roger Bacon really flourished in the time of Henry III, however, and was really a friar. This term applies to four great mendicant orders, finally established by the Church while Henry III was on the throne: the Dominicans (Black Friars); the Franciscans (Gray Friars); the Carmelites (White Friars); and the Augustinians (Austin Friars). Bacon, a Franciscan, appears to have been among the most learned men of his period, to have been important in the history of science, and consequently to have been suspected of dabbling in black arts and to have been traditionally remembered as a magician. The most familiar legend of him, which duly recurs in Greene's play, tells how he made a brazen head and then, after instructing his attendant to wake him when the head spoke, went to sleep. Though the head spoke three times,—saying first "Time is," next "Time was," and last "Time has been,"—the attendant let the tired friar sleep on. So the head fell down, and was broken to pieces; and the friar never knew the truths it might have told him. Fantastic it seems again, this England of Henry III, far-off and indistinct.

In his time, however, the last three Crusades occurred; and they are associated with sovereign names more memorable than his—the Fifth with that of the Emperor Frederic II, the Sixth and

Seventh with that of Louis IX, King of France and sainted.

Frederic II, grandson of Barbarossa and of the Norman King Roger of Sicily, royal in childhood, imperial while still a youth, is perhaps the most brilliant figure of the Middle Ages; and the golden-grounded mosaics of Palermo and of Monreale still preserve some ruined trace of the soft Southern delights amid which this heir to the strongest strains of Northern blood passed the pleasantest days of his adventurous life. His history is a pageant of magnificence, luxury, bravery, intrigue, and war. He led a Crusade which for a while reconquered Jerusalem; the splendour and the manners of his court were rather Oriental than European; he was far too powerful and headstrong to stay at peace with the Pope; and in the end the persistent diuturnity of the Church was too much for him. In his time, the Italian struggles between Guelphs and Ghibellines were at their fiercest. He died, while planning a new attack on the States of the Church, in the year 1250.

There could hardly be a more profound contrast with such a figure and a character as Frederic's than that presented by Saint Louis. The historic record of this French king happens to be unusually distinct. Joinville, a devoted follower, wrote a reminiscent history of him which may fairly be counted among the memorable biographies of European literature. As a matter of history it is not always clear; as a matter of anecdote it may very likely tend rather toward loyal legend than toward inconvenient fact; but as a matter of atmosphere you can hardly help believing it true. If so, here for once was a historic saint who fully deserved to be sainted: faithful to his royal charge, yet filled with humility of Christian spirit; brave and just, yet tender and merciful; thoughtful for the welfare of men, yet resolved to do all in his power that the Cross of Christ should prevail; simple in life, yet sovereign in resolve. His Crusades came to grief—the first at the Delta of the Nile, where he was made prisoner; the second at Tunis, where he died. But besides his holy memory he has left in France at least two wondrous monumental traces—the Sainte Chapelle in Paris, sometimes held the masterpiece of Gothic aspiration, and the deserted walls of Aigues Mortes, at the mouth of the Rhone, built, they say, as a base for his hapless expeditions consecrated to the Cross. In his days, too, the Cathedral of Rheims was growing to that noble completeness which endured until the German barbarism of the Twentieth Century made it a target.

Before passing from this long reign of Henry III, we may perhaps prudently notice at least two other matters then taking shape in foreign distance. The first is that sturdy instrument of Catholic orthodoxy, the Inquisition, which appears to have clearly defined itself at about this time, although its special development in Spain did not occur until some two hundred years later. The second is the swift career of the Tartar conqueror Kublai Khan, who was making himself master of all northern Asia. But for most of us nowadays these things are only names.

The chief traditions which make Edward I more distinct than his father are legendary. In all likelihood, to be sure, he was really tall and alert, so his nickname of "Longshanks" may be as old as his own time; we should remember, however, that it could hardly have been understood either by the king himself or by his courtiers, whose language was still French. And George Peele's dreary Elizabethan play about him carries us far away from any realities, for it turns partly on the story that his first and unpopular wife, Eleanor of Castile, was abominably wicked, that accused of crime she impiously desired if guilty to sink into the earth, that the earth proceeded presently to swallow her up and to disgorge her at another spot thenceforth called Queenhithe, and that she thereupon confessed her sins and was duly punished. Another story, which at first sounds more genuine, relates that when the king's son, who became Edward II,[1] was born at Carnavon in Wales, he was forthwith presented to the Welsh as their Prince, in the arms of his royal father. The tale is now said to be without historical foundation; in maturity, however, Edward of Carnavon was really proclaimed Prince of Wales, and ever since that time the title has been conferred on the eldest sons of the English kings. Edward I, in point of fact, subdued a good deal of Wales, and later came near subduing a good deal of Scotland; when the Thirteenth Century ended, he was at arms with Scottish forces under the celebrated William Wallace. To follow his historical career, adventurous, for a little while crusading, at odds with France, with the Church, with his barons, would take us beyond our province. It is enough now to remember that good authorities trace to the circumstances and the politics of

[1] Marlowe's play, Edward II, is more powerful than the lesser historical plays of Shakspere.

his reign the firm establishment of that parliamentary government which in greatly modified form still controls the British Empire.

Of the continental traditions which came into existence under Edward I, during the last quarter of the Thirteenth Century, none are very distinct among English-speaking peoples. The death of Frederic II had been followed by a confused and turbulent period of imperial history, in which the heirs of his own race perished. Just about the time when Edward succeeded to the English throne, Rudolf of Hapsburg was made King of Germany; and, as we all know, the sovereign history of the House of Hapsburg came to the end of its widely fluctuating fortunes only during the World War which has made chaotic the first quarter of our own Twentieth Century. To linger over the Hapsburgs, however, would lead us astray; for our purposes we shall do better to collect our vague notions of what was happening in Twelfth Century Italy.

Two facts which belong to the time of Edward I may help us to do so. This was when the Venetian adventurer Marco Polo made his way to China through the dominions of Kublai Khan, and brought back to Europe its first real notions of the previously almost legendary civilisation of Eastern Asia, little altered since the remote times when Pericles for a little while dominated Athens. And this was when the oppression of Sicily by French occupiers exploded in the revolutionary massacres remembered as the Sicilian Vespers. Slight as the names of Marco Polo and of the Sicilian Vespers may seem, they imply two things which we cannot neglect—the persistent power of Venice, and the anarchic confusion of the rest of Italy, vexed not only with bewildering internal dissensions but with the recurrent presence of alien invaders.

To touch on the details of these dissensions and invasions would be to confuse confusion. We may do well, however, to remind ourselves that the fall of the Roman Empire in the Fifth Century did not destroy the local existence of the chief Italian cities; that through the centuries these tended to become more or less independent and often mutually hostile centres of petty political existence, generally at once aristocratic and republican, as Rome had been from the days of Tarquin to those of Augustus Cæsar; that by the Thirteenth Century powerful families, almost sovereign locally, like the Scalas at Verona, were beginning here and there to appear established; that in the contentions between Emperors and Popes for the sovereignty of sovereignty, if one city took either side the next was apt to take the other; that sometimes, as in Thirteenth Century Florence, the struggle between Guelphs and Ghibellines broke out between factions within the cities themselves; and that stronger foreign powers were now and again called in to assist the weaker Italian contestants.

The Emperors, by this time, were Germans; little love has ever been lost between the Germans and the French; but you cannot console yourself with so simple a conclusion as that Italian Popes summoned French aid to oppose the armies of German Emperors. In 1300, for example, the Pope was Boniface VIII, who held himself as high as Innocent III a century before; it was only fifty years since, at the death of Frederic II, the pretensions of the Emperors had been humbled by the sovereign successors of Innocent; but in 1303, a year or so after Boniface had declared the papal see supreme over all earthly thrones,—including that of Philip the Fair, King of France, who ten years later suppressed the Templars,—the luckless Pope himself, almost undefended, was seized by French knights at Anagni. His death has been attributed to his indignant mortification. This Thirteenth Century Italy is really and bafflingly confused; but it was the Italy where Cimabue, at Florence, had wakened the art of painting into new semblance of life, and where Giotto, already surpassing him,[1] planned the Campanile, or belfry, still perhaps the most marvellous fusion of painting with architecture ever conceived by man. In that Thirteenth Century Florence, seven years before Edward became King of England, Dante was born.

II

THE ROMANCE OF THE ROSE

The centuries, we must remember, are accidents of chronology, as unreal as the lines of latitude and longitude on maps, but almost as convenient to think with; and their never too distinct boundaries have seldom been less marked than where we now find ourselves. Almost every phase of literature at which we glanced in the Twelfth Century persisted well into the Thirteenth, and some of them throughout it. By 1300,

---

[1] See Purgatorio, XI, 94-5.

at the same time, certain more sophisticated
works, clearly derived from the traditions of a
hundred years before, had come to the front. At
two or three of these we must now glance. None
is more characteristic of its period than the courtly
poem then most widely admired—the Romance of
the Rose.

This gracefully fantastic allegory was begun
by a French court poet, William de Lorris, who
died somewhere about 1250; at the end of Henry
Adams's chapter "Nicolette and Marion" you
will find two or three pages about it. For our
purposes here, the opening lines are worth attention. The brief preface to the First Canto—

> Ci est le Rommant de la Rose,
> Où l'art d'Amors est tote enclose—

needs no translation: The Romance of the Rose
comprises the whole art of Love. The actual poem
then begins:

> Maintes gens dient que en songes
> N'a se fables et mençonges;
> Mais l'en puet tiex songes songier
> Qui ne sunt mie mençongier.

(They tell you that dreams are only fables and lies; but you
can dream such dreams as are not a bit lying.)

And thereupon, in his easy and swift couplets,
the poet goes on to tell how one night, at twenty,
when he was peaceably asleep in bed, he dreamed
a beautiful dream which pleased him very much.
It was May, the buoyant month of young leaves
and flowers. He strayed to the walls of a park,
where ugly figures were painted—Hatred, Felony,
Villainy, and the like. He found a gate, opened

to him by an agreeable young person called Idleness. "In the Park," to quote a convenient summary in the Encyclopædia Britannica, "he finds Pleasure, Delight, Cupid, and other personages, and at length the Rose"—by kissing which he may solace the pains of love. "Welcome grants him permission to kiss the Rose, but he is driven away by Danger, Shame, Scandal, and especially by Jealousy, who entrenches the Rose and imprisons Welcome, leaving the Lover disconsolate."

The moment you stop to think, you will see that this fantastic and now faded prettiness is just such as you might have expected to develop from the kind of fantasies at which we glanced a little while ago—the exquisite artifices of the troubadours, for example, and the airy symbolism of the Bestiary. The convenient device of a dream is not new, either. You will find something like it in the Consolation of Philosophy of Boethius; and if you are disposed to retrospection you may like to look at Cicero's Dream of Scipio,[1] and thence perhaps to be led back to Plato's Vision of Er.[2] Here, to be sure, is no respectably unbroken literary pedigree; but here is a tendency recurrent throughout literature. The last lines of the Sixth Book of the Æneid will remind you how dreams are always flitting from another world to ours. For all this, the shape assumed by the dream in the Romance of the Rose has a distinct character which we might be tempted to call its own, except that the dainty convention occurs again and again, about it and

[1] Republic, IX *seq*. There is a translation in Longfellow's notes on the Inferno of Dante.
[2] Republic, X, 614 *seq*.

for hundreds of years thereafter. This was a Thirteenth Century device which long harmonised with human imagination and fancy. So did the whole notion of Allegory, and not least those personifications of Virtues and Vices, still alive when

> Hope for a season bade the world farewell,
> And Freedom shrieked when Kosciusko fell.[1]

William de Lorris wrote thirty-two cantos of his allegory, comprising almost 4300 lines. This would seem long enough. The Thirteenth Century, however, so eagerly wanted more that after an interval another poet felt called to answer the demand. The Thirty-third Canto is prefaced as follows:

> Cy endroit trespassa Guillaume
> De Loris, et n'en fist plus pseaulme;
> Mais, aprés plus de quarante ans,
> Maitre Jehan de Meung ce Rommans
> Parfist, ainsi comme je treuve;
> Et ici commence son œuvre.

(At this point William de Lorris passed away and made no more psalmody; but, after more than forty years, Master Jean de Meung finished this Romance, as I find; and here begins his work.)

Once begun, Jean de Meung continued the work until it extended to 22,608 lines, of which the last four are

> Explicit li Rommans la Rose
> Où l'art d'Amours est toute enclose:
> Nature rit, si com moi semble,
> Quant *hic* et *hec* joignent ensemble.

[1] Campbell: Pleasures of Hope (1799), I, 387. And look, if you like, at Collins's Ode to the Passions (1747), where personification is at its English height.

(So ends the Romance of the Rose
Where all the Art of Love lies close;
All Nature laughs, it seems to me,
When *he* and *she* together be.)

If this reference to the Art of Love, or that by
William de Lorris forty or fifty years earlier, lead
you to expect that the poem is a bit like Ovid's
on this delicate subject, you will be disappointed.
Jean de Meung knew Ovid, to be sure, as at least
one passage imitated from the Metamorphoses[1]
would instantly show. For that matter, so did
William de Lorris, who imitated at least one passage from the Art of Love[2] itself. The Thirteenth Century, too, was not squeamish; it was
ready to grin and to laugh at things quite as unmentionable as Ovid wallowed in at his worst.
Its notions of how Love should be poetically celebrated, however, assumed the symbolic idealism
of the troubadours as a code of manners. Instead of Lesbia's sparrow so tenderly made undy-
ing by Catullus,[3] you will find troubadour fancy
trying to make alive the song of the generalised
nightingale. And so on. Not to allegorise would
then have been unseemly. Both William de
Lorris and Jean de Meung allegorise as if allegory
were the only conceivable form of human expression.

Those who have read and enjoyed them, however,—and they may still here and there be read
and enjoyed,—agree that their use of allegory
differs. In the four thousand lines of William de
Lorris it appears almost pure, tending toward
nothing much darker than sentimental sadness.

[1] Bartsch, 381.   [2] Bartsch, 317.   [3] II and III.

In the nineteen thousand lines of Jean de Meung, it becomes now and again elaborately philosophic, and its temper turns satirical. You cannot reflect much about life and stay youthfully cheerful. Jean de Meung would not have been a man of his time if he had not at least pretended to reflect. So the Romance of the Rose, beginning with a short and bright dream, ends with a dream grown long drawn out and murky.

III

REYNARD THE FOX

At the time when the Romance of the Rose was at the height of its fashion, many traditional stories clustering about the name of Reynard the Fox were widely known, and relished wherever discontent lurked or gathered. Their origin we may take to be partly popular and partly literary; they may here and there be traced to fables, bestiaries, and the like, and again to such folk-lore as obscurely gathers anywhere and everywhere. They have perhaps been most widely current among the Germans; Caxton's prose English version of them, printed in 1479, was translated from the Low German, or Dutch. By the Thirteenth Century, however, they existed and were widely known in French verses, something like those of the Romance of the Rose but much less polished, collected under the name of the Roman de Renart.

Though just here we need hardly consider them in any detail, we had best remind ourselves of their general character. Each beast is presented as a type—a generalised individual. Broadly speaking, as is true in Nature, beasts survive the struggle for life by virtue either of strength, which we like to call brute force, or of intelligence, which when we dislike it we call trickery. Rightly or wrongly, the far from strong Fox is traditionally held a miracle of slyness. He accordingly became the fabulous or satirical type of oppressed humanity outwitting stupid power. Unable to destroy or to overcome it, he could at once evade it and make it ridiculous. He did so through the ages, and never more viciously than when a little before the French Revolution Beaumarchais made French fashion laugh with Reynard, still typical, but humanised into Figaro.

Wherever you find him, you will find something to laugh with and to laugh at. Your laugh, though, will be neither full-throated nor kindly. So far as it is at all sympathetic, it will sympathise not with the hardships but with the knavery of the downtrodden; so far as it derides the great, it will ignore the beneficence potentially theirs, and often persistent even when those who do us good by keeping the world policed prove, as human beings, no better than our miserably sinful selves. Without order, such as Virgilian Empire dreamed of, there can be no such thing as civilisation. If you doubt this, ponder a little on what happened to Europe between the fall of Rome and the rise of modern nationalities at the period where we have now arrived. If you wish to puzzle your wits, try to decide whether the beginning of our Twentieth Century looks like the dawn of a new civilisation, serenely democratic, or like the dusk of what men have imagined to be civilisation during the last eight hundred years. Then turn back, wherever you like, to Thirteenth Century tales of Reynard the Fox. You can hardly help feeling that then, as now and always, there floated in the air, often more than half recognised, the germs, poisonous to society and therefore to what we have supposed civilisation, of not sublime but malignant discontent, the more venomous when it moves you to sneering laughter.

In lasting English literature there is one familiar example of such deliberately elaborated and allegorised fable as you will find in the stories of Reynard the Fox; and not long ago there was a desperate attempt to make another in French. Though, very likely, neither is directly taken from work of the Thirteenth Century, both imply the kind of tradition at which we have just been glancing. The first is the Nun's Priest's Tale of Chaucer, which tells how Chanticleer, the cock, after relating an ominous dream to his favourite wife Partlet, the hen, gets the better of a fox, after all. The second is the fantastic effort of Edmond Rostand to outdo the exuberant romanticism of his Cyrano de Bergerac with the laboured allegory of his abortive Chanteclere.

But we begin to wander. We must turn back to the Middle Ages.

IV

THE GOLDEN LEGEND

Those of us who by this time have pondered over Henry Adams's Mont Saint Michel and Chartres will have been rewarded by such saturation with Twelfth and Thirteenth Century spirit as they will hardly find elsewhere. If they have sometimes found the process a little arduous, for Adams generally demands attention, let them now turn to his chapter on "Les Miracles de Notre Dame"—the Miracles of Our Lady. This can be read like a fairy-tale.

The stories he collects and so puts together that each gives new savour to the others he has mostly found in easy Old French verse, like that of the Roman de Renart and of the Roman de la Rose. His translations take you into the very heart of the words he translates, and that heart is the heart of Thirteenth Century legend. These were the fancies which peopled the dim, religious light of the cathedrals when the cathedrals were still new. Once come to feel them, and thus become possessed of the heart of this olden time, you need vex yourself little more about its body.

Hearts, though, are bound to be enshrouded with bodies; and for one who has known the heart of Thirteenth Century legend, where Our Lady reigns, girl and mother at once, unreasoning, capricious, loving, comforting, and sovereign, thousands have known the body of that legend enmisting her with the miracles of unnumbered saints who on earth were only human and faithful. The book which tells their stories was perhaps the most popular of all the Middle Ages. Written in easy monkish Latin, it was very soon translated into the living languages of simple men; and an English version of it, printed in 1483, at once attests how long human beings eagerly turned to it and is said to have been the most considerable undertaking of Caxton's press.

The Golden Legend—Legenda Aurea—it had come to be called by that time. Its original and less pretentious title was the Legends of the Saints. By the Thirteenth Century, legends had mossily gathered about venerated names anywhere and everywhere. Some of the names, and on the whole the greatest, belonged to Apostolic times, twelve hundred years before; some—like Ambrose and Augustine, for example, Chrysostom and Benedict—though later were fully historical; a far greater number, such as Nicholas and Lawrence, Agatha and Agnes, had little or no historical existence; a few, like Bernard and Thomas of Canterbury, Dominic and Francis, were at least comparatively contemporary. Whether the names were historical or not, however, and even when they were within the range of personal memory, the stories gathering about them in monkish fancy had very little to do with anything so negligible as fact.

At least by the Thirteenth Century, a great many generations of simple-minded cloistered human beings, devout and unquestioning abominators of infidelity and heresy, and bound—often from childhood—by the vows of earthly poverty and of chastity which should assure them the boundless and pure delights of heaven, had found pleasure and comfort in letting fancy play with the edifying virtues of the Christian past, rewarded above and miraculously attested below. This world, they believed, is vain, transitory, and evil; the Devil and his angels, together with their infidel and heretical ministers,—such as the persecuting Cæsars and the lying gods of both civilised and barbarian antiquity, such as Mahomet and his followers, such as the Arians of old and the Albigensians a little while ago,—are always alert to snatch the souls of men; but persevere in the faith, and in loyalty to your vows of poverty, chastity, and obedience, and with heavenly help— after a decent interval of purgation—you may confidently hope to attain real and everlasting joy and felicity. The Saints enjoyed it already, as the stories of their miracles attested. At the same time you were in no spiritual need of believing the legends as if they had been gospel; they were not matters of doctrine, on which the future of immortal souls depends. This element of innocent vagrancy gave an added charm to pious tales which could harm nobody and if only by reason of their obvious and simple morals might very possibly do many people good.

Such appears to have been the opinion of Jacopo da Voragine, a good Dominican monk who finally became Archbishop of Genoa. He put together a great many stories about Saints which came to him from study, from reading, from pious gossip, or from wherever else. His apparently accidental arrangement of them may perhaps be based on some Thirteenth Century calendar of their feasts.[1] As a casual example of what he liked to set down, you may look at the story, pleasantly translated by Henry Adams, of how Our Lady mended a torn hair-shirt of St. Thomas of Canterbury— incidentally, according to a French version, with red silk.[2] Julian the Apostate, the Golden Legend tells us,[3] began his career as a monk, was intrusted

---

[1] Into this question I have not had patience to look. The present official Calendar of the Church was not fixed until later times.

[2] Légende Dorée (Paris, 1843), I, 61.   [3] *Ib.*, 127.

by a woman with some pots of gold concealed under layers of ashes, stole the gold, and therewith purchased the imperial crown of the Cæsars. The legend of how St. Barlaam with the help of divine grace converted the holy King Josaphat[1] is evidently derived, the learned inform us, from Indian legends of Buddha, duly Christianised in transmission to Thirteenth Century Italy. What is more to our present purpose is that the legends of the Saints, as Jacopo da Voragine wrote them, are the sources of many saintly figures familiar to us all in later painting—Sebastian[2] with his arrows, for example, George and the dragon,[3] Denis carrying his own severed head,[4] and Catherine tortured on the wheel before the voice of Our Lord summons her to heaven as His beloved bride.[5] To feel the quality of these childish, monkish, often grotesque yet often sweet stories, you must browse among them for yourself. If you can keep yourself from deriding them, you may still faintly enjoy them. When you can somehow enjoy them you will begin to know something of Thirteenth Century spirit in its most elementary phase.

This world it conventionally assumes to be as full of evil and misery as the snarling or jeering tellers of tales about Reynard the Fox ever pretended. Evil and misery are not wisely to be outwitted, though; it is better to recognise them, and to overcome them by persistent exercise of the Christian graces, Faith, Hope, and Charity. These are divinely eternal; whoever thinks otherwise proves himself a minister of the Devil, and if he refuses to be converted ought to be abominated. And the joys of the flesh—such as wealth and plea-

[1] *Ib.*, II, 230.   [2] I, 92.   [3] II, 75.   [4] II, 286.   [5] II, 207.

sure—being earthly are at best naughty, deserving only the disdain of the poor and chaste righteous. If you doubt this, ponder right and left on the miraculous attestation of the merits of the Saints. Here they are in the Golden Legend for us all to read about and choose from. Rightly understood, the height of human happiness is martyrdom, sealing assurance of happiness in that other world, close at hand, which is a world without end.

Like the Romance of the Rose and the tales about Reynard the Fox, the stories of the Golden Legend may be opened at random. You can read all three best with no thought of beginning or end or system. Very likely, too, you must turn to them often, and in different moods, before you can come to feel them a bit familiar. Until they seem so, you will hardly guess how men felt in that Thirteenth Century when things like these were really popular. Until you somehow enter into this long-past state of human feeling, it may well seem silly, remote, and negligible. Once let it possess you, though, and you will find it both human after all and like though unlike the moods of a century before, at which we glanced not long ago. Without them—the first definite utterance of Christian Europe—it could never have taken its actual form, so strangely different from any known to European antiquity. Yet compared with them, you can hardly help feeling it no longer spontaneous but rather deliberate, almost thoughtful. The allegory of the Romance of the Rose is ingeniously so, the satire of Reynard the Fox maliciously, the simplicity of the Golden Legend impotently if you will and ridiculously. But all three bespeak a swiftly ripening world, perhaps already past its ripeness.

V

THE SAINTS

DOMINIC; FRANCIS OF ASSISI; LOUIS;
THOMAS AQUINAS

In this Thirteenth Century world, there lived
and died four men recognised and venerated almost from their own time as orthodox saints.   Two
of them, on whom we have touched already, St.
Dominic and St. Francis, grown men when the
Century began, did not survive its first quarter.
The others—St. Louis, on whom we have touched
at a little more length, and St. Thomas Aquinas—
were of a younger generation.   St. Louis died at
fifty-five, in 1270; St. Thomas, at somewhere
about fifty, in 1274.

Contemporary records of St. Francis and St.
Louis have survived in literature; and the writings
of St. Thomas Aquinas are still held by many to
be the greatest intellectual achievement of the
Middle Ages.   In this respect, St. Dominic is
less fortunate.   As neither records of him nor
works of his have enduring literary existence, his
gravely great name is the least distinct of the four.
A Spaniard, about thirty years old in 1200, he
was deeply stirred by that fervid passion of Christian revival which seems in perspective to suffuse
his period.   The world is very evil and out of
joint; it always has been and always will be; it
was never more so than in the Crusading centuries.
Then, however, those who believed saw their way
very clearly.   Stimulate faith, awake the convic-
tion which is the human soul of the Church, and

good should triumph over evil. So Dominic
was moved to preach, and his preaching, vagrant
in missionary body, orthodox in devout heart,
gave rise to what soon grew into an order of earnest preachers, uncompromising enemies of heresy
in all its forms. They still exist. Their centuries
of history have now accumulated about them,
as about their saintly founder, a great body of
tradition, such as in the minds of those who do
not accept their teaching distorts their character.
True missionary impulse is charitable, springing
from that love of men which longs to save souls.
The means of missionary salvation, however, is
apt to be the destruction of idols and the confusion
of idolaters. Even though your missionary begin
by proclaiming truth, he soon falls rather to denouncing and, if he can, to extirpating falsehood.
Those who have most studied the story of Dominic
therefore love him best. In other than orthodox
tradition his name has come to stand for the phase
of orthodoxy most far from winning. Rightly or
wrongly, it is darkly associated with the merciless
ferocity of the Albigensian Crusade, uprooting at
once the heresies and the civilisation of Provence.
It is thus associated, as well and more, with the
later terrors of the Inquisition. A grim play on
words implies the story: the brothers of the order
he founded are called Dominicans, in Latin
Dominicanes; this Latin word, split in two, becomes *Domini canes,* the hounds of the Lord;
and, at least among Protestants, Dominic has been
remembered as the leader of the pack, chasing
from the temple and to perdition whoever will not
heed the call to righteousness.

Dante saw him at once thus and otherwise.

In the Paradiso,[1] St. Bonaventura, on earth a
Franciscan, speaks a wonderful tribute to St.
Dominic,

> l'amoroso drudo
> Della fede Cristiana, il santo atleta,
> Benigno a suoi, ed ai nemici crudo.[2]

The portrait he thus begins to draw, though too
stern to be winning, is austerely and inspiringly
noble. Bonaventura goes on to lament, rather in
Dominican spirit than in Franciscan, the lapses
of men and churchmen from the path pointed
out by Dominic; but he refers at least twice[3] to
the celestial courtesy of St. Thomas, which has
moved him to speech, and incidentally to recipro-
cation.

For in the previous Canto,[4] St. Thomas Aquinas,
in life a Dominican, has ecstatically discoursed
about St. Francis, a rising sun of holiness, for
whose sake whoever names his birthplace

> Non dica Ascesi, che direbbe corto,
> Ma Oriente, se proprio dir vuole;[5]

and has dwelt on the mystic union of Francis with

---

[1] XII, 31–111.
[2] Ib., 55–7.
> the amorous paramour
> Of Christian Faith, the athlete consecrate,
> Kind to his own and cruel to his foes.—Tr. Longfellow.
Longfellow's careful translation is throughout thus line by line; and his
notes are always excellently literate.
[3] Ib., 109–11, 142–5.   [4] Par., XI, 43–122.
[5] Ib., 53–4.
> (Let him)
> Say not Assisi for he would say little,
> But Orient, if he properly would speak.—Tr. Longfellow.
The old form Ascesi suggests only a notion of ascent, as distinguished from
sunrise. This devout play on words is characteristic of the Middle Ages.

Poverty—so constant in loyalty to those who cherish her that in days of old, even

> when Mary still remained below,
> She mounted up with Christ upon the cross![1]

So, in the glowing Heaven of the Sun, eternal happy followers of the two greatest Thirteenth Century saints celebrate each the leader chosen on earth by the other. This, St. Bonaventura tells us, is courtesy; and here we may come to feel courtesy no longer a gracious convention of troubadour manners but something essentially divine. A little earlier Dante has proclaimed it so. In the Seventh Canto of the Paradiso, where Beatrice is expounding to Dante theologic doctrine, she points out that man once fallen could nowise redeem himself, and so could be saved only by

> Dio, solo per sua cortesia.
> (God, through His courtesy alone.)[2]

Nothing compelled God to grant salvation; He did so with voluntarily gracious consideration for his creatures. Gratefully sensible of this Divine Grace, Franciscans and Dominicans in Paradise exercise to one another something like the courtesy of God. Here below, they might have been less thoroughly illuminate; for the essence of Dominic's mission was orthodoxy, and the essence of the mission of Francis was charity, and human heads are not often quite at one with human hearts.

[1] *Ib.*, 71–2.
> dove Maria rímase giuso
> Ella con Cristo salse in sulla croce.

[2] Par., VII, 91. Here Longfellow, who translates *cortesia* by *clemency*, fails to imply something of what the term suggests.

Particularly nowadays, when the notions of
Democracy make so wide an appeal, Francis of
Assisi is by far the most popular of mediæval
saints. The literature about him, already boundless, is constantly increasing. He was by birth a
gentleman of Assisi, some ten years younger than
St. Dominic; but their influence took root and
grew at about the same time, the first quarter of
the Thirteenth Century, and St. Dominic had
been dead only about five years when St. Francis
closed his eyes at Assisi. Much of the little city,
still surrounded by its hillside walls, looks as it
looked when he was alive. He must have known
well the portico of the small Roman temple in
the market-place and the narrow mediæval streets
with tall shapeless houses ready to withstand petty
local attack; they linger in your pilgrim memories
as clearly as the great mother-church of the order
which St. Francis founded, or the domed sanctuary in the valley below, marking the spot where
he passed from this world. So at Assisi he seems
almost of yesterday. He might recognise everything now, you feel, except that because of him
it has all become consecrate; you forget the lapse
of the centuries.

The story of him is a matter of history. Very
briefly, he was moved by love—divinest, if so may
be, of all divine attributes—to abandon the comforts of this world, and to give himself, in irradiate
joyousness of spirit and with no care for the morrow, to the succour of the poor and wretched. Followers flocked about him. Stories grew into legend
around him and among them. The overflowing
happiness of his heart appears wonderfully in his
Canticle of the Sun, which you will find set forth
in its primitive old Italian by Henry Adams, and

rendered into simple English by Matthew Arnold,[1]
who places it contrastingly beside the pagan hymn
to Adonis, from the Idylls of Theocritus. The first
of its stanzas runs thus:

> Laudato sie, misignore, con tucte le tue creature
> Spetialmente messor lo frate sole,
> Lo quale iorno et allumini noi per loi
> Et ellu e bellu e radiante cum grande splendore
> De te, altissimo, porta significatione.[2]

Its later stanzas give like thanks for Sister Moon
and the Stars, for Brother Wind and the Air and
the Clouds, for Sister Water and Brother Fire,
for our Sister and Mother Earth, and for Sister
Death of the Body. How he was remembered, and
his earlier followers too, you may find for yourself
in the little book of Franciscan legend, the Fio-
retti, or the Little Flowers of Saint Francis.
You need hardly be reminded that his virtues were
rewarded by a seraphic vision which left on his
body the testimony of Stigmata—or scars on hands,
feet, and side like those made on the body of Christ
in the agony of the Cross. And close by waits
the tender figure of St. Clara, who loved him
purely, and followed his example, first of "Poor
Clares," and longed to see him before he died, and
had only the message that she should put aside grief
now and be assured that she and her nuns should
see him before they died,[3] and found the promise
fulfilled when the brethren bore his body past the

---

[1] Pagan and Mediæval Religious Sentiment: Essays in Criticism, I, vi.

[2] Here is Arnold's rather too literate rendering: Praised be my Lord
God with all his creatures; and specially our brother the sun, who brings
us the day, and who brings us the light; fair is he, and shining with a very
great splendour: O Lord, he signifies to us thee!

[3] Speculum Perfectionis, X, 108. Here is the Latin of his message:
Vade et dic sorori Claræ quod deponat omnem dolorem et tristitiam quia
me modo videre non potest, sed in veritate sciat quod ante obitum suum
tam ipsa quam sorores suæ me videbunt et de me plurimum consolabuntur.

window of her convent. In the Speculum Perfectionis, or Mirror of Perfection, you will find the Canticle of the Sun again. These early books about him will bring you nearest him, perhaps; but Henry Adams's chapter on the Mystics will help you toward his pure, simple, loving, and ecstatic heart.

At about the time when St. Francis died, Louis IX, then a boy of ten or so, became King of France. He lived on for more than forty years; we have touched on his history already; but those who love an olden time cannot be too often reminded of the delightful book in which years later Joinville set down his memories of the justly sainted sovereign whom he knew and loved. It is no monkish chronicle, such as Jacopo da Voragine was fond of digesting; it is an honest record of how a French gentleman of the Thirteenth Century remembered both a character which had almost fulfilled its ideals, and the restless circumstance by which that character was moulded and chastened. Furthermore it is among the few books always readable. Vague though the name of St. Louis may be to most of us, it will always be familiar.

Unlike St. Louis, and indeed unlike the two earlier Thirteenth Century saints as well, St. Thomas Aquinas is remembered not so much for what he did as for what he wrote. Born about the time when St. Francis died and St. Louis became king, he lived until Dante was a boy of eight or nine. An Italian at once of high rank and of remarkable intellect, he studied under the best teachers of his time, partly at the University of Paris; he became a Brother of the Dominican order; he consecrated his life to the exposition of truth; and he has been known through the centuries as the Angelic Doctor—who reasoned, as it were, with the heavenly wisdom of an angel. In the history of thought and of philosophy his name is important; even those who have supposed his power wasted have never denied it. Among the masters of scholastic philosophy he is the most memorable.

What scholastic philosophy was, and where it got to, is another question, variously beyond our present scope. All we can now do is to remind ourselves that it was fundamentally orthodox, and therefore would not suffer the human mind to contradict the divine authority of the Church. Its generally accepted masterpiece is the Summa Theologica of St. Thomas Aquinas. If you are willing to read hard for an hour or two, you will not waste the time you may thus give to what is written about him in the Catholic Encyclopædia and in the chapter bearing his name with which Henry Adams ends the book at which we have now glanced so often. Though nothing but prolonged study, in paths divergent from literature, can begin to make you understand what all this means, even a little while with it will give you a deep sense of its calmly dogmatic atmosphere. Strangely enough, too, one aspect of this atmosphere looks piercingly clear. The thought of St. Thomas is at once subtle and sustained to the limit of human power; but his words are so simple that you hardly realise his Latin not to be your own living language. Take, for instance, the Conclusion, or Answer, to the Tenth Article of his First Question. This article discusses

Utrum Sacra Scriptura sub Una Littera habeat Plures Sensus

(Whether Holy Scripture Single in Utterance[1] has Many Meanings);

and the formal answer, supported by some two closely printed and reasoned pages, is

Cum sacræ Scripturæ auctor Deus sit, qui omnia simul suo intellectu comprehendit, ea ipsa doctrina sub una littera plures sensus habet; litteralem multiplicem, spiritualem triplicem; videlicet allegoricum, moralem et anagogicum.

(As the author of Holy Scripture is God, who in his understanding embraces all things at once, that doctrine single in utterance has many meanings; in the letter multiple, in the spirit triple; that is allegorical, moral, and spiritual.)

The words of Scripture, like all words, have a literal meaning; but, coming from the infinitude of God, they will be found also to have an allegoric meaning, whereby they throw light far and wide on other things than themselves; a moral meaning, whereby they guide conduct; and a spiritual or transcendental meaning, whereby they reveal the truths of eternity. Even though all this appear far from the common sense of our own not fervently faithful period, nobody can fail to recognise its compact ease of statement. It is a fair example of the style of the Summa Theologica throughout.

The object of the philosophy comprised in this colossal work was, if so might be, to reconcile revealed truth with human reason, always tempted to stray from it. Truth is revealed by God in Scripture and through the Church; reason, the highest of human faculties, was held in the Thir-

[1] Literally "under One Letter."

teenth Century to have reached its most lofty
achievement in the work of Aristotle—then known
only through Latin versions, said mostly to have
been made from Arabic versions sanctioned by
Averroës and used at the universities of Mahometan Spain. When faith and reason—Scriptural doctrine and Aristotle—agreed, each fortified the other. When they disagreed, one or the
other must evidently be mistaken. Here, the
Thirteenth Century maintained, is no ultimate
difficulty; for, as the divinely revealed truth of
faith is absolute, any divergence from it must be
error. When you find reason leading you astray,
accordingly, you need only inquire and discover
what for the moment is the matter with reason.
The whole task of theology and philosophy, thus
regarded, has been summarised in three words:
Fides quærens intellectum (Faith searching reason).

Agreeable to the Thirteenth Century, this
formula no longer commands instant assent; between that time and ours, indeed, it has pretty
steadily tended to reverse itself. At least from
the period of the Reformation, in any event,
the characteristic thought of Europe has been
apt so to exalt reason that if any one should ask
us now to summarise the philosophic and indeed
the general tendency of moderns we might rather
be disposed to do so in the words *Intellectus quærens
fidem* (Reason searching faith). This new turn
of the phrase was lately used in conversation by
an eminent American ecclesiastic, trained in the
doctrine of St. Thomas Aquinas at the time when
it was most vigorously revived by the most learned
of recent Popes, Leo XIII. If those who listened
to his friendly talk understood him rightly, fur-

thermore, he candidly acknowledged that, in any given dispute, the case of reason must usually be the more instantly attractive to unprejudiced minds. Having made this concession, however, he smilingly suggested that there are few more illuminating subjects of inquiry than whether, between the time of St. Thomas Aquinas and our own, faith or reason has altered most or oftenest. Consider for yourself; whatever else, you can hardly deny increased respect for the Angelic Doctor.

For in its own way, and within its accepted limits, his intellectual power has hardly been surpassed; and the smug assumption of our passing democracies that the mind of the Thirteenth Century was asleep has basis only in their superstitious addiction to the legends of reason—now and again as childish as any of the pious tales collected by Jacopo da Voragine.

VI

LYRICS

LATIN, FRENCH, AND PROVENÇAL

Though the lyric poetry of the Thirteenth Century may seem at first very like that of the Twelfth, one soon comes to feel it as different as any other form of literature. This is perhaps most evident when we compare the two great Latin hymns generally attributed to the Thirteenth Century with the Latin hymns thought to be a hundred years or so earlier.[1] It is by no accident that the Dies Iræ and the Stabat Mater Dolorosa are the

---

[1] *Cf.* pp. 519–523.